Debt Capital Markets

Debt Capital Markets

Law, Regulation, and Policy

VINCENZO BAVOSO

OXFORD
UNIVERSITY PRESS

OXFORD
UNIVERSITY PRESS

Great Clarendon Street, Oxford, OX2 6DP,
United Kingdom

Oxford University Press is a department of the University of Oxford.
It furthers the University's objective of excellence in research, scholarship,
and education by publishing worldwide. Oxford is a registered trade mark of
Oxford University Press in the UK and in certain other countries

Published in the United States of America by Oxford University Press
198 Madison Avenue, New York, NY 10016, United States of America

British Library Cataloguing in Publication Data

Data available

Library of Congress Control Number: 2024945803

ISBN 978–0–19–889325–7

DOI: 10.1093/oso/9780198893257.001.0001

Printed and bound by
CPI Group (UK) Ltd, Croydon, CR0 4YY

MIX
Paper | Supporting
responsible forestry
FSC® C013604
www.fsc.org

*This monograph is dedicated to my father, Judge Alessandro Bavoso,
who passed to a better life before this work reached its printed form,
but inspired much of the thinking behind it.*

Preface

In the spring of 2014, with memories of the global financial crisis of 2008 still relatively fresh in the minds of scholars interested in capital markets regulation, I came across a short paper jointly published by the Bank of England and the European Central Bank. It argued for the resurrection of the securitization market in Europe as the fulcrum of integrated EU-wide capital markets and the necessary development to spur a post-crisis economic boom. This was soon followed by the fully fledged Green Paper for an EU Capital Markets Union in 2015, and the eponymous ambitious policy project. I ended up writing on, and critiquing, these initiatives in the subsequent years, and that led to my direct participation in a number of policymaking exercises with major EU think tanks. The main concerns I expressed at the time revolved around one fundamental question: why revive a segment of financial markets that had been widely recognized as the main engine of instability in the years before 2008? Other, more technical questions that I posed focused on the manner in which EU policymakers were envisaging the new regulation of these critical segments of capital markets that only few years earlier had been recognized as part of the shadow banking system.

The period between 2014 and 2020 coincided with a sharp resumption of debt capital markets, particularly of segments that had remained moribund in the years after 2008. The other very visible phenomenon of the post-2008 years is the relentless growth of private debt creation, a pattern that in fact never really subsided after the global financial crisis. What we started witnessing in that period is also the migration of these dynamics, and attendant risks, from large banks to entities in the non-bank financial system (such as private equity funds, insurance firms, asset managers). This shift presented renewed challenges for regulators, because while the banking system was reflecting a healthier image, with much reduced balance sheet exposures to the shadow banking system, the global financial system as a whole was showing problematic increases in private debt and leverage. The reason for this ambivalent picture may be found in the narrow regulatory focus of post-2008 reactions, which were chiefly directed at large banks. The Basel III framework for instance focused on enhancing capital requirements for banks (together with a leverage ratio and new liquidity requirements), but did not set similar standards for entities operating in the shadow banking system.

The reality though was that banks remained highly interconnected with the wider non-bank financial ecosystem, in ways that were not always clear to regulators and market participants. In spite of this, policy efforts in the post-2008 period were aimed at further empowering market-based forms of financial intermediation, which in essence became a more palatable way to refer to the shadow banking system. Many regulatory initiatives in the same period need to be understood in that vein, as a way to facilitate debt capital markets (as exemplified by the EU capital markets union).

Eventually, red flags were raised by the International Monetary Fund and the Financial Stability Board in 2019 about the level of risks in the financial system, and these pointed to the unsustainable level of private debt, against the reduced capacity of economic actors to meet payment obligations under debt contracts. Moreover, it became clear that notwithstanding the new regulatory safeguards, large systemic banks were still highly interconnected with entities in the non-bank financial system, and exposed to shocks emanating from those alternative channels of intermediation.

Those warning signs materialized in the spring of 2020, when the economic slowdown induced by the Covid-19 pandemic revealed the deep-seated fragility of the financial system, burdened by unsustainable levels of private debt, and over-dependent on a system of public backstops via governments and central banks liquidity support. The panic of 2020 was followed by prolonged uncertainties, which culminated more recently with a string of banking failures in the US and Europe. It is precisely this current age of turbulence that warrants a study on debt capital markets. Because, even if turbulence today comes from several different aspects of our social life—geopolitical fault lines, ecological disasters, widening social inequalities, among others—the very source of financial instability flows from the unfettered expansion of the riskiest segments of capital markets.

This monograph explores these themes from the perspective of law, regulation, and policy-making. Its central argument is that the present instability in financial markets is the result of a process of transformation that started in the 1980s. The evolution and growth of debt capital markets in particular was propelled by the undisputed belief in the validity of neoclassical economics, and more specifically in assumptions of efficient markets. These in turn informed the regulatory changes that, between the 1980s and 1990s, shaped the regulatory edifice of capital markets. This book ultimately contends that the regulatory reactions to the 2008 crisis have not gone far enough in re-evaluating those underlying beliefs and assumptions, which in fact remain at the heart of current policy designs.

Work on this book commenced during the 2018/19 academic year, particularly during a period of research leave that allowed me to set out the historical and conceptual framework of debt capital markets. The remainder of the monograph was written more recently, between 2022 and 2023, again coinciding with another period of research leave, and in the midst of a wave of financial instability that seems to vindicate my contentions in this book.

Writing a research monograph represents such a prolonged endeavour that one cannot imagine seeing the end of the road without a certain degree of support, and luck—it is a bit like winning a five-set tennis match. The list of debts I incurred over the past years is therefore a long one, and what follows in the next paragraphs cannot amount to a comprehensive list of acknowledgments. First, I have benefited from an amazing network of friends and colleagues in the School of Law at the University of Manchester, and particularly within the Manchester Centre for Law and Business which has become a truly inspiring home and a platform to share ideas and get them constructively shredded. Special thanks are owed to Orkun Akseli, Nicolette Butler, Alan Cunningham, Michael Galanis, Ashley Hannay, Geraint Howells, Pinar Oruc, Niyoosha Shishehgar, Jasem Tarawneh, and Kyriaki Vasileiou. Finding good colleagues is in itself something to be thankful for; having colleagues who are also friends off-the-court is a blessing, and over the years the School of Law has remained a very collegial setting. I therefore thank my colleagues, past and present, for their friendship and support, and particularly Hazel Carty, Neil Cobb, Jean d'Aspremont, Javier Gacia-Oliva, John Haskell, Yenkong Ngangjoh Hodu, Joseph Jaconelli, and Graham Smith and Robert Thomas .

During my periods of research leave I have been fortunate to find great working environments, and homes away from home: at the National University of Singapore, particularly the Centre for Banking and Finance Law, where Sandra Booysen, Christian Hofmann, and Dora Neo have always offered great hospitality and opportunities to present my research, both in 2019 and in 2023, and at the Chinese University of Hong Kong, where Jyh-An Lee, Chao Xi, and Lutz-Christian Wolff welcomed me in the best possible way during my visit in 2023. My time in Singapore and Hong Kong has always been incredibly productive and happy, and I have to thank in particular Alessio Azzutti, Giuliano Castellano, and John Murphy for their friendship and academic advice during my time in Asia.

Friends, both in the UK and in Italy, and family more significantly, have also had to cope with the peculiar attitude that accompanies such a task. Academics are an odd species, and our life is not always easily understood outside of the academic bubble that we live in. My family in particular has been extremely supportive, providing during my prolonged stays in Neapolis a very comfortable setting, the necessary distractions, and constant encouragement. Special thanks are owed to my mother, my brother, and my sister-in-law.

It would be unfair to leave out of this list the PhD students at Manchester, the grassroots of our research community: not only those who have had to withstand my pedantic supervision, but the PhD population at large falling under the aegis of the Centre for Law and Business. The truth is that we are enriched by them as they are by us. Likewise, teaching LLM courses in Securities Law and Financial Regulation gave me great opportunities to test ideas. I am therefore thankful to those students who, year after year, sit patiently in my classes and keep asking questions.

Last but not least, I must acknowledge the very valuable inputs of the anonymous reviewers who read my book proposal and earlier drafts of chapters. Their comments have been instrumental to steering my understanding of how this book should be structured and where focus should be placed. It goes without saying though that all errors and inaccuracies in this book should be attributed to myself only. I am also thankful to the editorial team at Oxford University Press, particularly Rachel Mullaly and Kim Vollrodt who followed me through this process and always gave me good guidance and advice. The law is stated as it stands on 30 November 2023.

Vincenzo Bavoso
Manchester, January 2024

Advance praise for *Debt Capital Markets*

'Vincenzo Bavoso explores the origins of the rise of modern debt capital markets and the risks they pose to the financial system. He skilfully explains how substantial growth and innovation in debt capital markets contributed in Europe and the US to a highly-leveraged banking and financial system and how post-2008 regulatory reforms have not addressed the underlying systemic risks. His call for a redesign of capital markets regulation that moves away from the assumptions of efficient capital markets to a more realistic assessment of the market failures and financial stability risks caused by the growth of private debt in capital markets and its transmission through the shadow banking system will certainly draw the attention of regulators and policymakers. This book will lead the field in addressing the financial stability risks posed by debt capital markets.'

Kern Alexander, Professor of International Financial Law, University of Zurich

'Debt capital markets are the breeding ground for financial crises. *Debt Capital Markets: Law, Regulation, and Policy* will be the go-to resource for practitioners, policymakers, and scholars looking to better understand this crucial area of modern finance.'

Morgan Ricks, Herman O. Loewenstein Chair in Law, Vanderbilt Law School

Overview of Contents

Contents

PART II TRANSACTIONAL DYNAMICS AND RISKS IN DEBT CAPITAL MARKETS

PART III UNDERSTANDING HOW DEBT CAPITAL MARKETS ARE REGULATED

Figures

Table of Cases

UNITED KINGDOM

UNITES STATES

Table of Statutes

EUROPEAN UNION

UNITED KINGDOM

UNITES STATES

Abbreviations

ABCP	asset-backed commercial paper
ABS	asset-backed securities
AFME	Association for Financial Markets in Europe
ATM	automated teller machine
BCBS	Basel Committee on Banking Supervision
BIS	Bank for International Settlements
BoE	Bank of England
CAPM	capital asset pricing model
CCP	central clearing counterparty
CDO	collateralized debt obligation
CDS	credit default swap
CBT	Chicago Board of Trade
CfD	contract for difference
CFTC	Commodities Futures Trading Commission
CLN	credit-linked notes
CME	Chicago Mercantile Exchange
CMO	collateralized mortgage obligation
CMU	capital markets union
CLO	collateralized loan obligation
CRA	credit rating agency
DCO	derivatives clearing organization
DTC	Depository Trust Corporation
EBA	European Banking Authority
ECB	European Central Bank
EIOPA	European Insurance and Occupational Pensions Authority
EMH	efficient markets hypothesis
ESA	European Supervisory Authority
ESG	environmental, social, and governance
ESMA	European Securities and Markets Authority
ESRB	European Systemic Risk Board
ETF	exchange traded funds
FCA	Financial Conduct Authority
FSA	Financial Services Authority
FSB	Financial Stability Board
FSMA	Financial Services and Markets Act 2000
G10	Group of 10
G20	Group of 20
G30	Group of 30
GDP	gross domestic product

GFC	global financial crisis
GSE	government-sponsored enterprise
GSIB	global systemically important banks
HFT	high-frequency trading
HoL	House of Lords
HQLA	high-quality liquid asset
ICO	initial coin offering
IMF	International Monetary Fund
IOSCO	International Organization of Securities Commissions
IPO	Initial Public Offering
IRB	internal risk-based
IRS	interest rate swap
ISDA	International Swaps and Derivatives Association
ITS	implementing technical standards
LCR	liquidity coverage ratio
LDI	liability-driven investment
LFIs	large financial institutions
LSE	London Stock Exchange
MIH	Minsky instability hypothesis
MBS	mortgage-backed securities
MMF	money market mutual fund
MPT	modern portfolio theory
MTF	multilateral trading facility
MTS	Mercato dei Titoli di Stato
NASDAQ	National Association of Securities Dealers Automated Quotations
NSFR	net stable funding ratio
NYSE	New York Stock Exchange
NRSRO	nationally recognized statistical rating organization
OTC	over-the-counter
OTF	organized trading facility
P2P	peer-to-peer
PRA	Prudential Regulation Authority
PSM	Professional Securities Market
RoE	return on equity
RTS	regulatory technical standards
RWA	risk-weight assets
S&L	savings and loans
SEC	Securities and Exchange Commission
SFT	securities financing transactions
SME	small and medium-sized enterprise
SPE	special purpose entity
SPV	special purpose vehicle
STC	Simple, Transparent, Comparable

STS	Simple, Transparent, Standardized
TRA	transnational regulatory actors
TRS	total return swap
UCC	Uniform Commercial Code
UCITS	Undertakings for the Collective Investment in Transferable Securities
VaR	value at risk

1
Introduction

1 Why a book on debt capital markets?

The purpose of this book is to re-evaluate this area of law and regulation which, for multiple reasons, has progressively risen to prominence over the past forty years. The most immediate reason is represented by the soaring levels of private debt, which, counterintuitively, have kept increasing even in the post-2008 years.[1] Globally, between 2007 and 2020, private debt grew from 164% to 178% of global GDP.[2] Rising levels of private debt were also recognized by the International Monetary Fund (IMF), from 2019, as a source of fragility in the financial system.[3] In particular, warning signs emerging from the IMF report referred to: a) the weakened debt servicing capacity of the corporate sector in the face of soaring levels of private debt and volatile economic conditions; and b) the concentration of private debt origination among non-bank financial intermediaries (ie shadow banks).[4]

Going back to the global financial crisis of 2008 (GFC), debt capital markets were duly recognized as the epicentre of those cataclysmic events. The causal connection between the GFC and debt capital markets was emphasized by prominent policy responses, such as the Turner Review in the UK in 2009,[5] the De Larosiere Report in 2009 at the EU level,[6] and the Financial Crisis Inquiry Commission (FCIC) in the US in 2011.[7] In different ways, they all focused on aspects of debt capital markets as causes of the GFC: the Turner Review pointing to the uncontrolled process of financial innovation that shaped debt markets in the period leading up to the GFC;[8] de Larosiere looking at the complexity of structured

[1] In the period between 1991 and 2007, private debt in the US increased from \$10.4tr to \$41.6tr, and as a percentage of GDP, it went from 169% to 288%; in the UK private debt reached 400% of GDP in 2007. Arthur Wilmarth, 'The Pandemic Crisis Shows that the World Remains Trapped in a "Global Doom Loop" of Financial Instability, Rising Debt Levels, and Escalating Bailouts' (2021) 40(8) Banking & Financial Services Policy Report 1.

[2] Vitor Gaspar, Paulo Medas, and Roberto Perrelli, 'Global Debt Reaches a Record \$226 Trillion', IMF Blog, 15 December 2021.

[3] IMF, 'Global Financial Stability Report', Washington 2019, chapter 1 and 2; IMF 'Global Financial Stability Report', Washington, 2024, chapter 2.

[4] See on this point Financial Stability Board, 'Global Monitoring Report on Non-Bank Financial Intermediation', 20 December 2022, chapter 1.

[5] Adair Turner, 'The Turner Review—A Regulatory Response to the Global Banking Crisis', FSA, March 2009.

[6] Jacques de Larosiere, 'The High-Level Group on Financial Supervision in the EU', Brussels, 25 February 2009.

[7] The Financial Crisis Inquiry Commission, 'Financial Crisis Inquiry Report', January 2011.

[8] Turner Review (n 5), chapter 1.

Debt Capital Markets. Vincenzo Bavoso, Oxford University Press. © Vincenzo Bavoso 2024.
DOI: 10.1093/oso/9780198893257.003.0001

products and the difficulty of governing this new area of financial markets;[9] the FCIC dedicating a substantial portion of its analysis to developments in debt capital markets,[10] specifically segments such as securitization and the ensuing growth of what is referred to as shadow banking.[11]

Another reason justifying the focus of this monograph is the centrality that debt capital markets have attained in the regulatory space since the mid-1980s. This is perhaps a less tangible aspect of this story, but effectively the wave of liberalizations that shaped financial markets since the 1980s—such as the 1986 'Big Bang' in the UK—had profound effects on the size and shape of debt capital markets. Not only did new regulations liberalize specific segments of capital markets, but importantly they elicited their growth, which critically occurred through waves of financial innovation. It is vital to stress that legal and contractual structures permeating debt capital markets became particularly susceptible to changes informed by market practices. Ultimately, this dynamic further facilitated financial innovation.

Regulatory changes over recent decades had the effect of altering the nature of both banks and capital markets. If traditionally these two areas of finance were seen as a dichotomy, the transformation of finance that occurred since the 1980s resulted in a functional integration of banks and capital markets, whereby the former have become the main participants in the latter, with large banks profiting enormously from their capital markets operations. This shift started with the regulatory changes (detailed in Chapter 2 of this monograph) which ushered in the emergence of the global megabanks: financial institutions combining the business of banking together with other, historically separate, aspects of financial intermediation, such as insurance and investment. The business of these megabanks, no longer confined within the boundaries of 'banking', became central to scholarly debates on the law and regulation of capital markets.[12] Moreover, as explained throughout this monograph, large banks are at the centre of transactions that interconnect different segments of and participants in financial markets, bringing together as a result banking and shadow banking. It is worth noting that current policy discourses no longer refer to shadow banking—that is, forms of intermediation that are conducted outside the banking system and attendant regulatory standards, despite presenting features of banking intermediation—but to market-based finance, or non-bank intermediation.[13]

Finally, this book's focus is prompted by the direction of policy-making in the post-2008 years. This has become apparent at the global level with the new (third)

[9] De Larosiere, 'High-Level Group' (n 6), chapter 1.

[10] See FCIC 'Financial Crisis Inquiry Report' (n 7), part II.

[11] For a seminal analysis on shadow banking, see Zoltan Pozsar, Tobias Adrian, Adam Ashcroft, and Hayley Boesky, 'Shadow Banking', Federal Reserve Bank of New York, Staff Report N.458, 2010.

[12] This is aptly dealt with by Arthur Wilmarth, *Taming the Megabanks*, Oxford University Press, 2020.

[13] To grasp the emphasis on this policy shift, see G30, 'Shadow Banking and Capital Markets: Risks and Opportunities', Washington, 2016.

iteration of the Basel Accord, a system of standards aimed at coordinating and harmonizing the supervision of globally active banks. Basel III[14] was designed to correct the failures associated with the GFC, and while some of its elements are still in the implementation stages, it has already attracted criticism from various angles. What is particularly controversial about the Basel approach is the underlying policy directed at fostering resilient market-based channels of intermediation.[15] These are exactly the forms of intermediation that before 2008 were branded as shadow banking, where hidden and unquantifiable risks were being created and transmitted to market participants through opaque transaction chains. More to the point of debt capital markets, since 2015 the EU Commission has been actively promoting the further integration of capital markets across the EU, through the Capital Markets Union (CMU).[16] This is centred on the expansion of market-based transactions and products, vis-à-vis banking ones. Critically, much of the CMU hinges on revived bonds and securitization markets, thus presenting a clear emphasis on debt.

This monograph explores the role of debt capital markets in fuelling crises and episodes of financial instability. The approach to this study is multifaceted and contextual, and while focused primarily on relevant aspects of law and regulation, it hinges on a more rounded understanding of capital markets, particularly insofar as theoretical discussions are conducted. The themes signposted so far in this section are all reprised in greater details in different parts of this monograph, as is illustrated in the last section of this chapter. Before doing that, some fundamental questions need to be addressed in relation to the meaning and functions of debt capital markets.

2 Drawing the perimeter: what are debt capital markets?

Following from the discussion started in the previous section, it is necessary to briefly define the meaning and functions of debt capital markets, for the purpose of situating them in the wider context of the financial system. Generally speaking, the financial system tends to be divided into two broad forms of intermediation, one revolving around banks, and the other centred on capital markets. This distinction hinges on the means by which finance is raised, namely, through the intermediation of banks providing loan-type products, or by issuing securities to investors in capital markets.[17] The latter is a nomenclature that often escapes specific legal

[14] Basel Committee on Banking Supervision, 'Basel III: A Global Regulatory Framework for More Resilient Banks and Banking Systems', 2011.

[15] G30, 'Shadow Banking and Capital Markets: Risks and Opportunities', Washington, 2016.

[16] EU Commission Green Paper, 'Building a Capital Markets Union', Com(2015) 63 Final.

[17] For an illustration of different functions, and particularly the different source of intermediation of each model, see Jakob de Haan, Dirk Schoenmaker, and Peter Wierts, *Financial Markets and Institutions*, Cambridge University Press, 2020, chapter 1.

and regulatory provisions because capital markets refer to the ultimate markets where securities (broadly conceived) are traded, and not to a specific segment or exchange. As an illustration, shares and some types of bonds are typically issued on stock exchanges, while there are other regulated markets where other bonds and debt securities are traded. Moreover, some securities, such as shares, are actively traded on stock exchanges in their secondary market, whereas the secondary market for debt securities is chiefly over-the-counter (OTC).

Within capital markets, a key distinction arises as to the means of raising finance, pointing in other words to the type of securities issued to the public: equity securities (shares), giving the holder a right in the issuing entity,[18] as opposed to debt securities (such as bonds), resulting in a right against the issuing firm.[19] It needs to be borne in mind though that between these two categories, hybrid securities exist, which combine in the same product some of the properties of equity and debt. Preference shares for instance carry a right to a fixed dividend, unlike ordinary shares, and similarly to bonds.[20] On the opposite side of the spectrum, convertible debt offers investors the possibility to convert the debt into a share. These debt securities can sometimes provide issuers too with the conversion right, so that the conversion from bond to share is triggered automatically upon the occurrence of specific events.[21] Importantly, contingent convertible bonds (CoCos) became widely employed in European banks post-2008, as a 'bail-in' mechanism to facilitate the recapitalization of distressed banks.[22] Incidentally, CoCos were very much at the heart of the Credit Suisse debacle in March 2023.[23]

With respect to debt capital markets, they include segments such as the bond market, commercial paper, covered bonds, securitization, as well as more innovated debt securities that have proliferated in recent decades. Moreover, innovations in market-based channels of finance have expanded the above markets, fostering interconnections with adjacent areas of the financial system. Most prominent instances, for the purpose of this book's analysis, are the repo market and credit derivatives. These areas have progressively become an integral part of capital

[18] Shareholding typically entails a right to vote and to receive dividends, which is subject to the board of directors declaring a distribution, and the availability of distributable profits.

[19] Bondholders have a right to receive the payment under the bond (coupon) regardless of the issuer's profitability. They also enjoy a priority of payment, relative to shareholders, in the event of the issuer's insolvency.

[20] Eilis Ferran and Look Chan Ho, *Principles of Corporate Finance Law*, Oxford University Press, 2014, 50–51.

[21] ibid, 51.

[22] The rationale of bail-ins is the participation of bank creditors in bearing the costs of restoring the financial health of the ailing bank. See Emilios Avgouleas and Charles Goodhart, 'Critical Reflections on Bank Bail-ins' (2015) 1(1) Journal of Financial Regulation.

[23] For a critical overview, see Patrick Bolton, Wei Jiang, and Anastasia Kartasheva, 'The Credit Suisse CoCo wipeout: Facts, misperceptions, and lessons for financial regulation' (2023) 35(2) Journal of Applied Corporate Finance.

markets, and the relevant synergies they propose with debt capital markets are detailed in this book (particularly in Chapters 4 and 7).

Four cautions about the scope of this book need to be made. First, technology has historically played a significant role in the innovation of financial markets, and recent developments revolving around the application of blockchain technology in securities markets (referred to as FinTech) have shaped numerous academic and policy discussions.[24] This book takes stock of these innovations insofar as they are relevant to the analysis of debt capital markets, as is the case for instance with the securitization of P2P loans originated by online technology platforms (discussed in Chapter 4).

Another important caveat relates to the very limited coverage that this monograph offers to areas such as green bonds and environmental, social, and governance (ESG) securitization. They both refer to an expanding field within financial markets seeking to endorse environmental sustainability. Green bonds do not present legal and regulatory features that warrant a specific treatise in the context of this monograph (beyond the further expansion of capital markets to new asset classes), and their size remains limited relative to the overall size of bond markets.[25] Despite the rather facilitative regulatory framework,[26] ESG securitization volumes have remained modest, firstly, as a proportion of the wider green-labelled market, and secondly, relative to the overall securitization market.[27]

A third caution is the jurisdictional reach of this book. While debt capital markets have developed to a substantial degree also in jurisdictions such as China,[28] this monograph is concerned with their growth, and attendant law and regulation, in the UK, the US, and EU.

Lastly, a fundamental distinction needs to be drawn between privately denominated (and issued) debt products, and public ones. The latter category refers primarily to sovereign debt and sovereign bonds. While they are a central component of bond markets as they represent a benchmark for their valuation, questions revolving around public debt are squarely outside the remit of this monograph, simply because they would move it towards the field of economics and political economy. As a result, in this book problems of excessive debt (and ensuing

[24] See for reference Ross Buckley, Douglas Arner, and Dirk Zetzsche, *FinTech: Finance, Technology and Regulation*, Cambridge University Press, 2023.

[25] As an illustration, green bonds represented 0.6% of all bond issues in the EU in 2014, rising to 8.9% in 2022. See European Environment Agency, 'Green Bonds', 28 April 2023.

[26] The European Green Bond Standards include provisions that facilitate its application in the context of securitization. See for a discussion Maddie Burrell, Mikhail Kleptsov, Adam Craig, Jonathan Lewis, and Julia Tsybina, 'ESG Securitisation: Weathering the Storm?' (2023) June Clifford Chance, Securitisation Markets and Regulation: Choosing Different Paths? 35.

[27] ibid.

[28] Interestingly, a shadow banking system has also developed in China, with some peculiar features. See on this Robin Hui Huang, 'The Regulation of Shadow Banking in China: International and Comparative Perspectives' (2015) 30 Banking & Finance Law Review 481.

leverage) refer conceptually to private debt creation, and not to increases in the level of public debt.

3 The urgency of re-evaluating capital markets regulation

It has become increasingly evident that certain segments of capital markets, while having the potential to advance financial deepening and economic development, can also augment the riskiness of the financial system. This fragility is rooted, as is argued throughout this book, in the excessive levels of private debt creation, which foster an environment of high leverage, in turn leading to financial instability and crisis situations. This type of concern was raised in 2019 by the IMF, in a report that stressed that the financial system was burdened by unsustainable levels of private debt, pointing to uncertainties in the economic cycles and questioning the capacity of market participants to face interest payment obligations.[29] This scenario eventually materialized in the spring of 2020 when the economic slowdown induced by the Covid-19 pandemic unveiled the fragilities of the global financial system.

At the time of writing this book a new period of instability is surfacing, with banking failures emerging in the US and in Europe. In March 2023 the Swiss giant Credit Suisse was on the brink of collapse, following the last of a long string of regulatory violations, and fundamental weaknesses emerging in their financial reporting. This forced the Swiss regulator to coordinate (or rather coerce) a merger with national rival UBS.[30] At the same time, fear of a panic spread throughout the US too, with the collapse of two small regional banks, Silicon Valley Bank and Signature Bank.[31] It is important to stress that these crises, while emanating from banking institutions (as was the case in 2008), are very much the reflection of the interdependence between banks and capital markets that was highlighted earlier, and of the functional integration of these channels of intermediation.[32]

This period of financial instability could be configured as a seamless continuation of the GFC of 2008, whose impact and gravity were only temporarily attenuated in the years after 2008. This line of argument is often used to critique post-2008 regulatory reactions. One contention in this sense is rooted in the fact that most financial institutions (Lehman Brothers aside, of course) were bailed-out, either directly or in less overt ways, in the years during and after the GFC. This

[29] IMF 'Global Financial Stability Report', 2019 (n 3), chapter 2. Similar concerns are also raised in the eponymous 2024 report (n 3).

[30] For an account of the Credit Suisse collapse, see Rebecca Stuart, 'Why did Credit Suisse fail and what does it mean for banking regulation?', *Economics Observatory* (13 April 2023).

[31] See on the failure of Silicon Valley Bank John Turner, 'Why did Silicon Valley Bank fail?', *Economics Observatory* (17 March 2023).

[32] On the concept of functional integration, see Robert Hockett and Saule Omarova, 'The Finance Franchise' (2017) 102 Cornell Law Review 1143.

behaviour on the part of regulators in the US, the UK, and EU had the effect of first, increasing the debt burden (both the public one, and more critically, the private one) and fostering an environment of ever-increasing private debt creation; secondly, it advanced the expectation among market participants that privately originated liabilities would be backstopped by central banks in worst-case scenarios, in order to prevent further disruptions in the financial system. This expectation provided more impetus to the build-up of excessive risk-taking through private debt creation.[33] Eventually, this scenario manifested itself between 2019 and 2020, where it became evident that post-2008 regulation had not adequately dealt with the root causes of the GFC—particularly to the extent that structural reforms were deemed unnecessary.

These fears are somewhat legitimized by the fact that in the post-2008 period central banks have extended their bailouts beyond banks, to entities in the shadow banking system. Effectively, central banks have increasingly been acting as market-makers of last resort, facilitating the provision of liquidity to wholesale segments of financial markets (the repo market, analysed in Chapters 4 and 7).[34] Such a system of public backstops in the shadow banking system reinforced the expectations (prevalent in the pre-2008 period) that money claims issued by shadow banking entities can be treated at par (just like bank liabilities, ie deposits).[35] Moreover, it entrenched the functional integration mentioned earlier, between banks and non-banks, extending the problematic 'finance franchise', theorized by Hockett and Omarova, to the shadow banking system.[36]

Despite being recognized as the epicentre of the GFC,[37] shadow banking has instead continued to grow, with many large banks becoming more interconnected with money market mutual funds (lenders in the repo market), which are in fact often sponsored by the same banks for regulatory arbitrage purposes.[38]

As stated earlier in this section, this situation became particularly visible during the panic of 2020 and the Covid-19 pandemic, with central banks engaging in programmes that provided liquidity assistance (ie asset purchase programmes) to a

[33] In this sense see the critique put forward by Wilmarth, 'The Pandemic Crisis' (n 1), 1. Wilmarth observes correctly that the so-called panic of 2020 shows the increased operational interlinks between banks and shadow banks.

[34] See Benjamin Braun and Daniela Gabor, 'Central Banking, Shadow Banking and Infrastructural Power', in *International Handbook of Financialisation*, edited by Philip Made and others, Routledge, 2020.

[35] For a definition of money claims, and the problems associated with their issuance in the shadow banking system, see Morgan Ricks, 'Regulating Money Creation after the Crisis' (2011) 1 Harvard Business Law Review 103.

[36] See Hockett and Omarova, 'The Finance Franchise' (n 32).

[37] As clearly contended for instance by Gary Gorton and Andrew Metrick, 'Securitized Banking and the Run on the Repo' (2012) 104(3) Journal of Financial Economics.

[38] Wilmarth, 'The Pandemic Crisis' (n 1), 7. Regulatory arbitrage in this case represented by banks avoiding capital and liquidity regulation, and also more basic deposit insurance, by moving some of their institutional clients to the money market mutual funds. Wilmarth further observes that between 2008 and 2020 the repo market expanded from $6 trillion to $11 trillion.

variety of participants in market-based channels of intermediation. In many cases, these facilities amounted to bailing out counterparties that large banks were exposed to, effectively allowing the large banks to escape bailouts.[39] Beyond exposing the lack of resilience of the financial system, these policies further entrenched the creation of private debt by financial institutions, fuelling a credit boom that is inevitably further inflating a bubble and leading to financial instability.[40]

Lastly, it needs to be emphasized that both the endless increase in private debt and the growth of the shadow banking sector are rooted in legal technologies, such as the bond market and securitization. Critically, it is the unfettered innovation of these transactions and products that elicited the relentless rise of risk-taking in the financial system through private debt creation.

4 The structure of the monograph

This monograph develops the legal and regulatory questions raised in the preceding sections of this introductory chapter. It puts forward the argument that debt capital markets have been the main locus of financial instability over the past decades, and remain the chief source of fragility in the financial system. This monograph argues that this is the result of the undisputed reliance on a set of theories reliant on ideas of efficient markets that still inform the governance of the financial system, and make its regulation ever more problematic. To substantiate these overarching claims, this monograph proposes a three-part structure, divided into eight chapters, including the present introductory chapter.

The first part of the monograph comprises Chapters 2 and 3. Chapter 2 charts the historical development of debt capital markets, showing their growth since the mid-1980s in connection with sweeping regulatory changes, leading to the liberalization of financial markets in the UK and the US (and eventually globally). This analysis uses data showing that much of the transactional innovation in debt capital markets started in that period, reaching its climax in the early 2000s, only to subside in the post-2008 years and restart again after 2014.

Chapter 3 develops a conceptual framework to understand the dynamics and trends in debt capital markets that are illustrated in Chapter 2. This analysis explores the conceptual link between the neoclassical theories that became dominant in the 1970s and 1980s, and the way in which they informed capital markets development through neoliberal policies. Chapter 3 effectively clarifies the feedback

[39] ibid, 12.

[40] In the UK, the House of Lords criticized the post-2008 policies enacted by the Bank of England (often referred to as quantitative easing, QE), observing that these policies had the effect of encouraging the financial industry to take excessive risks through private debt creation, given that QE was effectively reducing debt servicing burdens. See House of Lords, 'Quantitative easing: a dangerous addiction?', Economic Affairs Committee, 16 July 2021.

loop between the concept of market efficiency and attendant assumptions, and how it was employed to inform policy-making and eventually regulation in debt capital markets.

The second part of the book includes Chapters 4 and 5. Chapter 4 focuses on the legal and transactional aspects of debt capital markets, analysing in detail the relevant segments and markets. This is a wide-ranging discussion that starts with the foundations and mechanics of the bond market, and ends with the most recent innovations, such as collateralized loan obligations, passing also through the relevant aspects of credit derivatives and repo transactions. In doing so, this chapter sheds light on the specific processes of financial innovation that have come to characterize debt capital markets, pointing to the relevant risks arising in each context.

Building on this analysis, Chapter 5 draws attention to the causal links between the recurring periods of financial instability that swept financial markets over the past three decades, and the underlying common denominators, identified in this book with abuses of debt capital markets. This is done by constructing a taxonomy of crises and scandals, situating the role that debt capital markets play in the process. This chapter focuses on aspects that fuel instability and crises and particularly on the risks associated with financial innovation and the way it has prospered in a lightly and indirectly regulated environment.

Questions of regulation are at the heart of Part III of this monograph, which is developed across Chapters 6 and 7. Chapter 6 provides a critical analysis of the regulatory framework governing debt capital markets. It explores the key principles that shape the architecture of this area of finance, with some emphasis on disclosure, market discipline, and private ordering. This focus helps understand that a large part of the debt capital market, especially its most innovated segments, prospered largely outside the perimeter of financial regulation and supervision.

Chapter 7 analyses the specific regulatory instruments that are relevant in the context of debt capital markets—mirroring the analysis developed in Chapter 4 where specific markets are explored. Much of this exercise is aimed at assessing the regulatory initiatives that were undertaken in the post-2008 years, primarily in the UK (through EU law before Brexit), and also in the US, and at the transnational level (with Basel III). This chapter not only seeks to critically evaluate the regulatory reactions to the GFC, and how they withstood the periods of instability that came afterwards, but it also offers an opportunity to discuss the broader policy direction that currently drives debt capital markets. This is an exercise informed by transnational initiatives, such as the already cited Basel III, but importantly also the EU CMU, with its thrust on debt channels of intermediation.

Building on the arguments laid out throughout this monograph, Chapter 8 points to its fundamental findings and conclusions. It provides in particular a final assessment to the analysis conducted in Part III, as to whether post-2008 regulation is suited to create a more stable and resilient financial system, and whether policy-making has sufficiently departed from pre-2008 orthodoxies. Ultimately, these reflections lead to further questioning the scope of debt capital markets, and the necessary degree of regulatory intervention that would be necessary to stabilize this area of financial markets.

PART I

THEORIZING THE DEVELOPMENT OF DEBT CAPITAL MARKETS

2
A historical overview of debt capital markets

1 Introduction

The purpose of this chapter is to draw a historical evolution of debt capital markets from the 1970s to the present day. This excursus allows an appreciation of the growth of specific segments of securities markets, and particularly debt capital markets. The focus of this historical analysis therefore is chiefly on the bond market, the commercial paper market, securitization and its more innovative offshoots such as CDOs and CLOs, highlighting how they became the backbone of capital markets activities. This was the case especially in the US and the UK, and this chapter lays emphasis chiefly on these two jurisdictions, and when relevant on the EU too. Charting the development of securities markets over the past four decades further shows the increasing prevalence of debt transactions and products over equity.

In the context of this historical enquiry, this chapter firstly examines the main regulatory changes that shaped financial markets in the US, the UK, and globally. Secondly, it uses data to show the measure of growth in different segments of debt capital markets and the contextual limited increase in the level of IPOs in the main financial centres. This multifaceted analysis provides a clearer understanding of how financial markets evolved, and critically how they became engines of unprecedented levels of private debt creation. More specifically, the level of private debt as a percentage of GDP has kept increasing in most financialized economies. This process was for a long time perceived to be conducive to economic development and financial stability. At the heart of this belief was a deep-rooted ideological orthodoxy, still reflected today in the fundamental construction of financial regulation.

The last statement leads to the critique developed in the next chapter, which clarifies the extent to which neoclassical economic theories underscored the development of capital markets in the last forty years. Importantly, the discussions laid down in these two chapters (together forming Part I of this monograph) also expose a conceptual link between the regulatory changes highlighted in this chapter and the intellectual dimension that informed those changes. Part I assesses whether regulatory and supervisory arrangements reflected an undisputed reliance on that set of theories recognized as neoclassical economics.

Debt Capital Markets. Vincenzo Bavoso, Oxford University Press. © Vincenzo Bavoso 2024.
DOI: 10.1093/oso/9780198893257.003.0002

This line of enquiry becomes particularly important in conjunction with the analyses conducted later in this monograph. It provides the necessary background to reflect critically on the pre-crisis regulatory infrastructure for debt capital markets, pointing at the fault-lines and the incorrect assumptions that were the premise of that edifice. Part III of this book discusses post-crisis policy and regulatory initiatives, and it is even more central to that analysis to evaluate whether policy-making has moved away from the axioms that have permeated financial markets since the 1970s.

This chapter is divided into two main sections: section 2 charts from a historical perspective the regulatory changes that spurred the growth of capital markets, detailing the different stages of that development, and also pointing to the more recent emergence of alternative capital markets channels. Section 3 uses data to corroborate the claim on the growth of capital markets and especially the pattern of that growth, characterized by increases in private debt creation.

2 The development of bond markets and the rise of debt (market-based) financial products

The purpose of this section is to contextualize the growth of debt capital markets, from the 1970s to the present day. Due to the focus of this research, which is on law, regulation, and financial markets, the development of modern capital markets needs to be understood through its most poignant regulatory changes, and particularly those that occurred from the early 1970s. This historical timeline contributes to unpacking the direction and pace of change, as well as the trends that characterized the past four decades in financial development. What is most central to this enquiry is thus: a) tracing the growth of debt capital markets; b) understanding the size of this phenomenon (especially vis-à-vis equity markets) and its consequences on the creation of increasing levels of private debt.

2.1 The centrality of debt capital markets

Following from the general definitions provided in Chapter 1, this section details the historical developments of debt capital markets, and the process of innovation that characterized them. Importantly, product and transaction innovation led to fundamental changes in debt finance. By the end of the twentieth century, bonds and more sophisticated securitized products had become the centrepiece of what is referred to as market-based finance. In essence, this reflected a system of financial intermediation that progressively became detached from the more traditional banking system—hence disintermediated[1]—because both borrowers/issuers and

[1] On the concept of disintermediation in financial markets, see Steven L Schwarcz, 'Framing Address: A Framework for Analyzing Financial Markets Transformation' (2013) 36 Seattle University Law Review 299, 303.

lenders/investors could tap capital markets in order to either access sources of finance, or invest in products with a more customized profile for risks and returns.

What is also necessary to appreciate is that bonds became part of a more intricate and interconnected system. Through product innovation, derivatives were progressively combined with bonds in order to create synthetic exposures, which eventually became notorious in the pre-crisis years in connection with the rise of collateralized debt obligations (CDOs). More sophisticated debt products became also highly demanded assets, with a number of financial institutions holding them due to their presumed liquidity and safety (traditionally attributed to government bonds). The employment of these assets as collateral in the money market further increased the interdependence and correlation of different segments of financial markets.[2]

To appreciate the evolution of securities markets and the emergence of market-based finance, it is necessary to go back to the 1970s and start this account by detailing how earlier regulatory changes in that decade prompted shifts in financial markets.

2.2 The end of Bretton Woods and the early regulatory changes

The process of financial transformation that this book is concerned with starts in the mid-1970s. There is some agreement that the innovation of transactions and products that underscored the global financial crisis (GFC) of 2008 has its roots in regulatory changes that took place between the 1970s and the 1990s.[3] Between the post-WWII years and the mid-1970s, the Bretton Woods Agreements were widely identified as the main regulatory impediments to the processes of financial integration and financial innovation. In particular, Bretton Woods established a system of regulated fixed exchange rates, coupled with national controls of cross-border financial flows, which effectively resulted in 'closed' national financial markets.[4] Moreover, from a regulatory perspective Bretton Woods coincided

[2] And critically, with what in the mid-2000s became known as the shadow banking system, of which more will be said later in this monograph. See for an early definition Laura Kodres 'Shadow Banks: Out of the Eyes of Regulators', IMF, available at www.imf.org/en/Publications/fandd/issues/Series/Back-to-Basics/Shadow-Banks (last accessed on 17/04/2024).

[3] As observed by Ranald Michie, despite a number of financial innovations developed during the industrial revolution, the dynamism of global finance had reached a standstill in connection with the start of WWI. Even after WWII, Michie argues, tighter financial regulation and government control of financial markets pre-empted the flourishing of financial innovation. See Ranald Michie, 'Financial Capitalism', in *The Cambridge History of Capitalism*, edited by Larry Neal and Jeffrey G Williamson, Cambridge University Press, 2014, Vol 2, chapter 8.

[4] Barry Eichengreen, *Globalizing Capital: A History of the International Monetary System*, Princeton University Press, 2008, chapter 4.

with the acceptance of Keynesian political economy, predicating the centrality of government intervention for the purpose of supervising and regulating financial markets.[5]

The collapse of Bretton Woods in the early 1970s was the first regulatory milestone that prompted the re-emergence of financial globalization, and with it financial innovation.[6] It elicited foreign participation in other countries' capital markets, and more generally the post-Bretton Woods financial architecture was one centred on free capital markets and the prominence of supranational regulatory actors (such as the IMF, the World Bank, and the Bank for International Settlements).[7] From a transactional perspective, the fixed exchange rate system had facilitated free trade under a regime that required national currencies to be pegged with a reserve currency, which was the US dollar.[8] With the end of Bretton Woods, trade and investments came to be characterized by a regime of floating exchange rates,[9] which posed the challenge of managing exchange fluctuations and related risks. This period saw the initial expansion of the derivatives market, and the progressive introduction of new products that were designed to deal with new types of financial risks.[10]

The United States pioneered a number of relevant regulatory changes in the 1970s. First, in 1975 the New York Stock Exchange (NYSE) abolished fixed commissions. The contextual gradual disappearance of exchange controls imposed by national governments elicited increased competition in US financial markets.[11] The mid-1970s also saw in the US mergers between members of the NYSE, which created larger brokerage houses[12] that were keen to exploit the advantages of free commissions. Importantly, these changes went hand in hand with the permission

[5] See on this, Yuri Biondi, 'Empowering Market-Based Finance: A Note on Bank Bailouts in the Aftermath of the North Atlantic Financial Crisis of 2007' (2016) 6(1) Accounting, Economics and Law: A Convivium.

[6] For a discussion on cycles of regulation, see Robert Boyer, 'The Global Financial Crisis in Historical Perspective: An Economic Analysis Combining Minsky, Hayek, Fisher, Keynes and the Regulation Approach' (2013) 3(3) Accounting, Economics and Law: A Convivium.

[7] See Eichengreen, *Globalizing Capital* (n 4), chapter 4.

[8] This meant that member states had to establish a parity of their reserve currencies and maintain it within a band of + or −1%. This was often done by intervening in foreign exchange markets.

[9] Eichengreen, *Globalizing Capital* (n 4), 136.

[10] See Donald MacKenzie, *Material Markets*, Oxford University Press, 2009, chapter 4, where the author explains that the derivatives market in the 1970s was relatively small, existing in the fringes of the stock market. For an example of how new classes of derivatives were designed to deal with emerging risks, see Vincenzo Bavoso, 'Financial Innovation, Derivatives and the UK and US Interest Rate Swap Scandals: Drawing New Boundaries for the Regulation of Financial Innovation' (2016) 7(2) Global Policy.

[11] Ranald Michie, *The Global Securities Market—A History*, Oxford University Press, 2006, 253.

[12] One distinction that was more relevant to UK financial markets was that between brokers and dealers. Brokers were agents acting on behalf of investors and were remunerated through fees, and could only trade for others and not on their own account (what is referred to as proprietary trading). Dealers could trade on their own account, their profits normally being generated from the trading that they make. See Jakob de Haan, Sander Oosterloo, and Dirk Schoenmaker, *Financial Markets and Institutions—A European Perspective*, Cambridge University Press, 2012, 132.

that the NYSE granted its members to incorporate and obtain a public listing.[13] Between 1976 and 1977 then, in response to its growing competitiveness, NYSE started accepting foreign securities for trading and then foreign brokers as members.[14]

With respect to the United Kingdom, exchange controls were finally removed in 1979, and this exposed the City of London to external competition, particularly from across the Atlantic. It is believed that it was primarily this competition that drove subsequent policies in the UK, aimed at gradually dropping restrictive practices, eventually leading to the 'Big Bang' of 1986 and to a new relationship between the UK government and the City of London.[15] In the same period the London Stock Exchange (LSE) accepted corporate members as well as foreign ones. This change was accompanied by the end of the fixed commission system and the end of the distinction between dealers and brokers that had traditionally characterized the LSE.[16] These changes resulted in a totally new securities market in London, increasingly dominated by large financial institutions, freed of regulatory constraints.[17] Importantly, in the 1980s large financial institutions started internalizing a number of trading operations, without the need to rely on a centralized trading platform such as the stock exchange. This was especially the case for bonds, whereby the position of London as a global hub became increasingly important, also due to the emergence of the eurobond market.[18]

In the 1980s the eurobond market reinforced its position as the preferred venue for the trading of government bonds, with increasing numbers of international investors providing depth and liquidity, which many European national markets did not have. The progressive rise of the eurobond market was also part of a broader process of globalization that saw sharp increases in transactions in foreign securities.[19] It was with the inception of the single currency in the EU though that bond markets in Europe ceased to be fragmented along national borders. Towards the end of the 1990s the global growth of bond issues saw euro-denominated bonds

[13] Michie, *The Global Securities Market* (n 11), 256–257. It is worth noting that at that stage commercial banks were still excluded from membership.

[14] ibid, 269–270.

[15] ibid, 275–276. For a different perspective on the relationship between the City and the UK government, and the historical privileged position of the former towards the latter, see George Gilligan 'Bad Behaviour in International Financial Markets: National and Multilateral Perspectives', in *Integrity Risk and Accountability in Capital Markets: Regulating Culture*, edited by J O'Brien and G Gilligan, Hart, 2013.

[16] This in particular meant the disappearance of 'stockjobbers', bearing in mind that all transactions in London had to be made through a dealer. See Michie, *The Global Securities Market* (n 11) 253.

[17] It needs to be remembered that unlike in the US, the UK never had any Glass-Steagall-type restrictions related to the activities of commercial banks and investment firms, and separation between the two.

[18] The development of the eurobond market is discussed in more details in Chapter 4 of this book.

[19] This was so especially in the US. See Michie, *The Global Securities Market* (n 11) 292.

increasing their share of global net issuances, especially with respect to private-sector issues.[20]

It is important to remember that with the end of Bretton Woods, the newly liberalized and progressively global financial industry was lacking a regulatory infrastructure that could co-ordinate and oversee financial markets at the global level. Instead, reliance was laid on transnational regulatory actors, or in other words international bodies such as the International Monetary Fund (IMF), and the Bank for International Settlement (BIS, the Basel Committee on Banking Supervision being part of it). These however, never possessed the attributes of hard law regulatory authorities and in fact performed roles that never amounted to the effective regulation and supervision of financial markets.[21] In this environment the market for debt securities thrived and it progressively moved away from the more regulated stock exchanges, towards more specialized ones, or altogether over-the-counter (OTC).[22]

2.3 Towards the new world of finance

The handling of bond trading became progressively more central to the operations of large financial institutions. The evolution of bond-type products and their trading needs therefore to be examined in connection with the last stage of regulatory changes that occurred between the 1990s and the early 2000s. The first sweeping change is related to derivatives. As mentioned earlier, the evolution of derivatives from a small niche market revolving around physical assets—such as agricultural products in Chicago, or raw materials in London—to one more squarely concerned with the management of complex financial risks, was a gradual one. Donald MacKenzie provides an insightful analysis of these changes which in fact started in the late 1960s.[23] The first relevant development was the move from agricultural derivatives, to financial derivatives, namely a derivative that was based not on the value of a real asset (ie, bananas or gold) but rather on the value of other financial products/instrument. Even more drastic was the possibility to

20 See Marco Pagano and Ernst-Ludwig Von Thadden, 'The European Bond Markets under EMU' (2004) 20(4) Oxford Review of Economic Policy 533–534.

21 This is explained by Emilios Avgouleas in *Governance of Global Financial Markets—The Law, the Economics, the Politics*, Cambridge University Press, 2012, 165, where the origins of the most influential transnational regulatory actors are drawn. On the soft law character of international financial law, see Chris Brummer, Soft Law and the Global Financial System', Cambridge University Press, 2015, especially chapters 2 and 5.

22 This assertion will become clearer in Chapter 6 of this monograph where the regulatory framework of debt capital markets is analysed closely. It suffices at this stage to say that beyond the move to more specialized markets, sophisticated bond issues such as securitization chiefly fall within the scope of regulatory exceptions and thus outside the perimeter of financial regulation.

23 Donald MacKenzie, *An Engine, Not a Camera—How Financial Models Shape Markets*, MIT Press, 2008.

enter derivatives that were based on a financial index, such as the Dow-Jones or the Standard and Poor's 500.[24] What crystallized these changes, however, were extreme shifts in the law and regulation of derivatives.

At the heart of these changes there was a fundamental distinction between commercial or hedging derivatives on the one hand, which were considered legitimate, and speculative derivatives on the other hand, which were associated with gambling and thus considered illegal. The basis for this distinction rested for many years on a characterization developed by US courts, whereby the discerning elements was the deliverability of the underlying asset. Under this doctrine, courts would deem unenforceable any contract where delivery was not possible.[25] This common law distinction was effectively abandoned in 2000 with the enactment in the US of the Commodities Futures Modernization Act, which had the effect of further liberalizing derivatives trading, by essentially making them all legal and enforceable (which had huge implications on the OTC market and on securitization, as is explained in section 2.2).[26]

A similar provision limited the application of speculative derivatives in the UK, where prohibitions under the Gaming Act 1845 extended to financial investments. As a consequence, derivative contracts entered into as wagers were deemed void because they were assimilated to gambling. The already mentioned Big Bang[27] in 1986 exempted 'investments', broadly defined, from the purpose of the Gaming Act, thus effectively liberalizing the use of speculative derivatives.

It was noted earlier that the role of large banks started to change, specifically with respect to the bond market, but more generally with respect to their organizational and business model. While UK financial markets were never affected, unlike their US counterparts, by a statutory prohibition to combine commercial and investment businesses,[28] organizational changes did take place with the Big Bang

24 ibid, 143–145.

25 This is very well explained by Lynn Stout in 'Derivatives and the Legal Origin of the 2008 Credit Crisis' (2011) 1 Harvard Business Law Review 1–38. Professor Stout stressed how the removal of the traditional distinction between hedging and speculative derivatives gave way to the mass liberalization of over-the-counter speculative derivatives. The common law doctrine at the heart of the distinction between derivative contracts was established by a US Supreme Court case, *Irwin v Williar* 110 US 499 (1884). In the UK, a similar doctrine was established in *Universal Stock Exchange v Strachan* [1896] AC 166, para 18-22, where the House of Lords held that contracts for difference, that is where participants speculate on the performance of the underlying price, were void as they were considered gaming contracts.

26 Commodities Futures Modernization Act 2000, Pub. L. No. 106-554, 114 Stat. 2763. Central to the liberalization of derivatives was the head of the US Federal Reserve at that time, Alan Greenspan, who famously praised the quality of derivatives, especially in times of financial distress, due to their capacity to unbundle risks and allocate them optimally across the financial system. See The Federal Reserve Board, 'Remarks by Chairman Alan Greenspan', before the Futures Industry Association, Boca Raton Florida, 19 March 1999, available at www.federalreserve.gov/boarddocs/speeches/1999/19990319.htm (last accessed on 17/04/2024).

27 More specifically, the Financial Services Act 1986, s 63.

28 In the US, this prohibition was recognized with the Banking Act 1933, the so-called Glass-Steagall Act, which was part of the broader regulatory package engineered with the New Deal.

of 1986, which had the effect of aggregating into larger institutions different businesses that had traditionally remained distinct and compartmentalized.[29] Critical organizational changes in the UK banking environment were also caused by the demutualization of building societies[30] which represented another regulatory response to the increasing competitiveness of securities markets.[31]

The result was similar to what happened in the US, with the progressive and relentless abrogation of the aforementioned New Deal prohibitions,[32] culminating with its final repeal in 1999 through the Gramm-Leach-Bliley Act.[33] What followed was a wave of mergers between commercial banks and investment firms, which elicited the combination under the same institution of traditional retail functions together with advisory ones.

So far, this section has focused on regulatory changes that took place in the US and the UK. At the international level, the Basel framework played an important role since its first Accord in 1988 that sought to coordinate the regulation of bank capital[34] for internationally active banks. The first Basel framework was aimed at reducing systemic risk by requiring banks to hold minimum amounts of capital against risk, and at providing a level playing field for banks, thus also mitigating problems of regulatory arbitrage.[35] While a closer critique of Basel I is outside the scope of this chapter, it is relevant to stress how its mechanics of risk calculation

[29] Mention was made earlier of the traditional distinction between dealers and brokers. From a different perspective, stockbrokers as wholesalers, and stockjobbers as market-makers were occupying different compartments of UK financial markets. Moreover, in 1986 the London Stock Exchange agreed to accept corporate members, whereas previously stockbroking firms and stockjobbers were partnerships of individuals. See Colin Bamford, *Principles of International Financial Law*, Oxford University Press, 2011, 176.

[30] Traditionally, building societies were mutual organizations, owned by their members, and the range of their activities was restricted to personal savings and/or home mortgages. With their demutualization under the Building Societies Act 1986, they adopted a corporate organizational model (shareholder-owned instead of member-owned) that allowed them to list their shares and diversify their range of activities.

[31] See on this Graham Tayler, 'UK Building Society Demutualisation Motives' (2003) 12(4) Business Ethics: A European Review.

[32] As highlighted by Emilios Avgouleas, 'The Reform of "Too-Big-To-Fail" Bank: A New Regulatory Model for the Institutional Separation of "Casino" from "Utility" Banking', February 2010, available at SSRN, specific attention needs to be paid to a number of sections of the original Act, in particular ss 16 (prohibition of proprietary trading), 20, 21, and 32 (on the prohibition of affiliation and engagement with investment activities and entities).

[33] Financial Services Modernization Act, Pub. L. No. 106-102, 112 Stat. 1338 (1999). See on this Arthur Wilmarth, 'The Dark Side of Universal Banking: Financial Conglomerates and the Origins of the Subprime Financial Crisis' (2009) 41(4) Connecticut Law Review 963; see Avgouleas, 'The Reform of "Too-Big-To-Fail" Bank' (n 32) 12–13.

[34] Capital adequacy is defined under Principle 16 of the Basel Committee 'Core Principles for Effective Banking Supervision' issued in September 1997 (revised in October 2006, and then in 2012). Under this definition, capital requirements are set to reflect the risk undertaken by a bank in the context of the markets and the macroeconomic conditions in which it operates. The capital is therefore set by the relevant supervisor in order to absorb the related losses. For a general understanding of bank capital regulation, see Simon Gleeson, *Gleeson on the International Regulation of Banking*, Oxford University Press, 2018, 20–21.

[35] Douglas Arner, 'The Global Credit Crisis of 2008: Causes and Consequences', AIIFL Working Paper no.3, January 2009, 13.

allowed off-balance sheet assets to qualify as total risk-adjusted assets for the purpose of capital. More on the pre-crisis regulation of securitization will be said in Part III of this book, but the conclusion shared among a number of academics is that the Basel framework represented a regulatory incentive for the wider growth of securitization in the late 1980s. The contextual development of the originate-to-distribute model that is discussed later in this section was also a consequence of that, namely it was the result of the employment of securitization for the purpose of gaming capital requirements.[36]

At the European level, the organizational structure of banks was liberalized with the Second Banking Directive.[37] The Directive in particular allowed banks that had been authorized in their home state, to conduct their activities and provide related services across the EU, subject to mutual recognition. It will be remembered that a legal separation between commercial and investment activities was not present across all EU states, and as the mutual recognition extended to all types of banking activities, it created pressure on member states to permit such activities, or impose a competitive disadvantage upon the local banking sector.[38]

Before diving in the next section into the world of securitization, it is necessary to understand another segment of debt finance that grew exponentially after the 1980s: the commercial paper market. Commercial paper was introduced in the US over a century ago as a short-term unsecured funding tool, chiefly designed to allow corporations to raise finance by selling their short-term obligations. One of the benefits of this market was its cost-effective regulatory regime, which falls within the exemptions of the US Securities Act 1933 with respect to the registration of securities.[39] What is interesting for the purpose of this discussion is that from the 1980s onwards, new categories of issuers, such as foreign financial institutions, started to participate in this market, due to the progressive liberalization of global financial markets.

The higher volume of issuance was also due to other factors such as the notorious wave of mergers and acquisitions that characterized the 1980s, and the development of the swap market that allowed issuers to combine liabilities (for instance with other currencies, in the case of foreign exchange swaps).[40] What was

[36] ibid, 14–15. As explained in Chapter 4, by legally transferring assets off-balance sheet, securitization became a means to improve regulatory capital, essentially enabling banks to increase their assets base without at the same time increasing their capital.

[37] 89/646/EEC [1989] OJ L386/1, later consolidated into the Credit Institutions Directive 2000/12/EC [2000] OJ L126/1.

[38] See Stephen Valdez and Philip Molyneux, *An Introduction to Global Financial Markets*, Palgrave Macmillan, 2013, 43.

[39] Under the Act, s 3(a)(3) allows commercial paper to be sold without the disclosure protection (both prospectus and registration) that is typically mandated by the Act. This is due to the short-term nature of commercial paper, whose maturity normally ranges between three days and 270 days, with most issuances being within a ninety-day maturity. The exception includes a security with a maturity of not more than nine months.

[40] Mitchell Post, Michael Schoenbeck, and Joyce Payne, 'The Evolution of the U.S. Commercial Paper Market since 1980' (1992) 78 Federal Reserve Bulletin 879, 879.

probably the most important innovation in this market was the introduction of asset-backed commercial paper, which ushered in the advent of off-balance sheet financing. This new transactional form would go on to become the emblem of the financial world that took shape in the 1990s, as is explained in the next section. Lastly, it is important to note that the evolution of commercial paper in the 1980s coincided with the development of money market mutual funds, which became increasingly important as the largest source of funding for borrowers in the commercial paper market.[41]

2.4 The origins of securitized banking

Regulatory changes were the necessary prerequisite for transactional and product innovation to reach a high climax. This happened with the blossoming of securitization[42] in the 1990s. In its modern format, securitization was engineered in the US in the 1970s, in order to facilitate lending towards home ownership, boosting in essence the liquidity of the secondary market for mortgages.[43] This market revolved at that time around the operations of two government-sponsored enterprises (GSEs), Fannie Mae and Freddie Mac, which were channelling liquidity from the secondary market back to originators of home mortgages.[44] The privatization of the GSEs in the 1970s gave pace to the evolution of securitization and its more widespread application to different areas of capital markets—effectively the rise of private-label securitization.

Firstly, a number of originators (banks, corporations, public entities) started to enter the securitization market, broadening the range of assets that could be securitized and converted into more liquid bonds.[45] Different maturities and risk profiles of these underlying assets meant that the appetite of a more diverse range of investors could be attracted to this market and its products. One transactional innovation that in the 1980s broadened the investor base of the securitization market

[41] ibid, 879.

[42] The mechanics of securitization will be detailed in Chapter 4 of this monograph.

[43] Initially home ownership was facilitated through the establishment of the Federal National Mortgage Association (more widely known as Fannie Mae) in 1938, a government-sponsored agency with the function of buying mortgage loans from originators, thus pumping federal money into the mortgage market. See Frank Fabozzi and Franco Modigliani, *Mortgage and Mortgage-Backed Securities Markets*, Harvard Business School Press, 1992, 19–20; Leon Kendall, 'Securitization: A New Era in American Finance', in A Primer on Securitization, edited by L Kendall and M Fishman, MIT Press, 2000.

[44] Government-sponsored agencies were instrumental in creating uniform underwriting standards, monitoring the market, and offering a quasi-government guarantee to the investors of securitized bonds. See Kendall, 'Securitization' (n 43), 6; see also Joseph Shenker and Anthony Colletta, 'Asset Securitization: Evolution, Current Issues and New Frontiers' (1990–1991) 69 Texas Law Review 1369.

[45] Kendall, 'Securitization' (n 43), 7. Among the assets securitized during the 1980s and 1990s for instance, one can find different categories of mortgages (fixed-rate, adjustable-rate, second mortgages), auto loans, real estate loans, credit card receivables, equipment leases, marine loans, junk bonds, student loans, aircraft leases.

is what we today call 'tranching', which was then known as collateralized mortgage obligation[46] (CMO, later replaced by the more general collateralized debt obligation, CDO). CMOs provided the opportunity to issue a securitized bond that instead of having a unique cash-flow, had different tranches, each corresponding to a different risk, subordination and yield.[47]

As anticipated earlier in this section, the liberalization of OTC derivatives, and the contextual opening up of new channels of business for large banks, created huge opportunities for the use of securitization. The application of derivatives to plain vanilla securitizations,[48] elicited by the regulatory changes signposted in this section, led to the massive growth of synthetic securitizations at the end of the 1990s. At the same time, as large financial institutions embraced securitization, this led to a twofold transformation of their business model (and of financial markets as a whole), namely the adoption of the originate-to-distribute model instead of the traditional originate-to-hold,[49] and the emergence of the securitized banking model.[50]

As regards the adoption of the originate-to-distribute model, this refers to the practice whereby banks increasingly originated mortgages and other loan assets and instead of holding these assets on their balance sheet to maturity, they repackaged them and sold them off-balance sheet, to a specifically created corporate vehicle.[51] This practice fundamentally changed the way in which banks interfaced with their clients and with capital markets. In fact, it represented the functional integration that at the beginning of the new century tied together banking and capital markets.[52] What is important to stress is that following the last stage of regulatory changes, the newly established large financial conglomerates moved towards a completely new model of business. They could rely on implicit government guarantees, due to their large depositor base (once the domain of commercial banks), while at the same time pursuing short-term profits by conducting high-risk activities (traditionally the prerogative of investment firms).[53] Changes in business

[46] See Lewis Ranieri, 'The Origins of Securitization, Sources of its Growth, and its Future Potential', in *A Primer on Securitization*, edited by L Kendall and M Fishman, MIT Press, 2000, 36–37.

[47] This is explained in greater detail in Chapter 4.

[48] In the context of securitization, 'plain vanilla' refers to the earlier and simpler transactional structure.

[49] See Vitaly Bord and Joao Santos, 'The Rise of the Originate-to-Distribute Model and the Role of Banks in Financial Intermediation', Federal Reserve Bank of New York, Economic Policy Review, July 2012.

[50] On securitized banking, see Gary Gorton and Andrew Metrick, 'Securitized Banking and the Run on the Repo' (2012) 104(3) Journal of Financial Economics 425–451.

[51] Referred to as a special purpose vehicle (SPV) or special purpose entity (SPE). This area is expounded in Chapter 4 of this book.

[52] On the functional integration of banks and capital markets, see Robert Hockett and Saule Omarova, 'The Finance Franchise' (2017) 102 Cornell Law Review 1143.

[53] See on this Sue Jaffer, Nicholas Morris, and David Vines, 'Why Trustworthiness is Important', in *Capital Failure: Rebuilding Trust in Financial Services*, edited by N Morris and D Vines, Oxford University Press, 2014; Sue Jaffer, Nicholas Morris, Edward Sawbridge, and David Vines, 'How Changes to the Financial Services Industry Eroded Trust', in *Capital Failure: Rebuilding Trust in Financial Services*, edited by N Morris and D Vines, Oxford University Press, 2014.

models moved banks away from more traditional sources of earnings, such as interest on clients' loans, and led them to embrace more risky practices, such as proprietary trading[54] in complex derivatives products.[55]

Moreover, Basel I and II had established a regulatory system that relied heavily on micro-prudential approaches to capital requirements, and generally on a firm-specific focus on risk-taking and liquidity. In essence, Basel I and II ignored the interplay between banks and capital markets, and specifically the off-balance sheet network of liabilities that securitization elicited. From a different perspective, due to Basel's narrow focus, securitization became an arbitrage tool for banks to increase their asset base, while allocating less capital to the related risks.[56]

In the pre-crisis years the increased employment of the originate-to-distribute model, facilitated by the Basel regulation of capital requirements, led to soaring levels of leverage in the financial system and levels of risk-taking that could only be quantified in hindsight in the aftermath of the 2008 crisis.

The second transformation mentioned earlier, namely the rise of securitized banking, is of course closely related to the growth of securitization. The focus here is on the interconnections between the banking system—or rather the banks that were originating assets—and the other non-bank entities in the financial system that were buying securitized bonds. Between the 1980s and 1990s, financial liberalization, and the dismantling of the post-war regulatory infrastructure, enabled the progressive globalization of financial activities, most of which were not conducted on organized and regulated exchanges. This latest development coincides with what at the outset of the GFC was termed the shadow banking system, explained by Perry Mehrling and Zoltan Pozsar in their seminal works.[57]

In the context of this discussion on the development of debt capital markets, it is useful to point out that the so-called shadow banking system signalled the emergence of a new model of financial intermediation. Large financial institutions (LFIs—universal banks, sometimes recognized as systemically important financial institutions) slowly abandoned the model whereby they were originating loan-type assets on the assets side of their balance sheet, while relying primarily on depositors' money on the liabilities side of their balance sheet.[58] This model had

[54] This refers to the bank's practice of trading on its own account as opposed to its clients' account.

[55] Jaffer, Morris, Sawbridge, and Vines, 'Changes to the Financial Services Industry' (n 53), 51.

[56] A clear explanation of the shortcomings of the Basel framework is provided by Emilios Avgouleas, *Governance of Global Financial Markets: The Law, the Economics, the Politics*, Oxford University Press, 2012, 238–240; see also Markus Brunnermaier, 'Deciphering the Liquidity and Credit Crunch 2007–2008' (2009) 23 Journal of Economic Perspectives.

[57] See on this Perry Mehrling, Zoltan Pozsar, James Sweeney, and Daniel Neilson, 'Bagehot Was a Shadow Banker: Shadow Banking, Central Banking and the Future of Global Finance', 2013, available at SSRN http://papers.ssrn.com/sol3/papers.cfm?abstract_id=2232016 (last accessed on 17/04/2024); and Zoltan Pozsar, Tobias Adrian, Adam Ashcroft, and Hayley Boesky, 'Shadow Banking' (2010) 458 Federal Reserve Bank of New York Staff Reports.

[58] This is a simplification of course. For a less simplified representation of banks' balance sheets, see the table provided by *Gleeson on the International Regulation of Banking* (n 34), 5.

for many years characterized the operations of commercial banks, generating relatively low but steady income represented by the difference (spread) between the interest charged for the loans originated and that paid to depositors. The removal of regulatory barriers allowed banks to absorb investment firms, and then engage with new and more profitable channels of intermediation. Instead of loans or mortgages on the assets side, LFIs held bonds and other securitized assets (purchased from other entities or manufactured in-house and warehoused), whereas on the liabilities side, instead of relying on depositors' cash, they increasingly funded their operations through short-term lending from the money market, primarily through repo transactions.[59]

The shortcoming and riskiness of this (wholesale) funding system will become clearer with the analysis conducted in Chapter 4. At this stage it suffices to say that under the securitized banking model LFIs profited greatly from loan intermediation and other advisory and consulting services.[60] While this proved highly lucrative in the short term, as we learned in the aftermath of 2008, it also increased the interconnectedness between the banking system and the unregulated shadow banking sector, exposing as a result the fragility of the financial system as a whole.[61]

Lastly, it becomes clearer at the end of this excursus that the model of intermediation described above was grounded on securitization and repo transactions. More specifically, it was centred on LFIs manufacturing or purchasing securitized bonds and then pledging them as collateral in return for short-term funding from the money market. This is the process that Mehrling aptly explained as 'money market funding of capital market lending',[62] which has also become known as market-based finance.[63]

2.5 Debt capital markets post-2008

After the turmoil of 2008, much of the securitized banking system came to a near standstill. As is demonstrated in the second part of this chapter, both securitization and the repo market remained moribund in the post-crisis years, more so across Europe than in the US. The situation started to change around 2014, with a number of policy initiatives that were aimed at restarting capital markets, and

[59] See Zoltan Pozsar, 'Shadow Banking: The Money View', Office of Financial Research Working Paper 14-04, July 2014.

[60] See Mehrling and others, 'Bagehot Was a Shadow Banker' (n 57).

[61] On the fragility of the shadow banking system and the lack of regulation therein, see Morgan Ricks, 'Regulating Money Creation after the Crisis' (2011) 1 Harvard Business Law Review 75.

[62] Mehrling and others, 'Bagehot Was a Shadow Banker' (n 57).

[63] For a critique and full explanation on market-based finance, see Vincenzo Bavoso, 'Market-Based Finance, Debt and Systemic Risk: A Critique of the EU Capital Markets Union' (2018) 11(3) Accounting Economics and Law: A Convivium; and also the work of the Financial Conduct Authority (FCA) 'Market-Based Finance: Its Contribution and Emerging Issues', Occasional Paper 18, May 2016.

rebranding the shadow banking system as resilient market-based finance.[64] What became particularly interesting in the post-crisis years was the way in which intermediation chains shifted, moving the origination of risky loans partly away from banks. After 2014 in particular, there was a sharp increase in the involvement of non-bank financial institutions as originators of leveraged loans. This happened primarily through collateralized loan obligations (CLOs).[65]

While the technique at the heart of CLOs is part of the broader innovation of securitization,[66] its application showed some interesting evolving features. In particular, the CLO market has developed a synergy with another asset market, namely highly leveraged loans, the latter having risen in value from $554 billion in 2007 to $1.2 trillion in 2019.[67] Beyond the problems associated with these rising risks[68] there is an underlying trend whereby private equity (PE) firms have become pivotal in the origination of these risky loans, chiefly through their leveraged acquisitions. PE firms have also been acting as managers of these structured transactions, playing in some ways the role that investment banks were covering in the CDO market before 2008.[69] Critically, this evolving market is at the very heart of the private debt crisis that exploded during the spring of 2020, in conjunction with the Covid-19 pandemic.[70]

It is important to note that notwithstanding the regulatory adjustments enacted in the post-GFC years, some areas of the financial system have remained insufficiently reformed, thus allowing the re-emergence of practices that are redolent of pre-2008 years. This phenomenon is visible in the CLO market. Chapter 4 of this monograph explains in greater detail how the CLO market prospered. To a great degree, this was permitted by risk management mechanisms that incentivised investors to take on counterparty credit risk that they could not properly gauge, and that remained beyond the radar of regulators' scrutiny. Much like CDSs before

[64] See G30, 'Shadow banking and capital markets: Risks and opportunities', Washington, November 2016.

[65] See Financial Stability Board, 'Vulnerabilities associated with leveraged loans and collateralized loan obligations', 19 December 2019, 1.

[66] See for an overview, Andreas Jobst, 'Collateralized Loan Obligations (CLOs): A Primer', CFS Working Paper, No. 2002/13, Goethe University, Center for Financial Studies, 11, 12, where Jobst explains that in principle CLOs are a subset of CDOs, whereby the issuer combines a selection of loan-type assets of similar characteristics in order to create a credit-enhanced claim against the portfolio's cashflow.

[67] See Joe Rennison and Rober Smith, 'CLOs: ground zero for the next stage of the financial crisis?', *Financial Times* (13 May 2020).

[68] See on this IMF, 'Global Financial Stability Report', October 2019, chapter 2, highlighting how financial risk-taking and the riskiness of lending had risen in previous years, and how the high level of corporate leverage could exacerbate the vulnerability of the financial system in the event of a downturn.

[69] See Rod Dubitsky, 'CLOs, Private Equity, Pensions and Systemic Risk' (Spring 2020) The Journal of Structured Finance.

[70] Some commentators may argue that the pandemic, and the ensuing economic slowdown, were the main cause of the rising defaults in CLOs, but a closer look into this market shows that rising levels of corporate debt had already been identified as possible determinants of an economic slowdown well before the pandemic. IMF, 'Global Financial Stability Report' (n 68).

2008, total return swaps (TRSs) allow institutional investors to leverage their balance sheet by gaining access to the return of financial assets, without however owning the underlying assets.[71] What is particularly controversial about the application of these derivatives is that the layers of counterparty credit risk that they create have remained poorly monitored due to the delay in implementing relevant rules on swaps and margin requirements.[72]

2.6 The importance of technology and the emerging world of FinTech

Product and transactional innovations as they are discussed in the previous sections were all made possible by advances in information technology (IT). Especially in the post-WWII years the pace of that innovation allowed geographical and temporal restrictions that had in the past constrained financial markets within local dimensions to be minimised or annulled altogether. In other words, the liberalization and ensuing globalization of securities markets that is illustrated in this chapter was elicited by a number of IT innovations that contributed to connecting financial markets around the world.

The impact of technology on the world of finance is receiving renewed attention in legal and financial literature due to the impetus of words such as FinTech (a contraction for 'financial' and 'technology') and blockchain. The reality is that the synergy between technology and finance is not a new phenomenon. It has certainly increased its momentum since the inception of the automated teller machine (ATM) in 1969 in the UK, due to the pace of the innovations that ensued. For instance, in the 1960s and 70s, digitalized ledgers had already contributed to integrate financial institutions at a global level because they represented the necessary infrastructure on which cross-border payments could work.

Trading on stock exchanges in the 1980s was facilitated by the progressive use of electronic quotes, which eventually led to new ways to distribute information faster and more widely. Eventually, in connection with the Big Bang of 1986, the London Stock Exchange (LSE) moved from face-to-face dealings on the market floor, to computer and/or telephone dealings.[73] Earlier, in the 1970s,

[71] Under a total return swap two parties exchange the returns from a financial asset. The contractual structure of this derivative is similar to other swaps (such as credit default swaps), and it sees one party (the investor) making payments based on a set rate, while the other party (say a bank holding the financial asset) makes payments based on the return of the underlying assets. See for an illustration Corporate Finance Institute, 'What is a Total Return Swap (TRS)?', available at https://corporatefinanceinstitute.com/resources/knowledge/finance/total-return-swap-trs/ (last accessed on 17/04/2024).

[72] Joe Rennison, Eric Platt, Colby Smith, and Philip Stafford, 'US put off derivatives rules for a decade before Archegos blew up', *Financial Times* (12 April 2021), www.ft.com/content/7819e714-bf9d-4f83-a6e4-497df534f77c (last accessed on 17/04/2024).

[73] See London Stock Exchange, 'Our History', available at www.londonstockexchange.com/discover/lseg/our-history (last accessed on 17/04/2024).

over-the-counter automated trading became possible with the establishment of the National Association of Securities Dealers Automated Quotations (known as NASDAQ), which created the preconditions for the making of the digital marketplace.[74] More recent advances in this sphere have revolved around computer programs that allowed the wide application of trading and investment techniques known as high-frequency trading (HFT) and dark pools. These represent a form of algorithmic automated trading and take advantage of high order-to-trade ratios, thus maximizing high volumes of financial data through electronic trading tools. The modernization of the bond market was equally spurred by the application of data science and computing, which led to the progressive electronification of bond trading, and the increased efficiency that is associated with this process.[75]

Blockchain is chronologically the latest example of technology applied to finance. It represents an improvement of public-private key encryption originally developed in the 1970s.[76] In its current form, blockchain allows coordinating individual activities conducted on the Internet, ensuring that the data has not been altered.[77] In essence, it is a chronological database of transactions recorded by a network of computers, whereby each blockchain is encrypted and organized into smaller datasets.[78] What is probably the most relevant application of blockchain is the possibility to create digital assets, or cryptographic tokens that can represent property interests in specific services. The legal and financial classification of these tokens is becoming the subject of academic debates, specifically with respect to the emerging questions surrounding initial coin offerings (ICOs).[79]

What needs to be stressed about the rise of FinTech in the period following 2008 is the new dimension of the symbiosis between finance and technology. Before 2008, the innovations in FinTech had taken place within large financial institutions, which had also benefited directly from the application of new technologies (translating into new processes, transactions and products). The post-crisis years saw an increasing level of distrust of LFIs, largely because of the role that they played in the build-up of the GFC, and also because of their lending behaviour

[74] See NASDAQ, 'NASDAQ's Story', available at www.business.nasdaq.com/discover/nasdaq-story/index.html (last accessed on 17/04/2024).

[75] See Robin Wigglesworth and Joe Rennison, 'Bond trading: Technology Finally Disrupt a $50tn Market', *Financial Times* (9 May 2018). The authors also observe that the biggest disruptive force in recent years has been the rise of exchange traded funds (ETF) which rely on algorithmic trading.

[76] See Whitfield Diffie and Martin Hellman, 'New Directions in Cryptography' (1976) 22 IEEE Transactions on Information Theory 644.

[77] See Aaron Wright and Primavera De Filippi, 'Decentralized Blockchain Technology and the Rise of Lex Cryptographia', 10 March 2015, available at SSRN, 6. They explain that blockchain protocols ensure that transactions on a blockchain are valid and never recorded to a shared repository more than once. Therefore, blockchain enables people to coordinate individual transactions in a decentralized manner without the need to rely on a central authority to verify and clear all transactions.

[78] ibid, 7.

[79] See on this Wulf Kaal and Marco Dell'Erba, 'Initial Coin Offerings: Emerging Practices, Risk Factors, and Red Flags', in *Fintech Handbook* edited by F Moeslein and S Omlor, Verlag C.H. Beck, 2008.

in the years leading up to 2008.[80] These factors led in the past fifteen years to an increasing number of start-up technology firms engaging directly with the delivery of financial services and products to end-users, bypassing therefore the service traditionally provided by banks.[81] The most prominent intermediation role conducted by FinTech platforms in this sense is related to peer-to-peer (P2P) lending, which represents a disintermediation of lending facilities, from banks towards non-bank entities. The growth of P2P lending has been significant, especially in the US, China, and the UK, where facilitative regulatory frameworks were initially enacted to encourage this practice in the post-2008 period.[82] This segment of financial markets has become particularly relevant for the purpose of this book, given its increasing interplay with wholesale capital markets, and the regulatory questions that emerge from this channel of market-based intermediation.

3 Illustrating the growth of debt capital markets

Throughout this chapter reference has consistently been made to the growth of debt capital markets and the attendant development of a number of debt markets, such as bonds and securitization. The purpose of this section is to provide some backing to that claim and illustrate the measure of that growth. In light of the analysis that is conducted later in this book on the future direction and regulation of debt capital markets, it is also useful to reflect on the increase in the level of private debt creation that ensued, and the attendant regulatory challenges associated with this phenomenon.

One key driver behind the growth of debt capital markets—not just in Europe but globally—was the development of the eurobond market in the 1980s. This phenomenon needs to be understood in conjunction with the liberalization of national financial markets in most jurisdictions, and with the ensuing opportunities to participate in other countries' capital markets.[83] The eurobond market increased from

[80] See on this: Douglas Arner, Janos Barberis, and Ross Buckley, 'The Evolution of FinTech: A New Post-Crisis Paradigm?' (2016) 62 University of New South Wales Law Research Series 6–7. See also on the evolution of banking Ross Buckley, 'The Changing Nature of Banking and Why it Matters', in *Rethinking Global Finance and its Regulation*, edited by Buckley, Avgouleas, and Arner, Cambridge University Press, 2015; more specifically on the lending behaviour of banks in the pre-crisis years, see Sue Jaffer, Nicholas Morris, Edward Sawbridge, and David Vines, 'How Changes to the Financial Services Industry Eroded Trust', in *Capital Failure: Rebuilding Trust in Financial Services*, edited by N Morris and D Vines, Oxford University Press, 2014.

[81] The range of services provided by these firms can be wide, but a growing phenomenon is that of peer-to-peer lending, whereby technology platforms bring together lenders and borrowers, allowing them to bypass the role of banks. See on this Vincenzo Bavoso, 'The Promise and Perils of Alternative Market-Based Finance: The Case of P2P Lending in the UK' (2019) 21 Journal of Banking Regulation 395–409.

[82] On the regulatory trajectory of P2P lending, see Bavoso, 'The Promise and Perils of Alternative Market-Based Finance' (n 81).

[83] Of course the eurobond market as such did not start in the 1980s. One early prominent example dates back to 1963, when Autostrade SpA, the public company managing Italy's motorway network,

321 issues for a value of $19.8 billion in 1980, to 1692 issues for a value of $221.7 billion in 1989. Contextually, the secondary market also grew, from turnover of $240 billion in 1980, to $8,833 billion in 1991.[84] This represented an invaluable platform for sovereign borrowers (but also for private issuers) to access large pools of investors (especially those sovereign borrowers that could not count on deep and liquid national markets); investors in turn could rely on debt securities denominated in a currency that was not the issuer's.

A different concept that emerged in more recent times with the adoption of the single currency in the European Union, is that of sovereign bonds denominated in the euro (thus eurobonds, vis-à-vis eurobonds which are bonds issued in a currency different from the issuer's). While a discussion on the problems and challenges associated with the EU monetary union is beyond the scope of this book, it suffices to recall here that the EU architecture did not include a fiscal union, therefore a complete mutualization of debt across all member states is still absent.[85] Overall, between 1999 and 2006 the outstanding nominal amount of eurobonds increased by 84%, more specifically from EUR 6,381 billion in 1999, to EUR 11,725 billion in 2006.[86]

Despite the fact that the above numbers reflect a large majority of EU issuers, the global attractiveness of the eurobond market cannot be neglected. Generally speaking, the globalization of financial markets has entailed a progressive increase in debt securities denominated in a foreign currency (overall 140% between 1999 and 2006).[87] As will be observed later in this section, bond markets experienced a rapid growth globally in the 1990s and early 2000s, exceeding the rise of world GDP. In this context, the eurobond market grew even faster, and by mid-2007 euro-denominated debt securities accounted for 27% of all debt securities (against 43% US dollar and 14% yen).[88]

The key claim put forward in this section is also concerned with how debt securities became the most important tool to raise finance in global financial markets, and how their growth was not mirrored by that of equity markets. Looking at the NYSE listings, in 1970 there were 636 stocks against 113 bonds; in 1989 numbers had gone up, with 3030 stocks against 1412 bonds.[89] Listings on a regulated

issued dollar-denominated bonds. See International Capital Markets Association, 'History of the Eurobond market', available at www.icmagroup.org/About-ICMA/history/history-of-the-eurobond-market/ (last accessed on 17/04/2024).

[84] Michie, *The Global Securities Market* (n 11), 274.

[85] This is so, despite a number of arrangements designed to achieve inter-governmental fiscal support, especially in times of crisis, such as the sovereign debt crisis of 2010–11, or the Covid-19 pandemic of 2020. Examples of such arrangements are the European Financial Stability Facility, or the European Stability Mechanism. See on this Stijn Claessens, Ashoka Mody, and Shahin Vallee, 'Paths to Eurobonds', Bruegel Working Paper 2012/10, July 2012.

[86] European Central Bank, 'The Euro Bonds and Derivatives Markets', June 2007, 7.

[87] ibid, 7.

[88] ibid, 8.

[89] Michie, *The Global Securities Market* (n 11), 281.

exchange, however, only provide part of the picture, because the trading (and to some extent also the listing) of debt securities started in the 1990s to move to alternative trading venues, such as multilateral trading facilities (MTFs), or also OTC (which is the case especially for the secondary market in bonds that takes place off exchanges).[90]

From a broader perspective, looking at both the US bond and stock markets relative to nominal GDP provides a clear picture of the disproportionate growth of the former vis-à-vis the latter.[91] As far as the US market is concerned, data focusing on the period between 1988 and 2012 shows a wide divide between debt and equity securities, with the former being 104% larger at the end of 2012.[92]

Similarly, a chart produced by the Federal Reserve Bank of San Francisco (Figure 2.1)[93] looked at corporate securities issued in the US between January 1996 and July 2005. Against about $18 billion of corporate stock, in the same period the value of corporate bond issues amounted to $218 billion.

Looking at the European market, the size of the bond market in the period between 1999 and 2010 rose consistently from just below EUR 10 trillion, to around EUR 23 trillion[94]; over the same period (2000–10) the equity market experienced some major fluctuations, particularly between 2000 and 2002, and then in 2007–08, and it moved from a market value of almost EUR 10 trillion in 2000, to just above EUR 8 trillion in 2010.[95]

It is thus correct to say that from the 1990s the main component of global securities markets has been the bond market—and more generally the market for debt securities.[96]

[90] The regulatory implication of this move will be explained in Chapters 6 and 7 of this book. On this see generally Guido Ferrarini and Paolo Saguato, 'Reforming Securities and Derivatives Trading in the EU: From Emir to MiFIR' (2013) 13(2) Journal of Corporate Law Studies; Nis Jul Clausen and Karsten Engsig Soerensen, 'Reforming the Regulation of Trading Venues in the EU under the Proposed MiFID II—Levelling the Playing Field and Overcoming Market Fragmentation?' (2012) 9(3) European Company and Financial Law Review.

[91] Kurt Shrout, 'The U.S. Bond Market May Be Much Different Than You Think It Is', 30 May 2013, available at https://learnbonds.com/93027/how-big-is-the-bond-market/ (last accessed on 17/04/2024). For an overview of statistics and data related to both the bond market and the stock market, see the Securities Industry and Financial Markets Association (SIFMA) website at: https://sifma.org/resources/archive/research/statistics/ (last accessed on 17/04/2024).

[92] From a different angle, it has also been noted that from 1996 to 2015 total corporate bond issues in the US have quadrupled, while equity issues have barely doubled since 1996. See Cullen Roche, 'The rise of the Bond Market and its Impact on Portfolio Allocations', Pragmatic Capitalism, 25/02/2015, available at www.pragcap.com/the-rise-of-the-bond-market-its-impact-on-portfolio-allocation/ (last accessed on 17/04/2024).

[93] Federal Reserve Bank of San Francisco, 'What are the differences between debt and equity markets?', October 2005, available at www.frbsf.org/education/publications/doctor-econ/2005/october/debt-equity-market/ (last accessed on 24/04/2024).

[94] This is in terms of amounts outstanding. See De Haan, Oosterloo, and Schoenmaker, *Financial Markets and Institutions* (n 12), 136.

[95] ibid, 135.

[96] See Michie, *The Global Securities Market* (n 11) 310. Interestingly Michie also observes the increase in the trade of international bonds, and the importance of the City of London in this market.

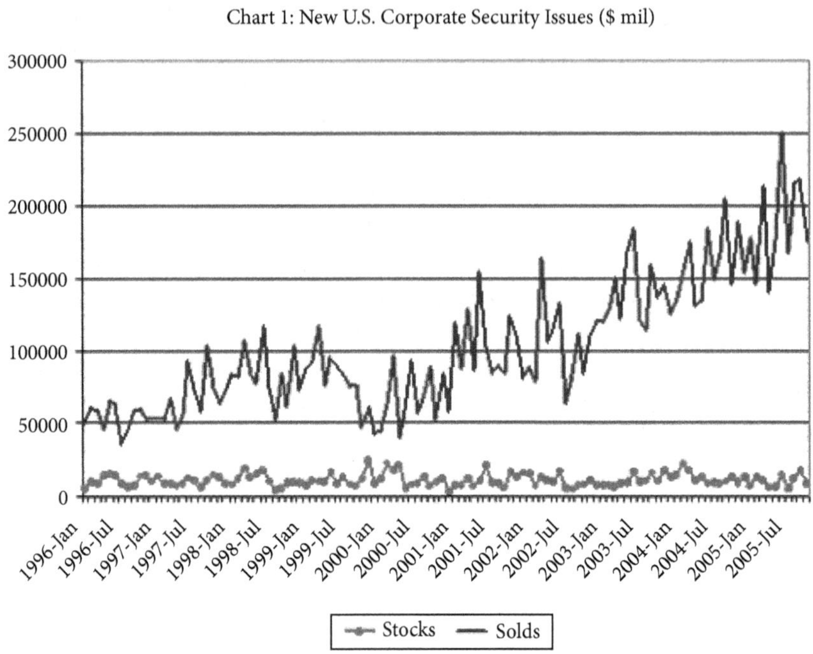

Figure 2.1 US corporate securities issues (Federal Reserve Bank of San Francisco, 2005)
Source: Federal Reserve Bank of San Francisco/Haver Analytics, 'What are the differences between debt and equity markets?', October 2005

A similar trend can be recognized in the more specific context of debt products, from commercial paper, to securitization and other structured products. More than other debt securities markets, though, securitizations suffered greatly the effect of the 2008 GFC, where a mix of investor bias and tentative regulatory changes drastically hindered new issues. Looking at historical European data from 2003 to 2017, two trends emerge clearly, namely an upswing in growth that culminated in 2008 with new issues for over EUR 800 billion (whereas in 2003 they amounted to about EUR 180 billion)[97]; and a downward trend from 2009 to 2013, when values of new issues went down again to EUR 180 billion.[98] Over the four years between 2013 and 2017 the European securitization market showed timid signs of life, with values of new issues oscillating between EUR 216 billion (2016) and EUR 239 billion (2017).[99] It is worth noting that even after the inception of the EU capital markets union (CMU), securitization volumes in Europe (including

[97] De Haan, Oosterloo, and Schoenmaker, *Financial Markets and Institutions* (n 12), 151.
[98] See Association for Financial Markets in Europe, 'Securitisation Data Report', Q1:2018, 7.
[99] ibid.

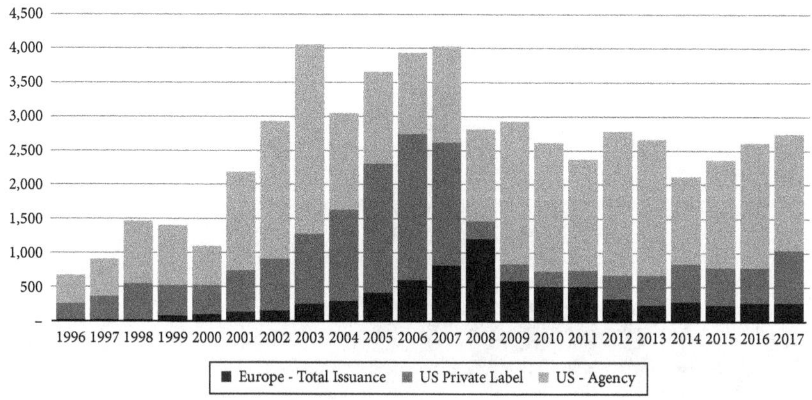

Figure 2.2 US and Europe securitization issues (Kara and Deku, 2018)
Source: Alper Kara and Solomon Deku, 'Securitisation—the complex financial product that fuelled the financial crisis is making a comeback', *The Conversation* (14 September 2018)

the UK) are shrinking as a percentage of US volumes.[100] Chapters 6 and 7 of this monograph focus on the different regulatory frameworks within which debt capital markets developed, before the GFC and after it. The regulatory angle will be particularly useful to appraise the role that new policy initiatives within the EU CMU may have, especially as regards bond and securitization markets.

The US securitization market presents a slightly different picture. While the freezing of structured finance also appeared across the Atlantic, especially in 2008, it experienced a quicker recovery, albeit not reaching pre-crisis levels. It is also worth noting—as clearly illustrated in Figure 2.2[101]—that overall, the US securitization market has been highly subsidized in the post-crisis years by government/agency-backed issues, while the market for private label securitization shrank dramatically in the US too post-2008.

This also shows—confirming what was explained in the previous section—that structured finance grew much earlier in the US, and that it also developed around a number of different market segments. As the 2008 crisis unfolded, certain structured finance markets froze in the US too, some almost completely, as was the case with CDOs, for instance. Figure 2.3[102] outlines the specific components of the

[100] See George Matlock, 'Reviving Securitisation in Europe for CMU', European Stability Mechanism, 15/07/2021.

[101] See Alper Kara and Solomon Deku, 'Securitisation—the Complex Financial Product that Fuelled the Financial Crisis is Making a Comeback', The Conversation, 14 September 2018, available at https://theconversation.com/securitisation-the-complex-financial-product-that-fuelled-the-financial-crisis-is-making-a-comeback-93807 (last accessed on 17/04/2024).

[102] Grahame Johnson and Eric Santor, 'Central Bank Liquidity Provision and Core Funding Markets', Reserve Bank of Australia, Conference 2013, available at www.rba.gov.au/publications/confs/2013/johnson-santor.html (last accessed on 17/04/2024).

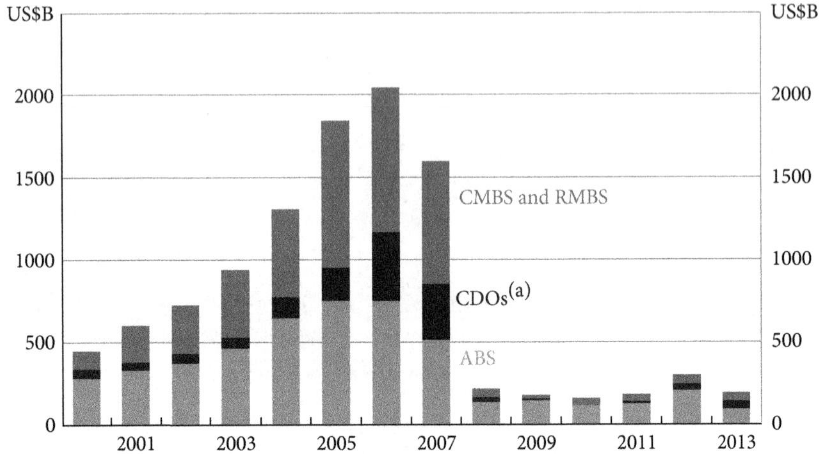

Notes: Year to july 2013; CMBS denotes commercial mortgage-backed securities, RMBS denotes residential mortgage-backed securities, ABS denotes asset-backed securities
(a) Collateralised debt obligations (CDO) issued in US dollars
Source: Securities Industry and Financialv Markets Association

Figure 2.3 US non-agency securitization (Reserve Bank of Australia, 2013)
Source: Grahame Johnson and Eric Santor, 'Central Bank Liquidity Provision and Core Funding Markets', Reserve Bank of Australia, Conference 2013

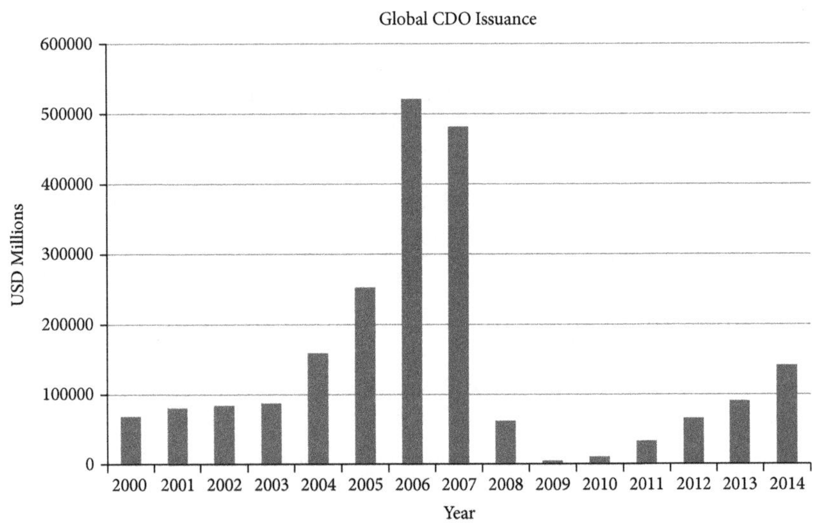

Figure 2.4 CDO issues (Buchanan, 2018)
Source: Bonnie Buchanan, *Securitization and the Global Economy—History and Prospects for the Future*, Palgrave Macmillan, 2017, 115.

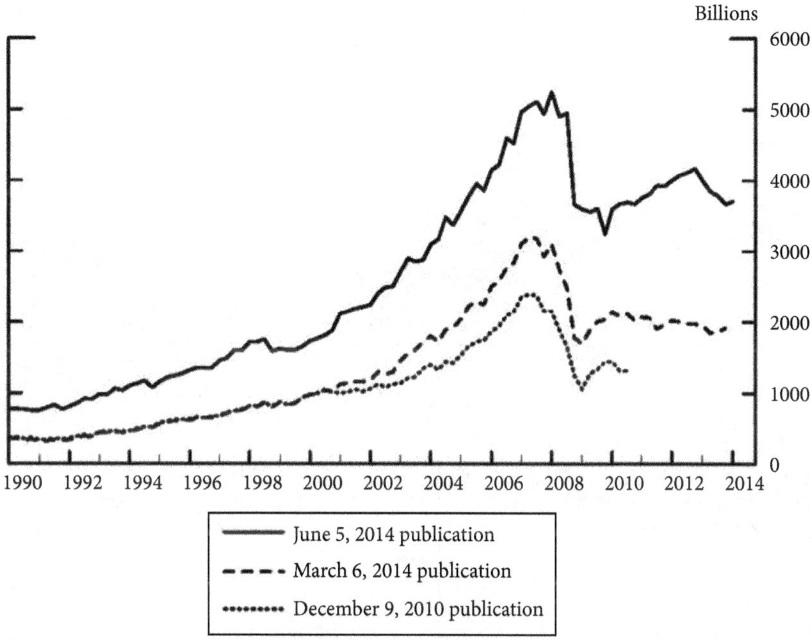

Figure 2.5 Repo liabilities (Holmquist and Gallin, 2014)
Source: Elizabeth Holmquist and Josh Gallin, 'Repurchase Agreements in the Financial Accounts of the United States', FEDS Notes, 30 June 2014

private-label securitization market in the US, with the near collapse of its more problematic segments.

From a global perspective, Figures 2.4 and 2.5 highlight the collapse of the securitized banking model. As explained, securitized banking grew exponentially in the pre-crisis years in connection with the booming of CDOs. Beyond facilitating the creation of virtually unlimited amounts of credit (and therefore asset expansion) for LFI, the top tranches of CDOs were in high demand as collateral for short-term funding from the money market, through repo transactions. Figure 2.4[103] shows the near collapse of CDOs, especially in 2009 and 2010, with a slow but steady process of restart in the subsequent years.

A very similar trend can be recognized by looking at the fluctuations in the repo market,[104] which also experienced a sharp collapse at the end of 2008. Figure 2.5

[103] See Bonnie Buchanan, 'Securitization and the Global Economy—History and Prospects for the Future', Palgrave Macmillan, 2017, 115.

[104] Elizabeth Holmquist and Josh Gallin, 'Repurchase Agreements in the Financial Accounts of the United States', FEDS Notes, 30 June 2014, available at www.federalreserve.gov/econresdata/notes/feds-notes/2014/repurchase-agreements-in-the-financial-accounts-of-the-united-states-20140630.html (last accessed on 17/04/2024).

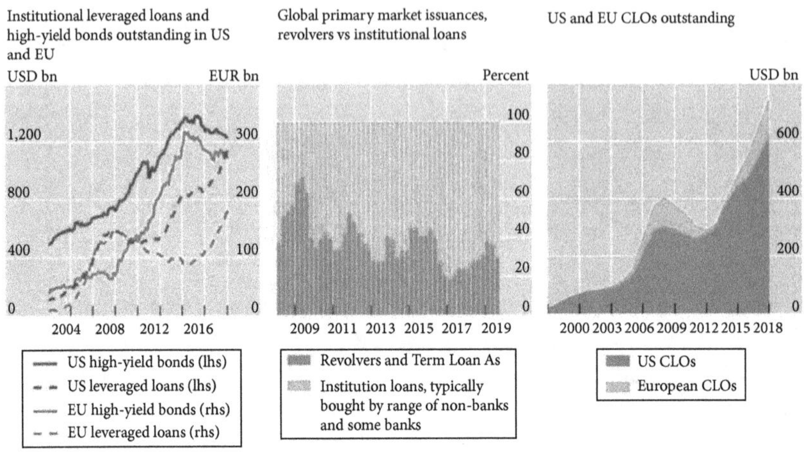

Figure 2.6 Volumes of CLOs and leveraged loans (FSB, 2019)
Source: © 2019 Financial Stability Board, 'Vulnerabilities associated with leveraged loans and collateralised loan obligations', December 2019, 7.

illustrates what Gorton and Metrick suggested,[105] namely that the systemic crisis of 2008 was caused by a run on the repo market, triggered in turn by a liquidity dry-up for the collateral used in repo transactions.[106]

In light of some of the themes that are expanded in later parts of this monograph, namely the post-crisis regulatory developments and the way forward in the global regulation of debt capital markets, it is worth further reflecting on the previous two charts. The trend in fact points to a slow restart of some of the more risky and opaque segments of debt capital markets. While efforts have been made, especially within the EU, to restart the securitization market in a stable and transparent environment (under the Simple, Transparent and Standardized (STS) label), there is some disagreement among policymakers about the desirability of more complex products such as CDOs and synthetic CDOs. As said, this discussion is part of the analysis conducted later in this monograph.

As anticipated in the previous section, the post-2008 period coincided with a rapid increase in the volume of the CLO market, which mirrored the growth of leveraged loans originated both in the US and in Europe. It appears in other words that CLOs became the vehicle for the transmission of risks through new, partially uncharted, transactional avenues. Figure 2.6 illustrates the parallel pattern of growth of leveraged loans and outstanding CLOs.[107]

105 See Gorton and Metrick, 'Securitized Banking (n 50).

106 The mechanics of the repo market and the dynamics related to its collapse in 2008 are examined closely in Chapter 4 of this monograph.

107 FSB, 'Vulnerabilities associated with leveraged loans and collateralised loan obligations', December 2019, 7.

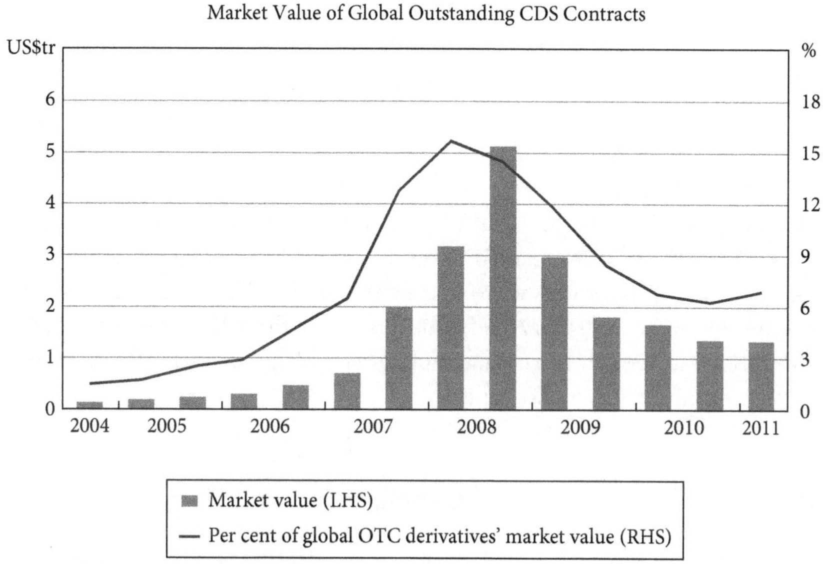

Figure 2.7 Outstanding CDS contracts (Reserve Bank of Australia, 2011)
Source: 2011 Reserve Bank of Australia and Daniel Fabbro, 'The Australian Credit Default Market', Bulletin December 2011, graph 2.

Finally, it is worth also illustrating the expansion of the specific segments of derivatives that contributed to the growth of debt capital markets, and the attendant increase in debt creation and leverage. From 1998, the global development of derivatives followed a bifurcated path: on the one hand, OTC instruments went from a market of around $80 trillion in 1998 to just under $600 trillion in 2010 (with a peak of around $680 trillion in 2007); on the other hand, exchange-traded instruments grew from less than $10 trillion in 1998, to around $80 trillion in 2010.[108] Consistent with these numbers is the more specific development of the market for credit default swaps (CDS) which in the pre-crisis years became the main tool for risk-management and risk-transfer in capital markets. Figure 2.7 shows the sharp increase in the market value of outstanding CDS contracts before and during the GFC.[109] The contextual analysis conducted in chapter seven, on the post-crisis regulation of the relevant aspects of OTC derivatives, clarifies the extent to which this market has been more recently affected by regulatory constraints such as clearing obligations.

Before concluding, it is necessary to stress that all the developments discussed thus far can be reconceptualized as transactional and product innovations.

[108] De Haan, Oosterloo, and Schoenmaker, *Financial Markets and Institutions* (n 12), 159.

[109] See Daniel Fabbro, 'The Australian Credit Default Market' (December 2011) Reserve Bank of Australia Bulletin, graph 2.

Critically, they all contributed, among other things, to increasing the level of private debt in the financial system and ultimately at the social level too. Former chairman of the UK Financial Services Authority (FSA; now Financial Conduct Authority, FCA) Adair Turner provided a powerful statement on this problem.[110] He observed that during the decade before the GFC almost all developed economies experienced rapid growth in credit creation, in the US at a rate of 9% per year, and in the UK 10% per year. What is more important to note is that credit creation grew much faster than GDP, resulting therefore in huge increases in private leverage.[111] Turner goes on to suggest that in the US, private sector leverage grew from 53% in 1950 to 170% in 2007, while in the UK it grew from 50% in 1964 to 180% in 2007.[112] Attendant regulatory problems are further expounded in Chapters 6 and 7 of this monograph.

4 Conclusion

This chapter charted the growth of debt capital markets from the 1970s until present, and in so doing highlighted some of the engines of this trend, as well as the regulatory problems that ensued. It became clear that capital markets have chiefly evolved around debt products, which emerged as a result of a process of innovation. This process in turn was elicited by a series of regulatory changes that resulted in the overall liberalization of financial markets. Advancements in information technology contributed to give further pace to this phenomenon, which is today most prominently recognized with new trends in the FinTech industry. The other important trend to note is the shift in the post-2008 years towards non-bank channels of intermediation.

Discussions conducted in this chapter are instrumental to correctly frame the regulatory questions that are addressed later in this monograph. The background that this part of the book provides is complemented by the enquiry developed next, in Chapter 3. This follows from the findings delineated in this chapter related to the growth of debt capital markets and analyses their intellectual underpinnings. That contextualization allows in turn appreciating the policies and regulatory changes that from the late 1970s favoured the development of larger debt capital markets.

110 See Adair Turner, *Between Debt and the Devil*, Princeton University Press, 2016.

111 ibid, 51. Leverage, and the risks associated with it, are explained in Chapter 5.

112 ibid, 52. Turner questions the usefulness of such levels of private debt creation and whether they achieved the promised economic growth. He suggests in his work instead that the above trend coincides with 'too much of the wrong sort of debt', and that a large chunk of private debt went to fuel consumption and the purchase of already existing assets (largely real estate). Turner argues that these patterns of credit creation lead to inequality and financial instability.

3
The conceptual foundations of debt capital markets

1 Introduction

This chapter reinforces the argument that the growth of debt capital markets took place from the 1970s onwards in connection with a very specific intellectual consensus. Many of the developments in bonds, commercial paper, securitization and attendant markets were triggered by regulatory changes during this period. These changes in turn came as a result of a fundamental belief in what can be called a 'market orthodoxy', under which market forces and market mechanisms were considered more effective than traditional legal and regulatory tools to govern financial markets.

Reference to 'efficient markets' started to abound in policy discourses from the 1970s, in particular when these efficient markets started being seen as antagonistic to government regulation and government intervention, the latter being identified with the process of rule-making not flowing from market mechanisms.[1] The central contention brought forward in this chapter is that debt capital markets thrived and grew as a result of the progressive removal of regulatory barriers. Moreover, the orthodoxy centred on efficient markets entailed replacing state regulation (which had become the centrepiece of financial governance in the post-war years) with market mechanisms. This pre-2008 regulatory framework will be closely analysed in Chapter 6 of this monograph.

To fully appreciate the regulatory changes explored in Chapter 2, and their intellectual roots, a contextual analysis of the theoretical foundation upon which financial markets developed and operated from the 1980s is required. That theoretical foundation is often associated with neoclassical economics, which is actually not one single theory, but rather a bundle of theories, some of which started being developed academically as early as the 1950s. Before engaging with the analysis of the theories that informed financial regulation over the past four decades, a brief discussion on the dynamics of financial regulation is required, and this is done in

[1] See as a paradigmatic example of this intellectual orientation, Milton Friedman, *Capitalism and Freedom*, The University of Chicago Press, 1962; see also for an example of how the idea of efficient markets became embedded in the financial economic literature Frederic Mishkin and Stanley Eakins, *Financial Markets and Institutions*, Addison Wesley, 2000; Richard Brealey, Stewart Myers, and Franklin Allen, *Corporate Finance*, McGraw-Hill, 2006.

Debt Capital Markets. Vincenzo Bavoso, Oxford University Press. © Vincenzo Bavoso 2024.
DOI: 10.1093/oso/9780198893257.003.0003

section 2. Section 3 starts uncovering the idea of efficient market, and it does so by looking into a number of specific theories and how they informed market developments. Section 4 provides further context to these theories, by explaining the feedback loop between market orthodoxy, policy-making, and regulation.

2 The dynamics of financial regulation

The complex web of laws and regulations that govern financial markets do not necessarily generate from the same law-making processes that characterize other areas of law and other industries. One first peculiarity that distinguishes financial markets is that over the past four decades, as illustrated in chapter two, regulatory changes have facilitated the integration of financial centres around the world and the ensuing globalization of financial markets. The consequence of this process is that national laws, emanating from conventional national processes, may in many cases not be effective in addressing issues that have become by nature transnational. The global nature of financial markets has been most critically epitomized by the increasing significance of transnational regulatory actors (TRAs)[2] in the governance of finance.

The second peculiarity links with the first one, and it relates to the way in which TRAs determine the scope and character of financial regulation. Global finance lacks the legitimacy that is commonly associated with international law, because international financial standards do not emanate from legally binding treaties and are instead promulgated by international organizations with sui generis legal identities, such as the TRAs.[3] This architecture has often led commentators to characterize international financial law, unlike fields such as international trade or tax law, as soft law, due to the non-binding nature of international financial standards.[4] The problem though is not so much about the type of obligations stemming from these agreements and standards,[5] but rather the legitimacy of the underlying process that flows into international financial rules and standards. The question therefore

[2] Such as most prominently the Basel Committee on Banking Supervision (which is part of the Bank for International Settlements), the International Organization of Securities Commissions (IOSCO), the G20, the Financial Stability Board (FSB).

[3] This problem is expounded by Chris Brummer, *Soft Law and the Global Financial System*, Cambridge University Press, 2012.

[4] The use of soft law is clearly explained by Iris Chiu as a necessary compromise in international financial regulation, where intergovernmentalism prevails over institutionalization: 'Prospects for International Financial Deglobalisation and its Potential Impact on International Financial Regulation' (2022) 16 Law and Financial Markets Review 4.

[5] Brummer explains that despite their non-binding, soft-law character, standards can still be backed by mechanisms that enforce compliance. So, even though they are not promulgated in line with traditional and democratic treaty processes, they may still have coercive force. See Brummer, *Soft Law* (n 3), 5. One such example is the impact that Basel has on EU legislation, which in turn becomes hard law once it is implemented by EU member states.

lies in the proximity that TRAs maintain with market participants, and the way they represent the interest of the industry vis-à-vis a broader public interest when promoting policies and regulations.

The dynamic of financial regulation is closely bound to the role that market participants play in the process of promulgating or supporting certain standards. This is true when it comes to the TRAs mentioned earlier, but also with respect to the EU, whose Regulations and Directives are not the result of a democratic law-making process.[6] Market participants, in other words, either through industry associations or powerful lobbies, have traditionally been able to exert pressure on the regulatory architecture of financial markets.

One justification for this is typically found in the intrinsic complexity of finance and financial law, which makes it a topic that ostensibly escapes the concern and scrutiny of common citizens. Following this line of argument, it has often been posited that the governance of financial markets is best left to experts. This approach has led to the delegation by legislature to specialized regulatory agencies that are entrusted with the regulation and supervision of financial markets.[7] These agencies are typically staffed with 'experts' (sometimes known as 'technocrats')[8] whose specialized skills are validated through their experience in the industry. Yet again, this shows how market participants can retain a powerful grip on the regulation of financial markets. Most typically, this can occur due to regulatory capture or the process of 'revolving doors'.

The former refers to situations where regulators are susceptible to capture by the industry that they regulate, due to the bias and interest that they have towards the industry (rather than towards the broader public interest).[9] This capture could lead to the regulator drafting rules and regulations that minimize the regulatory costs incurred by market participants, or it may also result in a supervisory strategy based on light-touch intervention. Revolving doors is a slightly different phenomenon but it is interrelated causally with the concept of capture. It means that regulators, due to their required expertise, are recruited from the industry that they have to regulate.[10] This has become increasingly common in the financial sector,

[6] The Commission (which is not an elected body) maintains a strong influence on the legislative process which in fact it initiates, whereas the Parliament (which is elected) has the final say in ratifying EU legislations.

[7] The question of the democratic legitimacy of non-majoritarian regulatory agencies is beyond the scope of this book. For a discussion see Giandomenico Majone 'Europe's "Democratic Deficit": The Question of Standards' (1998) 4(1) European Law Journal.

[8] While a critique of technocracy is beyond the scope of this chapter, some elements of this discussion are reprised in Chapter 6. For an interesting, and critical, perspective on technocracy, see Miguel Angel Centeno 'The New Leviathan: The Dynamics and Limits of Technocracy' (1993) 22(3) Theory and Society.

[9] The idea of regulatory capture is associated with the work of George Stigler, 'The Theory of Economic Regulation' (1971) 2(1) The Bell Journal of Economics and Management Science.

[10] Macroscopic examples of revolving doors can be found in most central banks presently, where chairs are former members of prominent banks—the Bank of England and the European Central Bank offer paradigmatic examples. Another controversial example is that of Henry Paulson who was in 2008 US Treasury Secretary and was instrumental for the bailout of AIG, whereas he had previously rejected

where professionals from large financial institutions go on to occupy top positions in regulatory bodies, only to return to the industry once their tenure ends. This tends to reinforce problems of capture, because regulators inevitably will be bound by their previous ties, and may also be motivated to cultivate those ties in light of future opportunities.[11]

Beyond the problems of capture and revolving doors, the dynamics of financial regulation are characterized by the pervasiveness of the banking lobby. In theory, lobbyists are any interest groups (public or private) that aim to sway political opinions and ultimately attempt to influence legislators on specific sensitive issues.[12] While they have been a typical feature of US (and also EU) policy-making, their influence in complex areas of financial regulation has become increasingly problematic. This is so because of what was explained earlier, namely that the complexity of finance-related policies offers lobbyists greater discretion and limited public scrutiny.[13]

One example of this broader problem—capture caused by lobbying—may be represented by an international body such as the Basel Committee, which is highly relevant in global finance and whose standards are examined in Chapter 7 of this book. To reconceptualize what was said earlier, the standards (Capital Accords) promulgated by Basel are not legally binding on any state as they are soft-law frameworks. The Basel Committee in turn is an informal group of central bankers and financial regulators drawn presently from twenty-eight jurisdictions.[14] However, domestic regulators adopt these standards as legally binding capital requirements, and they are employed to set the amount of risk-taking that banks can engage with. Critically, Basel II in 2004 afforded banks the possibility to self-determine the risk weight of their assets in order to calculate how much capital they would have to

pledging public money to prevent the bankruptcy of Lehman Brothers. The controversial aspect of this story is that the bailout of AIG proved vital for the survival of another bank, Goldman Sachs, of which Paulson was formerly Chairman and CEO. For an insightful overview, see Adam Levitin, 'The Politics of Financial Regulation and the Regulation of Financial Politics: A Review Essay' (2014) 127(7) Harvard Law Review 2011–2013.

[11] A discussion on this is conducted in John Armour, Dan Awrey, Paul Davies, and others, *Principles of Financial Regulation*, Oxford University Press, 2016, 91–93.

[12] Common tools to achieve this are the use of expertise, network connections, persuasion, public relations, but also on a more concrete level, through policy research, think-tanks, and also drafting bills or assisting relevant agencies. See on this, Deniz Igan and Thomas Lambert, 'Bank Lobbying: Regulatory Capture and Beyond', in *The Political Economy of Financial Regulation*, edited by E Avgouleas and D Donald, Cambridge University Press, 2018.

[13] ibid, 129–130. While the authors in this article focus on the US, a prominent and recent example comes from the EU, in the context of the consultation for the Simple Transparent and Standardised Regulation (analysed in Chapter 7). The debate within the consultation was dominated by the relevant banking lobby, represented in that forum by the European Banking Authority Banking Stakeholder Group, which put forward the economic benefit of securitizing high-risk assets, and the necessity to resort to synthetic securitization in order to do so. See Vincenzo Bavoso, 'High Quality Securitisation and EU Capital Markets Union—Is it Possible?' (2016) 7(3) Accounting Economics and Law: A Convivium 9.

[14] At the time of Basel II, the Committee was based around the members of G10 jurisdictions only.

set aside; this determination was the result of risk models developed internally by each bank. The same approach remains within Basel III, which was agreed upon in 2010 as a response to the global financial crisis (GFC).[15] Beyond allowing banks a great degree of discretion in determining how risky their business should be, this approach is firmly grounded on the idea of market discipline[16], which is in fact embedded in the third pillar of the Basel framework (both Basel II and III).

The question of how market discipline became an undisputed tenet of financial regulation is tied to some of the functions of lobbying, namely swaying the opinion of legislators and regulators, by providing policy research, sometimes through think-tanks.[17] As regards the Basel framework and its use of market discipline as one of its pillars, this appears to be consistent with the 'market orthodoxy' that was highlighted in the previous section, and that was becoming more dominant in financial regulation at the time the Committee was established in 1974. The following sections provide some ground to understand how the ideology centred on market efficiency became the mainstay of financial regulation, and how that regulatory architecture spurred the growth of debt capital markets.

3 Genesis and development of the idea of efficient markets

The concept of efficient markets was developed in connection with the question of understanding the movements of securities' prices. The seeds of that quest lie in statistical work conducted in 1953 that looked at the behaviour of stock and commodities' prices. Instead of finding regular patterns of price cycles, evidence showed that prices were following a wandering pattern, or a 'random walk'.[18] The randomness here implies the unpredictability of future price movements. In the attempt to predict the behaviour of prices, financial economists have used two tests, namely one looking at whether changes in market prices are systematically related to previous changes and could therefore be predicted; and second, whether publicly available information, other than past stock prices, could have been used to predict price changes.[19]

Before discussing the main implications of the efficient market hypothesis (EMH), it is interesting to note that the concept of efficient markets seems to be intractably linked with that of expectations. In the case of securities markets,

[15] The details and mechanics of the Basel framework are discussed in the more appropriate context of Chapter 7.

[16] The mechanics of market discipline are analysed in Chapter 6 of this book.

[17] See Igan and Lambert, 'Bank Lobbying' (n 12), 129.

[18] The 1953 study was conducted by Maurice Kendall, 'The Analysis of Economic Time Series, Part I, Prices' (1953) 116(1) Journal of the Royal Statistical Society; on the randomness of stock market prices, see Paul Cootner, 'The Random Character of Stock Market Prices', MIT Press, 1964; and also Burton Malkiel, *A Random Walk Down Wall Street*, WW Norton and Company, 1973.

[19] Mishkin and Eakins, *Financial Markets* (n 1), 167–168.

expectations about risk, return or liquidity underscore the way in which market participants operate and take decisions.[20] As explained by Mishkin and Eakins, the theory of rational expectations describes how expectations are formed and also how the price of securities moves over time.[21] According to this theory, expectations will be identical to optimal forecasts using all available information.[22] Critically, a key caveat is introduced here, namely that forecasts do not need to be accurate in order to be rational, which implies that even optimal forecasts will never be completely accurate (even when based on all available information).[23] The availability of information of course plays a crucial role, because if market participants were not aware of relevant information, or if they were to find it too difficult to incorporate it into their decision-making, this would hinder the rationality of the expectation.

The discussion thus shifts towards the question of informational efficiency. Financial economists have maintained in this sense that the price of securities fully reflects all available information in an efficient market. The last condition, of markets being efficient, is central to this proposition, and it holds that all unexploited profit opportunities should be eliminated in an efficient market, that being the essence of arbitrage trading.[24] What should thus be understood is that the idea of efficient markets is built upon a number of assumptions[25] that need to be in turn critically analysed in this section.

3.1 Efficient market hypothesis

Empirical research started being conducted in the mid-1960s on the efficiency with which securities' prices were incorporating all available information, and on the attendant randomness of price changes.[26] Much of the early work on efficient

[20] ibid, 157.

[21] ibid, 158.

[22] ibid, 158–159. Here reference is made to the author of the theory of rational expectations, namely John Muth, 'Rational Expectations and the Theory of Price Movements' (1961) 29 Econometrica 315–335.

[23] Mishkin and Eakins, *Financial Markets* (n 1), 159.

[24] ibid, 164. This is further clarified by explaining that for the proposition of efficient markets to hold, it is not necessary that all market participants are well informed or have rational expectations. All that is needed is for a few market participants to become aware of unexploited profit opportunities as they appear, so that by trading on them and making a profit, the profit opportunity will be eliminated from the market.

[25] These assumptions can all be reconceptualized under what Dan Awrey calls 'conventional finance theory' in 'Complexity, Innovation, and the Regulation of Modern Financial Markets' (2012) 2 Harvard Business Law Review. In this work, Awrey provides a critique of the assumptions centred on perfect markets and recognizes a number of theories built on those assumptions, namely, Markowitz's modern portfolio theory, the Modigliani and Miller capital structure irrelevance principle, the capital asset pricing model, and the efficient market hypothesis.

[26] See Eugene Fama, 'The Behaviour of Stock Market Prices' (1965) 38(1) The Journal of Business 34–105; Eugene Fama, 'Random Walks in Stock Market Prices', *Selected Papers of the Graduate School*

markets was attributed to Eugene Fama, who hypothesized efficient markets as being characterized by competition among rational actors, whereby prices converged towards their fundamental value.[27] Fama therefore introduced two major assumptions into his hypothesis, namely the competitiveness of markets, and the rationality of market-players; moreover, Fama also referred to the concept of fundamental value, which, while being related to efficiency, remains a different notion.[28] Fama's earlier conclusion on price randomness was that successive price changes were consistent with the idea of an efficient market for securities, where, given the available information, actual prices at every point in time represent a very good estimate of their fundamental value.[29]

It is worth noting that at the same time Paul Samuelson proposed a slightly different idea of efficient markets, namely one where the randomness of price fluctuations could be explained through the competition between rational market-players, with no regard to fundamental value.[30] In essence, Samuelson's claim was simply that the valuation of present securities' price is the best estimate of their future price (not of their fundamental value).[31] Critically though, both statements relied on the same set of assumptions, namely on: 1) a market sufficiently competitive and populated by a large number of participants; 2) market participants driven by rational behaviour (or rational choices as explained earlier) and by a profit maximization goal; 3) free availability of information.[32]

In a later paper reviewing theoretical and empirical work on efficient markets, Fama distinguished three degrees (or forms, as he put it) of efficiency, in order to assess the extent to which the current price of securities fully reflects all available information.[33] Essentially, a market is deemed efficient if investors cannot make abnormal returns by trading on public information. This definition incorporates both weak forms of efficiency, whose information set includes only historical prices, and semi-strong efficiency, which requires that all public information

of Business, University of Chicago, 1965; Paul Samuelson, 'Rational Theory of Warrant Pricing' (1965) 6(2) Industrial Management Review 13–39.

27 See Fama 'The Behaviour of Stock Market Prices' (n 26).

28 On the difference and relationship between informational efficiency and fundamental efficiency, see the critique by Ronald Gilson and Rainer Kraakman, 'Market Efficiency after the Financial Crisis: It's still a Matter of Information Costs' (2014) 100 Virginia Law Review 313. They explain that the fundamental value of a security is the true present value of its expected future cash flow. The market therefore is fundamentally efficient if prices accurately reflect the fundamental value of securities, which in itself is a condition that hinges on the capacity of traders to act on the basis of private information—which is impossible. Thus, the authors here state, fundamental value is an approximation upon which the EMH is judged.

29 See Fama, 'The Behaviour of Stock Market Prices' (n 26), 90–94.

30 See Samuelson 'Rational Theory of Warrant Pricing' (n 26).

31 ibid, 44.

32 ibid.

33 Eugene Fama, 'Efficient Capital Markets: A Review of Theory and Empirical Work' (1970) 25(2) The Journal of Finance 383–417.

is reflected into prices. Strong forms of efficiency would require that market prices also reflect private information, which is not a realistic prospect.[34] At the same time, Fama reiterated some necessary conditions for markets to be efficient, namely: a) the absence of transaction costs for the trading of securities, b) the free availability of all relevant information to all market participants, c) the agreement about the implication of current information for the formation of current prices and the distribution of future securities' prices.[35]

Critiques of the empirical validity of the EMH started to emerge in the 1980s, especially with respect to its capacity to capture the reality of financial markets and particularly the pervasiveness of transaction costs.[36] Doubts were also raised as regards the role attributed to arbitrage traders in correcting prices when they move away from their fundamental value.[37] Moreover, the findings of behavioural finance provided ever stronger empirical evidence against the presumed rationality of market participants.[38]

Another critical empirical problem was the absence of a reference point against which market prices could be measured. As was observed by Gilson and Kraakman in their more recent work, informational efficiency refers to the concept of fundamental efficiency, which occurs when prices accurately reflect the fundamental value of a security (in turn this is the true present value of securities' expected future cash flow).[39] They argue that first, perfection is impossible here because traders only act on the basis of public information (semi-strong efficiency). This results in an approximate fundamental efficiency, which they argue should be the standard by which the EMH is to be judged. Secondly, they observe that there is nothing against which to measure market prices, so if market prices differ from their fundamental value, this would be due to either an informationally inefficient market, or incorrect pricing mechanisms.[40] In other words, informational efficiency is a precondition of fundamental efficiency, which in turn is grounded on the idea that market participants use information to estimate values and set prices.[41] This leads to the analysis of a pricing model that is associated with similar assumptions employed by the EMH, namely the capital asset pricing model.

[34] ibid, 415. This implies that a relative efficiency is what is most realistic to attain, as would be later postulated by Gilson and Kraakman.

[35] ibid, 389.

[36] See Ronald Gilson and Rainer Kraakman, 'The Mechanisms of Market Efficiency' (1984) 70(4) Virginia Law Review 549.

[37] See Lynn Stout, 'The Mechanisms of Market Inefficiency: An Introduction to the New Finance' (Summer 2003) The Journal of Corporation Law 635.

[38] ibid; on the findings of behavioural finance, see also Emilios Avgouleas, 'The Global Financial Crisis, Behavioural Finance and Financial Regulation: In Search of a New Orthodoxy' (2009) 9(1) Journal of Corporate Law Studies; Daniel Kahnemann and Amos Tversky, 'Prospect Theory: An Analysis of Decision under Risk' (1979) 47 (2) Econometrica.

[39] Gilson and Kraakman, 'Market Efficiency after the Financial Crisis' (n 28), 321–323.

[40] ibid, 324–325. Here, Gilson and Kraakman reiterate that testing fundamental efficiency is impossible unless the standard of rigour is lowered by inter alia using proxies.

[41] Stout, 'The Mechanisms of Market Inefficiency' (n 37), 651.

3.2 Capital asset pricing model

In the context of this discussion, the analysis of the capital asset pricing model (CAPM) is useful to understand investor behaviour when selecting portfolios of securities. In particular, under CAPM investors are assumed to value securities according to two criteria, namely expected returns, and expected non-diversifiable market risks. This question was initially tackled by William Sharpe,[42] whose main concern was to ascertain the prices that securities would command once capital markets have reached equilibrium,[43] and assuming that investors were to behave optimally. In this quest, Sharpe assumed that all investors had the same estimates of expected returns, and overall employed a set of simplified assumptions that led to a mathematical formulation of equilibrium.[44]

The problem with Sharpe's model is that it embedded the idea—empirically untested—that all investors would hold exactly the same set of securities, and in the same proportions. Moreover, in a later paper, Sharpe went on to state that the optimal combination of risky securities is that existing in the market, thus an idealized market portfolio.[45] A proposition that, following from Harry Markowitz's theory on portfolio diversification,[46] implied a further layer of abstraction, namely that investors' expected return could be predicted on the basis of the exposure of the investment (share or bond) to market movements, disregarding therefore the specific and individual risks flowing from the underlying corporation/entity associated with the investment.[47]

In essence, the validity of CAPM was rooted in a number of assumptions that are common across neoclassical economics, and can be summed up as follows: a)

[42] See the original paper by William Sharpe, 'Capital Asset Prices: A Theory of Market Equilibrium under Conditions of Risk' (1964) 19(3) The Journal of Finance.

[43] The concept of equilibrium for the purpose of this discussion can be understood as the price at which the quantity of a commodity that is for sale is equal to the quantity that is being purchased by buyers. If the market price is below that equilibrium level, there is excess demand; whereas if the price is above equilibrium, there will be an excess of supply. See on the context of this discussion Donald MacKenzie, *An Engine, Not a Camera*, MIT Press, 2008, 53.

[44] See on this the discussion conducted by MacKenzie on the relationship between Sharpe's model and Markowitz' earlier work, which also employed a simplified assumption, namely that the correlation between securities arose because they were each correlated with one underlying factor, the general prosperity of the market, represented by some index. MacKenzie, *An Engine* (n 43), 52–23.

[45] See William Sharpe, *Portfolio Theory and Capital Markets*, McGraw-Hill, 1970, 82. On the assumptions used by Sharpe, it is interesting to note that, like some of his contemporaries, he did not allow unrealistic assumptions to 'disturb' his models. It was also clear that when discussing the validity of the theory, Sharpe used the wording 'acceptability of a theory's implications', rather than 'accuracy'. The underlying idea behind Sharpe's assumption derived of course from Harry Markowitz's theory on portfolio diversification, where he postulated that the risks associated with investments in a specific stock could be diversified away, and that the only non-diversifiable risks were those inherent in the market as a whole and therefore common across all securities. See for a critique Lawrence Mitchell, *The Speculation Economy—How Finance Triumphed over Industry*, Berrett-Koehler 2007, 274–275. See also MacKenzie, *An Engine* (n 43), 55.

[46] This has gone on to be known as modern portfolio theory (MPT) which started with Markowitz's early work 'Portfolio Selection' (1952) 7(1) The Journal of Finance.

[47] Mitchell, *The Speculation Economy* (n 45), 275.

investors all seek a mean-variance optimal portfolio;[48] b) securities markets are sufficiently large and liquid; c) securities markets are characterized by the absence of transaction costs; d) all assets are publicly traded; e) in this idealized market, any amount can be borrowed at a fixed risk-free rate. These assumptions in the specific context of CAPM imply that all investors hold identical risky portfolios.

As Lynn Stout observed, both EMH and CAPM were based on a prediction that in informationally efficient markets, prices will also be fundamentally efficient. It will be remembered that this predicament also relied on the role of arbitrage traders to spot prices that were not fundamentally efficient and trade the difference away.[49] Moreover, another problematic assumption was that all investors would share homogeneous expectations on future returns and risks of specific securities, something that is not realistic to hypothesize, especially given the lack of empirical evidence to that end.[50]

Other theories that were developed in the same period, and also part of what is conventionally referred to as neoclassical economics, were similarly grounded on assumptions of perfect markets that were never empirically proven.[51] The methodology that led to such assumptions and abstractions was captured by George Stigler, who stressed that economic theories were conceived as simplified and analytical representations of the real world. Such simplifications, however, led economic theories in most cases to flow into unrealistic models and problems.[52]

3.3 The option pricing formula

Some of the assumptions at the heart of EMH and CAPM were also employed for the pricing of derivatives. Fisher Black started theorizing on this, trying to apply CAPM to a broader range of assets than corporate stock. In approaching the problem, Black assumed the riskless rate of interest and volatility to be constant, leaving three variables in his equation, namely the option price, the stock price, and time. At the heart of this model, though, there were a set of simplifying assumptions, common to other hypotheses, namely that options and shares could

48 Mean-variance refers to the portfolio of assets where the expected return is maximized for a certain level of risk.

49 See Stout, 'The Mechanisms of Market Inefficiency' (n 37).

50 ibid, 653–655. Lynn Stout goes on to state that the reasoning behind these conjectures becomes circular. In other words, if CAPM had to account for heterogeneous investor estimates, while still assuming a situation of perfect markets, it would become difficult to still hold the role of arbitrage, and as a consequence, that of market equilibrium. In the same paper Stout goes on to argue against the assumption centred on the role of arbitrage traders, observing that in real-life scenarios there are severe limits to arbitrageurs' powers to correct prices.

51 See Awrey, 'Complexity' (n 25). One example is the Modigliani and Miller hypothesis on capital structure, where the authors claimed the irrelevance of firms' capital structure. This irrelevance conjecture was itself an abstraction from the real world (not contemplating for instance the role of tax).

52 See George Stigler, *Memoirs of an Unregulated Economist*, Basic Books, 1988, 75.

be bought and sold at low transaction costs. Black's work was eventually complemented by Myron Scholes, who had conducted research on specific types of hedged portfolios and their related risks.[53]

Initially Black and Scholes encountered problems in that their hedged portfolio was not entirely risk-free. The hedging, they argued, would not be rigorous if the stock price changed significantly, with the value of an option varying as expiration drew closer. They observed that the risk of the hedged portfolio was the sort of risk that could be diversified away. Effectively, the option-pricing equation devised by Black and Scholes in 1970 started from a simple manipulation, given that the expected return on the hedged portfolio was known, the manipulation eventually led to the differential equation that came to be known as the Black-Scholes equation.[54]

Interestingly, the Black-Scholes equation attracted the interest of another prominent economist of that time, Robert Merton, who among other things, had worked on warrant pricing. Merton had been critical of CAPM, and in particular he pointed out that the formula did not incorporate anything about risk, as if it were reflecting a risk-neutral world.[55] Consistently with this critique, Merton found that the key aspect of the Black-Scholes equation was an assumption that continuous trading, in other words the capacity to adjust a portfolio at all times and instantaneously, could get rid of all risk, not just the systematic risk, and thus realize the perfect hedge.[56] As observed by MacKenzie, this latter assumption resulted in a complete abstraction and, as a consequence, the equation never really corresponded to reality when it was tested empirically.[57]

Above and beyond this more specific conjecture, the work conducted by Black, Scholes and Merton relied on the same set of assumptions encountered earlier in this section, namely, that stock prices follow a random walk, that there are no transaction costs related to the buying or selling of securities, that it is possible to borrow any fraction of the price of a security to buy or hold it at the riskless rate of interest, and that there is unrestricted possibility of short-selling.[58]

The definite application of the option-pricing formula not only represented another abstraction from the real world of finance, as is the case with the other theories explored previously, but it signalled a further move towards the mathematization of finance and economics.

[53] MacKenzie, *An Engine* (n 43), 130. See also Alice Bamford and Donald MacKenzie 'Counterperformativity' (2018) 113 New Left Review 103.

[54] ibid, 131–132. See for the original work on the formula Fisher Black and Myron Scholes, 'The Pricing of Options and Corporate Liabilities' (1973) 81(3) Journal of Political Economy.

[55] Robert Merton, 'Theory of Rational Option Pricing' (1973) 4 Bell Journal of Economics and Management Science 141–183, 162.

[56] ibid.

[57] MacKenzie, *An Engine* (n 43), 137 and 142. See also Fisher Black and Myron Scholes 'The Valuation of Option Contracts and a Test of Market Efficiency' (1972) 27 Journal of Finance 399–417, 413.

[58] In this sense, see Fisher Black and Myron Scholes, 'The Pricing of Options and Corporate Liabilities' (1973) 81(3) Journal of Political Economy 637–654, 640.

3.4 The mathematization of finance and other abstractions

Admittedly the process of mathematization referred to at the end of the previous section started well before the inception of the option pricing formula. As critically pointed out by MacKenzie, it probably began with the portfolio selection theory published by Harry Markowitz in 1952, which was highly based on mathematical models that assumed rational investors.[59] What is also interesting to note about the Black-Scholes equation is that it had an immediate effect on the trading of derivatives. Notwithstanding its mathematical abstraction (and the lack of empirical proof), the formula contributed to changing the perception of derivatives at the Chicago Board Options Exchange, where the long-standing association between options and gambling started to diminish.[60]

What also transpires from this analysis is that progressively from the 1950s onwards, economics started to take the shape of natural science. Of course, this was more of an aspiration than an effective morphing of economics into science.[61] The fundamental difference between the two was aptly highlighted after the crisis of 2008 by a physicist who laid emphasis on the different use of models in the two disciplines. He observed that when physicists come to the realization that empirical tests do not corroborate models, the latter have to be discarded or amended. Economists on the other hand tend to be in thrall to the mathematical elegance of models, and the conceptual convenience they entail. This attitude results in models prevailing over empirical observation in economics, which is something that has been confirmed by the events preceding the GFC, and the repeated failure of economic models to predict those events.[62]

Effectively, mathematical models have come to dominate the financial system, from the theorems discussed earlier in this section, to the more general approaches to risk-management.[63] These models were all premised on some fundamental

[59] The concept of a mean-variance optimal portfolio, encountered in the previous section, was the result of this type of mathematical modelling. MacKenzie interestingly notes that in the issue of the Journal of Finance where Markowitz published his paper, no other article included any equation. See MacKenzie, *An Engine* (n 43), 50.

[60] ibid, 158. It will be remembered from the previous chapter that at this time in history, speculative derivatives were still deemed void by US courts, in line with the precedent set by *Irwin v Williar*.

[61] This is well documented in the work of Philip Mirowski, who explained the influence that physics had historically had on the development of economic theories, and particularly the need to employ mathematical methods in order to resemble science. See Philip Mirowski, *More Heat Than Light: Economics as Social Physics, Physics as Nature's Economics*, Cambridge University Press, 1989. Of course, the mathematization of economics and finance happened progressively, and while it started in the early 1900s with economists such as Leon Walras and Irving Fisher, it was only in the 1980s that the process reached a climax.

[62] Jean-Philippe Bouchaud, 'Economics Needs a Scientific Revolution', *Nature* (30 October 2008) 1181.

[63] Think about the value-at-risk (VaR) formula, which is still used to calculate the maximum loss expected on an investment, over a given time period, and given a specific degree of confidence. But another example of the pervasive application of mathematical models is related to the idea of risk mitigation and the ensuing application of credit default swaps (CDS).

constructions. First of all, it was assumed that the economy is a physical system, which could therefore be modelled theoretically just as it is done in physics. However, the main problem here is that the neoclassical concept of equilibrium[64] could not be compared to its physics counterpart, because the latter only refers to systems that are by nature closed, whereas economics systems are open.[65] Secondly, mathematical models developed under neoclassical economics were based on simplifications (abstractions), such as for instance the number of market actors involved in a given transaction.[66] Lastly, the economic theories that informed these models were assuming—as was explained earlier—that all market participants could rely on the same set of information. In real world scenarios, though, markets will include different types of actors, each having access to different types of information, and at different times. In other words, this sort of heterogeneity, which was never accounted for in mathematical models, made risk-management very problematic in the pre-crisis years.[67]

The employment of science into economics was most spectacularly epitomized by the application of the Brownian motion theory in the field of risk-management and attendant techniques. The original theory was developed by Robert Brown, a botanist, in 1827, and it was concerned with the movement of particles in the physics world, where some quantity of particles is showing constant, small, rapid, and random fluctuations.[68] Initially, the model theorized by Brown found application in a number of fields, such as air pollution, electromagnetic fields, the movements of atoms, or the penetration of calcium into bones. In the 1970s though, financial economists concluded that the mathematical model behind Brownian motion could be used to predict stock price fluctuations.[69]

While the most notorious financial formula that incorporated the Brownian mathematical model was the one finalized by Black, Scholes, and Merton,[70] later adaptations flowed into the models that have become widely employed by financial institutions to forecast price fluctuations in different securities markets, and to manage the risk of their investments.[71] The immediate critique here is that the original scope of these formulae was to observe fluctuations in the scientific world,

[64] This was introduced earlier in section 3.

[65] See on this, Luciano Gallino, *Finanzcapitalismo*, Einaudi, 2011, 91–92.

[66] ibid. Gallino explains that often models were developed to deal with simple systems, sometimes comprising as many as two actors, whereas in a real-life scenario the same model would have to be applied to situations involving millions of market participants.

[67] ibid, 93.

[68] More technically, it is the irregular movement of small particles suspended in gas or liquid, caused by the bombardment of the particles by molecules of gas or liquid. See definition at www.dictionary.com/browse/brownian--motion (last accessed on 18/04/2024).

[69] Gallino, *Finanzcapitalismo* (n 65), 97–98.

[70] See Fisher Black and Myron Scholes, 'The Pricing of Options and Corporate Liabilities' (1973) 81(3) Journal of Political Economy 637–654.

[71] Gallino, *Finanzcapitalismo* (n 65), 98. Earlier in this section, mention was made of the VaR formula that is still widely employed by financial institutions.

in ambits whose boundaries were clearly delineated. To apply the same type of method to the world of economics, where variables (such as the number of market participants and their behaviour) could not be predicted represented a clear leap of faith, an abstraction.

Possibly even more controversial is the case of the Gaussian copula function, a complex mathematical formula that was more recently used in the context of synthetic securitizations. It specifically facilitated the process of modelling risk through a correlation coefficient, which effectively determined the bundling of very heterogeneous (and often high-risk) assets into securities that would receive triple-A ratings—regardless of the credit risk of the underlying assets bundled together.[72]

What emerges clearly from the analysis conducted in the last few pages is that developments in financial-economic theories were crucial in determining the way in which markets evolved from the 1970s onwards. Theories were in most cases constructed in advance of empirical work, and when tested empirically they showed severe shortcomings. In essence, they were presenting a prescriptive nature, rather than a descriptive one as may be expected, given the nature and scope of these theories: instead of portraying the reality of financial markets, they were telling investors what to do.[73] An illustration of this phenomenon is the risk modelling employed by banks to control their exposures. Risk modelling techniques started being used by financial engineers in order to create securities with specific risk profiles, reversing therefore the process of risk analysis. Instead of assessing the riskiness of a portfolio of securities, large banks and their financial quantitative analysts started with a target level of riskiness and then structured a portfolio that could replicate that level of risk. Effectively, risks and prices in those markets were predetermined by risk models.[74] This is a phenomenon that Donald MacKenzie called the 'performativity of theories'. In other words, the models did not contribute to describing how markets operated, they were actually designed to create markets in a certain fashion. In that process, traders and investment firms that were employing those models, and believed in them, were contributing to make the whole abstraction a reality.[75]

[72] Felix Salmon, 'A Formula for Disaster', *Wired* (March 2009) 74–75. This correlation formula was at the heart of the collateralised debt obligation (CDO) industry, and it is what elicited the incredible growth of the CDO market in the pre-crisis years. This process will be closely analysed in Chapter 4.

[73] MacKenzie, *An Engine* (n 43), ch.2 and 3.

[74] Simon Gleeson, *Gleeson on the International Regulation of Banking*, Oxford University Press, 2018, 26.

[75] See on this Donald MacKenzie and Yuval Millo, 'Constructing a Market, Performing Theory: The Historical Sociology of a Financial Derivatives Exchange' (2003) 1 American Journal of Sociology.

4 The feedback loop between market orthodoxy and the growth of debt capital markets

The set of theories discussed in the previous section contributed to portray an idea of financial markets that, towards the end of the twentieth century, had become widely considered efficient. The belief (or faith, one may say) in efficient markets had repercussions beyond the academic world, and it spread to create a social imaginary whereby 'the market' came to represent the archetype of efficiency, something to be understood as a socially desirable outcome. In this social imaginary, anything flowing from outside of the market would be labelled as an inefficient and undesirable outcome, particularly with respect to regulation.[76] The purpose of this section thus is to reconcile the theoretical orthodoxy examined in the previous section, and its attendant assumptions, with the policy-making that characterized the period from the 1970s to the crisis of 2008. The analysis on the pre-crisis regulatory architecture, conducted in Chapter 6 of this monograph, ties conceptually with this discussion.

To expound on the previous statement, the idea of efficiency, despite its limited empirical validity, went on to influence very critical legal and regulatory developments—some of which were at the heart of the regulatory changes illustrated in the previous chapter. To understand this process, it is important to remember that the interpretation of efficiency portrayed by neoclassical economics was very generously endorsed by certain political circles in the 1970s and 1980s. Gilson and Kraakman go on to state that the idea of efficient markets was 'hijacked' by the Reagan and Thatcher governments in the 1980s, and was then transformed into an ideological justification for bringing about legal and regulatory changes aimed at favouring market outcomes.[77] Political endorsement of neoclassical economics created what is commonly referred to as the neoliberal ideology. Through neoliberalism, neoclassical economics entrenched its supremacy as the undisputed theoretical orthodoxy, not only in the field of economics education, but also in business management, in the way financial institutions operated, the policies of central banks, and of course the objectives of transnational regulatory actors.[78]

[76] Concepts of efficiency in relation to regulation are expounded in Chapter 6 of this book. In this context, it is important to highlight that the widespread acceptance of the theories discussed earlier among policy-makers advanced the role and primacy of the market for regulatory purposes. This was in turn rooted in the concept of competitive equilibrium (often referred to as Pareto efficiency), which prescribed a normative framework that limited the scope of regulation, because this was seen as a form of government interference. See on this Kenneth Arrow and Gerard Debreu, 'Existence of an Equilibrium for a Competitive Economy' (1954) 22 Econometrica 3.

[77] Gilson and Kraakman, 'Market Efficiency after the Financial Crisis', 315–316; the authors stress that the validity of the EMH in particular was largely inflated, that instead of simply being a theory about informational underpinnings of market prices, it became a scientific justification for the validity of market valuations.

[78] In this sense, Gallino, *Finanzcapitalismo* (n 65), 87.

While this chapter is not closely concerned with the way in which law validated neoclassical economics,[79] its main thrust is on the regulatory consequence of this endorsement. Namely, the quest here is to clarify how theory informed policy-making, and how that in turn informed the regulatory changes that were explored in Chapter 2, bearing in mind that those changes were instrumental to the development of debt capital markets.

The increased acceptance of neoliberal policies in the 1970s advanced the role of the market for regulatory purposes and beyond. More specifically, in that period it was the work of Milton Friedman[80] (and more broadly of the Chicago School of Economics) that championed the idea of the 'free market', an orthodoxy that was grounded on the same unverified assumptions upon which neoclassical theories were constructed.[81] Friedman's proposition hinged on the idea of individual freedom, and more specifically on the belief that individuals were to be left free to make economic, utility-maximizing decisions. For this individual economic freedom to be attained, Friedman argued, it was essential that the economic sphere remained separate from any political intrusion. In other words, the actions of utility-maximizing individuals would have been best coordinated through the functioning of the market, with little or no intervention at all from political circles.[82] It is important to remember that regulatory intervention here was conceived as the by-product of political interference, thus external to the market. The neoliberal idea of free markets was therefore reliant on a framework of laws and regulation that was fundamentally facilitative, that aided and complemented market mechanisms in coordinating individual behaviour. It can be observed that neoliberal policies were centred on two pillars (assumptions), namely efficient markets and rational individuals.

Beyond the theoretical justifications discussed in the earlier part of this chapter, the neoliberal idea of individual freedom was also rooted in the proposition that

[79] This is illustrated for instance in Yesha Yadav, 'How Algorithmic Trading Undermines Efficiency in Capital Markets' (2015) 68(1608) Vanderbilt Law Review 1637. The author here stresses that the underlying proposition of securities law is that efficient markets reflect all available information in the prices of traded securities. In the US, the application of Rule 10b-5 is grounded on a presumption that is a direct consequence of the tenets of EMH. Arguably, the use of disclosure as a regulatory mechanism to ensure informational efficiency is also a direct consequence of the EMH (as will be discussed in Chapter 6).

[80] Of particular relevance to this discussion is Milton Friedman, *Capitalism and Freedom*, University of Chicago Press, 1962 (reissued in 1982). It needs to be borne in mind that the beginning of what we call neoliberism can be ascribed to Friedrich Von Hayek's *The Road to Serfdom*, Routledge, 1944, where the Austrian economist started arguing in favour of 'market economies', whereby he attributed to the market the power to coordinate the activities of individuals for the wider social benefit. Von Hayek however, was writing at a time where totalitarian regimes characterized much of Europe's political landscape, and his arguments were particularly directed at the risks associated with centrally planned economies.

[81] See on this Rob Van Horn and Philip Mirowski, 'The Rise of the Chicago School of Economics and the Birth of Neoliberalism', in *The Road from Mont Pelerin The Making of the Neoliberal Thought Collective*, edited by Philip Mirowski and Dieter Plehwe, Harvard University Press, 2009, 139–181.

[82] Friedman, *Capitalism and Freedom* (n 80), 27.

in a competitive and efficient market, the actions of rational utility-maximizers would lead to a state of competitive equilibrium (also referred to as Pareto optimality).[83] Attaining competitive equilibrium was a further reason for preferring policies, and normative frameworks, that limited the scope of regulation—again regulation to be understood here as government interference. From a different perspective, the concept of efficiency under neoliberal policy-making came to coincide with the possibility for market participants to directly interact with the market and its mechanisms in order to reach equilibrium.[84] The application of Pareto optimality (or Pareto efficiency) led neoliberal proponents to further argue that, holding the two conditions (or rather, unproven assumptions) of competitive markets and optimal use of resources by market actors, the interaction between rational individuals and the market would result in a state where everyone in the economy would reach the highest possible standard, that being Pareto efficiency. Pareto efficiency in turn would critically coincide with an optimal allocation of resources. Once this equilibrium is reached, the hypothesis goes, resources cannot be reallocated without making somebody worse off.[85]

The above proposition is instrumental to understanding policies aimed at facilitating the unfettered growth of capital markets. The idea of Pareto efficiency became a central tool to evaluate the efficiency of the economy, and more specifically the cost of information therein and how resources are allocated. The underlying belief, flowing from the above assumptions, was that given the existence of an efficient market and the rationality of the actors within it, a state of equilibrium would be reached without any external intervention.[86] Thus, the regulatory changes highlighted in the previous chapter, which resulted in the reduction/removal of regulatory and supervisory constraints in capital markets, can be reconciled with the policy direction informed by efficiency. And in fact, they did broadly mirror Milton Friedman's propositions[87], analysed earlier in this section.

Likewise, the idea of allocative efficiency, a corollary of Pareto optimality, presupposed large enough capital markets, a platform where all the assumptions of neoclassical economics could come to life. In particular, deep and liquid capital

[83] Competitive equilibrium is a theorized situation where demands equals supply, and the economy achieves Pareto optimality. In turn, Pareto optimality refers to a state where making one person better off comes at the expense of making another person worse off. See on this Kenneth Arrow and Gerard Debreu, 'Existence of an Equilibrium for a Competitive Economy' (1954) 22(3) Econometrica 265.

[84] In this sense see the explanation by Joseph Stiglitz, 'The Cases and Consequences of the Dependence of Quality on Price' (1987) 25(1) Journal of Economic Literature 13.

[85] See on this discussion Joseph Stiglitz, 'Credit Markets and the Control of Capital' (1985) 17(2) Journal of Money, Credit and Banking 133–152, 135.

[86] ibid. That intervention in other words would not lead to any Pareto improvement. Stiglitz does pose the question that if markets are not complete as hypothesized, and if information is not efficient, then an economy cannot be Pareto efficient. In the article, which is mainly concerned with agency problems, the author also suggests that some forms of intervention in the market (such as taxes or subsidies) can in fact make everyone better off, but he does not address the question as to whether political intervention would be Pareto improving.

[87] Friedman, *Capitalism and Freedom* (n 80), 28.

markets were considered the essential mechanism to facilitate the optimal allocation of resources (capital) in the economy, and consequently, the growth of the economy.[88] As a result, neoliberal policies in the US and the UK were strongly driven by the goal of expanding capital markets. One exemplification of this policy was the 'Big Bang' of 1986 in the UK, which ushered in regulatory changes that proved to be instrumental in the development of the City of London as a global financial centre.[89]

To fully appreciate this idea of efficiency, and how it is pursued, Pareto optimality needs to be understood in conjunction with the legal mechanisms of private ordering, which became particularly relevant in capital markets.[90] Generally speaking, private ordering is a delegation of certain aspects of regulation from public authorities to private market actors. The rationale for this delegation rests in the opportunity to reduce costs of regulation,[91] particularly in the broad area of business law. In this more specific context, market actors are traditionally deemed capable to operate more efficiently than public authorities[92], and are therefore better placed to attain allocative efficiency goals.

The development of debt capital markets, especially as illustrated in Chapter 4 of this book, provides a picture of how transactions and products have developed according to dynamics that are consistent with private ordering. Such transactional and product developments were characterized by very limited (if any) legislative intrusion, and unfettered contractual developments shaped by market practices and market participants.[93] Reliance on private ordering in debt capital markets was of course justified by the pursuit of economic efficiency[94], and it is in the name of that efficiency that financial deepening became a policy priority.

[88] It is not within the scope of this chapter, and this book as a whole, to expand on a critique of growth as a policy goal. Suffice to state though that there is an expanding body of literature that questions the validity of this orthodoxy. See for instance Serge Latouche, *Farewell to Growth*, Polity Press, 2010.

[89] Critically, these changes were perpetuated by subsequent governments in the UK, particularly at the turn of the millennium. See for an overview of those regulatory changes Laurence Gower, 'Big Bang and City Regulation' (1988) 51(1) The Modern Law Review.

[90] Private ordering is also analysed in Chapter 6 as one of the central regulatory techniques in financial markets.

[91] On the more general scope and aims of private ordering, see Clark Havinghurst, 'Foreword: The Place of Private Accrediting Among the Instruments of Government' (1994) 57 Law and Contemporary Problems 9–10.

[92] See Steven Schwarcz, 'Private Ordering' (2002) 97(1) Northwestern University Law Review 319, 322. Schwarcz explains that this is why in the sphere of business law this delegation has occurred with very limited procedural constraints.

[93] See Vincenzo Bavoso, 'Regulating Complex Financial Products Post-Crisis: Between the STS Regulation and ESMA Product Intervention Powers', in *Regulation and the Global Financial Crisis*, edited by Daniel Cash and Robert Goddard, Routledge, 2021.

[94] See Awrey, 'Complexity' (n 25), 258.

4.1 Explaining the loop

On the back of the neoliberal agenda, economic growth became in the 1970s and 1980s a central goal to justify policies aimed at capital markets development.[95] Moreover, financial deepening, particularly the availability of a wider range of financial products, and easier access to credit, was a central tenet of these policies, which ultimately led to the liberalization of derivatives markets in both the UK and the US.[96] Chapter 5 of this book, dealing specifically with the development of debt finance, and more generally with the question of financial innovation, provides an illustration of how financial deepening had undesired consequences, and did not contribute to economic growth as promised, creating instead financial stability risks. However, as is discussed in Chapters 6 and 7, the policy objectives at the heart of the EU capital markets union (CMU), and also common to broader global policy trends, are still informed by the same set of assumptions revolving around the idea of efficiency, and the ensuing objective to grow debt capital markets.[97]

The link that should be established at the end of this discussion is one clarifying the conceptual ties between the theories illustrated earlier in this chapter, and the regulatory infrastructure of debt capital markets, that eventually elicited their growth. Increasingly, post-2008 scholarship has focused on the intellectual foundations of capital markets, and on the centrality of conventional finance theory in shaping how financial markets are viewed, and their role in the economy. As suggested by Katarina Pistor, the way financial markets are conceived ultimately determines how they are regulated, and admittedly the set of theories identified under neoclassical economics has swayed policy discourses since the 1970s.[98] The utmost importance of efficiency within that theoretical construction led to the pursuit of policies that were centred on ensuring efficient markets. This goal was reflected in: a) rules and regulations aimed at maximizing informational efficiency (such as disclosure mechanisms, for instance); and b) regulatory measures designed to replace state intervention (or its proxy represented by more adversarial

[95] See Christoph Kaserer and Marc Rapp, 'Capital Markets and Economic Growth—Long-Term Trends and Policy Challenges', Research Report, March 2014; the authors of this report found a positive impact of the increased size of capital markets on economic growth and they stress that equity markets in particular can provide the ideal platforms to access finance for long-term risky investments.

[96] See on this Alif Darrat, 'Are Financial Deepening and Economic Growth Causally Related? Another Look at the Evidence' (1999) 13(3) International Economic Journal 19. Ideally, wider availability of financial products would improve lending conditions and access to credit. The increased availability of credit, according to these propositions, would improve allocative efficiency, and ultimately the availability of capital for new investments. See on this also Peter Rousseau and Paul Wachtel, 'What is Happening to the Impact of Financial Deepening on Economic Growth?' (2011) 49(1) Economic Enquiry 276.

[97] For an overview of these themes, see Vincenzo Bavoso, 'Market-Based Finance, Debt and Systemic Risk: A Critique of the EU Capital Markets Union' (2018) 11(3) Accounting Economics and Law: A Convivium.

[98] Katharina Pistor, 'On the Theoretical Foundations for Regulating Financial Market', Columbia Law School Public Law & Legal Theory Working Paper Group, 12–304, June 2012.

agencies, as was the case in the US) with market mechanisms and/or light-touch styles of regulation—what is commonly referred to as deregulation.[99]

Ultimately, it is interesting to reconsider the pre-crisis policy agenda as one rooted in a sort of liturgy, where the agenda was clearly the neoliberal one, and the liturgy was the panoply of assumptions flowing from neoclassical economics, analysed earlier in this chapter. The liturgy took the shape of ritual stories shared among communities of politicians, regulators, and market participants.[100] These stories were very successful in creating a narrative, and eventually an undisputed orthodoxy. The liturgy was also instrumental to the formation of the social imaginary that was referred to at the beginning of this section, that instilled upon the 'congregation' a belief in the powers of the market, in the positive effects of financial innovation and financial deepening. These liturgies critically served the purpose of also reassuring masses, convincing them that everything was fine, even at a time when financial markets were about to collapse.[101] As was repeated throughout this chapter, this orthodoxy drove the regulatory agenda in the pre-crisis decades, and one of the goals of this monograph is to assess the extent to which post-2008 narratives have changed, if at all.

5 Conclusion

This chapter has provided a conceptual basis to understand the trajectory and growth of debt capital markets in the last four decades. The first goal of this chapter was to reconceptualize the intellectual drive that underscored the regulatory changes examined in Chapter 2, and that led to the relentless development of debt capital markets. Emphasis in this discussion was laid specifically on the concept of efficiency under neoclassical economics, because this represents the pillar and justification for much of neoliberal policy-making. Understanding theoretical claims of efficiency, in other words, helps identifying the rationale behind the regulatory changes that led to the growth of debt capital markets.

[99] The concept of deregulation reflects in essence the regulatory changes that were analysed in the previous chapter. Deregulation can be said to represent a devolution of regulatory powers from the public to the private, which in turn rested on three fundamental ideological assumptions: a) a belief in the self-correcting power of the market, and its ability to allocate resources; b) a belief in the social desirability of unfettered market; c) a belief that market participants were able to manage risk, by inter alia employing quantitative models and financial innovation. On this see Awrey, 'Complexity' (n 25).

[100] See Julie Froud, Adriana Nilsson, Michael Moran, and Karel Williams, 'Stories and Interests in Finance: Agendas of Governance before and after the Financial Crisis' (2012) 25(1) Governance: An International Journal of Policy, Administration, and Institutions 35–59, 36. The authors here refer to the traditional meaning of the word 'agenda', which referred to liturgical forms and rituals.

[101] ibid, 43. Reference here is made to a speech by Ben Bernanke, head of the US Federal Reserve, who reiterated in a speech he gave in May 2007 the enormous economic benefit flowing from financial innovation and its role in promoting economic growth, capital allocation, and risk dispersion, among others.

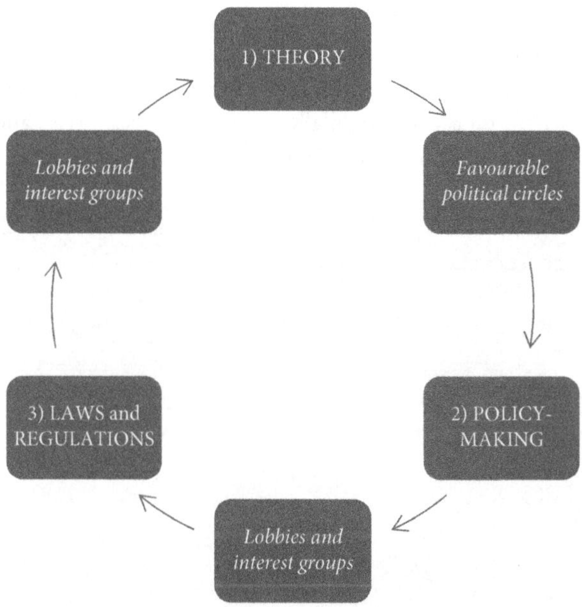

Figure 3.1 The feedback loop between theory, policy-making and regulation (Vincenzo Bavoso, 2024)

Exploring neoclassical economics in this context also highlights some of the underlying assumptions that are common to the bundle of theories (some of which are discussed in this chapter) commonly referred to as conventional finance theory. Despite the lack of empirical validation, these assumptions still form the basis for much of the policy-making in the area of financial markets, and particularly, debt capital markets. This chapter drew particular attention to the role attributed to the idea of the market under these assumptions, again an orthodoxy that explains policy-making and regulatory agendas in the years before 2008, and critically, also after it.

Ultimately, this chapter draws the contours of the feedback loop (Figure 3.1) that ties together three different, yet interlinked, functions in financial markets. Namely, 1) the formulation and subsequent interpretation of theories (in this case hypothesizing the role of efficient markets); 2) the design of policy agendas that, to differing degrees, find legitimization in a certain set of theories and attendant assumptions (such as neoliberal policy-making centred on the role of free markets); 3) the promulgation of laws and regulations that reflect a specific policy agenda, as was the case most typically with the regulatory changes in the US and the UK between the 1980s and the late 1990s.

While the neoliberal agenda received harsh criticism, particularly after the events of 2008, its policies still permeate current trends in debt capital markets.

This contention is made clearer in Chapter 7, where post-crisis regulatory initiatives are discussed in greater detail. In particular, global and regional regulatory developments reflect some of the beliefs analysed in this chapter, such as the idea of efficient markets, their capacity to allocate financial resources, and the ensuing need to achieve financial deepening. The EU CMU is the most striking example in this sense.

This chapter links conceptually to a number of discussions developed later in this book and serves in fact as their necessary background.

PART II

TRANSACTIONAL DYNAMICS AND RISKS IN DEBT CAPITAL MARKETS

4
Transactional dimensions of debt capital markets

1 Introduction

Part II of this monograph moves to an in-depth examination of debt capital markets. This is designed to show how the micro-structures of debt capital markets, that is their transactional dimension, caused legal and regulatory problems that eventually led to systemic stability concerns. Systemic, crisis-related concerns are in turn explored in Chapter 5, which discusses from a macro perspective the propensity of debt capital markets to be engines of crises, scandals, and financial instability.

The analysis conducted in this chapter reveals how different segments of debt finance elicited, in particular since the 1980s, the relentless increase in private debt and leverage, resulting in waves of financial instability. This is done by delving into the transactional design of a number of techniques that have characterized past crises (most prominently, the global financial crisis of 2008). The chapter also charts more recent developments, some of which are at the heart of the FinTech 'revolution' that has occurred over the past fifteen years, as well as the morphing of structured finance into collateralized loan obligations (CLOs), which have become the main technique to repackage highly leveraged loans. Discussing the micro-structures of debt capital markets helps in understanding the risks created in these segments of financial markets, and eventually the extent to which these risks are adequately mitigated by law and regulation—an assessment that is conducted in Part III of this monograph.

In order to understand present-day debt capital markets and their mechanics, this account starts with the bond market and its expansion in the 1980s. While the history of bonds is rich and goes back centuries,[1] if not millennia,[2] the analysis

[1] Wars in the European Middle Ages were typically funded with bonds. An early example is provided by the Venetian 'war bonds' in the twelfth century, issued by the city-state's government. More typical forms of sovereign bonds emerged in England in the late 1600s during the war with France. See Douglas Gabriel, 'The History of Italian Banking', American Almanac, 4 September 1995, at https://truthbitsblog.files.wordpress.com/2019/03/history-of-italian-banking.pdf (last accessed on 19/04/2024); Paul Gallagher 'How Venice Rigged the First, and Worst, Global Financial Collapse', reprinted from Fidelio Magazine 1995, at https://archive.schillerinstitute.com/fid_91-96/954_Gallagher_Venice_rig.html (last accessed on 19/04/2024).

[2] There is consensus that contractual forms similar to bonds have been employed as far back as Mesopotamian times, around 2400 BC. These bonds were used to guarantee the payment of grain and

Debt Capital Markets. Vincenzo Bavoso, Oxford University Press. © Vincenzo Bavoso 2024.
DOI: 10.1093/oso/9780198893257.003.0004

conducted in this monograph is focused on the growth of the bond market following the inception of eurobonds, first in the 1960s[3] and then with greater impetus in the 1980s with the initial liberalization of national capital markets.[4] Innovations in transactional designs were enabled in the 1980s by a facilitative legal and regulatory environment (discussed in Chapter 2). As a result, market participants led a process of financial engineering that was aimed at minimizing legal and regulatory costs associated with bond issues, particularly through repackaging and collateralization techniques. Evolutions in these contractual schemes, combined with the pervasive employment of special purpose vehicles (SPV) as issuing entities, further disintermediated the process of accessing the ultimate source of finance in capital markets.

Securitization became, from the late 1980s onwards, the fulcrum of capital markets, initially in the US and the UK, and progressively across all booming financial centres around the world. As is explained in this chapter, securitization combined the technique of bond issues, together with aspects of the commercial paper market, particularly in its secured forms.

The pace of innovation in the years before 2008 hit new zeniths, and in the space of few years plain vanilla securitizations were largely replaced by more complex and opaque structures, such as collateralized debt obligations (CDOs), CDO squared, and synthetic CDOs. While these new products were all singled out as among the culprits of the 2008 global financial crisis, synthetics in particular represented another layer of innovation, with derivatives (specifically credit default swaps (CDS)) intertwined into the structure of securitization, and giving rise in the process to new levels of complexity, interconnectedness, and hidden risks. Despite remaining moribund in the post-2008 period, structured finance bounced back after 2014, with new vigour and under the aegis of new contractual structures.

The post-2008 evolution of debt capital markets reveals policy and regulatory dynamics that are closely analysed in Part III of this book, where the rationale for restarting specific segments of capital markets is discussed.

This chapter ultimately provides the necessary micro-view of debt capital markets, zooming into the transactional features that elicited sharp increases in private debt, leverage and overall risk-taking. This micro-view informs the understanding of financial crises that is provided in the next chapter, as well as the regulatory and policy discussions developed in Part III. Section 2 of this chapter provides an

other agricultural commodities. Fast-forward to Babylonian times, the Code of Hammurabi, around 1770 BC, went as far as codifying earlier Sumerian practice by setting the interest payable on the bonds at 20%. See Jared Cummans, 'A Brief History of Bond Investing', 1 October 2014, at http://bondfunds.com/education/a-brief-history-of-bond-investing/ (last accessed on 19/04/2024); Edward Chancellor, 'The Price of Time: The Real Story of Interest', Penguin, 2023, chapter 1.

[3] The first eurobond was issued in 1963 by Autostrade. See Ian Kerr, 'A History of the Eurobond Market: The First 21 Years', Euromoney Publications, 1984.

[4] This was discussed in Chapter 2.

overview of the development of present-day capital markets by looking at the evolution of bond markets and their more specific legal structures. Some of the legal issues analysed in the context of bonds are important for understanding debt capital markets generally, and section 3 explores relevant synergies and evolutions (commercial paper, covered bonds, credit derivatives). This narrative paves the way for the examination of what became the centrepiece of debt capital markets: asset securitization. Section 4 analyses transactional and legal structures of securitization, together with various waves of innovation, including CDOs and synthetics, as well as CLOs and the securitization of P2P loans. Section 5 concludes.

2 Developing present-day capital markets: the bond market

The modern understanding of a bond market has its roots in Medieval Europe, where in Venice first and then in Amsterdam, interest-bearing debt was issued in order to allow cities and states to pursue commercial ventures or military campaigns.[5] It was in Amsterdam that active trading in these debt securities arose in the late 1600s, because of two converging factors: first, the increasing wealth of the local merchants, seeking avenues to invest their surplus; second, the growing tendency of European states to fund part of their budget deficits by issuing bonds to international investors. Amsterdam became the first market where the exchange of these capital flows was facilitated by the intermediation of professional agents (early forms of merchant banks).[6] The first truly international bond transaction occurred some time later, in connection with the so-called Louisiana purchase in 1801. This was a territory that Napoleonic France was willing to cede to the then expanding United States of America. The latter though did not have the means to finance the purchase and sought the advice of two merchant banks (Barings in London and Hope & Co in Amsterdam) who in essence structured the first US government bond.[7] This means of financing government expenditures became widely accepted in the mid-nineteenth century, particularly in connection with the emergence of the City of London as the main venue for the issuance of sovereign bonds denominated in pound sterling.[8]

Eventually, with the industrial revolution in the nineteenth century and the expanding networks of merchant banks across Europe and North America, international bond markets flourished as a source of corporate finance for governments

[5] Chris O'Malley, *Bonds without Borders*, Wiley, 2015, chapter 1.

[6] The Amsterdam Stock Exchange was founded in 1602 and is considered to be the first stock exchange in history. See Ludewijk Petram, *The World's First Stock Exchange*, Columbia University Press, 2014.

[7] O'Malley, *Bonds without Borders* (n 5), 5. The bond was issued in 1804, and the French government sold it to Barings and Hope at a discount.

[8] See Ranald Michie, *The Global Securities Markets: A History*, Oxford University Press, 2006, 67.

as well as corporations.[9] This is also a period of history characterized by the expansion of securities markets due to further factors: first, the rapid rise of corporations as the main vehicle of business association (as opposed to the partnerships employed until the mid-1800s); second, the transnational dimension of bond markets, no longer constrained by national boundaries, aided in this process of globalization by an ever-increasing network of intermediaries with a presence in most financial centres.

The outbreak of WWI halted the international development of bond markets (and securities markets as a whole), which remained confined to national economies until well after WWII—bearing in mind that WWII was preceded by the Great Crash of 1929 and the ensuing Great Depression.[10] In the immediate post-WWII years some international activity was represented by bonds issued by the World Bank or by government agencies and municipalities. It was only in the 1960s that the market acquired, again, a truly transnational dimension with the development of the eurobond market.[11] Two preconditions for the development of this market were the dollar becoming the global reserve currency in the post-war years, and the lingering centrality of the dollar (through the Marshall Plan) in the context of growing European economies. Bonds issued in Europe and denominated in dollar (so-called Eurodollar) became particularly attractive due to the availability of, and demand for dollars among both borrowers and investors. This trend was consolidated by what is regarded as the first eurobond, issued by the Italian state-controlled Autostrade in 1963, and listed in both London and Luxemburg, with a maturity of fifteen years.[12]

Without repeating the analysis of historical trends in Chapter 2 of this monograph, the more recent integration of securities markets needs to be understood through the regulatory changes of the 1970s. The collapse of the Bretton Woods system was followed by the liberalization of regulatory infrastructure, that was centred on capital controls and strong oversight of domestic markets by national regulators. The intellectual dimension of that movement, explored in Chapter 3, helps us understand how the neoliberal consensus pushed policy-makers and regulators towards more integration, lower regulatory constraints, more competition among financial institutions from different countries, and product innovation.

[9] O'Malley, *Bonds without Borders* (n 5), 8; Michie, *The Global Securities Markets* (n 8) 125.

[10] The consequences of the Great Crash of 1929 were manifold, but key among them was the disruption of the liberal securities markets that had again emerged for a short period of time after the end of WWI. These were replaced after 1929 by close financial markets, characterized by heavy government supervision. New Deal legislation enacted in the US in the early 1930s, and similar standards adopted in other major jurisdictions, further reduced opportunities for speculation in securities markets, and thus reinforced national supervision over financial markets.

[11] O'Malley, *Bonds without Borders* (n 5), 14–15.

[12] The dynamics of the Autostrade bond issue are representative of the economic climate of post-war Europe, characterized by reconstruction and an economic boom, which particularly in Italy is remembered as 'The Italian Miracle'. Ibid, 24–25; see also Ian Kerr, *A History of the Eurobond Market: The First 21 Years*, Euromoney Publications, 1984.

These forces were conceived as the necessary elements of more efficient financial services, particularly in the European context where the goal was always to develop stronger capital markets vis-à-vis systems of financial intermediation dominated by banks.[13]

The introduction of the single currency in the EU represented a huge shift towards the further integration of EU capital markets and the creation of a market for euro-denominated bonds that eventually started attracting issuers and investors globally.[14] It is important to stress that European bond markets have historically been dominated by sovereign issues, with the market for sovereign bonds often overwhelming the corporate bond market in the past. This trend shifted progressively, particularly with the increased involvement of financial institutions as issuers.[15] Two aspects need to be noted here, despite being only marginally relevant to the discussion. First, sovereign bonds across Europe remain national operations that involve the relevant organs of each member state (finance ministries and central banks). In other words, there is no mutualization of debt in the EU, and individual sovereign bond issues, despite being denominated in the single currency, expose investors to different credit risks and yield spreads, which vary according to the issuing government.[16] The second aspect is the strong centrality that government bonds have traditionally played in the functioning of the repo market, because they have for a long time been the main type of security pledged against short-term lending.[17] More will be said about the interplay between debt securities and the repo market later in this chapter.

2.1 The legal structures of bond markets

Bonds need to be understood as a type of debt financing, as a means to access finance via a debt contract. In this sense, bonds involve two main parties, namely the issuer who is accessing the bond market to borrow money, and the lender who

[13] See Jean-Pierre Casey and Karel Lannoo, *Europe's Hidden Capital Markets: Evolution, Architecture and Regulation of the European Bond Market*, Centre for European Policy Studies, 2005, chapter 1. The challenges related to capital markets integration in Europe are of course still very present, as evidenced by the recent initiative promoted by the EU Commission, the EU Capital Markets Union, which is discussed in more details in Part III of this book. European financial markets remain to this day dominated by banks and bank-based intermediation, and capital markets remain fragmented along national borders.

[14] Casey and Lannoo, *Europe's Hidden Capital Markets* (n 13) 8–13.

[15] ibid, 23. For an overview of current trends in European debt markets, see ESMA, 'EU Securities Markets', ESMA Annual Statistical Report, 18 November 2020, 24.

[16] Having said that, between the late 1990s and 2008, there was a convergence of bond yields across the eurozone, whereas, before the inception of the single currency, interest rates on long-term government bonds would vary greatly across European economies, with German bonds at around 7.84%, Italian at 13.28% and Greek at 24%. See Kevin Featherstone, 'The Greek Sovereign Debt Crisis and EMU: A Failing State in a Skewed Regime' (2011) 49(2) Journal of Common Market Studies.

[17] Casey and Lannoo, *Europe's Hidden Capital Markets* (n 13) 24.

is investing in bonds (hence bondholder).[18] In essence, this is a sophisticated form of lending, whereby borrowers choose to tap capital markets, instead of more traditional (and in most jurisdictions still predominant) bank lending channels.[19] It is often called a disintermediated access to funding for that reason, namely the opportunity to access finance from its ultimate source (investors in the capital markets) instead of banks.[20]

It is important to stress that the parties involved in a bond issue are both sophisticated: the issuer can be a government, a municipality, a large corporation or financial institution. Investors in bonds are typically sophisticated organizations, such as pension and insurance companies (historically, the backbone of the investor population in the UK), investment funds, and banks. A critical role in the context of bond issues is provided by investment banks as lead managers of the issue. This interposition facilitates the organization of the bond issue, its subscription, and marketing to investors.[21] As is discussed elsewhere in this chapter and Part III of the monograph, bonds are typically listed on a stock exchange. A number of bond issues though fall outside this listing requirements, and are traded directly between counterparties, over-the-counter (OTC). Listing bonds expands the scope of the issue and the wider marketability of bonds to more classes of investors. Some large investors for instance, such as municipalities or mutual and pension funds, are restricted from buying securities that are not listed on a regulated exchange. OTC trading instead offers advantages in terms of speed and economy of transactions (which override questions of market liquidity and price discovery typically attained through the exchange), particularly given that these bond issues are directed at a specific pool of large, professional investors.[22] Trading bonds OTC is possible due to exemptions that apply to prospectus regulations across most jurisdictions. These exemptions can be grouped under five categories, namely: 1) private offerings, 2) offerings to sophisticated investors, 3) offerings by governments, 4) commercial paper issues, and 5) foreign transactions.[23]

The marketability of bonds is in any case supplemented by their credit rating, which is conducted by credit rating agencies (CRAs). All debt securities need to receive two ratings from two recognized agencies, whereby the rating indicates the measure of the bonds' creditworthiness. Ratings are divided into different classes, with slight differences in nomenclature provided by different agencies, but the key

[18] Bearing in mind that a bond issue involves the participation of many more parties outside issuer and investor/bondholder, as will be seen later in this section.

[19] Due to the volume of money that is involved with bond issues, the realistic alternative is not really a loan from a bank, but a structure called syndicated lending, arranged by a pool of commercial banks.

[20] In this sense, Steven Schwarcz, 'Framing Address: A Framework for Analysing Financial Markets Transformation' (2013) 36 Seattle University Law Review 299, 303.

[21] Philip Wood, *International Loans, Bonds, Guarantees, Legal Opinions*, Sweet & Maxwell, 2019, chapter 25.

[22] ibid, 263–264.

[23] ibid, 286–287. The relevant legislation in the EU is the EU Prospectus Regulation 2017; in the US the Securities Act 1933 and Rule 144A published under it.

issue is that some investors are only permitted to buy securities that are rated investment grade or above, meaning that they are prevented from investing in riskier assets.[24] Credit ratings are by law mere opinions provided by the agencies as to the issuer's ability to meet payment obligations in due time and in full. They are not recommendations to buy or sell, nor are they opinions about the price of the bond or its future yield. They are however strongly relied upon by investors because the rating effectively relieves investors of the risk assessment that should be conducted before securities are purchased.[25]

While most legal and regulatory problems in relation to credit rating agencies have arisen in the context of structured finance, they pertain to debt capital markets as a whole and the way CRAs have become, effectively, their arbiters. Attendant regulatory problems are analysed in Chapters 6 and 7 of this book and can be summed up here by: 1) the CRAs' business model[26] and 2) the regulatory paradox under which they operate.[27] These regulatory problems have been further augmented by the difficulty in attributing legal liability to the agencies for the ratings they provide.[28]

The trading of bonds is further facilitated by clearing systems. Most debt securities, once issued, are held in a clearing system[29] which contributes to the custody,

[24] While this governance model has attracted widespread criticism over the past twenty years, CRAs remain the arbiters of international debt markets and their ratings are relied upon by investors. The sector has been regulated since the global financial crisis of 2008, as seen in Part III of this book, but its mechanics have not changed. For a critique, see: Vincenzo Bavoso, *Explaining Financial Scandals*, Cambridge Scholars Publishing 2013, 142–157; Frank Partnoy, 'How and Why Credit Rating Agencies Are Not Like Other Gatekeepers', University of San Diego Legal Studies Research Paper, 07-46, 2006; Harry McVea, 'Credit Rating Agencies, the Subprime Mortgage Debacle, and Global Governance: The EU Strikes Back' (2010) 59 International & Comparative Law Quarterly 701; Andrew Johnston, 'Corporate Governance is the Problem, not the Solution: A Critical Appraisal of the European Regulation on Credit Rating Agencies' (2011) 11(2) Journal of Corporate Law Studies.

[25] Again, this is a regulatory problem that post-crisis regulation has attempted to tackle. These regulatory questions are discussed in Part III of this monograph.

[26] Partnoy, 'How and Why Credit Rating Agencies Are Not Like Other Gatekeepers' (n 24), 60; Steven Schwarcz, 'Private Ordering of Public Markets: The Rating Agency Paradox' (2002) 1 University of Illinois Law Review.

[27] This is particularly evident in the US, where CRAs were granted regulatory licences. See Frank Partnoy, 'Rethinking the Regulation of Credit Rating Agencies: An Institutional Investor Perspective', University of San Diego Legal Studies Research Paper, No. 09-014, 2009; Schwarcz 'The Rating Agency Paradox' (n 26).

[28] There is no liability in contract between investors and the CRAs of course, and there is an established difficulty to bring a successful claim for tortious liability (based on misrepresentation or negligence) in this type of scenario, where the plaintiff/claimant would have to prove 'proximity' to establish whether a duty of care arises on the agency. In the UK, this test is informed by the ruling in *Caparo Industries Plc v Dickman* [1990] UKHL 2, where the House of Lords upheld the Court of Appeal's test of proximity, denying such a relationship between the auditor and either existing shareholders or future investors. This excluded any duty of care owed by the auditors. This test was employed in later cases, among which *Her Majesty's Commissioner of Customs and Excise v Barclays Bank Plc* [2006] UKHL 28. Similar obstacles arise in US cases, where rating agencies' opinions are treated as such under the First Amendment, which effectively shields them from any liability they may incur in the exercise of their conduct, except in cases of fraud. A relevant US case where CRAs' liability was litigated is *Newby v Enron Corp.* 2005 US Dist. Lexis 4494 (SD Tex., Feb 16 2005).

[29] Most typically, in Europe these are Euroclear in Brussels and Clearstream in Luxemburg, while in the US the Depository Trust Corporation. Wood, *International Loans* (n 21), 296.

administration and transfer of the bonds. Clearing houses are interposed between issuers and investors, and they typically hold the bonds on trust for the benefit of investors (who hold an account with that clearinghouse).[30] The clearing system plays a key role in augmenting the overall negotiability of bonds, which is a key characteristic of debt capital markets instruments. One key distinction for instance between loans and bonds is the free transferability of the latter, which is what enhances their liquidity, particularly in the secondary market. As explained by Philip Wood, the concept of negotiability, which is traditionally an attribute of bonds, needs to be distinguished from mere assignability, and is derived either by statute or mercantile usage.[31] While historically negotiability was a feature of bearer bonds (bearer as in transferable by delivery), the advent of clearing systems represented a huge innovation involving the abolition of bearer bonds as well as the irrelevance of related rules of delivery. These were eventually supplemented by the transfers between account holders at clearing houses, which affected the negotiability of bonds and their overall marketability.[32]

Beyond transferability, a key aspect of the bond market is liquidity, which is reflected in the secondary market. Developing a secondary market was initially a priority particularly in the context of sovereign bonds, in order to attract large investors and reduce the cost of borrowing for states. Due to its traditionally large deficit, Italy was always a big participant in the sovereign debt market (together with Japan and the USA), and this led to the creation of an electronic system for the trading of sovereign bonds through an inter-dealer platform in Italy, called MTS.[33] The platform attracted most of the secondary market activities, particularly from OTC trades, and in the process improved the liquidity of Italian government bonds.[34] Eventually, the MTS system was first extended to thirteen EU member states, and then in 1999 the London-based EuroMTS was launched as a pan-European platform.[35] The establishment of the MTS system was the springboard

[30] The system is further intermediated because often account-holders at clearing houses are brokers who hold the bonds for the ultimate interest of their clients, the owners of those bonds. On the other side of the transaction too, issuers represent the entire bond issue to a large bank acting as a common depository, which in turn holds the bonds on trust for the benefit of the clearinghouse. Ibid.

[31] Wood, *International Loans* (n 21), 291–292. The relevant statute under English law is the Bills of Exchange Act 1882, which attributed negotiability to bills of exchange, promissory notes and cheques, whereas the US Uniform Commercial Code Art 8 states that any instrument in bearer or registered form which is commonly recognized as a medium for investment is a negotiable instrument. Mercantile practice in England provided some clarity though in recognizing the negotiability of bearer bonds as a matter of practice, both as regards cases involving English parties (in 1824) and foreign ones (in 1892), the relevant cases being *London Joint Stock Bank v Simmons* [1892] AC 201, and *Edelstein v Schuler* [1902] 2 KB 144.

[32] ibid, 291.

[33] Casey and Lannoo, *Europe's Hidden Capital Markets* (n 13) 38. MTS SpA (Mercato dei Titoli di Stato) was founded in 1988.

[34] See European Central Bank, 'Trading European Sovereign Bonds: The Microstructure of the MTS Trading Platform', ECB Working Paper Series No 432, 2005.

[35] Casey and Lannoo, *Europe's Hidden Capital Markets* (n 13) 39. It is observed that one of the features that contributed to improving liquidity was the requirement for primary dealers to quote two-way prices on the platform, effectively creating a 'mandatory pool of liquidity'.

for a progressive and wider modernization of trading in the secondary markets through electronic facilities. This extended beyond sovereign bonds, to corporate bonds, and across different segments of bond markets and market participants.[36]

An important legal structure in bond markets, and in debt capital markets as a whole, is the function of trustees. In the context of a bond issue the role of trustee is akin to that of a regulator, with the specific trustee's duties stipulated in the trust deed, which is the relevant documentation for each transaction. Moreover, the appointment of trustees is a listing requirement in London, which highlights the importance of the trustee to represent all bondholders collectively, and coordinate the actions of individual bondholders (who may otherwise take disparate enforcement decisions, which would be detrimental to the bond issue).[37] The function of this legal institution is to coordinate the interest of all bondholders, in accordance with the term of the bond, and the trust deed. This becomes particularly relevant in the context of complex structured transactions, where the bond encompasses different classes of bondholders, often with conflicting interests.[38] In essence, trustees ensure the proper performance of the bond through their discretionary powers to enforce obligations under the transaction documents.[39] In most cases though, the power of trustees is only triggered in post-default scenarios, where funds have to be collected and distributed among bondholders.[40]

Lastly, to fully appreciate the legal structures of bond markets, it is necessary to briefly delve into the contractual clauses (often referred to as financial covenants) that are employed in bond issues. This becomes particularly central to the discussion conducted in Part III of this book, where emphasis is laid on the role of private ordering in disciplining this area of financial markets and the ensuing centrality of financial covenants in the governance of debt capital markets. It firstly needs to be remembered that the terms employed in bond issues are the same typically used in large international loan agreements, bearing in mind the substantially different

[36] ibid, 43.

[37] See Geraint Thomas and Alastair Hudson, *The Law of Trusts*, Oxford University Press, 2010, 1370; Philip Rawlings, 'The Changing Role of the Trustee in International Bond Issues' (2007) 43 Journal of Business Law 47. see also Wood, *International Loans* (n 21), 389–390, who explains that the practice of appointing a trustee is typical of Anglo-American-style jurisdictions, whereas in different countries, corporate law establishes bondholder communities with voting rights similar to shareholders.

[38] Rawlings, 'The Changing Role of the Trustee' (n 37), 47–48. When bonds are secured, the security trustee represents the interests of secured creditors.

[39] ibid, 49–50. Trustees can often act without bondholders' consent, provided they are satisfied that there is no material prejudice to bondholders' interests.

[40] This is the case both in the UK and in the US, also because of the common practice whereby the powers and obligations of trustees are informed by the transaction documents, and tend to be narrower than the powers and duties typically attributed to trustees in other areas. Moreover, trustees' duties in the context of debt capital markets are in most cases limited by exclusion clauses, whose effect is to limit the full applicability of statutory duties that emanate in the UK from the Trustee Act 2000 (particularly section 3), and in the US from the Trust Indenture Act 1939 (section 315 in particular). See on this, Thomas and Hudson, *The Law of Trusts* (n 37), 1388; Steven Schwarcz, 'Structuring Responsibility in Securitization Transactions' (2012) 40 Capital University Law Review 803; Steven Schwarcz, 'Fiduciaries with Conflicting Obligations' (2010) 94 Minnesota Law Review 1867.

relationship and bargaining power that parties have in the two contexts. While borrowers are similarly sophisticated entities in both scenarios, there are some fundamental differences in the configuration of lenders. In international loan agreements, the lender (or lenders, in the case of a syndicated loan) maintains a strong grip on the negotiation of the terms of the agreement, sometimes imposing certain clauses.[41] Conversely, in the context of bonds, the position of a lender is taken up by a multitude of bondholders who, despite having collective representation through a trustee, have limited individual rights. Crucially, their capacity to negotiate the terms of the bond is non-existent, as investors buy bonds with standardized terms and conditions that apply to all bondholders.[42] In essence, bondholders do not have ex-ante governance and monitoring powers, unlike lenders in international loan agreements.

Some degree of details though is retained with two specific clauses, namely pari passu and the negative pledge. The latter is widely used in many areas of finance and commercial law, and it purports to limit the level of the borrower's indebtedness in both secured and unsecured debt. More specifically, the lender seeks to protect its creditor interests by limiting the capacity of the borrower to create new security interest or to increase the amount secured by existing securities.[43] As observed by Philip Wood though, negative pledge clauses in bonds usually have 'no teeth', as they only prevent the issue of comparable secured debt by the issuer to the effect that the new security may directly affect bondholders' interest by distorting the value of their unsecured bonds.[44]

As to the pari passu clause, this is typically an insolvency law principle that aims at the equal treatment of creditors with respect to the distribution of available assets.[45] In the context of bonds, the extent of this clause is embedded in two main principles: one internal, whereby the bonds rank without any preference among themselves (indeed pari passu); the other external, whereby the bonds rank at least pari passu with other unsecured debt of the issuer. Critically though, in both cases,

[41] It could be argued that this will depend on the negotiating power of the borrowing entity, and their capacity to tap alternative sources of finance. From the lender's perspective, this can be explained in different ways, among which, the difficulty to transfer loan agreements once they are originated (for a transfer, the borrower's consent would be necessary), but also the corporate governance function played by specific clauses that are designed to facilitate the lender monitoring role over the borrower's financial situation. For a discussion, see Eilis Ferran and Look Chan Ho, *Principles of Corporate Finance Law*, Oxford University Press, 2014, 295–300.

[42] As Philip Wood explains, these terms used to be printed on the back of bearer bonds, when these still had physical form. Presently, terms and conditions are incorporated by reference, and are set out in the trust deed, as well as in the offering circular. See Wood, *International Loans* (n 21), chapter 28.

[43] Ferran and Ho, *Principles of Corporate Finance Law* (n 41), 288.

[44] Wood, *International Loans* (n 21), 311–312. It is noted by Wood that in the US a fuller version of the negative pledge may apply, whereby all borrowings would be captured by the clause, which would extend to the broader US understanding of security interest.

[45] For a critical discussion on the general application of pari passu, see Gerard McCormack, *Secured Credit under English and American Law*, Cambridge University Press, 2004, chapter 1.

the clause only hinges on the equality in terms of priority of claims, rather than on payment.[46]

More critical questions related to the regulation of the bond market are explored in Part III of this book, where the discussion also examines issues of private debt creation through the lens of financial stability risks, and how existing regulation mitigates those risks.

3 Synergies and evolutions

The relentless growth of debt capital markets, as portrayed in chapter two of this book, could not simply hinge on the use of plain vanilla bonds. Financial innovation and legal engineering have been at play particularly in this area of capital markets, largely because of the malleable legal structure of transactions and products, characterized by a governance centred on private ordering (explained in Chapter 6). As a result, debt capital markets have been particularly fast in adapting to ever-changing commercial scenarios and regulatory challenges. The remainder of this section draws a map of the key relevant areas of debt capital markets which help explaining their current structures as well as highlighting legal and regulatory risks.

3.1 The commercial paper market

Together with bonds, the commercial paper market has traditionally represented an important corporate finance alternative to bank loans, and a crucial element of debt capital markets. While its origins are rooted in the US,[47] evolutions in the commercial paper market made it, in the years prior to the 2008 GFC, a truly global segment of capital market.

In its simple form, the legal structure of commercial paper can be understood as an unsecured promissory note issued by a business entity.[48] Typically, this note has a short-term maturity, which varies between 30 and 270 days, and it represents a low-cost alternative to bank loans, partly because of the lack of regulatory costs

[46] Wood, *International Loans* (n 21), 109, 310–311.

[47] A parallel in the UK could be found in the debenture market. 'Debenture', however, lacks any precise definition in UK practice, and it is often used to refer to all debt, including loan agreements (as for instance is the case in the context of s 738 of the Companies Act 2006). A similarly wide approach was endorsed by the Court of Appeal in *Fons HK (In Liquidation) v Corporal Ltd, Pillar Securitisation Sarl* [2014] EWCA Civ 304, where it was accepted that in the absence of contractual terms and circumstances limiting the definition of debenture in the contract, the term meant an acknowledgment of debt recorded in a written document, whether secured or not. See for an explanation Paul Davies, Sarah Worthington, and Christopher Hare, *Gower's Principles of Modern Company Law*, Sweet and Maxwell, 2021, 1140.

[48] For a definition, see Marcia Stigum, *The Money Market*, Dow Jones-Irwin, 1983, 625.

associated with prospectus and registration requirements.[49] Traditionally, commercial paper was used by issuers to finance current transactions, such as payroll obligations, receivables and other inventories; investors were typically large wholesale institutions looking for short-term and low-risk investments. Historically, there is a low credit risk attached to these notes,[50] which are issued at a discount, with the difference between the face value and the price paid by investors being the interest on the note.[51]

A number of important distinctions characterize different applications (and transactional forms) of commercial paper. Generally speaking, there are three broad categories that need to be singled out: non-financial, financial, and asset-backed. The difference between the first two categories draws on the type of borrowers in the commercial paper market, which was initially characterized chiefly by industrial firms. The shift towards financial commercial paper occurred with the introduction, initially in the 1920s in the US, of consumer finance, and the increasing demand for short-term credit that led to the growth of consumer finance companies.[52] The third category of commercial paper moves away from the typical transactional structure already explained. It involves specific assets attached to the issue of the note, and with it, the interposition of so-called conduits[53] that issue the commercial paper to investors.[54] The essence of asset-backed commercial paper closely resembles securitization, which is analysed in details in section 4 of this chapter. It is centred on the setting up of a special purpose vehicle (SPV) which holds the pool of receivables, and issues commercial paper to investors, whereby the notes are secured over the asset pool.[55]

Interestingly, the market for asset-backed commercial paper was always associated with lower levels of transparency, precisely because of the interposition of the SPV, and the opaqueness associated with it. This is reflected in higher yields than in unsecured commercial paper, despite the higher level of security provided

[49] Exemption from registration requirements arises when three conditions are met: maturity of less than 270 days; notes must be of a type not ordinarily purchased by the general public; and the issue of commercial paper must be used to finance current transactions. See Thomas Hahn, 'Commercial Paper', in *Instruments of the Money Market*, edited by Timothy Cook and Robert Laroche, Federal Reserve Bank of Richmond Special Report, 1998, 105–127.

[50] It is observed for instance that between 1971 and 1989 the commercial paper market was free of defaults, the single exception represented by a litigation-driven default. See Mitchell Post, 'The Evolution of the US Commercial Paper Market since 1980' (1992) 78(12) Federal Reserve Bulletin 888.

[51] Richard Anderson and Charles Gascon, 'The Commercial Paper Market, the Fed, and the 2007–2009 Financial Crisis' (November/December 2009) Federal Reserve Bank of St Louis Review 590. Due to the low credit risk, yields on commercial paper notes have typically been only slightly higher than on Treasury bills with similar maturity.

[52] A classic example of this type of company is General Motors Acceptance Corporation, which financed the purchase of General Motors cars. See Stigum, *The Money Market* (n 48), 627.

[53] These are the special purpose vehicles that are analysed in greater detailed later in this chapter, in the context of securitization.

[54] Anderson and Gascon, 'The Commercial Paper Market' (n 51), 590.

[55] Post, 'The Evolution of the US Commercial Paper Market' (n 50), 886; and Anderson and Gascon, 'The Commercial Paper Market' (n 51), 591.

by the collateral.[56] This is also a market that was from the outset more reliant on the intermediation of advising banks, providing some degree of reassurance about the liquidity and creditworthiness of the asset pool. This is particularly the case in those asset-backed issues where the underlying receivables pooled into the SPV are originated by more than one entity. In such instances in particular, a further layer of credit enhancement of the asset pool becomes necessary because credit rating agencies base their ratings on the presence of such arrangements.[57]

Critical shifts in the structure of the commercial paper market became significant in the mid-1980s, when the majority of transactions were financial or asset-backed, and with an increasing volume of foreign issuers. This was caused by the increased interplay of large banking organizations with financial markets[58] and by the opportunity for fee-earning income that banks were taking. As is explained in section 4 of this chapter, by the mid-1990s the commercial paper market converged closely towards the booming securitization business, as both provided through the off-balance sheet technique the opportunity for businesses to economize on capital and profit from expanding their asset portfolio.[59] As an illustration of this trend, in 2008, 90% of outstanding commercial paper was either asset-backed or financial.[60]

An important and long-lasting change in the commercial paper market was the inception in the early 1970s of money market mutual funds (MMMF).[61] As will become clearer throughout this chapter, the interconnections and synergies between the MMMF and different channels of capital markets became one of the main causes of the instability and risk-taking that led to the 2008 GFC. In the context of the commercial paper market, MMMFs increased dramatically their holdings between the 1970s and the years before 2008.[62] In turn, financial institutions issuing or intermediating commercial paper became exposed to money market funds, creating a layer of interconnectedness, the risks of which only became fully exposed in 2008.

[56] See Moody's Investor Service, 'ABCP 2008 Year in Review and 2009 Outlook', Structured Finance: Special Report, February 2009.

[57] Credit enhancements in the shape of letters of credit, surety bonds by insurance companies, or supply of liquidity. See Post, 'The Evolution of the US Commercial Paper Market' (n 50), 884 and 886; Anderson and Gascon, 'The Commercial Paper Market' (n 51), 593 and 599.

[58] It will be remembered from Chapter 2 that between the 1980s and 1990s the restrictions of the Glass-Steagall Act were being progressively eroded in the US, and similar processes were taking place in the UK, culminating with the 1986 'Big Bang'.

[59] Post, 'The Evolution of the US Commercial Paper Market' (n 50), 886.

[60] Anderson and Gascon, 'The Commercial Paper Market' (n 51), 593.

[61] MMMFs attracted the interest of savers and investors on the one hand because their shares represented an alternative to bank deposits; while they were also attracting borrowers looking for alternatives to bank loans. The growth of MMMF assets between 1980 and 1991 was sixfold. See Anderson and Gascon, 'The Commercial Paper Market' (n 51), 596.

[62] As Marcia Stigum explains, commercial paper became a natural investment for MMMFs because of the short-term maturity and the low credit risk, and the opportunity to diversify risks in an expanding market for commercial paper. See Stigum, *The Money Market* (n 48), 631.

3.2 Covered bonds (*Pfandbrief*)

In the aftermath of the 2008 GFC, when the structured credit market became moribund both in the US and even more so in the UK and Europe, Steven Schwarcz suggested that a possible candidate to fulfil the role of securitization in capital markets could be covered bonds.[63] While the discussions conducted in Part III of this book explore some of the reasons why this has not been the case, this chapter situates the market for covered bonds in the wider context of debt capital markets. The legal structure of covered bonds is not too dissimilar from bond issues, because in essence covered bonds are long-term debt securities issued by an entity (a corporation or a bank) and secured over an asset pool. What is distinctive about this transactional structure is the way in which the security is achieved for the benefit of bondholders, because the designated asset pool (covered pool) which serves as collateral for the bond is ringfenced on the balance sheet of the issuer.[64] In essence, the ringfencing provides some degree of bankruptcy remoteness—a critical feature of asset-backed commercial paper, and more prominently of securitization, as seen later in this chapter.[65]

Instead of employing SPVs, covered bonds provide protection to bondholders against the issuer's bankruptcy by ringfencing assets on-balance sheet. In this way, bondholders have a secured claim over this segregated pool of assets, whose level of collateralization is further enhanced by the timely replacement of the assets throughout the lifecycle of the covered bond.[66] Bondholders further enjoy an unsecured claim over the issuers' assets outside of the covered pool, which entails a dual recourse: one, secured over the covered pool, and a second, unsecured, over the remainder of the issuer's assets, in the event of the first becoming insufficient.[67]

It is important to highlight that while the law and practice of debt capital markets found its roots in Anglo-American practice, covered bonds originated in eighteenth-century Prussia (where they were known as *Pfandbrief*). This market was primarily engineered as a system of access to finance for agricultural credit, whereby the bonds had full recourse to land that served as collateral. The modern contours of covered bonds emerged in 1900, when the German Mortgage Bank Act codified the practice into law, by establishing a legal framework for the ringfencing of the covered asset pool on the issuer's balance sheet.[68] In more recent times, the

[63] Steven Schwarcz, 'The Conundrum of Covered Bonds' (2011) 66 The Business Lawyer 562.

[64] What the ringfencing means for bondholders here is that they have priority of claim over the other creditors of the issuers against the covered asset pool.

[65] See generally Moody's Investors Service, 'A short guide to covered bonds' (2010) Structured Finance in Focus 1.

[66] ibid.

[67] ibid.

[68] Schwarcz, 'The Conundrum of Covered Bonds' (n 63), 564. see also Steven Schwarcz, 'Securitization, Structured Finance, and Covered Bonds', 39 Journal of Corporation Law, 130–154, 2014. Schwarcz explains that the ringfencing is accomplished by statute through a fiat separation of the covered asset pool from the issuer's estate, for the purpose of isolating the covered asset pool in the event of the issuer's insolvency. Covered bondholders therefore are granted a priority of claim against

market for covered bonds has grown substantially, and particularly in the EU area, where the issue of covered bonds is specifically regulated by statute[69] in ways that define the assets that are eligible to be part of the covered asset pool, as well as other specific aspects of the transaction (such as the ringfencing of assets in the pool, their over-collateralization, and bondholders' recourse to the asset pool).[70] It is also observed that covered bonds have become fairly popular across common law jurisdictions too, where the same transactional features are achieved through contractual structures rather than by statute. This, however, brings covered bonds closer to the practice of securitization, which is examined in the next section.[71]

It is also important in the context of this discussion to draw the necessary distinctions between ordinary bonds (as seen earlier in this chapter) and covered bonds. Some differences can be blurred in the case of secured corporate bonds, where bondholders have security over the issuer's assets. The distinctive features of covered bonds, relative to secured corporate bonds, are the ringfencing of assets on the issuer's balance sheet, and the dynamic nature of the asset pool, whereby the issuer is required to maintain a certain level of over-collateralization, by replacing weak assets with good-quality ones throughout the life of the covered bond.[72]

What is also critical to this transaction, particularly in light of the analysis of securitization conducted later in this chapter, is its on-balance sheet character, which dispenses with the use of SPVs. As a result, in achieving bankruptcy remoteness on-balance sheet through the ringfencing, covered bonds provide issuers with an important funding and liquidity tool. However, the absence of the SPV prevents the credit risk shifting off-balance sheet, and the opportunity for the issuer to originate more assets without a corresponding increase of capital, which refers essentially to the capital efficiency traditionally associated with securitization.[73] This is a key difference with securitization which will become relevant for the purpose of understanding the different regulatory treatment that they have received in the post-2008 years.

the asset pool, and only once their claim is satisfied can the covered asset pool be used to satisfy the issuer's other creditors.

[69] This was originally fostered though the implementation of the UCITS Directive and member states' specific implementation of article 22(4). See 85/611/EEC of 12/20/1985.

[70] See Renzo Avesani, Antonio Garcia Pascual, and Elina Ribakova, 'The Use of Mortgage Covered Bonds', IMF Working Paper Series, January 2007, 4–5.

[71] Schwarcz, 'The Conundrum of Covered Bonds' (n 63), 569–570, where it is explained that in jurisdictions such as the US, UK, or Canada, issuers may achieve the ringfencing by creating a wholly owned SPV for the purpose of acquiring the asset pool.

[72] Schwarcz, 'The Conundrum of Covered Bonds' (n 63), 568. See also Schwarcz, 'Securitization' (n 68), 142.

[73] The capital efficiency of securitization has been mitigated by the implementation of Basel III (explored in Part III of this book), but it is important to stress here that shifting assets off-balance sheet has the effect of reducing in principle on-balance sheet leverage, while increasing system-wide leverage.

3.3 The use of credit derivatives

While the study of derivatives is not at the heart of this book—chiefly because derivatives by nature are not debt products and fall outside the scope of this book's focus—they have progressively become an important component of debt capital markets. This has become more clearly the case due to their development from the 1980s onwards, a phenomenon that was discussed in some details in Chapter 2 which explored the impact of regulatory changes on the progressive liberalization and growth of derivatives markets. Chapter 3 also highlighted how the neoliberal consensus from the 1980s advanced the idea that derivatives would be essential elements of efficient financial markets, contributing to their liquidity, risk-management, and price discovery.[74]

Financial derivatives were at the heart of the process of innovation that characterized much of debt capital markets, as will become clearer in section 4 of this chapter. Financial engineering often entailed embedding derivatives into the structure of debt transactions, for purposes related to the hedging of risks or the diversification of investment portfolios.[75] More importantly though, these new transactional techniques created opportunities for acquiring synthetic exposures to specific underlying asset (or asset classes, or portfolios, or also indexes).[76] This means that counterparties in derivative transactions can gain exposure to a specific asset (say a bond) without actually acquiring that asset. While this strategy is consistent with goals related to transactional efficiency (as they imply lower transaction costs), it is also synonymous of higher risks, due to the leveraged positions acquired in the process. Counterparties effectively gain exposure to the price swings of specific underlying assets, without owning those same assets. Those swings can lead to a multiplication of profits, but also to unexpected losses, beyond what counterparties can predict and sustain.[77]

The evolution of derivative markets along these lines presents problems and legal risks. It is important to stress that as derivatives grew under the guise of OTC

[74] This was embedded in the words of Alan Greenspan, 'Risk Transfer and Financial Stability: Remarks by Chairman Alan Greenspan to the Federal Reserve Bank of Chicago's Forty-first Annual Conference on Bank Structure', 5 May 2005, available at www.federalreserve.gov/Boarddocs/Speeches/2005/20050505/default.htm (last accessed on 19/04/2024).

[75] Casey and Lannoo, *Europe's Hidden Capital Markets* (n 13) 2. The authors observed how the early stages of financial innovation were characterized by derivatives expanding opportunities to hedge risk on the supply side, and diversifying portfolios on the demand side. In essence, the application of derivatives allowed more sophisticated forms of risk mitigation, through, for instance, interest rate-linked derivatives (futures, options and swaps). These products at that time were traded over-the-counter, but more critically perhaps, they allowed increasing returns for a specific level of risk, something that was hailed as a form of portfolio efficiency.

[76] See Donald MacKenzie, *Material Markets: How Economic Agents are Constructed*, Oxford University Press, 2009, particularly chapter 4.

[77] This is explained by Margaret Blair, 'Financial Innovation, Leverage, Bubbles and the Distribution of Income' (2010–2011) 30 Review of Banking and Financial Law.

transactions after 2000,[78] liberated from the legal and regulatory constraints that had previously existed in the UK and the US, they became instruments that facilitated the creation of private debt, leverage, and hidden risks. The mechanics of derivatives post-2000 allowed firms to increase their debt exposures, or in the case of financial institutions, facilitated the origination of more debt.

It is worth reiterating that two main contractual functions are achieved through derivatives. First, as is the case in many instances, derivatives have been used in accordance with their more traditional function, which is pre-eminently commercial, resulting in the hedging of risks. Counterparties have for centuries resorted to derivatives for the purpose of fixing the price of specific assets in the future, by effectively hedging specific risks related to the underlying assets (such as currency risks, interest rate risks, or more simply risks flowing from unpredictable weather patterns). This is a function that is reminiscent of insurance, with counterparties having a proprietary interest in the underlying assets and managing relevant risks by entering into a derivative contract.[79] In the more specific context of financial institutions holding portfolios of assets such as bonds, derivatives are used to perform a critical function of 'cleaning' these assets of their risks,[80] by for instance swapping risks attached to one financial obligation, with another set of risks flowing from another financial obligation.[81]

The second function emerging vigorously from derivatives markets, particularly after 2000, is the speculative one. This is more critically the effect of the legal and regulatory changes implemented between the 1980s and the early 2000s, which progressively distanced derivatives from the exchange of the underlying assets, permitting what was referred to as a synthetic exposure. Under this contractual scheme, counterparties do not have a proprietary interest in the underlying assets, which never change hands among the derivative counterparties, who effectively place a 'bet' on the value of the same assets.[82] This is the realm of so-called naked derivatives, as opposed to the covered derivatives illustrated above.[83] It needs to be

[78] An illustration of the reforms that shaped and liberalized derivatives, particularly in the US and UK, was provided in Chapter 2 of this book.

[79] See on this Don Chance, 'A Brief History of Derivatives', in *Essays in Derivatives*, Hoboken, 1998; Ernst Juerg Weber, 'A Short History of Derivative Security Markets', University of Western Australia, Discussion Paper 8/10, 2008.

[80] This is explained by the Financial Conduct Authority, 'Market-Based Finance: Its Contribution and Emerging Issues', Occasional Paper 18, 2016.

[81] This is the example of an interest rate swap, whereby two counterparties exchange two pecuniary obligations, say a fixed interest in exchange for a floating interest, on an underlying reference asset, such as a bond. See Vincenzo Bavoso, 'Financial Innovation, Derivatives and the UK and US Interest Rate Swap Scandals: Drawing New Boundaries for the Regulation of Financial Innovation' (2016) 7(2) Global Policy.

[82] The settlement of these contracts is performed with the payment of the difference (hence the nomenclature contracts for difference) between the market price of the underlying asset at maturity, and the price stipulated in the derivative contract. In this sense, see the House of Lords pronouncement in *Universal Stock Exchange v Strachan* [1896] AC 166, para 18–22.

[83] See Lynn Stout, 'Derivatives and the Legal Origin of the 2008 Credit Crisis' (2011) 1 Harvard Business Law Review 1–38.

remembered that the distinction between hedging and speculative derivatives was well preserved in law and regulation until the 1980s, both in the UK and the US.

In the UK, general prohibitions in relation to speculative activities flowed from the Gaming Act 1845, a Victorian law aimed at capturing a wide range of activities characterized as gambling, and thus considered socially destabilizing and morally undesirable.[84] The Financial Services Act 1986 had the effect of abrogating section 18 of the Gaming Act, creating an exemption for investment activities, such as derivatives, which could be entered into as pure wagers for speculative purposes.[85] In the US, the distinction between hedging and speculative contracts was operated at common law by courts. The distinguishing element between the two contractual functions was the delivery (or at least the deliverability) of the underlying reference assets, which in turn represented the proprietary interest of the contracting parties in the physical assets.[86] Derivatives contracts where one party was expected to take delivery of the underlying physical assets were enforced by courts, whereas contracts between two parties speculating on the future price of the underlying assets, which they did not own nor were expected to own, was deemed a wager and as such legally unenforceable.[87]

As was the case in the UK, market developments and reforms in the US led to a progressive acceptance of speculation through derivatives, initially, with the development of commodity exchanges dominated by traders exchanging contracts (such as futures) based on the price of underlying goods (rather than buyers and seller of the same goods);[88] and then more recently, with the passing of the Commodities Futures Modernization Act 2000[89] which, by giving legal certainty to all speculative derivatives traded by a wide range of eligible counterparties, created the perfect environment for the widespread employment of OTC derivatives.

This new scenario became the incubator of much greater and hidden risks, particularly due to two critical features of the OTC market, namely, the lack of transparency as regards the obligations of counterparties, and the related counterparty credit risk, pertaining to the impossibility for market participants to assess the

[84] Section 18 of the Gaming Act included a wide range of prohibited gambling activities, among which were financial contracts that resulted in gambling. Such contracts, according to the Act, would be void and not recognized by law.

[85] For an overview of the 'Big Bang' in the City of London, see Laurence Gower, '"Big Bang" and City Regulation' (1988) 51 The Modern Law Review 1.

[86] This is explained in detail by Stout, 'Derivatives' (n 83), 11–12.

[87] This approach was embedded in *Irwin v Williar* 110 US 499, 508–09 (1884). In this case the court reiterated that a contract for the sale of goods to be delivered in the future would be valid even if the seller had no goods (nor any means of getting the goods other than buying them on the market). This type of contract would only be valid if the parties agreed for the goods to be delivered by the seller and paid by the buyer. Conversely, if the real intent under this type of contract was to speculate on the rise or fall of the price of goods, and the goods were not to be delivered (with one party paying the other the difference between the contract price and the market price of the goods), then the transaction would be deemed a wager and as such would be void before the courts.

[88] Stout, 'Derivatives' (n 83), 15–17.

[89] Pub. L. No. 106–554, 114 Stat. 2763 (2000).

creditworthiness of counterparties in the financial system.[90] As is analysed in Part III of this monograph, these problems have been partly mitigated after 2010 by regulatory adjustments that have mandated the interposition of a central clearing counterparty (CCP) in derivative contracts. Notwithstanding post-2008 regulation though, unquantified risks and hidden leverage remain a very urgent problem in capital markets,[91] and derivatives remain instruments that foster interconnectedness and hidden correlations in debt capital markets.

4 The alchemy of securitization

The development that most drastically shaped the dynamics of debt capital markets is the evolution of the securitization market in the 1980s and 1990s. As the title of this section suggests, the securitization of receivables was hailed in the early 1990s as a process that would fundamentally change financial intermediation, in the US initially and then globally, due to its capacity to mobilize financial resources by turning illiquid loans into liquid securities.[92]

Earlier experiments in this sector go back to the late 1970s in the US, where the mortgage market was largely dominated by so-called thrift institutions, the equivalent of UK building societies. At that time, increasing demand for new mortgages was putting pressure on the balance sheet of thrifts, which were typically funding the origination of mortgages with deposits, and were thus constrained by intrinsically limited funding sources. The idea that emerged at that point was to aid the thrift industry by using mortgages as collateral for long-term bonds, which would be used to fund more lending operations. The result of these earlier innovations came to be known as mortgage-backed pass-through securitization, the first of which was issued in 1977 with the intermediation of Solomon Brothers.[93]

[90] See Emilios Avgouleas, 'Regulating Financial Innovation', in *The Oxford Handbook of Financial Regulation*, edited by Moloney, Ferran, and Payne, Oxford University Press, 2015, 679.

[91] This was recently evidenced by two cases, first the collapse of a small US hedge fund, Archegos, and then the more problematic crisis of liability-driven investments in the UK pension system. See ESMA, 'Leverage and Derivatives—The Case of Archegos', May 2022; speech by Sarah Breeden, 'Risks from Leverage: How did a small corner of the pension industry threaten financial stability?', Bank of England, 7 November 2022.

[92] In this sense, Steven Schwarcz, 'The Alchemy of Asset Securitization' (1994) 133 Stanford Journal of Law, Business and Finance; Vinod Kothari, *Securitization: The Financial Instrument of the Future*, Wiley Finance, 2006; Frank Fabozzi and Vinod Kothari, 'Securitization: The Tool for Financial Transformation', Yale ICF Working Paper no 07-07; Leon Kendall and Michael Fishman (eds), *A Primer on Securitization*, MIT Press, 2000.

[93] See Lewis Ranieri, 'The Origins of Securitization, Sources of Growth, and Future Potential', in *A Primer on Securitization*, edited by Kendall and Fishman, MIT Press 2000, 31–32. Ranieri, identified as one of the people behind this innovation at the time he was at Solomon Brothers, stressed that the involvement of Wall Street in this nascent business was always conceived to remain at its margin. As is illustrated in the following pages, this was not to be the case.

The funding and liquidity problems experienced by the thrift institutions, and their limitations as sources of mortgage lending, would eventually be mitigated by the wider use of government-sponsored enterprises (GSEs), and particularly the Federal Home Loan Mortgage Corporation (known as Freddie Mac). The GSEs effectively helped creating a secondary market for mortgages, by acquiring home mortgages from lending institutions, and issuing mortgage-backed securities, distributed by Wall Street investment banks.[94] Already in the 1980s the disintermediation accomplished by securitization was converting millions of dollars of loan-type assets into securities: in essence, securitization was financing home mortgages through capital markets investors. In the process though, instead of supporting the activity of thrift banks, securitization fundamentally shaped the market and ended up replacing them.[95] Soon, the securitization market grew to include a wide range of rights to payment, from credit cards to auto loans, and beyond, to encompass as many asset types as can be fathomed. This practice progressively expanded across most jurisdictions with developed capital markets.[96]

Crucial to the securitization process from the outset was the valuation of the mortgage-backed bonds, and the placement of these securities relative to other more conventional debt securities. The challenge, in other words, was to issue securitized bonds that received a better credit rating than corporate bonds, something that hinges on two factors, namely the transactional design, which is further explored in the next paragraph, and the credit rating, which was discussed earlier in the context of bond issues. These two aspects are in fact highly interdependent, because in gauging the creditworthiness of the asset pool (in other words, the risk of default on the underlying mortgages), credit rating agencies look at specific steps of the securitization structure, and how they are executed.

From a transactional point of view, securitization is centred on the assignment of receivables from the entity that originates them (the originator). While this is common to other commercial law techniques, most prominently factoring, securitization features the involvement of a special purpose vehicle (SPV) as the assignee (the entity that purchases the pool of receivables).[97] The SPV in turn funds the purchase of receivables by issuing bonds on the capital markets, secured over the pool of receivables. The interposition of the SPV as issuing entity is critical because of various legal, accounting, tax, and regulatory problems that securitization addresses. Chiefly, transferring assets to the SPV ensures that the originator cedes property rights over the same receivables, which are moved beyond its reach in

[94] Philip Wood, *Project Finance, Securitisation, Subordinated Debt*, Sweet and Maxwell, 2007, chapter 6. The other two government-sponsored agencies are Fannie Mae (Federal National Mortgage Association) and Ginnie Mae (Government National Mortgage Association).

[95] Ranieri, 'The Origins of Securitization' (n 93), 35 and 42.

[96] ibid, 39.

[97] For a distinction between securitization and factoring, see Steven Schwarcz, 'The Alchemy of Asset Securitization' (n 92), 114; and Gerard McCormack, *Secured Credit under English and American Law*, Cambridge University Press, 2004, chapter 7.

the event of its insolvency.[98] This transfer also has the effect of segregating the asset pool into the SPV, for the unique benefit of the investors.[99]

For this transfer between originator and SPV to be effective, it needs to be qualified as a 'true sale'.[100] This is likely to avoid two legal risks from materializing: recharacterization and substantive consolidation. The former refers to the possibility of courts recharacterizing the transaction as secured financing (where the asset pool would be configured as collateral). This would have a detrimental impact on the treatment of securitization for tax, accounting and insolvency purposes,[101] because if the transaction were to be configured as a secured financing (instead of a sale), the assets would remain on the originator's balance sheet, together with the associated risks. Moreover, in the event of insolvency, the securitization's bondholders would have to compete with claims from all other originator's creditors. In short, the whole function of securitization would be impeded.[102] The second legal risk, substantive consolidation, pertains to the potential claim of the originators' creditors against the asset pool held by the SPV, seeking in essence the consolidation of the estates of originator and SPV.[103] It needs to be stressed that this is a risk affecting chiefly US courts, where assets and liabilities of an entity affiliated to the insolvent one can be merged in order to create a common estate for the benefit of creditors.[104] Again, should this risk materialize, bondholders' rights would be hugely frustrated because the cashflow from the asset pool would be directed at satisfying the originator's creditors.

What transpires from this discussion is that the main transactional purpose of securitization is the creation of bankruptcy remoteness, a concept that was encountered earlier in this chapter in the context of covered bonds. This is what limits investors' exposure to a specific class of assets, and therefore to a more specific credit risk than would be the case with corporate bonds. Achieving bankruptcy remoteness[105] counters the legal risks analysed in the previous paragraph, as it

[98] See Vincenzo Bavoso, 'Financial Innovation and Structured Finance: The Case of Securitisation' (2013) 34(1) The Company Lawyer 3–12.

[99] ibid. In essence, while the value of corporate bonds is based on the creditworthiness of the whole issuing corporation, securitized bonds are valued by reference to the creditworthiness of the assets held in the SPV.

[100] Wood, *Project Finance* (n 94), chapter 8. From a legal perspective the qualification of a transaction as a true sale hinges on satisfying three main criteria: 1) liability for the assets which should pass to the buyer, 2) exclusive control over the assets that should again be with the buyer, 3) non-revocability of the sale in case of buyer's insolvency.

[101] See Alan Berg, 'Recharacterisation after Enron' (2003) 3 Journal of Business Law 205.

[102] See Wood, *Project Finance* (n 94), chapter 8.

[103] See generally Patrick Sargent, 'Bankruptcy Remote Finance Subsidiary: The Substantive Consolidation Issue' (1989) 44 Business Lawyer 1223.

[104] Kenneth Kettering, 'Securitization and its Discontents: The Dynamics of Financial Product Development' (2008) 29(4) Cardozo Law Review 1553, 1622.

[105] This is typically achieved by ensuring that the SPV's assets are not subject to substantive consolidation with the originator's estate in the event of its insolvency, and by agreeing non-petition clauses with noteholders (effectively the SPV's only creditors) which will screen the SPV from insolvency proceedings. See Slaughter and May, 'Model Guide to Securitisation Techniques', February 2010,

ensures that the insolvency of the originator would not affect the rights of bondholders against the asset pool. It essentially refers to the legal status of the SPV. As was anticipated in the introduction of this chapter, the use of SPVs became, with securitization in particular, the main feature of debt capital markets. It is important therefore to define the legal attributes of this legal entity.[106]

SPVs are typically set up by the originator (or also by the transaction sponsor, a role covered by investment banks) as corporate entities or as trusts,[107] and often are incorporated in offshore jurisdictions due to the favourable tax and accounting treatment. The special purpose they are set up to fulfil is the issue of bonds to investors, so their business life is limited to the purchase of the asset pool from the originator and the issuance of bonds in the capital markets.[108] The SPV is likely to be a thinly capitalized shell entity, with shares held by a trust or a charitable foundation. While it has independent directors, these are not concerned with the management of securitization, but rather with more general and ministerial company duties. The management functions within the SPV, such as selecting the asset pool, paying bondholders, or replacing assets in the pool, is performed by trustees, asset managers and the originator's executives. This governance arrangement gives rise to an array of accountability and investor protection problems, that became evident particularly in the post-2008 years.[109]

An important structural aspect of SPVs is that in order to receive a favourable rating of the bonds, credit rating agencies need to be convinced that the cash-flow from the underlying receivables is sufficient to pay investors. In order to reinforce this mechanism, a number of credit enhancement techniques are in place, and typically they can consist in: over-collateralization by the issuer through a senior-subordinated structure;[110] a guarantee from a monoline insurer, whereby the issuer pays for the premium: a cash collateral loan provided by a commercial bank,

6. Contractual and governance arrangements also corroborate bankruptcy remoteness, among which, capitalization, books and accounts, no commingling of assets, independent directors.

[106] Bearing in mind that in other areas of commercial and finance law, the term SPV finance may well refer to slightly different uses of this entity.

[107] In case of a trust, a trustee is appointed over the assets held in the SPV; in a company, a trustee will act as custodian/manager of the assets. Alastair Hudson, *The Law of Finance*, Sweet and Maxwell 2013, 1299; Steven Schwarcz, 'Commercial Trusts as Business Organizations: Unravelling the Mystery' (2003) 58 Business Lawyer 559, 564.

[108] Complementary functions, in particular the servicing of the underlying assets, are conducted by the originator that maintains existing relationships with the underlying obligors. See Fabozzi and Kothari, 'Securitization' (n 92), 4.

[109] See for a specific analysis, Vincenzo Bavoso, 'Filling the Accountability Gap in Structured Finance Transactions: The Case for a Broader Fiduciary Obligation' (2017) 23(2) Columbia Journal of European Law 370.

[110] In essence this means that the issuer will place for instance \$100 million of mortgages into a trust and then issue securities for \$90 million, with the extra \$10 million serving as first-loss subordinated securities. These can be sold to investors interested in much greater yield and risks. See Neil Baron, 'The Role of Rating Agencies in the Securitization Process', in *A Primer on Securitization*, edited by Kendall and Fishman, MIT Press, 2000, 86.

or also a letter of credit.[111] While these techniques achieve similar economic goals, they also created the unintended consequence of greater interconnectedness in the financial system, a problem that is addressed later in this chapter.

4.1 Innovation 1.1: tranching and pooling heterogeneous (high-risk) assets, the birth of CDOs

The success of securitization rested in its capacity to accomplish functions that drastically shaped the balance sheet of originating entities, particularly those operating in the financial sector. For banks originating loan-type products, the employment of securitization changed their business model into so-called originate-to-distribute, whereby banks could continue originating mortgages, and instead of holding them to maturity, they could remove them from their balance sheet by selling them through securitization conduits.[112] This mechanism had profound consequences on the business of banking, and its regulation. Banks could profit from the process of loan intermediation, without having to hold mortgages to maturity, as was traditionally the case.[113] In the process, transferring assets off-balance sheet to the SPV created regulatory capital, which in turn elicited the origination of more mortgages.[114]

The advantages of employing securitization on a mass scale were rooted in regulatory incentives flowing from earlier iterations of the Basel framework. This becomes much clearer in the context of the regulatory discussion in Part III of this book, but in essence, by shifting assets and their risks off-balance sheet, securitization allowed banks to improve their regulatory capital—they could keep originating assets without a commensurate increase of their capital buffer.[115] Banks effectively were allowed under the Basel framework to manage their risk accumulation by separating it from credit origination, and in the process intensifying balance sheet management.[116]

Together with regulatory incentives, securitization advanced two key tenets of the then booming neoliberal ideology, namely the creation of liquidity, achieved

[111] ibid, 86–87. See also Wood, *Project Finance* (n 94), chapter 6.

[112] See Vitaly Bord and Joao Santos, 'The Rise of the Originate-to-Distribute Model and the Role of Banks in Financial Intermediation' (July 2012) Federal Reserve Bank of New York, Economic Policy Review 21–34; see also Emilios Avgouleas, 'Bank Leverage Ratios and Financial Stability: A Micro- and Macroprudential Perspective', Levy Economics Institute Working Paper No 849, October 2015, explaining how banks used securitization to engage with asset transformation and balance sheet management.

[113] See Gary Gorton and Andrew Metrick, 'Securitised Banking and the Run on the Repo' (2012) 104(3) Journal of Financial Economics 434.

[114] See Avgouleas, 'Bank Leverage Ratios' (n 112).

[115] Douglas Arner, 'The Global Credit Crisis of 2008: Causes and Consequences' (2009) 43(1) The International Lawyer 117–120.

[116] ibid, 120.

by turning a pool of illiquid mortgages into highly tradeable (and liquid) bonds, and the idea of private sector risk diversification. The creation of liquidity attracted many classes of sophisticated investors to the securitization market, all chasing the promise of higher yield and relatively low risks, but all essentially absorbing part of the credit risk of the securitized asset pool.[117] In this sense, it is correct to say that securitization represented the ultimate form of financial disintermediation, whereby issuers could tap the ultimate source of funding, outside the more traditional banking channels.

From the outset though, the challenge was to structure securitization in a way that could attract as wide a pool of investors as possible, particularly those investors holding large amounts of cash and restricted to investment-grade bonds (triple-A), such as mutual and pension funds. The challenge, in other words, was to create a more customized product, both in terms of yield, and maturity. The answer came from an innovation in the mid-1980s, called the collateralized mortgage obligation (CMO) which entailed a tranche structure, whereby each tranche carried a different coupon and maturity.[118] Traditionally, SPVs issued one type of security against the asset pool where investors acquired a pro-rata interest in that security, investing in the same yield and maturity. With tranching instead, SPVs started issuing a security sliced into a number of tranches, each providing investors with a different level of credit risk and subordination,[119] and attracting therefore a more diverse range of investor preferences.[120]

It was between the late 1980s and early 1990s that this innovation started taking a new shape in US capital markets, in connection with the boom in the market for junk bonds. The tranche structure, and the way in which risks could be diversified and distributed through that structure, led to new assets being pooled into the SPV, such as high-risk junk bonds.[121] Despite the underlying junk bonds being rated below investment grade (equivalent to B in the rating scale), the diversification of these bonds by industry, combined with the over-collateralization of the asset pool, and the originator retaining the equity interest in the securitized bond, led credit rating agencies to attribute triple-As to the top tranches of these securitizations. As

[117] Sarai Criado and Adrian Van Rixtel, 'Structured Finance and the Financial Turmoil of 2007-2008: An Introductory Overview', Banco de España Occasional Paper No 0808, 2008, 15, 16.

[118] See Ranieri, 'The Origins of Securitization' (n 93), 36, where Ranieri explains that this innovation drew on a structure that was already in use in the municipal bond industry.

[119] See Douglas Lucas, Laurie Goodman, and Frank Fabozzi, 'Collateralized Debt Obligations and Credit Risk Transfer', Yale IFC Working Paper No 07-06, 2006, who explain that first losses on the underlying pool are borne by the bottom (equity) tranche of the bond, while the top senior tranches are the most secure, and therefore rated AAA. See on this also William Bratton and Adam Levitin, 'A Transactional Genealogy of Scandal: From Michael Milken to Enron to Goldman Sachs' (2013) 86 Southern California Law Review 783, 800, who explain that while the average interest rate on the bond is constant, the distribution among different tranches is customized to match investors' appetite for specific risk/reward profiles.

[120] See Joshua Coval, Jakub Jurek, and Erik Stafford, 'The Economics of Structured Finance' (2009) 23(1) Journal of Economic Perspectives 5–6.

[121] Bratton and Levitin, 'A Transactional Genealogy of Scandal' (n 119), 801.

Bratton and Levitin observe, this was the beginning of what came to be termed collateralized debt obligations (CDO).[122]

The practice of tranching facilitated the origination of low-quality assets, but also the repackaging of already existing debt securities, including unsold tranches of previous securitization programmes.[123] Importantly, the resulting products would still receive triple-A ratings, and thus attract a plethora of investors, for a number of reasons. First, high-risk assets were pooled and bundled in the SPV in accordance with complex correlation formulae, that were thought to achieve the necessary level of risk diversification.[124] Second, credit enhancement mechanisms, such as guarantees provided by the originator, had the effect of minimizing the SPV's credit risk.[125] These transactional steps were deemed sufficient by credit rating agencies to award triple-As to CDO's senior tranches, further highlighting the problem with CRAs that was analysed in section 2.1 of this chapter.[126]

The transactional blueprint of CDOs proved to be instrumental to facilitate the avalanche of sub-prime mortgage origination that was experienced in the years before 2008.

4.2 Innovation 1.2: going synthetic and the rise of securitized banking

By the late 1990s, the securitization of receivables had become a critical engine of the banking business, not only in the US and the UK, but globally. One important reason for the rapid development of this market was the opportunity it created to optimize the cost of capital for lending institutions, particularly in light of the capital requirements prescribed under Basel I.[127] These regulatory incentives underscored much of the transactional innovation in the period leading up to the 2008 GFC.

The next stage of the innovation cycle was motivated by very similar goals. Large financial institutions were finding that bonds issued by SPVs would pay a

[122] ibid, 801–802.

[123] This is often termed securitization squared.

[124] Felix Salmon, 'A Formula for Disaster' (March 2009) Wired 79, explaining how the Gaussian copula formula allowed the creation of triple-A securities where none of the underlying assets were worth triple-A.

[125] See Viral Acharya, Philipp Schnabl, and Gustavo Suarez, 'Securitization without Risk Transfer' (2013) 107 Journal of Financial Economics 531–532.

[126] For a discussion, see Vincenzo Bavoso, *Explaining Financial Scandals: Corporate Governance, Structured Finance and the Enlightened Sovereign Control Paradigm*, CSP, 2013, chapter 4.3.

[127] Bratton and Levitin, 'A Transactional Genealogy of Scandal' (n 119), 813. They explain that under Basel I (the 1988 first iteration of the Accord), corporate loans would attract a capital cushion equal to 8% the value of the loan. Keeping this cushion while at the same time originating more loans became expensive for banks, limiting the bank's return on equity (RoE). Securitization represented a way to keep lending, bypassing capital rules. It needs to be anticipated that Basel II (the second iteration of the Accord finalized in 2004) did not address this regulatory incentive.

higher rate of interest than if they were issued by the bank directly; moreover, accomplishing the traditional true sale structure created transaction costs along the way.[128] The next big financial innovation was eventually directed at addressing precisely these costs, allowing large banks to originate future and high-risk assets, while removing related risks from their inventory. The answer to this puzzle came with the application of derivatives into the securitization structure, and specifically of credit default swaps (CDS),[129] giving way to what would be termed synthetic CDOs.[130] Synthetics represented from the outset a drastic departure from previous structures because the assignment of assets (true sale) is replaced by the CDS. The SPV here performs a different function, because instead of purchasing the asset pool, it serves as swap counterparty, and specifically as protection buyer under the CDS.[131] The swap in other words performs the function of moving the credit risk of the asset pool from the originator to the SPV, without the ownership of the same assets being transferred.[132]

Within this structure, the securities issued by the SPV are serviced out of the cash-flow from the CDS contract, instead of the payments made by the underlying obligors in the asset pool. Hence, the creation of securities backed by a synthetic exposure (the risk transfer under the CDS) rather than real assets. Importantly, to fully accomplish the credit risk transfer, the SPV issues credit-linked notes (CLN) to investors,[133] whose effect is to create an exposure to the risks in the asset pool, without however that asset pool having been transferred to the SPV.[134] By issuing CLNs, the SPV does not retain the risks acquired as protection buyer under the CDS, because that risk is effectively passed on to investors in capital markets.[135]

[128] ibid, 815. Transaction costs would materialize for instance due to the requirement to notify the assignment of receivables to the underlying obligors (the borrowers)—bearing in mind that in some jurisdictions the borrowers' consent is a legal requirement for the assignment to be perfected.

[129] In its typical form, a CDS is a bilateral contract, whereby one party agrees to sell protection to another party, over an underlying reference asset (such as for instance a bond). The protection is taken against a number of credit events (such as default or credit downgrades) that may affect the underlying asset. The protection buyer will make bi-annual payments under the contract for a fixed period of time, whereas the protection seller will have to make a payment corresponding to the value of the CDS in the event that one of the credit events is triggered. See for a concise example Michael Lewis, *The Big Short*, Penguin, 2010, 29.

[130] The inception of synthetic CDOs gave way to a fundamental distinction between cashflow CDOs, analysed in the previous section, and synthetic CDOs.

[131] See n 129 for an understanding of the CDS.

[132] Slaughter and May, 'Model Guide to Securitisation Techniques' (n 105), 19. See also Elisabeth Uwaifo, 'Key Issues in Structuring a Synthetic Securitisation Transaction—A European Perspective' (2001) 16 Journal of International Banking Law 98. In essence, the owner of the assets (the protection buyer) transfers the credit risk of the asset pool to another entity (the protection seller), while the actual ownership of the reference obligation remains on the balance sheet of the protection buyer (the originator).

[133] Credit-linked notes are typically employed in funded credit derivatives when the investor in the note is the protection seller and is making an upfront payment to the protection buyer when buying the note. The protection buyer therefore is the issuer of the note, and the buyer of the note is the protection seller. See Frank Fabozzi, Henry Davis, and Moorad Choudhry, *Introduction to Structured Finance*, Wiley, 2006, 181–182.

[134] Slaughter and May, 'Model Guide to Securitisation Techniques' (n 105), 19.

[135] ibid, 14.

In the years before 2008, synthetic CDOs had become the main technique to securitize assets, particularly for large financial institutions (former investment banks in the US and the big universal banks in Europe). This was proving to be an extremely profitable way to create cash-flow from high-risk assets, which were being pooled together in ever more complex ways, and were sold to investors in bespoke tranches, whose value was determined by the payments under the swap. While the swap structure (instead of the true sale) was still granting originators some degree of capital relief under the Basel framework at that time, the more immediate problem for banks was the level of on-balance sheet leverage that synthetics were creating[136], due to the time they were holding assets before they could repackage them and sell them to investors. The synthetic structure though remained highly profitable for banks, due to the lower transaction costs, and the more complex and opaque transaction chain which allowed exploiting arbitrage gains from the repackaging process. In other words, the opacity of these transactions allowed financial institutions to purchase large amounts of existing, low-quality debt securities, and repackage them as triple-A CDO tranches, remaining in the process unconcerned as to the creditworthiness of the underlying assets.[137] This was also the result of the 'rating game', with credit rating agencies advising originators on how to structure the transaction in order to achieve a triple-A, before actually rating the product.[138]

At this stage of the innovation process, just before the GFC of 2008 exploded, it had become apparent that synthetic CDOs were causing two main problems. First, they were contributing to a huge mispricing of credit in the financial system, and the economy too, partly because of the flaws associated with credit ratings, and also because of the intrinsic complexity of the transaction chain.[139] Second, complexity was fostering a market where sophisticated investors and transaction sponsors were able to manipulate the pricing of assets, due to their unique and inside knowledge of the structured credit market. These features were made possible by the widespread employment of derivatives—it is worth remembering that

[136] In this sense, Bratton and Levitin, 'A Transactional Genealogy of Scandal' (n 119), 817–818.

[137] See Bavoso, 'Filling the Accountability Gap' (n 109).

[138] See Andrew Johnston, 'Corporate Governance is the Problem, not the Solution: A Critical Appraisal of the European Regulation on Credit Rating Agencies' (2011) 11 Journal of Corporate Law Studies 395, 407, arguing how CDOs received AAA ratings even though the underlying assets were worth B or less. See also Bavoso, 'Explaining Financial Scandals' (n 126), discussing the increased conflict of interest resulting from credit rating agencies offering 'confirmation' services before the rating ones.

[139] Steven Schwarcz, 'Regulating Complexity in Financial Markets' (2009) 87(211) Washington University Law Review 216. Credit rating agencies insisted in the pre-crisis years in employing the same rating methodologies for both corporate bonds and structured ones, neglecting the fundamental differences between the two. See on this ESME's report to the European Commission, 'Role of Credit Rating Agencies', June 2008, 3. More recently, asset complexity has been recognized by the ECB and the BoE as among the problems associated with the lack of transparency in securitization and the concentration of risks, see BoE/ECB, 'The Case for a Better Functioning Securitisation Market in the EU', Discussion Paper May 2014.

derivatives were traded OTC before the GFC, and this increased the opacity of the market—which created perverse conflicts of interests between the many parties involved in CDO transactions, and more critically, incentives to destroy value.[140]

As is demonstrated by the volume of litigations initiated since the mid-2000s, investors in structured products found themselves at the end of transaction chains, having to bear risks (and losses) that they were unable to foresee and quantify.[141] This was most clearly epitomized by the Abacus CDO, which came to represent a widespread modus operandi among large financial institutions. Far from being a one-off case, the transactional dynamics that emerged from the Abacus CDO, sold and marketed by Goldman Sachs, proved to be a rather widespread phenomenon in pre-2008 practice.[142] It is interesting to look at some of the facts of the Abacus CDO to appreciate how this stage of financial innovation became completely detached from economic or social goals.

The portfolio of assets securitized in this case was selected with the aid of an asset manager,[143] and a hedge fund, and it comprised sub-prime mortgage-backed securities. Beyond contributing to the selection of the asset pool, the hedge fund invested in the CDO's equity tranche, which is a way to increase the marketability of the CDO. What was less conventional, though, was the adverse economic interest in the Abacus CDO that the hedge fund acquired through another CDS (outside the structure of the synthetic CDO), taking effectively a short position in the CDO's senior tranche. Critically, the hedge fund's role in the transaction, and its adverse economic interest in it, remained unknown to investors as well as the asset manager.[144] What clearly appears from the Abacus scheme, as well as the Magnetar trade,[145] is that large financial institutions were taking advantage of inside knowledge of deteriorating market conditions—they knew in other words that

[140] This type of incentive is typical of CDS, where investors can take a short position on an asset, without having any proprietary interest in that asset. Most prominent in this sense is the manipulation of a synthetic CDO structured by Goldman Sachs, where a hedge fund with a short position in the CDO participated in the selection of the CDO's portfolio. See on this *SEC v Goldman Sachs* 10-cv-3229 (2010) United States District Court, Southern District of New York.

[141] For a discussion on some of these cases, and the legal issues that arose in the process (such as inadequate disclosure of risks, conflicts of interest, misrepresentation of risks), see Bavoso, 'Filling the Accountability Gap' (n 109). Overall, the majority of these cases saw large commercial banks investing in structured products sold by investment banks.

[142] See for instance, Jesse Eisinger and Jake Bernstein, 'The Magnetar Trade: How One Hedge Fund Helped Keep the Bubble Going', *ProPublica* (9 April 2010).

[143] See Douglas Long, 'Converging Developments in ABCP Conduits and SIV Markets' in *Asset Securitisation and Synthetic Structures: Innovations in the European Credit Markets* edited by E Watson and J Carter, Euromoney, 2006, 124. Asset managers become an important feature of CDOs in the context of dynamic transactions, where the reference pool of assets moves in concert with maturity liabilities or with the occurrence of credit events that require restructuring the asset portfolio to maintain eligibility criteria.

[144] *SEC v Goldman Sachs* (n 140). This led eventually to another lawsuit by the asset manager against Goldman Sachs alleging Goldman's fraudulent misrepresentation of the hedge fund's position in the transaction. See *ACA Financial Guarantee Corp v Goldman Sachs & Co*, No. 650027/11, 2012 NY (NY Sup. Apr. 23, 2012).

[145] See Eisinger and Bernstein, 'The Magnetar Trade' (n 142).

the assets they were repackaging were in some instances valueless.[146] The legal structure of synthetic CDOs offered big market players opportunities to profit from the declining market (and particularly the imminent collapse of mortgage-backed securities), due to the structure of CDS and their unique capacity to elicit short-term and value-destroying incentives.

Lastly, the development of structured finance along the lines of synthetic securitization further entrenched interconnectedness in the financial system, well beyond what market participants and regulators perceived. Importantly, the transactional features of CDOs were recognized as the mechanisms that enhanced risk transmissions between large financial institutions and entities operating in the shadow banking system. Channels of transmissions hinged on the business model of large financial institutions which had become manufacturers and providers of collateral on the assets side of their balance sheet (through their engagement with the repackaging of assets into triple-A tranches), and participants in the repo market[147] for funding purposes on the liabilities side of their balance sheet.[148] The mass employment of this highly profitable business model in the pre-crisis years increased homogeneity in the financial system, and in particular the correlation between banks' portfolios. All this became evident with the collapse of Lehman Brothers in September 2008, showing the understated importance of systemic risk propagation.

To fully understand these dynamics, a brief analysis of the legal mechanisms characterizing the repo market is necessary. Repurchase agreements feature a borrower, typically a dealer bank seeking a high-volume short-term funding facility, and a lender, an MMMF.[149] The bank borrows money by transferring the legal ownership of collateral (ie, top tranches of CDOs) to the lender, promising at the same time to repurchase the collateral at a later date. A critical aspect of this contractual structure is that if the borrower is not in a position to honour its promise to buy back the collateral, the lender can sell it.[150] Lenders are in a safe position also due to haircuts, which refer to the difference between the value of the loan and the

[146] See for instance the evidence emerging during the trial involving Goldman Sachs, reported by the *Economist*, in 'Sachs and the Shitty', The Economist (29 April 2010).

[147] Discussed in the next paragraph.

[148] See Vincenzo Bavoso, *Market-Based Finance, Debt and Systemic Risk: A Critique of the EU Capital Markets Union*, Convivium, 2018, 16–19.

[149] MMMFs operate in the shadow banking system, given that they are not licensed as banks, are not bound by capital or liquidity requirements, but issue deposit-like liabilities, also known as money claims. The moneyness of these claims, that is to say their capacity to be paid at par, is the critical element that kickstarted the GFC of 2008, which was characterized by Gorton and Metrick as a run on the repo market. See Gary Gorton and Andrew Metrick, 'Securitized Banking and the Run on the Repo' (2012) 104 Journal of Financial Economics. To understand the concept of moneyness and money claims in the shadow banking system, see Morgan Ricks, 'Regulating Money Creation after the Crisis' (2011) 1 Harvard Business Law Review 75.

[150] See Jay Cullen, 'The Repo Market, Collateral and Systemic Risk: In Search of a Regulatory Coherence', in *Research Handbook on Shadow Banking*, edited by Iris Chiu and Iain MacNeil, Edward Elgar, 2018.

value of the collateral pledged against the loan. The value of the collateral is higher than the value of the loan, because the difference hedges the lender against the risks of that collateral.[151] Moreover, in the event the value of the collateral drops, margin calls are triggered to make sure the repo is fully collateralized.[152]

The dynamics of financial intermediation in the securitized banking system highlighted two specific features of repo agreements. First, transferring the collateral to the lender enables the lender to immediately sell or reuse the collateral in the event of the borrower's default, thereby greatly enhancing the lender's legal position in the repo.[153] Second, lenders' freedom to reuse the same collateral in other transactions, so-called rehypothecation, creates a virtually endless chain of transactions whereby the same asset is used as collateral for an unlimited number of repo agreements.[154] This system of intermediation magnified the creation of risk-taking and leverage in the pre-2008 period, because banks resorting to the repo market as a funding basis (instead of more traditional and stable deposits) could expand their assets base virtually without limits, beyond their core liabilities.[155] Effectively, the only limitation to this prerogative was the riskiness attributed to the assets pledged as collateral: the haircut.[156] The experience of 2008 showed, however, that the same CDO tranches that were considered safe collateral before 2007 (banks could borrow 90% on their value) turned into junk assets once the cycle shifted,[157] with lenders in the repo market either refusing to lend against those assets, or demanding haircuts than banks would be unable to afford. This market-driven dynamic of haircuts spirals is one of the factors that aggravated the crisis of 2008, reinforcing a liquidity crisis and spreading risks throughout the system.[158]

Rehypothecation further fuelled the idea of liquidity in the financial system,[159] but in the process it exacerbated the creation of leverage in the shadow banking

[151] See Gary Gorton and Andrew Metrick, 'Regulating the Shadow Banking System', Brookings Papers on Economic Activity, 2010, 264. A repo rate on the other hand refers to the difference between the loan and the amount of money received by the lender at the end of the repurchase agreement.

[152] See Carolyn Sissoko, 'The Collateral Supply Effect on Central Bank Policy', August 2020, 19, available at https://ssrn.com/abstract=3545546 (last accessed on 19/04/2024).

[153] Cullen, 'The Repo Market' (n 150), 8.

[154] ibid, 13. It needs to be noted that the practice of, and associated problems with rehypothecation are typical of bilateral repos, where collateral and cash are exchanged simultaneously. Tri-party repos instead feature the interposition of an agent bank between lender and borrower, which provides some degree of transparency and stability in the transaction.

[155] Effectively, banks could tap large sources of funding, whereby the only limitation was the quantity and quality of collateral that they could post—collateral that in most cases they were manufacturing in-house through the various securitization chains. See Vincenzo Bavoso, 'Basel III and the Regulation of Market-Based Finance: The Tentative Reform' (2021) 18(1) NYU Journal of Law & Business 107.

[156] See Richard Comotto, 'Haircuts and Initial Margins in the Repo Market', ICMA European Repo Council, 8 February 2012, 4.

[157] A brief discussion on the leverage cycle, and the problems associated with leverage, is conducted in the next chapter.

[158] This is well explained and documented in Gary Gorton and Andrew Metrick, 'Securitized Banking and the Run on the Repo' (2012) 104(3) Journal of Financial Economics.

[159] Eliciting in essence a form of money multiplier in the shadow banking system. See Hyejin Park and Charles Kahn, 'Collateral, Rehypothecation, and Efficiency' (2019) 39 Journal of Financial

system (outside of regulatory oversight) and the interconnectedness between banks and non-banks.[160] Again, once the crisis hit in 2008, the idea of liquidity became an illusion, because market participants were found to rely on liabilities issued by non-banks (repo counterparties) that, despite being money-like, were not covered by regulatory backstops, and whose value as a result dropped dramatically.[161]

This model of credit intermediation—referred to as securitized banking or market-based finance—was widely recognized as the main cause of the 2008 global crisis[162] and its reform has been at the heart of regulatory adjustments post-2008. A critique of these reforms is conducted in Part III of this book.

4.3 Innovation 1.3: shadow banking redux, the CLO market

The aftermath of the global financial crisis of 2008 was characterized by a clear slowdown of the securitization market (broadly defined), some segments of which remaining all but moribund.[163] In the US for instance, the market was kept alive by government-backed issues[164] and more complex segments of the structured finance market, such as for instance CDOs, remained defunct between 2008 and 2014.[165] A parallel trend materialized in the repo market,[166] which had been propelled in the pre-2008 years by the volume and availability of collateral. This period though was not to last very long, because in 2014 market-based channels of finance restarted, presenting elements of the pre-crisis securitized banking system.[167]

Intermediation; Zoltan Pozsar and Manmohan Singh, 'The Nonbank-Bank Nexus and the Shadow Banking System', International Monetary Fund, Working Paper no 11/289, 2011.

160 See Peter Breuer, 'Measuring Off-Balance-Sheet Leverage', International Monetary Fund, Working Paper no 00/202, 2000.

161 Ricks, 'Regulating Money Creation' (n 149), 103–104.

162 See Adair Turner, 'The Turner Review—A Regulatory Response to the Global Banking Crisis', FSA, March 2009, chapter 1; Financial Crisis Inquiry Commission, 'The Financial Crisis Inquiry Report', January 2011, part II. Specifically, part II dealt with shadow banking, securitization and derivatives, deregulation redux, and subprime lending.

163 The reason for this are chiefly found in 1) the bias against securitization, which was widely regarded as one of the chief culprit of the 2008 crisis, and 2) the increased regulatory costs brought by the Basel III and also by a number of specific regulatory requirements related to securitization (analysed in Part III of this book).

164 This is detailed in Chapter 2.

165 See Grahame Johnson and Eric Santor, 'Central Bank Liquidity Provision and Core Funding Markets', Reserve Bank of Australia, Conference 2013, available at www.rba.gov.au/publications/confs/2013/johnson-santor.html (last accessed on 19/04/2024); Bonnie Buchanan, *Securitization and the Global Economy—History and Prospects for the Future*, Palgrave Macmillan, 2017, 115.

166 Elizabeth Holmquist and Josh Gallin, 'Repurchase Agreements in the Financial Accounts of the United States', FEDS Notes, 30 June 2014, available at www.federalreserve.gov/econresdata/notes/feds-notes/2014/repurchase-agreements-in-the-financial-accounts-of-the-united-states-20140630.html (last accessed on 19/04/2024).

167 For instance, between the first quarter of 2015 and the first quarter of 2020, banks' cross-border claims on, and liabilities to non-bank entities grew from \$4.6 trillion to \$7.5 trillion (claims), and from \$3.7 trillion to \$5.6 trillion (liabilities). See Inaki Aldasoro, Wenqian Huang, and Esti

The renaissance of structured finance after 2008 was shaped by a rather different setting, mainly because of the regulatory framework enacted post-crisis, dominated by Basel III (partly implemented, partly yet to be implemented). Without anticipating what is analysed in part III of this book, Basel III focused on large financial institutions, because they emerged as the epicentre of the systemic instability that exploded in September 2008. The goal of the Accord in particular was to insulate large systemic banks from risks flowing from the shadow banking system, or rather from risks related to the interconnectedness between banks and non-banks. As most regulatory exercises inevitably are, Basel III was developed as backward-looking and reactive.[168]

This regulatory setting is important to appreciate the post-2008 development and innovation in structured finance. Financial innovation in particular manifested itself with a new version of CLOs. CLOs had initially emerged as an early innovation of plain vanilla securitization, and in fact as a sub-set of CDOs.[169] The transactional development that appeared more recently though, presents some different features (and in fact it has sometimes been termed CLO.2). It was driven by two main factors. On the demand side, the post-2008 economic environment, characterized by low interest rates, fuelled demand for high yields among institutional investors. By reproposing the tranche structure, CLOs satisfied different demands for risks and rewards (from triple-A to junior tranches). On the supply side, financial institutions profited for two main reasons, namely the opportunity to generate income from fees, for the repackaging of high-risk assets (leveraged loans),[170] and the possibility that CLOs created to extend credit to entities that are below investment grade.

The development of the CLO market post-2008 was fundamentally rooted in the parallel growth of leveraged loans, both in the UK and in the US,[171] whereby CLOs became the transactional structure that allowed these risky assets to be repackaged and sold on capital markets.[172] While the overall picture of this renaissance may seem reminiscent of pre-crisis patterns (particularly the use of CDOs to channel risks from the mortgage market into the capital markets), the new breed

Kemp, 'Cross-border links between banks and non-bank financial institutions' (2020) BIS Quarterly Review 62.

[168] For a discussion on Basel III and its impact, see Bavoso, 'Basel III' (n 155). A full analysis of Basel III is conducted in Part III of this book.

[169] See Andreas Jobst, 'Collateralised Loan Obligations (CLOs)—A Primer', CFS Working Paper no 2002/13, December 2002, 11.

[170] See S&P Global Market Intelligence, 'Leveraged Loan Primer', at www.spglobal.com/marketintelligence/en/pages/toc-primer/lcd-primer#sec1 (last accessed on 19/04/2024), chapter 2, reiterating that the greater the risk of the underlying assets, the higher the fees charged at each stage of the intermediation.

[171] ibid. As an illustration, as of 2019, the level of CLO issuance neared $120 billion in the US, whereas in the EU it was close to EUR 30 billion.

[172] Financial Stability Board, 'Vulnerabilities associated with leveraged loans and collateralised loan obligations', 2019, 7.

of CLOs has come under a new shape. The new transactional design is in fact what industry experts have hailed as the structure that can 'ride out cycles' and keep risks away from systemic institutions[173], refuting opposite claims and warning signs related to the problematic levels of leverage elicited by CLOs and the ensuing rise in systemic risks.[174]

The structure of CLOs is characterized by the pivotal role played by private equity firms, which have essentially replaced banks, acting as both transaction sponsors and managers of CLOs. The crucial difference here is that private equity firms do not originate the asset pool, because the underlying leveraged loans are originated through a process of syndication among a number of lenders, including both banks and non-banks. Instead, the transaction hinges on the rather ubiquitous role of private equity firms, which accomplish a number of functions: they set up and run the SPV; select the portfolio of assets to be securitized; facilitate the origination of the leveraged loans (often they own the firms that access the loans, or engineer the leveraged buy-outs that stand behind the leveraged loans); coordinate the syndication of the leveraged loans which are then pooled into the SPV.[175] As a result of this structure, large banks are not directly involved in any aspects of the CLO process, but, as is discussed later in this section, they remain exposed to different degrees to the CLO market.[176]

From a transactional point of view, CLOs present similarities with securitization-type structures. Bearing in mind what was already said about the absence of an originator, a true sale is completed whereby the asset pool is transferred to the SPV.[177] The SPV issues tranched securities to capital markets investors, whereby tranches are rated by credit rating agencies, which on paper should favour the higher levels of subordination of the CLO's senior tranches as well as their better quality of credit enhancement.[178] It is also important to point out that banks provide an indirect financial support towards the acquisition of the asset portfolio by the SPV, which means that the same banks remain exposed to the underlying assets for

[173] See on this Stephen Foley and Henny Sender, 'Private equity firms fuel demand for CLOs', *Financial Times* (20 December 2012), at www.ft.com/content/bd0081a8-4ab7-11e2-9650-00144feab49a (last accessed on 19/04/2024).

[174] See for instance IMF, 'Global Financial Stability Report', October 2019, chapter 2; and also Vincenzo Bavoso, 'Hail the New Private Debt Machine: Private Equity, Leveraged Loans and Collateralised Debt Obligations' (2020) 14(3) Law and Financial Markets Review.

[175] As it has been suggested, the private equity industry is fuelling demand for leveraged loans, which in turn require CLOs. See Foley and Henny Sender, 'Private equity firms' (n 173).

[176] See Bavoso, 'Hail the Private Debt Machine' (n 174).

[177] See Guggenheim Investments, 'Understanding Collateralized Loan Obligations', May 2019, 1–2. This sale typically includes between 100 and 250 secured leveraged loans.

[178] Rob McDonough, 'Collateralised Loan Obligations', Global Financial Markets Institute, 9 April 2016, available at www.gfmi.com/articles/collateralized-loan-obligations/ (last accessed on 19/04/2024), noting that while pre-2008 CLOs had a 20–25% level of credit enhancement, this has now gone up to 30–35%.

the whole warehousing period, until proceeds from capital markets investors are generated.[179]

What is important to point out in this discussion is that the innovation brought by CLOs had a significant impact on some of the legal and regulatory standards in place in the post-2008 years. Even more striking is that this new legal engineering reproposed forms of risk-taking that had been experienced before 2008. One starting factor that facilitated the huge growth of leveraged loans was the erosion of underwriting standards and the attendant changes in loan documentation.[180] As a result, covenant-lite loans (cov-lite) became the predominant practice both in the US and the UK.[181] Once again, the justification for this was twofold: on the supply side, originating leveraged loans was seen as an opportunity to extend credit to areas of the economy that were not receiving the necessary support. The CLO structure became the way to repackage high-risk assets into products that were perceived liquid. The demand side saw many investors attracted by the high yields of CLO tranches, combined with the promises of limited risk-taking. These perceptions were eventually shaken by the events of March 2020 and the ensuing panic, when the level of defaults in the underlying leveraged loans rose beyond expectations,[182] threatening (once again) the stability of the financial system.[183]

Another important aspect of CLOs is the way in which the transaction structure bypasses aspects of post-2008 regulation. An important regulatory development was the introduction of a formal skin-in-the-game provision, designed to align the interest of securitizers and investors and limit the concentration of risks in the repackaged asset pool. This provision imposed upon originators a 5% retention of the economic risk for all securitized assets.[184] The peculiar contractual structure of CLOs, which lacks originators, proves problematic in the context of the risk retention provision. The question arose in 2013 as to what party in the transaction

[179] Guggenheim, 'Understanding Collateralized Loan Obligations' (n 177), 3, noting that the warehousing period lasts on average between six and twelve months.

[180] Financial Stability Board, 'Vulnerabilities' (n 172), 1.

[181] Cov-lite loans are negotiated with a financial incurrence covenant that is normally associated with bonds, and requires that in the event of an issuer taking an action, the issuer would still need to be in compliance with the underlying covenant. In so doing, this type of clause limits the issuer's capacity to take on more debt in line with the incurrence limit. The incurrence limit though does not affect past actions, so for instance deteriorated earnings would not trigger a breach of the covenant. See S&P Global Market Intelligence, 'Leveraged Loan Primer' (n 170), chapter 15. It is observed here that what would be more appropriate in the context of loan agreements is a maintenance covenant, whereby the issuer is required to meet certain financial tests periodically, regardless of whether any action has been taken. In this case even a decline in earnings would cause a breach of the covenant.

[182] This concern was specifically highlighted by the Financial Stability Board (FSB). See Financial Stability Board, 'Vulnerabilities' (n 172).

[183] For a critical perspective on how the combination of relaxed underwriting standards and innovations in structured finance can interplay with a leverage cycle, see Vincenzo Bavoso, 'Market-Based Finance, Debt and Systemic Risk: A Critique of the EU Capital Markets Union', Accounting, Economics, and Law: A Convivium, 2018, DOI: https://doi.org/10.1515/ael-2017-0039 (last accessed on 19/04/2024).

[184] This was enshrined in the US in s 941 of the Dodd-Frank Act 2010; at the EU level, Regulation (EU) No 575/2013 (CRR) and accompanying Directive 2013/36/EU.

should bear the burden of the risk retention requirement, whether it should fall on the originator (or the syndicate of originators in the case of CLOs), or the CLO manager (the private equity firm). This question was resolved by the US Court of Appeal,[185] by introducing a distinction between open market CLOs and balance sheet CLOs, and stating that in the former, the obligation would be fulfilled by the loan syndicators and the lead arranger, instead of the CLO manager.[186] It needs to be noted that a similar dilemma arose in the EU, where new rules in 2014 rectified that collateral managers would only be under a risk retention obligation if they qualified as originators or sponsors.[187]

A final piece of the jigsaw emerging from the post-2008 renaissance is the level of risk-taking elicited by total return swaps (TRSs).[188] The employment of TRSs allowed institutional investors (such as hedge funds) to gain exposure to risky assets, such as CLOs, and particularly to the credit risk of the same assets, without actually holding them.[189] The structure of TRSs, which is similar to other swap contracts, recreated a problem that was present in the past, namely counterparty credit risk. This risk can materialize for instance when more investors enter into TRSs on similar underlying correlated assets. A decline in the value of the assets would cause a reduced return for investors, who would have to keep making payments under the swap. Under this situation, if investors were not adequately capitalized, their risk of default would translate into a risk for their counterparties too, leading to systemic concerns.[190]

It is important to note, without pre-empting the discussion conducted in Part III of this book, that after 2008 regulatory reforms were aimed at mitigating

[185] *The Loan Syndication and Trading Association v SEC and Board of Governors of the Federal Reserve System*, United States Court of Appeals, No 17-5004, 9 February 2018.

[186] Open market CLOs are limited to purchasing senior secured syndicated loans acquired directly from arrangers or syndicators. Where the CLO does not meet this definition, the risk retention requirement would have to be fulfilled by the CLO manager. This distinction was further clarified by the US Court of Appeal in *LSTA v SEC*, where it was explained that 'open market' CLOs acquire their assets from trading in the open market, whereas balance sheet CLOs are created by the originator of the underlying assets that are transferred to the SPV. The Court of Appeal also emphasized that the provision (implemented in the US with the Dodd-Frank Act) did not purport to bind open market CLO managers with the risk retention requirement, because managers are not securitizers, and could not be configured as transferors of the assets in the securitization structure.

[187] See on this the original broader risk-retention requirement in Art 122A CRD, which was later narrowed with the EBA/RTS/2013/12, Arts 4, 5, and 8. See also Latham and Watkins, 'EU Risk Retention Rules and CLOs—the Journey's End?' (2014) 1704 Commentary 2 and 4, where it was reiterated that the application of risk retention rules was designed with securitization-type transactions in mind, and it would remain problematic in the context of CLOs.

[188] Under a total return swap two parties exchange the returns from a financial asset. The contractual structure of this derivative is similar to other swaps (such as credit default swaps), and it sees one party (the investor) making payments based on a set rate, while the other party (say a bank holding the financial asset) makes payments based on the return of the underlying assets. See for an illustration Corporate Finance Institute, 'What is a Total Return Swap (TRS)?', available at https://corporatefinanceinstitute.com/resources/knowledge/finance/total-return-swap-trs/ (last accessed on 19/04/2024).

[189] ibid. This allows investors to maximize their investment capital—at the same time though it is synonymous of an increase in leverage.

[190] ibid.

counterparty credit risk by introducing clearing obligations via CCPs and margin requirements.[191] While these requirements come with a number of exceptions, both in the US and the EU, TRNs have remained outside the scope of these provisions, due also to the slow implementation of relevant rules.[192]

The analysis of this last phase of financial innovation could not end without a brief mention of the panic of 2020, triggered by the economic slowdown induced by the Covid-19 pandemic. While this was certainly an exogenous shock, it clearly showed the fundamental fault-lines in post-2008 capital markets, and the fragility of a financial system that is still built around very problematic levels of private debt and risk-taking.[193] The panic also showed that, despite regulatory efforts, financial markets are still highly interconnected, sometimes through hidden channels of transmission that have remained outside the scope of regulation. Without liquidity injections from central banks (in the US, UK, and EU), defaults in the CLO market would have affected systemic financial institutions.[194]

4.4 Innovation 1.4: the true (shadow banking) nature of FinTech

Some of the dynamics that underscored the growth of the CLO market are also at the heart of the FinTech[195] revolution that characterized the post-2008 period. After the GFC of 2008 a clearer and more widespread perception of large banks emerged, reflecting how their role in society had morphed in the previous decades.[196] In particular, increased distrust towards large financial institutions, together with their conservative lending patterns,[197] contributed to the emergence of alternative lending platforms. These revolve around the development of their own

[191] See Dodd-Frank Wall Street Reform and Consumer Protection Act, Title VII. Under EU law, total return swaps are covered under the Securities Financing Transactions Regulation, Regulation (EU) 2015/2365.

[192] Joe Rennison, Eric Platt, Colby Smith, and Philip Stafford, 'US put off derivatives rules for a decade before Archegos blew up', *Financial Times* (12 April 2021), at www.ft.com/content/7819e714-bf9d-4f83-a6e4-497df534f77c (last accessed on 19/04/2024).

[193] In this sense, see Adair Turner, *Between Debt and the Devil*, Princeton University Press, 2016, chapter 4; IMF, *Global Financial Stability Report*, 2019, chapter 2.

[194] For an analysis, see Bavoso, 'Basel III' (n 155)

[195] The FSB defined FinTech as 'technologically enabled financial innovation that should support new business models, new financial processes and products, and should thus result in more competitive financial markets'. See FSB, 'Financial Stability Implications from FinTech—Supervisory and Regulatory Authorities Issues that Merit Authorities' Attention', 27 June 2017, 1.

[196] See on the evolution of banking Ross Buckley, 'The Changing Nature of Banking and Why it Matters', in Buckley, Avgouleas, and Arner, *Rethinking Global Finance and its Regulation*, Cambridge University Press, 2015; more specifically on the lending behaviour of banks in the pre-crisis years, see Sue Jaffer, Nicholas Morris, Edward Sawbridge, and David Vines, 'How Changes to the Financial Services Industry Eroded Trust', in *Capital Failure: Rebuilding Trust in Financial Services*, edited by N Morris and D Vines, Oxford University Press, 2014.

[197] As will be explained in Part III, lending to the real economy became more expensive for banks following the implementation of new capital regulation under Basel III.

technology, which in turn facilitates cheaper and disintermediated forms of access to finance.[198]

As far as the UK is concerned, this move was encouraged, and even facilitated, by the Financial Conduct Authority (FCA), through the setting up of the 'Innovation Hub'[199] which was conceived as an incubator for the development of 1) more tech-based innovations, and 2) an appropriate regulatory framework.[200] It is important to stress that in the UK emphasis was also laid on the benefits that financial consumers would gain from FinTech. The policy narrative hinged on questions of access to finance, which have become more urgent in the post-2008 years, particularly for small and medium-sized enterprises (SMEs), and their difficulty to access lending facilities through conventional bank loans.[201] The widespread belief, especially at the time the Innovation Hub was set up in 2014, was that alternative, FinTech-based intermediation channels would be ideally placed to serve the financing needs of SMEs.[202] This materialized with 14% of new lending to SMEs provided by P2P platforms in 2015.[203]

The legal and transactional structure of P2P lending is straightforward and is conceived as a streamlined, middle-man-free form of financial intermediation. Platforms are essentially an online venue where prospective borrowers apply for a loan, and creditors (investors in the platform) can choose from the available loans those that match the risk profile they are seeking. The credit risk of each investment is determined by the information provided by the applicant borrower, and the credit risk assessment formulated by the platform—this being in principle the

[198] See Douglas Arner, Janos Barberis, and Ross Buckley, 'The Evolution of FinTech: A New Post-Crisis Paradigm?, University of New South Wales Law Research Series, 62, 2016, 6–7.

[199] See FCA, 'Innovate and Innovation Hub', 20/09/2018, available at www.fca.org.uk/firms/innovate-innovation-hub (last accessed on 19/04/2024).

[200] ibid. There is an idea of disruptive innovation at the heart of the Innovation Hub, and attendant policy and regulatory tools are directed at removing unnecessary barriers.

[201] As an illustration, between 2008 and 2012 bank loans to SMEs went down from £44.5 billion to £38 billion (the amount of loans went up between 2013 and 2017). From 2012 onwards, the amount of loans originated on P2P platforms started to increase, reaching in 2017 a value of £2.3 billion. See on this UK Finance, 'SME finance in the UK: past, present and future', December 2018, 11, at www.ukfinance.org.uk/system/files/UK-Finance-SME-Finance-in-UK-AW-web.pdf (last accessed on 19/04/2024). From a different perspective, it was suggested in 2017 that between 55% and 60% of borrowers on P2P platforms were denied, or would have been denied, a loan from a bank. See Mark Carney, 'The Promise of FinTech—Something New under the Sun', speech 25 January 2017. See also statistics on bank support to SMEs provided by the British Bankers Association at www.bba.org.uk/news/statistics/sme-statistics/ (last accessed on 19/04/2024).

[202] See Matteo Acquilina and Wladimir Kraus, 'Market-Based Finance: Its Contribution and Emerging Issues', FCA Occasional Paper No 18, May 2016; and European Commission, 'Building a Capital Markets Union—accompanying the Green Paper', COM 2015/63. At the heart of the idea to promote market-based financing channels there is the belief that banks would become more resilient as they would be able to free up regulatory capital and thus lower their costs. This would in turn lead to a more stable financial system according to this proposition.

[203] Carney, 'The Promise of FinTech' (n 201). In 2015, total loans originated by peer-to-peer lenders were $117 billion in China, $40 billion in the US, £4.5 billion in the UK and EUR 1.1 billion across Europe. At least in the UK, there are signs that the rate of growth for new lending has slowed recently; down from 100% to 30%.

technological advancement that platforms present vis-à-vis other forms of intermediation.[204] In line with their nature, platforms are not party to the loan agreement, which is instead established directly between the creditor and a number of borrowers.[205] Moreover, even though platforms engage with some form of credit risk assessment, they do not hold the borrowers' credit risk, which is held by lenders.[206]

What became evident at the early stages of development of this market is that platforms had to operate a secondary market for P2P loans, where these could be traded before their maturity. This became essential in order to attract investors, given that they hold the credit risk of the loans they invest in, and a secondary market was always the obvious way to create some degree of liquidity.[207] This was achieved through recourse factoring, and also through the securitization of P2P loans.[208] The importance of the secondary market is also a reflection of the type of investors that typically access P2P platforms. Notwithstanding the ambition to foster a retail-type market for financial intermediation, P2P lending has had to rely from the outset on wholesale institutional investors to satisfy the finance needs of consumers and SMEs. Notably, the (relative) scarcity of retail investors on these platforms is rooted in the lack of regulatory protection for investors, given that P2P platforms are outside the scope of banking regulation.[209]

The story of P2P lending was really shaped from the very beginning by the interconnectedness between platforms on the one hand, and larger banks or capital markets on the other. There has been evidence for instance of successful platforms becoming the interface of larger financial institutions, or being taken over by them.[210] Even more prominent is the emergence of P2P platforms securitizing loans originated through the platform.[211] Securitizing assets such as P2P loans

[204] See Paolo Giudici, 'Fin-Tech: Research Challenges in Financial Supervision and Technological Compliance', Frontiers in Artificial Intelligence, 5 November 2018, available at www.frontiersin.org/articles/10.3389/frai.2018.00001/full (last accessed on 19/04/2024).

[205] See World Economic Forum, 'The Complex Regulatory Landscape for FinTech: An Uncertain Future for Small and Medium-Sized Enterprises Lending', White Paper, August, 2016, 18–19.

[206] ibid.

[207] ibid, 15. Most typically the main avenue was that of invoice financing, whereby businesses investing in P2P platforms could trade their receivables and access liquidity.

[208] See Julian Craughan, David Palmer, and Emily Reid, 'Online lending platforms and securitisation: Bringing the wholesale market to the Individual' (2015) 6 Journal of International Banking and Financial Law 348.

[209] Platforms in particular are not recipient of deposit insurance protection or lender of last resort, which means that investors would have to bear losses in the event of default by borrowers they invest in, or in the event of the platform going out of business. See for a discussion on the impact of these regulatory protections Ricks, 'Regulating Money Creation' (n 149), 104–106.

[210] See for instance City AM, 'London fintech star Monzo is fending off one takeover offer each month' City AM, 10 October 2017.

[211] Peer2Peer Finance News, 'UK P2P set for securitisation boom', 5 October 2016, available at www.p2pfinancenews.co.uk/2016/10/05/p2p-securitisation-moodys/ (last accessed on 19/04/2024). Apparently, as of March 2018, this prediction of a securitization boom in P2P loans was yet to materialize, and one reason ascribed to the small numbers of securitization deals in the market was the size of each deal, which should be at least £1bn for a securitization to be economically viable. See Marc Shoffman, 'P2P securitisation boom still on the cards', *Peer2Peer Finance News* (27 March 2018),

presents legal and regulatory problems that are similar to those analysed in the previous section (in the context of CLOs), chiefly in relation to the poor level of credit information, the lack of data standardization, and the ensuing greater asymmetry of information between originators and investors.[212]

While a more straightforward application of securitization would see the sale of P2P loans to the SPV by the investor (originator),[213] a more problematic application of securitization has seen platforms directly tapping capital markets as originators. This practice became popular in the UK when two large platforms originated future loans that had not yet been matched on the platform by investors.[214] This more direct involvement of platforms in the securitization chain can potentially lead to their faster growth because they can inflate the volume of loans they originate. Loans, however, are securitized before their credit risk can be assessed on the platform and matched by investors. Moreover, concerns over the value of these assets throughout the business cycle have led to speculating that once the cycle turns (as has been the case since 2020), P2P loans may present the same problems experienced before 2008 with mortgages.[215]

Questions of interconnectedness and systemic risk become even more apparent by looking at the interplay between P2P platforms and wholesale channels of finance.[216] It was observed for instance that these concerns could materialize if a substantial percentage of investors in P2P platforms came from the banking sector, and their investments in P2P loans were funded through short-term repo exposures. Different stages of a business cycle could reinforce this interdependence

available at www.p2pfinancenews.co.uk/2018/03/27/p2p-securitisation/ (last accessed on 19/04/2024).

[212] See Giudici, 'Fin-Tech' (n 204). Compared with traditional banking institutions, P2P platforms have less information on their borrowers and therefore problems of asymmetric information tend to be greater than in the traditional banking system.

[213] In the US for instance this practice has seen large institutional investors (among which hedge funds, asset managers, banks) acquiring large portfolios of P2P loans and then securitizing them in order to increase their leverage positions. Kris Devasabai, 'A Loan in the Dark' (October 2014) Risk 18–21. It is observed in this article that P2P lending has turned in the US into 'hedge fund-to-consumer lending.'

[214] See Thomas Hale, 'Debut securitisation for Zopa loans,' *Financial Times* (26 September 2016), at www.ft.com/content/c401b6ef-5394-333c-bb9e-d89aa3845b91 (last accessed on 19/04/2024). In this case though, the situation seems to be closer to the previous scenario because the loans were being held by an institutional fund, P2P Global Investments PLC; Anna Brunetti, 'Funding Circle's SME securitisation wins higher ratings,' *Peer2Peer Finance News* (16 March 2017), at www.p2pfinancenews.co.uk/2017/03/16/funding-circles-sme-securitisation-wins-higher-ratings/ (last accessed on 19/04/2024): 'The platform kicked off a new business avenue for the whole UK sector when it became the first to package its loans into a multi-tranche bond, in collaboration with Deutsche Bank and KLS Diversified Asset Management.'

[215] Devasabai, 'A Loan in the Dark' (n 213), 18–21. See Vincenzo Bavoso, 'The Promise and Peril of Alternative Market-Based Finance: The Case of P2P Lending in the UK,' *Journal of Banking Regulation* (16 November 2019).

[216] Carney, 'The Promise of FinTech' (n 201). See also FSB and the Committee on the Global Financial System (CGFS), 'FinTech Credit: Market Structure, Business Models and Financial Stability Implications,' 22 May 2017.

(between P2P loans and wholesale markets), and expose the market for P2P loans to leverage and liquidity dynamics that are inevitable in capital markets.[217] In other words, while capital markets could initially boost the volume of finance available to P2P borrowers, dynamics that are integral features of capital markets may see sources of finance drying up during critical stages of the cycle, with problematic consequences for those entities that rely on P2P loans.

5 Conclusion

This chapter delved into the legal and operational aspects of debt capital markets, from plain vanilla bonds to CLOs. Unveiling the dynamics of financial innovation over different periods of time shows the engine and the rationale behind repeated exercises in product development. The same dynamics though also highlighted the dark side of financial innovation, and particularly how the continuous morphing of transactions and products led to complexity, interconnectedness and excessive risk-taking. While conceptually legitimized due to assumptions of market efficiency, financial innovation led to waves of instability in financial markets.

The nexus between debt capital markets and financial instability is developed in the next chapter, where, among other things, a taxonomy is constructed on the genesis of financial crises and scandals. This chapter provides the basis for that subsequent analysis, to the extent that it explains how most innovations were conceived with some degree of social and economic rationale, only to become an end in itself.[218] As an illustration, securitization was conceived as a way to aid thrift banks in mortgage lending, but it soon became the mechanism that supplanted them. Later innovations too proved, in hindsight, to be ways to create profit opportunities within the finance industry, with limited or no commercial rationale. In that sense, it is only fair to see the avalanche of cheap credit, both pre-2008 with sub-prime mortgages and post-2008 with leveraged loans, as a commoditization of debt that was engineered to keep the wheel of capital markets turning.

[217] In this sense, Alistair Milne and Paul Parboteeah, 'The Business Models and Economics of Peer-to-Peer Lending', Research Report, European Credit Research Institute, No 17/May 2016, 22; and also Vincenzo Bavoso, 'Financial Intermediation in the Age of Fintech: P2P Lending and the Reinvention of Banking' (2021) 2(1) Oxford Journal of Legal Studies.

[218] This argument is expounded by John Kenneth Galbraith, *A Short History of Financial Euphoria*, Penguin, 1990.

5

Debt capital markets, the genesis of crises and the role of regulation

1 Introduction

This chapter provides a conceptual link between the historical and theoretical arguments developed in Part I of this monograph, and the contention that capital markets, evolved and grown along the lines of debt transactions, have been the chief cause of financial instability and crises over the past thirty years. It is important to recall that the developments analysed in Chapters 2 and 3 were elicited by a facilitative regulatory environment, which is in turn more closely analysed in Part III of this monograph. In the context of the present discussion, it should be remembered that regulatory changes between the mid-1980s and the late 1990s were informed by policy priorities aimed at empowering market mechanisms. These mechanisms in turn were instrumental in fostering an enabling regulatory framework, whereby market participants could introduce new transactions and products into the market, without incurring regulatory barriers.[1]

The historical account drawn in Chapter 2 has a clear starting point in the mid-1980s. By that time, changes in the regulatory infrastructure of financial markets were well under way in the US and the UK; moreover, the intellectual environment, permeated by the tenets of neoclassical economics, became ripe for promoting policies that increasingly reduced regulatory constraints in financial markets. With market forces set in motion, the late 1980s provided a first episode of a series of scandals, the likes of which would eventually characterize the following decades. The story of Michael Milken and the surge in 'junk bonds' epitomized the changing nature of financial markets in the 1980s, particularly with respect to innovations in transactional models, and sharp increases in risk-taking.[2]

The former can be identified with advances in the transactional structure of bonds, and particularly the way in which bond issues became further disintermediated through the interposition of special purpose vehicles (SPV) as issuers. The new technology of bonds allowed the repackaging of a wider range of assets,

[1] An interesting perspective on financial innovation is provided in Ewald Engelen and others, *After the Great Complacence*, Oxford University Press, 2011, chapter 2.

[2] For an account of Micheal Milken and the junk bonds, see William Bratton and Adam Levitin, 'A Transactional Genealogy of Scandal: From Michael Milken, to Enron to Goldman Sachs' (2013) 86(4) Southern California Law Review 783.

Debt Capital Markets. Vincenzo Bavoso, Oxford University Press. © Vincenzo Bavoso 2024.
DOI: 10.1093/oso/9780198893257.003.0005

particularly high-risk junk bonds, held by the SPV, which would issue securities with different tranches. From a supply side point of view, this provided an invaluable tool to maximize the use of capital, particularly for financial institutions having to hold a percentage of capital commensurate to their assets' risk.[3] Assets were removed from the originator's balance sheet and transferred to the SPV. From a demand-side point of view, the new bond market appealed to a greater range of investors, due to the diverse risk profile of securities being offered. This was made possible by the innovation engineered by Michael Milken, because before then only investment grade bonds could be issued in the bond market. Effectively, the best (perhaps only) way to boost the liquidity and appeal of junk bonds was to repackage them, together with other assets, because in this way they could be purchased by those investors (such as pension funds) that were barred from buying below-investment grade bonds.[4] This business model represented the template for what would later be the securitization market.

The booming market for junk bonds was also the main tool to finance the corporate takeover wars that became common in the 1980s. The idea was that the junk bond market was a more attractive way to raise finance than more traditional bank loans, particularly due to the high yields attached to these bonds and the belief that the risk of default remained relatively low.[5]

The role of junk bonds in capital markets ties in with the problem of increased risk-taking, identified earlier in this introduction. At the heart of the innovations engineered in the 1980s there was an idea that was perfected in later years, namely that the process of repackaging assets could result in securities worth more than the underlying assets being repackaged.[6] While this alchemy defied logic, it became possible by virtue of two central features of capital markets that were particularly prominent in the 1980s. The first is the transactional innovation that went on to perfect underlying mechanisms of collateralization and risk diversification, something that was closely analysed in the previous chapter of this monograph. The second feature is one of regulation, analysed in great details in Chapters 6 and 7 of this monograph, and it refers specifically to the capacity of capital markets to

[3] See BIS, 'History of the Basel Committee', at www.bis.org/bcbs/history.htm (last accessed on 20/04/2024).

[4] See Robert Taggart Jr, 'The Growth of the "Junk" Bond Market and Its Role in Financing Takeovers', in *Mergers and Acquisitions*, edited by Alan J Auerbach, NBER Books, 1988, 5, 8.

[5] This belief reflects the scheme masterminded by Michael Milken, designed to inflate the value and market of junk bonds and thus create a more liquid representation of the market. Bratton and Levitin, 'A Transactional Genealogy of Scandal' (n 2), 795, 796; Taggart, 'The Growth of the "Junk" Bond Market' (n 4), 8.

[6] This process can be said to have been pioneered by Michael Milken in 1987, with the issue of something close to what we call today collateralized debt security (CDO). This was underwritten by investment bank Drexel Burnham Lambert to repackage a pool of junk bonds held by a savings and loans company called Imperial Savings. While the junk bonds were rated B- and triple-B, the securities issued by the SPV were rated triple-A by the credit rating agencies, chiefly due to the claim of diversification of the underlying bonds (being exposed to different industries), and the overcollateralization of the pool held by the SPV. Bratton and Levitin, 'A Transactional Genealogy of Scandal' (n 2), 801–803.

innovate in order to minimize the cost of regulation. As an illustration, the boom in securitization-type transactions in the 1980s coincided with the inception of capital regulation, initially under the Basel I Accord, and with the ensuing necessity for financial institutions to move assets off their balance sheet, thereby optimizing the cost of capital.[7]

The reduction of regulatory costs for market participants resulted however, in the dramatic increase in risk-taking in the financial system. The development of capital markets in the 1980s was accompanied by the contextual liberalization of derivatives, as was seen in Chapter 2. Derivatives progressively became employed for speculative purposes, and as instruments aimed at achieving regulatory arbitrage, rather than risk-management.[8]

The themes sketched in this introduction underscored various crises and scandals between the 1980s and the global financial crisis of 2008, and can be said to be at the heart of post-2008 dynamics, the most recent of which being the panic of 2020 and the banking crisis of 2023. This chapter expands on these same underlying themes, and explains how the relentless growth of debt capital markets, prospering in a lightly regulated environment, was conducive to the sequence of crises that shaped financial markets since the late 1980s. This discussion hinges on a taxonomy of crises and scandals developed in section 2, which is followed in section 3 by a contextualization of financial innovation. Section 4 concludes.

2 A taxonomy of crises and scandals

This part of the book is concerned with transactional innovation, and attendant legal and regulatory questions. While these themes were explored in the previous chapter, to fully appreciate the motives behind the underlying trends in debt capital markets, it is necessary to understand the extent to which they were conducive to instability and crises. This chapter does that by drawing a trajectory of the genesis of crises, seeking to find common denominators and patterns that explain the seemingly inevitable pendulum between financial peace and chaos. In particular, in the context of debt capital markets, the role of risk-taking that is intrinsic in debt contracts, and the perennial threat of financial instability, require some understanding of the underlying mechanics of credit supply, and how this leads to excessive levels of private debt creation in the financial system.

This analysis is necessarily grounded on some basic understanding of theories and models of instability. A paradigmatic theory of financial instability was

[7] See Douglas Arner, 'The Global Credit Crisis of 2008: Causes and Consequences' (2009) 43(1) International Lawyer.

[8] See Vincenzo Bavoso, 'Financial Innovation, Derivatives and the UK and US Interest Rate Swap Scandals: Drawing New Boundaries for the Regulation of Financial Innovation' (2016) 7(2) Global Policy.

provided in the 1980s by Hyman Minsky, whose model became particularly relevant (once again) in the aftermath of the 2008 global financial crisis as it provided a blueprint to understand its genesis.[9] Minsky's financial instability hypothesis can be explained as a type of leverage cycle,[10] which is worth briefly expanding upon here. Generally speaking, the dynamic of leverage cycles hinges on the procyclical supply of credit by financial institutions, and particularly the way they direct their investments in specific periods. It is observed in the literature that this supply of credit is influenced by expectations about the state of the economy; inevitably, optimism during boom periods leads to an expansion of the credit supply, because lenders become less cautious and provide a higher volume of credit with lower constraints (interest rates and margin requirements).[11] The general optimism and the cheap access to credit cause in turn an increase in the levels of borrowing, which becomes a driver of rapid asset price increases. Critically, asset prices increase at a faster rate than GDP and income, leading eventually to asset bubbles, and defaults in the underlying debt contracts.[12]

The inexorable swings in the economic cycle entail that periods of boom are followed by economic slowdowns, where the attitude towards risk-taking reverses.[13] This is a stage in the credit cycle whose fragility is caused by the prior credit expansion, and particularly by the behaviour of heavily indebted borrowers, especially those with short-term exposures. According to Charles Kindleberger, as distress follows the decline in asset price, the change in investor mindset represents in itself a cause of instability.[14] More specifically, the great riskiness of debt contracts entered into during boom periods is more likely to lead to borrowers' defaults once the economic cycle shifts, translating into losses suffered by lenders too.[15] In the words of John Geanakoplos, this becomes a self-reinforcing dynamic, because once economic prospects deteriorate, the behaviour of financial institutions adjusts

[9] See Hyman Minsky, 'The Financial Instability Hypothesis', Jerome Levy Economics Institute of Bard College, Working Paper No 74, May 1992; Hyman Minsky, 'The Financial Instability Hypothesis: An Interpretation of Keynes and an Alternative to "Standard" Theory' (1977) 20(1) *Challenge*.

[10] Leverage, and the problems associated with it, are discussed in the next section.

[11] See on the leverage cycle John Geanakoplos, 'The Leverage Cycle', in *NBER Macroeconomics Annual 2009*, edited by D Acemoglu, K Rogoff, and M Woodford, NBER, 2010; Sudipto Bhattacharya, Charles Goodhart, Dimitrios Tsomocos, and Alexandros Vardoulakis, 'Minsky's Financial Instability Hypothesis and the Leverage Cycle', London School of Economics FMG Special Paper, September 2011; John Geanakoplos, 'Solving the Present Crisis and Managing the Leverage Cycle' (August 2010) FRBNY Economic Policy Review.

[12] ibid. See also Charles Kindleberger, *Manias, Panics and Crashes*, Palgrave, 2011, chapter 5.

[13] This may be due to interrelated causes, among which are the lower pace of asset price increase; the fact that some professional investors may sell at this stage their exposures and cash in their speculative gains; or also the slower increase in the asset price may lead investors towards a more cautious approach. Kindleberger, *Manias* (n 12), chapter 5.

[14] Kindleberger, *Manias* (n 12), chapters 2 and 5, where he explains that both the expectations of borrowers and lenders determine the expansion of credit during the euphoric period, and its shrinking once the cycle shifts.

[15] These are known as loss-given defaults. See n 11.

accordingly, in the shape of higher interest rates, increased margin requirements, and overall a withdrawal from riskier investments.[16] At this stage of the cycle, asset prices fall drastically because many investors/borrowers exposed to short-term payments are forced to sell their assets in order to meet those payments.[17]

Within the context of the leverage cycle, Minsky proposed a specific reading of different stages and degrees of instability that eventually lead to a crisis. Central to his proposition is the idea that instability in the financial system is endogenous (something that fundamentally counters the neoclassical hypotheses and assumptions explored in Chapter 3 of this monograph, which are at the heart of capital markets development), because it is driven by the behaviour of financial institutions and the way they extend credit in the financial system.[18] This process is inevitably shaped by a period of euphoria, where memories of past crises progressively fade, and leave room for optimism and with it a drive towards financial innovation. In this context, more complex forms of innovation, a deeper financial system, and higher levels of private debt creation, are all contributing factors to the instability of the financial system.[19] It is also postulated that speculative fevers develop precisely at this stage, because of the availability of financial arrangements, and the belief that the amount of interest payments on debt contracts is lower than the profit available from the appreciation of the assets invested in.[20]

Critically, during the euphoric stage, three types of investment unit characterize the financial system, and the prevalence of one of them determines the degree of instability of the financial system, and eventually the gravity of the ensuing crash. Minsky configured three types of investment unit: hedge, speculative, and ponzi.

Hedge financial units are chiefly asset-based and consequently, the cash flow expected from the assets is sufficient to make all future payments on the underlying debt contracts, both principal and interest. These investment units are typically financially stable and withstand macroeconomic changes during the cycle.[21] Speculative financial units rely both on asset-based cash flows, and on refinancing arrangements of their existing debt exposures. Refinancing for these units is essential because their cash flow is not sufficient to repay the principal on their debt contracts. As a result, when access to credit supply becomes constrained in periods of deteriorating market conditions, these units become financially vulnerable.[22]

[16] Geanakoplos, 'Solving the Present Crisis' (n 11), 104; and Bhattacharya and others, 'Minsky's Financial Instability Hypothesis' (n 11), 15.

[17] Of course, this process is worsened in the event of a fire-sale. Geanakoplos, 'Solving the Present Crisis' (n 11), 105.

[18] See Minsky, 'The Financial Instability Hypothesis' (n 9); and Hyman Minsky, 'Capitalist Financial Processes and the Instability of Capitalism' (1980) 14(2) Journal of Economic Issues.

[19] See Minsky, 'Capitalist Financial Processes' (n 18), 517; and Hyman Minsky, 'Financial Instability Revisited: The Economics of Disaster', Prepared for the Steering Committee for the Fundamental Reappraisal of the Discount Mechanism Appointed by the Board of Governors of the Federal Reserve System, January 1970, 6.

[20] See Kindleberger, *Manias* (n 12), chapter 2.

[21] See Minsky, 'The Financial Instability Hypothesis' (n 9).

[22] ibid.

Ponzi financial units are so defined because they do not generate sufficient cash flow to meet either interest or principal payments on their debt contracts. Due to the way they are structured, they have to either keep borrowing in order to meet payment obligations (with obvious consequence on their leverage and overall fragility), or sell assets, with the expectation that asset prices keep appreciating over time. Inevitably, this type of investment unit is the most vulnerable when the cycle turns, due the constrained and disadvantageous access to credit, and the plummeting asset prices.[23]

In the context of this chapter, it is important to emphasize that the intermediate stage of the cycle—after levels of indebtedness have soared in the financial system, and credit conditions start worsening due to defaults—is critical to determine if and how manageable the financial system is. The type of investment unit that prevails during this phase determines the financial system's stability, or its fragility, once the cycle turns.[24]

Within both the leverage and the Minsky cycles, the euphoric period is particularly significant because that is the stage where the financial system is prone to adopt innovations and as a result incur more debt-creation dynamics. Inevitably, during this stage of optimism new financial products and services are hailed as the ultimate instruments to maximize the effectiveness of financial intermediation. Optimism and euphoria are consistent with another cycle that is worth briefly explaining here. The hype cycle was originally formulated by an IT consultancy called Gartner in 1995 and it has since been widely adopted in the wider context of decision-making and also to interpret technology strategies.[25] The latter is particularly interesting for the purpose of this discussion, as a way to position different types of financial innovations and how market participants react to them. Crucially, the hype cycle was recently used by the Basel Committee in a study that charted the reaction of investors and supervisors to FinTech-based innovations.[26]

The hype cycle presents five stages that are structured along a bell-shaped curve, representing the reactions at different points in time to the innovation. The first stage is the 'innovation trigger', where the new technology kicks off, and the interest around it is caused by publicity, even though at this stage the innovation is not yet available on the market.[27] The second phase of the cycle is the 'peak of inflated expectations', which follows from the early publicity and the related success stories, some of which start being accompanied by failures. Most market participants at

[23] ibid.

[24] It is important to stress that the type of investment unit determines the fragility of the individual financial institution, but at the macro level, the prevalence of an investment unit in the economy is an indicator of the overall system's stability.

[25] The Gartner hype cycle in its original explanation is available here: www.gartner.com/en/research/methodologies/gartner-hype-cycle (last accessed on 20/04/2024).

[26] BCBS, 'Implications of fintech developments for banks and bank supervisors' (February 2018) BIS Sound Practices 13.

[27] ibid.

this point in time remain oblivious of the failures.[28] Thirdly, with the 'trough of disillusionment', there is a more substantial loss of interest in the innovation as attendant experiments and implementations fail to deliver. At this stage, interest among investors continues only if the underlying innovation is improved and upgraded.[29] The fourth stage of the cycle is where the curve moves up again in what is defined the 'slope of enlightenment'. At this point in the cycle there starts being more clarity and understanding about the technology and how it can benefit the market, with a wider range of market participants adopting it.[30] The final phase of the hype cycle is the 'plateau of productivity' and it presents a mainstream adoption of the innovation, based also on clearer criteria for the assessment of new products and services.[31]

A revealing aspect of the hype cycle is that it presents similarities with both the leverage and Minsky cycles, particularly in the way they model reactions in the early phases, where phenomena such as 'irrational exuberance' drive the wider endorsement of the new innovation, notwithstanding the lack of any clear understanding of its long-term consequences, potential drawbacks, and risks. From a regulatory perspective, this is also an important model of crisis dynamic, because the 'plateau of productivity' indicates some degree of reliance on criteria and assessments, which often follow legal and regulatory intervention in the innovation process.[32]

The models illustrated in this section are also important because they put forward a view of financial markets that is in sharp contrast with some of the neoclassical assumptions that were explored in Chapter 3 of this monograph. Both the leverage cycle and the financial instability hypothesis are grounded on the somewhat irrational reactions of market participants to changes in the economic cycle, reactions that eventually affect the credit supply and the swings between euphoria and panic. In other words, while neoclassical economics assume that market participants are rational decision-makers, a historical view of financial crises shows the ubiquitous recurrence of manias.[33] Manias can be associated with the general irrationality permeating actors in financial markets, with hysteria and mob psychology resulting in herd behaviour.[34] The same behavioural patterns are of course at the heart of the hype cycle.

[28] ibid.
[29] ibid.
[30] ibid.
[31] ibid.
[32] For a discussion, see Michael Schillig, '"Lex Cryptographi(c)a," "Cloud Crypto Land" or What?—Blockchain Technology on the Legal Hype Cycle' (June 2022) Modern Law Review 5.
[33] Kindleberger, *Manias* (n 12), chapter 3.
[34] For a critical perspective on the standard neoclassical economics narrative, particularly in relation to the idea of value-maximizing decision-making by market participants, see Emilios Avgouleas, 'The Global Financial Crisis, Behavioural Finance and Financial Regulation: In Search of a New Orthodoxy' (2009) 9(1) Journal of Corporate Law Studies 23–59,; see also Robert Shiller, *Irrational Exuberance*, Princeton University Press, 2005, particularly chapters 8 to 11; and also Daniel Kahneman, *Thinking*

Understanding the patterns of financial crises reveals the centrality of financial innovation as a process that elicits credit expansion and access to credit, particularly in the euphoric periods. An over-expanded access to credit is in turn the prerequisite for increased speculative activities, where investors can more easily gain exposure to different markets and sectors. While speculation in the real estate sector (think about the innovations in the way mortgages were pooled into asset-backed securities) constitutes the main speculative fever of the twentieth century, the first relevant example in this sense is the surge in junk bonds in the 1980s, which was already highlighted in the introduction of this chapter. Section 3 expands on a common denominator between the crises that afflicted financial markets since the mid-1980s, by pointing at financial innovation in debt capital markets as the trigger behind increases in speculation and risk-taking. Before doing that, this section needs to be complemented by a brief discussion on the regulatory problems associated with leverage.

2.1 What is wrong with leverage?

The analysis conducted in Chapter 4 of this book, together with the historical overview in Chapter 2, show clearly that contemporary capital markets developed along the axis of debt transactions. Inevitably, this has led to a progressive increase in private debt (credit) creation in the financial system, as well as at the corporate and household levels.[35] One key problem with this trend is the attendant increase in the level of leverage. In simple terms, leverage refers to the percentage of debt in an investment, relative to equity.[36] In financial markets leveraged investments have traditionally been welcome, because they elicit maximizing returns on equity (RoE),[37] therefore under neoclassical economics thinking they represent an efficient use and allocation of capital. In this sense, leverage is seen as value-enhancing, and a contributor to deep and complete financial markets.[38]

Fast and Slow, Penguin, 2012, particularly part one explaining how judgements happen and how cognitive bias influences them.

[35] See Adair Turner, *Between Debt and the Devil*, Princeton University Press, 2016, chapter 4; Arthur Wilmarth, 'The Pandemic Crisis Shows that the World Remains Trapped in a "Global Doom Loop" of Financial Instability, Rising Debt Levels, and Escalating Bailouts' (2021) 40(8) Banking & Financial Services Policy Report 2.

[36] A straightforward example is that of the purchase of a house with a mortgage. In a situation where the house is valued £100, the buyer borrows £90 from the bank and pays a deposit of £10, the level of leverage can be represented by a debt-to-equity ratio, in this case 9:1. See for a critical discussion on leverage Margaret Blair, 'Financial Innovation, Leverage, Bubbles, and the Distribution of Income' (2010-11) 30 Review of Banking & Financial Law 225.

[37] Following the example in the previous footnote, if the value of the house increases by 10% after two years, to £110, the buyer will have realized a return on the initial equity investment of 100%. If the house had been bought with no leverage, the return on equity would have been 10%.

[38] On market completion as a policy goal, see for instance Andre Sapir, Nicolas Veron, and Guntram Wolff, 'Making a reality of Europe's Capital Markets Union', Bruegel Policy Contribution No 2018/07.

Moreover, leverage is also considered to be an important disciplining mechanism in the overall regulatory architecture of financial markets revolving around market discipline. The idea here, as is further examined in Chapter 6, is that investors in the financial system have an incentive to monitor counterparties' leverage and take corrective measures, when necessary.[39]

The problem is that while increases in debt and leverage can be profitable for individual firms, because they increase RoE for shareholders and more generally lead to quicker and cheaper asset growth, they inevitably result in excesses in credit supply and ultimately asset bubbles, with portfolios of investments rising in value chiefly due to leverage-driven asset inflation.[40] These distortions result in poor allocation of capital,[41] much against the ideas of efficiency and optimality postulated under neoclassical economic theories (explored in Chapter 3). Moreover, the abnormal increase in returns elicited by leverage during the good times is mirrored by equally unpredictable and multiplied losses that materialize when the cycle turns.[42] This, in other words, is the dark side of leverage that emerges inevitably with shifts in the economic cycles, as is explained through the theories discussed in the previous section. It has progressively become accepted that excessive levels of leverage are synonymous of instability: instability reflected both in the financial system's propensity to become prey of cycles of boom and bust,[43] and in its fragility in the event of external shocks.[44]

The problem with regulating and monitoring leverage is made ever more complex due to the engagement of large financial institutions with the shadow banking sector.[45] In essence, the transactions and channels of financial intermediation

[39] See for an explanation, and a critique of this stance, Emilios Avgouleas and Jay Cullen, 'Excessive Leverage and Bankers' Pay: Governance and Financial Stability Costs of a Symbiotic Relationship' (2015) 21(1) Columbia Journal of European Law.

[40] See Margaret Blair, 'Making Money: Leverage and Private Sector Money Creation' (2013) 36 Seattle University Law Review 417–454.

[41] ibid, 434–438.

[42] Looking again at the scenario in nn 36 and 37, should the house fall in value after two years, to £90, the buyer will have lost all its equity, and the loss on the initial investment would amount to 100%. In other words, a 10% price fluctuation on the underlying asset results in a 100% loss in the investment, due to the level of leverage the investor engaged with. This is the result of a 9:1 leverage ratio, whereas before 2008 large banks were trading on average with 35 or 40:1 leverage ratios. See Hyun Song Shin, 'Reflections on Northern Rock: The Bank Run that Heralded the Global Financial Crisis' (2009) 23(1) Journal of Economic Perspectives.

[43] This is consistent with the findings of Hyman Minsky and his financial instability hypothesis, explained in the previous section, where he contends that instability is endogenous in financial systems characterized by more complex forms of debt intermediation. See Hyman Minsky, 'Capitalist Financial Processes and the Instability of Capitalism' (1980) 14(2) Journal of Economic Issues 505–523.

[44] This was for instance the case during the Covid-19 pandemic, which revealed how high levels of private debt creation had impaired the resilience of the financial system. See Wilmarth, 'The Pandemic Crisis' (n 35).

[45] This is a process that started progressively, in the 1980s, and accelerated as a result of the functional integration of banks and capital markets activities. See on this Robert Hockett and Saule Omarova. 'The Finance Franchise' (2017) 102 Cornell Law Review 1143. For a discussion on market-based finance, and its impact on leverage creation, see Vincenzo Bavoso, 'Market-Based Finance, Debt and Systemic Risk: A Critique of the EU Capital Markets Union' (2018) 11(3) Accounting, Economics, and Law: A Convivium 7–9.

that create leverage are situated in the shadow banking sector—this is something that transpires from Chapter 4.[46] Moreover, in the post-2008 years, the increased regulatory focus on large banks (such as new leverage and liquidity requirements under Basel III, examined in Chapter 7) has caused a migration of certain activities away from banks, towards non-bank channels of financial intermediation. A first manifestation of this phenomenon was the panic of 2020, whose roots lay in the near-default of CLOs engineered by private equity firms;[47] a second episode in this sense is the liability-driven investment (LDI) crisis that brewed in the UK pension system in October 2022 and became a systemic issue warranting central bank intervention.[48] In both instances leverage propagated through 'hidden' corners of the financial system; large banks were indirectly affected by the instability caused by excessive levels of credit creation.[49]

In light of this, questions related to the regulation of leverage become more pressing, and they are reprised throughout Part III of this book.

3 Financial innovation: it's about debt, stupid!

This book draws an account of capital markets, starting in the 1980s, for reasons that were explained in Chapter 2. However, the history of financial innovation is much older than that. It can safely be posited that financial innovation began, in more rudimentary fashion, with the early development of urban societies based on agriculture, whereby social and commercial dynamics created the preconditions for the advance of early forms of commercial contracts.[50] One such prominent innovation was the development of credit relationships that would today be associated with basic derivative contracts. In Mesopotamian societies these ancestral forms of derivatives were chiefly employed to hedge harvest-based risks,[51] and contractual innovation more generally was conceived to address a variety of commercial realities related to the trading of agricultural commodities.

[46] Chapter 4 discussed in details some of the areas of debt capital markets that elicit huge increase in private debt creation and leverage. Emphasis was laid in particular on the combination of securitization and repo market (the securitized banking system), and also on credit derivatives that are employed to amplify gains, and critically losses too, once the cycle turns.

[47] See Vincenzo Bavoso, 'Hail the New Private Debt Machine: Private Equity, Leveraged Loans, and Collateralised Loan Obligations' (2020) 4(3) Law and Financial Markets Review.

[48] See Vincenzo Bavoso, 'The LDI (Liability-Driven Investment) Debacle, Derivatives and Systemic Risk: There You Go Again!', 2023 at https://papers.ssrn.com/sol3/papers.cfm?abstract_id=4372485 (last accessed on 20/04/2024).

[49] See speech by Sarah Breeden, 'Risks from leverage: How did a small corner of the pension industry threaten financial stability?', Bank of England, 7 November 2022.

[50] See in this sense, David Graeber, *Debt: The First 5000 Years*, Melville House, 2011, chapter 1.

[51] See on the history of derivatives Ernst Juerg Weber, 'Short History of Derivative Security Markets', The University of Western Australia, Discussion Paper 08.10, August 2008.

As correctly explained by Avgouleas, history teaches us that the evolution of finance is the result of a sequence of contractual innovations, which have typically been aimed at the improvement of two fundamental functions of financial systems, namely the management of risks, and the optimal allocation of resources.[52] The development of organizational structures around the facilitation of these functions is in turn traditionally associated with higher levels of economic development, thriving entrepreneurial environments, and technological breakthroughs.[53] As will be further emphasized later in this chapter, advances in information technology (IT) are the key engine behind the last wave of financial innovation.

It is incontrovertible that financial innovation has historically contributed to the wider development of financial markets, and more broadly, efficient commercial environments. In fact, it can be observed that innovative financial transactions were associated with advances in trade and commerce, particularly during the industrial revolution. By way of example, factoring and the floating charge became key contractual instruments in the nineteenth century, allowing manufacturers in the UK to continue trading while pledging their assets in ways that would allow them access to sources of finance.[54] Similarly, a much older instrument, the bill of exchange, became a critical means to settle transnational payments in the context of the expanding trade of the eighteenth and nineteenth centuries.

Notwithstanding the above narrative, it is difficult to argue in favour of the innovations that have swept financial markets since the 1980s. The most striking phenomenon that can be associated with post-1980s financial markets is the increasing absence of any economic or social goals behind new products and transactions that have proliferated over the past forty years. Some of the reasons behind this shift can be ascribed to new cultural and incentive structures that have gradually permeated financial markets and their players,[55] and the mechanics that have led to innovation processes becoming largely self-referential, abstract, and detached from economic reality.[56]

A synthesis of these problems was drawn by *The Economist* in 2012, in a special report on financial innovation. It specifically highlighted how the process of innovation was the result of private interests within the financial industry, whereby

[52] Emilios Avgouleas, 'Regulating Financial Innovation', in *The Oxford Handbook of Financial Regulation*, edited by Moloney, Ferran, and Payne, Oxford University Press, 2015.

[53] See generally Ross Levine, 'Financial Development and Economic Growth: Views and Agenda' (1997) 35(2) Journal of Economic Literature.

[54] Relevant commercial law schemes are analysed in Gerard McCormack, *Secured Credit under English and American Law*, Cambridge University Press, 2004.

[55] See Ismail Erturk, Julie Froud, Sukhdev Johal, Adam Leaver, and Karel Williams, 'The Democratization of Finance? Promises, Outcomes and Conditions' (2007) 14(4) Review of International Political Economy.

[56] Some of these explanations and themes were analysed in Chapter 3, particularly through the works of Donald MacKenzie, which are again relevant here, in particular: *An Engine, Not A Camera: How Financial Models Shape Markets*, MIT Press, 2008; *Material Markets: How Economic Agents Are Constructed*, Oxford University Press, 2009.

limited concerns were laid on fundamental questions of market efficiency (which is assumed as the main goal of financial innovation) or financial stability. Issues of wider social welfare would not even be contemplated. Such a disheartening picture was confirmed by a definition of financial innovation provided by the chief commercial officer of the Chicago Mercantile Exchange (CME), Julie Winkler, who pointed to three specific stages of innovation.[57] The first is the investigation, where market participants (typically, investment banks) assess whether there is demand for a certain product and level of risk-taking. The second stage is the creation, where the new product is designed contractually with the help of lawyers. This stage also involves some degree of validation among a sample of investors. Finally, there is the validation of the new product, which involves wider feedback from various stakeholders of the CME.[58]

Strikingly, none of the above stages of innovation involves any test as to the economic or social viability of the new product, its effects on consumer welfare, or the wider impact on financial stability. This, in other words, remains a privately orchestrated process, where the innovator (typically large financial institutions) remains mostly concerned with questions of legal compliance, and associated costs, and the profit-making opportunities flowing from the new product. Similarly, the standardization and marketization of new financial products hinges on inputs from the innovating financial institutions and the lawyers who advise them, in many cases leaving both consumers and regulators unable to understand the intricacies of new transactions and products, and thus to appraise attendant risks.[59]

Ultimately, the importance of financial innovation in a thriving financial system can be theorized on the basis of a trade-off, balancing on the one hand the benefits in relation to economic development through new trading techniques, more sophisticated risk-sharing opportunities and the resulting improved capital allocation; while, on the other hand, costs arise due to the financial instability that follows processes of innovation (as was already hypothesized in the previous section), and particularly as a consequence of the private debt that new products create, and the ensuing increase in risk-taking and leverage.[60]

It is important to stress that the benefits of financial innovation are closely linked with the idea of market completeness that has been widely advocated as a corollary of neoclassical economics. In particular, assumptions of rational individual

[57] The Economist Special Report: Financial Innovation 'The Ferment of Finance', 25 February 2012, 6–8.

[58] ibid.

[59] In this sense, Vincenzo Bavoso, 'Financial Innovation, Derivatives and the UK and US Interest Rate Swap Scandals: Drawing New Boundaries for the Regulation of Financial Innovation' (2016) 7(2) Global Policy 229.

[60] See Bruno Biais, Florian Heider, and Marie Hoerova, 'Risk-sharing or Risk-taking? Financial Innovation, Margin Requirements and Incentives', ECB working paper, 2010. As an illustration, contracts like CDSs create systemic risks because of the counterparty risk through contagion between otherwise unrelated asset classes. So effectively the opposite effect of risk diversification.

utility-maximizers in competitive and efficient markets[61] led policy-makers and regulators to pursue a system where market participants could directly interact with each other through market mechanisms, thereby attaining a state of competitive equilibrium.[62] Reaching this equilibrium, also referred to as Pareto efficiency, is associated with an optimal allocation of resources and risks.[63] In the context of debt capital markets, the customization of risks and rewards through innovated products hugely increased the depth of financial markets and facilitated the direct participation of a wider range of market participants.[64] The idea of market completeness was conceptually tied with two interrelated policy and regulatory agendas, namely the development of deep and liquid capital markets, and the opportunity for the diversification of risks. Both eventually legitimized the endless creation of unquantifiable private debt and leverage.

Questions on the costs of financial innovation have been raised, most prominently by two major post-GFC reports in the US and the UK.[65] In essence, the findings of these reports highlighted the shortcomings of the ideas and assumptions behind financial innovation, and how new products introduced in the pre-2008 years did not contribute to efficient risk diversification. From the account developed in the previous chapter, it will be remembered that the transactional structure of innovated products, such as collateralized debt obligations, elicited the origination of a wide range of high-risk assets that were being repackaged in a multi-tranche bond. The level of complexity that this process entailed caused, among other things, information failures[66] that resulted in losses for investors. This of course defied the ideas of risk diversification and allocation, because investors were unable to correctly value the products they were buying. More critically, the combination of credit derivatives with the securitization structure increased the interconnectedness between market participants with ever more homogeneous balance sheets.[67] This represented a further blow to the idea of efficient risk diversification, because, as the events of 2008 demonstrated, when the tide turned about

[61] These have been explored in greater details in Chapter 3.

[62] As explained in Chapter 3, competitive equilibrium is a theorized situation where demand equals supply, and the economy achieves Pareto optimality. This in turn refers to a state where making one person better off comes at the expense of making another person worse off. See on this Kenneth Arrow and Gerard Debreu, 'Existence of an Equilibrium for a Competitive Economy' (1954) 22(3) Econometrica 265.

[63] See for a discussion, Joseph Stiglitz, 'Credit Markets and the Control of Capital' (1985) 17(2) Journal of Money, Credit and Banking 133–152, 135.

[64] Avgouleas, 'Regulating Financial Innovation' (n 52), 668.

[65] The Financial Crisis Inquiry Commission, 'Financial Crisis Inquiry Report', January 2011, Part II, specifically dealing with shadow banking, securitization, derivatives, deregulation and subprime lending; Adair Turner, *The Turner Review—A Regulatory Response to the Global Banking Crisis*, FSA, 2009, chapter 1 dealing with financial innovation.

[66] On information failures caused by complex financial products see Steven Schwarcz, 'Controlling Financial Chaos: The Power and Limits of Law' (2012) Wisconsin Law Review 815.

[67] See Vincenzo Bavoso, 'High Quality Securitisation and EU Capital Markets Union—Is it Possible?' (2017) 7(3) Accounting, Economics, and Law: A Convivium, DOI 10.1515/ael-2016-0008.

the state of global financial markets, the opaqueness permeating them led to panic and herding behaviour on a mass scale.[68] Interconnectedness and homogeneous balance sheets were also the direct cause of the sequence of bank failures that occurred after the collapse of Lehman Brothers in 2008, resembling a domino effect. Not only financial innovation did not improve risk diversification, but it went on to create an unprecedented level of systemic risk and financial instability.[69]

Without placing excessive blame on financial innovation, it also became clear after 2008 that the contractual developments engineered in the previous decade had been chiefly aimed at creating avenues for regulatory arbitrage. The brief account of Michael Milken in the introduction of this chapter showed the early signs of this problem, and developments in securitizations in the 1990s have been more squarely recognized as intimately related to capital regulation (or rather as a way to minimize the cost of it).[70] Banks in particular started to heavily securitize their asset book, moving risks off their balance sheet. This allowed them to maximize the cost of their existing capital because they could originate more assets, without a corresponding increase of their level of capital (which is what Basel started implementing from the late 1980s, with the first iteration of the accords).[71] In essence, banks employed securitization to minimize the costs associated with capital regulation,[72] but in the process they increased exponentially the level of risk-taking that they were generating, because they kept originating assets of dubious credit quality (think of subprime loans) that were being processed into tranched securitized bonds. Risks, and leverage, were being created on an industrial scale, and shifted from the balance sheet of banks to institutional investors, again under the assumption that the latter had appetite for that level of risk-taking and were able to absorb it.[73]

[68] The events of 2008, as those of other financial crises, are clearly explained under the framework of behavioural finance theory, which is clearly illustrated in Emilios Avgouleas, 'The Global Financial Crisis, Behavioural Finance and Financial Regulation: In Search of a New Orthodoxy' (2009) 9 Journal of Corporate Law Studies 23.

[69] ibid. See also Steven Schwarcz, 'Systemic Risk' (2008) 97(1) Georgetown Law Journal.

[70] In this sense, see Douglas Arner, 'The Global Credit Crisis of 2008: Causes and Consequences' (2009) 43 The International Lawyer. From a different angle, see Charles Calomiris, 'Financial Innovation, Regulation and Reform' (2009) 29 Cato Journal 65.

[71] The first version of the Basel Accord was approved in 1988. For an overview of the road to the present-day Basel III, see www.bis.org/bcbs/history.htm (last accessed on 20/04/2024).

[72] A process that can be referred to as asset substitution, resulting of course in regulatory arbitrage, and critically in huge increases in the level of leverage in the financial system. See for a specific discussion Emilios Avgouleas, 'Bank Leverage Ratios and Financial Stability: A Micro- and Macroprudential Perspective', Levy Economic Institute, Working Paper no 849 2015, 9.

[73] In the context of this discussion, on the expansion of leverage and risk-taking through financial innovation, it is important to remember that the manufacturing of securitized bonds by large financial institutions allowed them in the pre-2008 years to have ready access to overnight liquidity facility in the repo market (where they pledged triple-A rated securitized bonds in returned for short-term funding). The exposure to such a short-term source of funding represented an increased risk on the balance sheet of banks, particularly as the repo market progressively replaced bank deposits as a source of funding. See Calomiris, 'Financial Innovation (n 70), 67. See also Vincenzo Bavoso, 'Basel III and the Regulation of Market-Based Finance: The Tentative Reform' (2021) 18(1) NYU Journal of Law and Business; Gary

Financial innovation, in its post-1980s form and shape, emerges as the main engine behind the unlimited credit expansion that has taken place via new debt contracts. The capacity of securitization technology to repackage illiquid loan-type assets into liquid (or at least so perceived) securities accelerated the process of financialization,[74] which in the specific context of debt capital markets manifested itself with the commoditization of debt and risk. In the words of Andrew Haldane, former chief economist at the Bank of England, long chains of debt contracts had the effect of slicing, dicing, and bundling risks in order to make them palatable to capital markets investors.[75] The reality was that commoditizing debt completely flipped the relationship between the securitization market and the idea of access to credit: while the former was initially conceived as an instrument to facilitate the latter, the manufacturing of debt, beyond economic and social needs, became an end in itself, aimed at feeding the securitization market.[76]

The locus of the unlimited expansion of private debt was that segment of capital markets intermediation that since 2007 is known as shadow banking.[77] While regulatory questions on shadow banking are addressed in Part III of this monograph, this proved to be a further reflection of the process of financial innovation, particularly in the contexts of securitization and repo.[78] Financial intermediation conducted in the shadow banking system was not falling under typical forms of banking regulation, despite creating bank-like risks.[79] Shadow banking, as a result, became an accelerator of risks and leverage, elements that are both inherent in debt contracts, and that were kept outside the scope of regulatory scrutiny.

Moreover, to reiterate a point made earlier, it became apparent that the shadow banking sector was profoundly linked with large banks,[80] and again the idea of risk diversification had to crash with the reality of interconnectedness, contagion, and systemic risk.[81]

Gorton and Andrew Metrick, 'Securitized Banking and the Run on the Repo' (2012) 104(3) Journal of Financial Economics.

[74] For an understanding of financialization, see Gerard Epstein, *Financialization and the World Economy*, Edward Elgar, 2005.

[75] Andrew Haldane, 'Rethinking the Financial Network', Speech, 2009, at https://www.bankofengland.co.uk/speech/2009/rethinking-the-financial-network (last accessed on 25/09/2024).

[76] An exemplification can be represented by the innovation of securitization into synthetic CDOs, analysed in Chapter 4.

[77] For a definition, see Financial Stability Board, 'Shadow Banking: Scoping the Issues', 11 April 2011.

[78] See Bavoso, 'Basel III' (n 73).

[79] Avgouleas, 'Regulating Financial Innovation' (n 52); see also Morgan Ricks, 'Regulating Money Creation after the Crisis' (2011) 1 Harvard Business Law Review.

[80] For an example of how this was the case, Viral Acharya, Philipp Schnabl, and Gustavo Suarez, 'Securitization without Risk Transfer' (2013) 107(3) Journal of Financial Economics.

[81] See on this, Andrew Haldane and Robert May, 'Systemic Risk in Banking Ecosystems' (2011) Nature 469.

3.1 Conceptualizing the impact of financial innovation on debt-creation and risk-taking

While it is often posited that financial innovation is welfare neutral,[82] the critique provided in the previous section pointed to a 'dark side' that has become prevalent when discussing financial innovation. In light of the regulatory and policy scope of this monograph, developed in Part III, it is important to clarify the nature of financial innovation, and how its excesses in terms of risk-creation can be reined in through regulation.

With that in mind, this section puts forward a conceptualization of financial innovation through four factors: a) theoretical consensus; b) regulatory environment; c) technological advance; d) finality.[83] These are expounded upon in the remainder of this section.

(a) Theoretical consensus

The theoretical and intellectual environment within which financial innovation takes place is something that has already been discussed in Chapter 3 of this monograph. It is worth reiterating here that some specific assumptions associated with the tenets of neoclassical economics legitimized the innovation process, as was analysed in the previous section, particularly with respect to the centrality of Pareto optimality. Beyond that, the development of debt products was hailed as the hallmark of efficient economic development.[84] The idea of efficiency was also what justified high levels of leverage that ensued the endless credit creation through debt contracts. It was widely believed that leverage could have a positive effect on the allocative efficiency of banks due to the resulting lower cost of capital.[85] This would allow banks to extend more credit at cheaper rates, fulfilling the already mentioned mission of ensuring economic development by widening access to finance.[86]

Linked to the above point is the function that debt played in neoliberal policies as a disciplining factor, through which bank management could be held to account. This is a regulatory mechanism that is more specifically explored in Chapter 6 of

[82] See Avgouleas, 'Regulating Financial Innovation' (n 52), 667.

[83] The word finality here is consistent with the meaning of something's faculty and purpose. See https://dictionary.cambridge.org/dictionary/english/finality (last accessed on 25/09/2024).

[84] This contention was justified by the overarching belief that deeper markets with more diversified products would lead to more efficient markets, with better allocation of resources and risk diversification. As was discussed in the previous section, and in Chapter 3, this ideology stems from the policy views of Milton Friedman in *Capitalism and Freedom*, University of Chicago Press, 1962, where the idea of the free market encompassing regulatory functions was put forward. This proposition is consistent with others explored earlier, such as the assumption of rational utility-maximizers, whose actions would naturally lead to a state of competitive equilibrium, and to an efficient allocation of resources.

[85] See Harry De Angelo and René Stulz, 'Liquid-Claim Production, Risk Management, and Bank Capital Structure: Why High Leverage is Optimal for Banks', Fisher College of Business Working Paper No 2013-03-08, 2014.

[86] ibid.

this monograph, and that is commonly associated with the idea of market discipline.[87] All in all, the underlying conceptual framework of neoclassical economics permeated the motives behind much of the innovation process between the 1980s and the early 2000s.

(b) Regulatory environment

With respect to the regulatory environment, it is unquestionable that the 'dark side' of financial innovation emerged in connection with the regulatory changes that were being implemented in the 1980s. These have been discussed in a historical context in Chapter 2 of this book, and are only briefly recalled here. One first critical element to remember is the structural changes in banks, which by the end of the 1990s were allowed to incorporate into the same organization different areas of financial services,[88] and very diverse forms of risk-taking. Moreover, mergers between commercial banks, insurance companies, and investment firms gave rise to megabanks, and to the so-called too-big-to-fail problem.[89] In a nutshell, these megabanks could still rely on the public regulatory backstop afforded to commercial banks (as deposit-taking institutions),[90] while taking different, and much greater risks related to the investment side of the business.[91]

Such new levels of risk-taking were made possible by the blunt legalization of speculation. In the context of derivatives for instance, this shift was caused by their facilitative legal treatment (explored in detail in Chapters 2 and 4), while in the more general context of debt capital markets the unchallenged application of private ordering has spurred the relentless innovation of debt contracts.[92] The result of this legal and regulatory orthodoxy was the abuse of contractual instruments, traditionally conceived as risk management tools, and transformed progressively into engines of speculation. Two examples can be drawn for the purpose of this discussion.

[87] For a discussion, see Emilios Avgouleas and Jay Cullen, 'Market Discipline and EU Corporate Governance Reforms in the Banking Sector: Merits, Fallacies and Cognitive Boundaries' (2014) 41 Journal of Law and Society 28; see Bavoso, 'Basel III' (n 73), 95–101.

[88] This change was sealed in the US with the final repeal of the old Glass-Steagall Act, and the enactment of the Gramm-Leach-Bliley Act of 1999; whereas in the UK part of the Financial Services Act 1986 achieved the same goal.

[89] See for a discussion Arthur Wilmarth, *Taming the Megabanks—Why We Need a New Glass-Steagall Act*, Oxford University Press, 2020, particularly chapters 7 and 8, where Wilmarth provides a detailed analysis of how the provisions introduced in 1933 with the Glass-Steagall were progressively eroded in the US, with a series of loopholes opened by regulators in the 1980s and 1990s.

[90] Specifically, regulatory protection consisting in deposit insurance protection and lender of last resort. The function of these public regulatory backstops is explained by Morgan Ricks, 'Regulating Money Creation after the Crisis' (2011) 1 Harvard Business Law Review.

[91] It is worth remembering that investment firms, both in the UK and the US, were constrained in their risk-taking activities by their form of incorporation, which until the mid-1980s was the partnership, involving unlimited liability of the firm's partners. See Chapter 2 for a discussion of these regulatory changes.

[92] Private ordering, and its relevance in regulatory discourse, is closely examined in Chapter 6.

The first is that of derivatives, which have traditionally existed as contracts conceived for the management of risk. Under that configuration, parties would enter derivatives to hedge a specific risk that they were exposed to in the underlying assets.[93] The precondition, in other words, was the direct proprietary interest in the underlying assets. With the evolution of derivatives markets in the 1980s, the distinction between hedging derivatives and speculative ones (essentially bets placed on the future value of underlying assets) progressively waned, due in particular to the legality conferred on the latter by legislative interventions, both in the US[94] and the UK.[95]

The second example is provided by the widespread abuse of special purpose vehicles (SPV)[96], or rather shell entities artfully incorporated by large financial institutions, largely for regulatory arbitrage purposes. It is well known that SPVs have been at the heart of the securitization structure, and beyond that they have been widely employed in other aspects of commercial law and financial services.[97] It is undeniable though, that in the pre-2008 years transactional innovations revolving around SPVs have become the catalyst for the multiplication of risks and hidden leverage. High-risk assets were being moved to areas of the financial system beyond the scrutiny of regulators, and outside the perimeter of rules governing

[93] A classic and straightforward example is a farmer who is exposed to fluctuations in the value of the harvest (which depend on a number of factors, such as weather) and the future sale price of crops. The farmer can obviate this uncertainty by entering, into a futures contract, the effect of which is to fix the sale price of the specific crop at a specified date in the future.

[94] In the US a distinction between hedging and speculative derivatives was in place at common law, with the rule set by *Irwin v Williar* 110 U.S. 499, 508-09 (1884), whereby contracts for the sale of goods in the future (such as derivatives) could be valid even where the seller was not in possession of the goods, and neither had the means to acquire them, if not by purchasing them from the market. Such a contract could still be valid as long as parties showed their intention in the contract, through the delivery of the goods by the seller and the payment of the purchase price by the buyer. Conversely, if the real underlying purpose of the contract was for the parties to speculate on the price of goods, and there was no intention to deliver the goods and pay the purchase price, and one party was to pay the difference between the price of the goods in the contract and the market price of the goods, in such a case the contract was deemed a form of speculation, and considered void by courts. This distinction was based on the actual delivery of the underlying goods. Later on, this criterion was first relaxed and eventually repealed under the Commodities Futures Modernization Act of 2000, which had the effect of validating speculative derivatives as a default contractual form, traded over-the-counter (OTC). See for a discussion Lynn Stout, 'Derivatives and the Legal Origins of the 2008 Credit Crisis' (2011) 1 Harvard Business Law Review 1.

[95] In the UK a similar distinction was in place. In *Universal Stock Exchange v Strachan* [1896] AC 166, the House of Lords held that contracts for difference (where parties speculate on the performance of the underlying price) would be void as wagers. This distinction was repealed by the Financial Services Act 1986; this abrogated section 18 of the Gaming Act 1845 which included financial wagers (such as derivatives) among its prohibited activities in relation to gaming and speculative bets. For a discussion of the 'Big Bang' in the UK, see Laurence Gower, '"Big Bang" and City Regulation' (1988) 51(1) The Modern Law Review.

[96] See on this topic Steven Schwarcz, 'Enron and the Use and Abuse of Special Purpose Entities in Corporate Structures' (2002) 70 University of Cincinnati Law Review.

[97] Typically, SPVs are employed to segregate a pool of assets, and related cash-flow, for the benefit of some creditors/beneficiaries. This is done in structured finance, but also in other areas, such as project finance, construction, and shipping.

financial intermediation.[98] SPVs were effectively at the very heart of what has come to be recognized as the shadow banking system, where some forms of financial intermediation are replicated, but without the regulatory costs typically associated with it. The legal and regulatory mechanisms that elicited this abuse are analysed closely in the next section of this chapter.

(c) Technological advances

Advances in information technology are the prerequisite for any process and form of financial innovation. The synergy between finance and technology is not a new phenomenon, and many of the payment, clearing and settlement facilities that today are taken for granted are rooted in fundamental technological breakthroughs. The development of earlier forms of digitalized ledgers in the 1960s and 1970s contributed for instance to the integration of financial institutions globally (particularly internationally active banks), thus facilitating cross-border payment services. Around the same time, in 1969, the inception of the automated teller machine (ATM) radically changed banking, particularly from the perspective of retail users.

More central to the thrust of this analysis are the recent advances in computer programs, which allowed the wide application of trading and investment techniques known as high-frequency trading (HFT) and dark pools. These are in essence forms of algorithmic automated trading that take advantage of high order-to-trade ratios, aimed at maximizing the volume of financial data through innovated electronic trading tools. Blockchain technology further developed the concept of a digital ledger, this time also independent of any central authority, and allegedly secret and secure by virtue of the technology deployed.[99]

The rise to prominence of the FinTech phenomenon, broadly defined, poses questions that are very relevant to this present debate, because in many respects the various applications of FinTech, whether in the shape of disintermediated platforms in the context of P2P lending, or cryptoassets issued via P2P networks, are a form of financial innovation. Assessing the merit and impact of the innovated activity without the benefit of hindsight, during the same lifetime of the innovation

[98] Banks for instance are subject to capital regulation, which means that they have to post capital as a percentage of the assets they originate, commensurate to the riskiness of those assets. This percentage of capital serves as a cushion to protect the stability of banks, should the value of the assets decrease. SPVs however, are not subject to the same regulatory measures, therefore by transferring assets to SPVs, banks were effectively bypassing capital regulation. The essence indeed of regulatory arbitrage.

[99] Blockchain is effectively a digitized, decentralized, public ledger that was initially developed as a method for the accounting of virtual currency such as bitcoin. It employs what is known as distributed ledger technology (DLT), which today has expanded to various commercial and financial applications. See for an overview Zibin Zheng, Shaoan Xie, Hongning Dai, Xiangping Chen, and Huaimin Wang, 'An Overview of Blockchain Technology: Architecture, Consensus, and Future Trends', IEEE 6th International Congress on Big Data, 2017, 557–564. See also Bank of England, 'What are Cryptoassets (cryptocurrencies)?', 19 May 2020, available at www.bankofengland.co.uk/knowledgebank/what-are-cryptocurrencies (last accessed on 20/04/2024).

process[100], is particularly difficult, and the diverging views on the merit of this last wave of technological disruption are testament to that.[101] In particular, in the post-2008 era it has become crucial to appraise the possible risks flowing from alternative FinTech-based channels of intermediation, their systemic stability concerns, and the appropriateness of the current regulatory oversight of this phenomenon.[102] In other words, understanding the wider impact of technology on financial innovation hinges on unveiling the ultimate finality of the innovation itself, something that is discussed below.

(d) Finality

New technologies, and the associated innovations, are in principle directed at maximizing the effectiveness of two fundamental processes that were mentioned in the previous section, namely the ability of the financial system to allocate resources and the attendant capacity to diversify risks efficiently.[103] Many examples of financial innovation in history have been aimed at addressing these goals, and have done it in practice. Examples can be drawn from some of the instruments signposted earlier in this chapter, such as factoring and the floating charge. These were conceived in the days of the industrial revolution as means to address specific commercial needs of entrepreneurs and manufacturing firms. The ultimate purpose of the underlying innovation was highly consistent with economic (and to some extent social) needs that were emerging in that specific period—namely the expansion of global trade, the industrialization of manufacturing processes, and the necessity to alleviate funding and liquidity problems of the parties involved in that trade.[104]

While similar claims are made by proponents of every innovation process, it is difficult to reconcile some of the more recent expressions of financial innovation with any real economy finality.[105] Drawing on what was explained earlier,

[100] A very interesting discussion on regulating during, and beyond, the hype cycle is conducted by Michael Schillig, 'Lex Cryptographi(c)a, "Clout Crypto Land" or What?—Blockchain Technology on the Legal Hype Cycle' (2022) Modern Law Review 1–36.

[101] See for instance, among some scholars expressing concerns on the merits of the FinTech and crypto revolution: Kelvin Low and Elisa Mik, 'Pause the Blockchain Legal Revolution' (2020) 69(1) International & Comparative Law Quarterly 135; Kelvin Law, 'Confronting Cryptomania: Can Equity Tame the Blockchain' (2020) 14 Journal of Equity 240; Edmund Schuster, 'Cloud Crypto Land' (2020) Modern Law Review 3; Vincenzo Bavoso, 'Financial Intermediation in the Age of FinTech: P2P Lending and the Reinvention of Banking' (2021) Oxford Journal of Legal Studies.

[102] See for instance Maria Teresa Chimianti, Urszula Kochanska, and Andrea Pinna, 'Understanding the Crypto-asset Phenomenon, its Risks and Measurement Issues' (2019) 5 European Central Bank Economic Bulletin.

[103] Avgouleas, 'Regulating Financial Innovation' (n 52), 666–667.

[104] More specifically, factoring addressed funding and liquidity problems, allowing manufacturing firms to receive fresh cash by selling invoices that would otherwise be payable at 90 days or more. With floating charges, firms could pledge a class of assets as security against a loan, whereby these assets were not fixed, and could still be used by the firm in the course of its business.

[105] The word finality here is consistent with the meaning of something's faculty and purpose. See https://dictionary.cambridge.org/dictionary/english/finality (last accessed on 25/09/2024).

the 'evolution' of derivatives from hedging contracts to speculative ones can serve as an illustration. The former were, from ancient times, the expression of a rather tangible commercial reality, where farmers for instance sought to fix the price of their harvest in the future. The same insurance-like rationale applied to derivatives until very recent times, as they were employed to facilitate trade and commerce, by hedging a variety of risks related to the underlying goods (such as raw materials, agricultural products, merchandise). The same goods were being traded by two parties in an underlying separate contract. The evolution of derivatives into speculative contracts, particularly since the late 1980s,[106] and then with the regulatory changes of the late 1990s,[107] led to a market that grew enormously in size (becoming in fact much greater than the underlying markets for the referred assets), but whose finality did not coincide with commercial needs. The justification for speculative derivatives lies in the panoply of assumptions flowing from neoclassical economics, grounded in ideas of efficiency and optimal resource allocation.[108] The legitimacy of these efficiency claims has however been greatly reassessed, particularly after 2008 and in the wider context of the risks that emanate from these transactions.[109] The idea of finality helps framing the risk-benefit analysis on this particular innovation, and it can contribute to the debate on the desirable regulatory approach in this area of financial markets.

A similar scenario may be that of securitization. Without repeating what was said in the previous chapter, securitization was developed in the US to boost the liquidity of the secondary market for mortgages, and to facilitate in the process easier access to home ownership for a wider spectrum of households. This finality seems to be consistent with social and economic dynamics—it will be recalled that at the heart of securitization there is a sale of receivables, as is the case with factoring. The evolution of plain vanilla securitization into CDOs and then into synthetic CDOs represented a clear departure from that finality, with the innovated transactions finding instead justification in abstract and unfounded assumptions of market completion and risk diversification. It became widely accepted, particularly after 2008, that innovated forms of securitization did not contribute to the purchase of homes or the more general access to credit. Neither did they

[106] See for an explanation of this dynamic MacKenzie, *An Engine, Not A Camera* (n 56).

[107] See nn 94 and 95.

[108] In particular, informational efficiency related to the price discovery of underlying commodities and markets. As an example of these claims, see Marc Bohmann, David Michayluk, and Vinay Patel, 'Price Discovery in Commodity Derivatives: Speculation or Hedging?' (2019) 39(9) The Journal of Futures Markets, where it is posited that increased speculation is conducive to better price discovery in underlying commodities markets.

[109] See on this Frank Partnoy and David Skeel, 'The Promise and Perils of Credit Derivatives' (2007) 75 University of Cincinnati Law Review 1020, 1032–1046. The authors identify problems associated with credit derivatives that can be summed up as: a) the incentives to destroy the value of the underlying asset/firm; b) the opacity of the market in speculative derivatives, which is ever more reliant on mathematical sophistication; c) the tendency of speculative derivatives to increase interconnectedness and systemic risks.

facilitate risk diversification, as the dramatic events of 2008 demonstrated. Instead, these innovated contractual structures were the very engine behind an unprecedented growth in private debt creation, ensuing leverage, and unquantifiable risks hidden in the shadow banking system.[110]

3.2 Debt creation through contractual innovation and entity disintermediation: the alchemy of the SPV

Before concluding this chapter, it is important to briefly focus on one key component of financial innovation that since the 1980s facilitated the evolution of transactions and the creation of unquantifiable amounts of private debt and leverage. SPVs were analysed in the previous chapter in the context of securitization, and the purpose of this discussion is to further explore the function of these legal devices in capital markets.

In the account provided by Bratton and Levitin of the genealogy of scandals, reference to the use of SPV abounds, and in fact the deployment of these vehicles in a range of structured finance transaction is perhaps the core underlying common denominator of the scandals they analyse. They refer to questions of 'corporate alter ego', and their vast use particularly given their regulatory treatment in both corporate and financial law, which creates regulatory arbitrage opportunities.[111] More specifically, in the field of structured finance, SPVs are entities set up for the purpose of segregating assets. These assets are removed from the books of the entity (typically the originator) that sets up the SPV, and the assets' cash-flow is used uniquely to pay investors in capital markets who buy bonds issued by the SPV. From the perspective of these investors, SPVs represent in principle a privileged access to cash-flow from a segregated pool of assets. That is after all why bonds issued by an SPV receive a better credit rating than corporate bonds issued directly by the originator. One reason is that the SPV achieves a separation between the source of payment (the assets) and the company (the originator), which has the effect of insulating investors from the insolvency of the originator.[112] That in essence is the idea of bankruptcy remoteness that is at the heart of the SPV.[113]

Against this transactional efficiency, SPVs present a number of legal question marks. They are peculiar legal entities, effectively with no shareholding

[110] See Turner, *The Turner Review* (n 65); Financial Crisis Inquiry Commission, 'Financial Crisis Inquiry Report' (n 65); Engelen and others, *After the Great Complacence* (n 1).

[111] See William Bratton and Adam Levitin, 'A Transactional Genealogy of Scandal: From Michael Milken to Enron to Goldman Sachs' (2013) 86(4) Southern California Law Review 783–868, 787.

[112] See on this Steven Schwarcz, 'Structured Finance: The New Way to Securitize Assets' (1990) 11 Cardozo Law Review 607.

[113] ibid, 613, 614. See also Gary Gorton and Nicholas Souleles, 'Special Purpose Vehicles and Securitization', in *The Risks of Financial Institutions*, edited by Mark Carey and René Stulz, University of Chicago Press, 2007, chapter 12.

(nominal shares are typically held by charitable foundations), and provided with very limited, if at all, equity capital. SPVs are in fact funded with debt, in the form of the bonds they issue to investors, the proceeds of which fund the purchase of the asset portfolio from the originator.[114] Originators nominate independent directors; however, these remain in charge of clerical activities only and the management of the structured transaction is in the hands of trustees, asset managers, or the originator's executives.[115] Questions of control surface at several stages during the life of SPVs, because for instance the originator remains in charge of servicing arrangements with the underlying obligors.[116]

As is correctly observed by Bratton and Levitin, SPVs never achieve the status of fully independent organizations, even within the narrow 'special purpose' for which they are incorporated.[117] As a matter of fact, control does not lie within the entity, but instead derives from a network of contractual arrangements, a number of which were detailed in the previous chapter. This bundle of contracts regulates key aspects of the SPV's life from the outside, so that equity ownership is replaced by functional control via contracts.[118] This form of control has attracted legal and regulatory questions, particularly in the post-2008 years, when investors in structured products sought to expand the scope of fiduciary duties in order to bypass the SPVs, and attach liability to the functional controllers of the SPV.[119]

Ultimately, a combination of private ordering (examined in Chapter 6) and corporate law formalism allowed the legal structure of SPV to remain unscathed through a number of crises and scandals, as is noted in the account provided by Bratton and Levitin. The legal alchemy of SPVs, particularly the way they are deployed in structured finance, allowed the sponsor/originating entity to effectively use the SPV as its extended arm, as if it were a subsidiary, without however qualifying as a controlled entity from the point of view of accounting or capital regulation.[120] Waves of financial innovation centred on the use of SPVs permitted the origination of unprecedented levels of credit, with associated risks being spread in the financial system, under the belief that they were efficiently allocated to investors capable of absorbing them.

[114] See Vincenzo Bavoso, 'Filling the Accountability Gap in Structured Finance Transactions: The Case for a Broader Fiduciary Obligation' (2017) 23(2) Columbia Journal of European Law 372–373.

[115] ibid, 377; Gorton and Souleles, 'Special Purpose Vehicles and Securitization' (n 113), 550.

[116] This means that despite the true sale of assets from the originator to the SPV, the originator keeps collecting payments on the underlying assets from the obligors, acting in essence on behalf of the SPV.

[117] Bratton and Levitin, 'A Transactional Genealogy of Scandal' (n 111), 788.

[118] ibid.

[119] For a discussion, see Bavoso, 'Filling the Accountability Gap' (n 114), 388; and Vincenzo Bavoso, 'HSH v. UBS—Lessons from New York' (2013) 28(6) Journal of International Banking and Financial Law. See for relevant litigation: *HSH Nordbank AG v UBS AG*, 2012 NY Slip Op 02276; *Northern Rock Plc v SGCIB, Cohen & Co Securities, Strategos Capital Management LLC*, Supreme Court of the State of New York, 2014 NY Slip Op 32155(U); *ACA Financial Guaranty Corp. v Goldman Sachs & Co.*, 2012 NY Slip Op 50723(U); *Cassa di Risparmio della Repubblica di San Marino SpA v Barclays Bank Plc* [2011] EWHC 484 (Comm).

[120] Bratton and Levitin, 'A Transactional Genealogy of Scandal' (n 111), 865.

One reason why regulation never caught up with SPVs is perhaps to be found in the same set of assumptions explored earlier in this chapter (and in Chapter 3), namely the capacity of these vehicles to facilitate high-leverage financing, to create safe and liquid assets by repackaging illiquid loan-type assets, and in the process completing markets, particularly thanks to the tranche structure of securitized bonds.

4 Conclusion and way forward: what role for regulation?

At the time of writing this monograph, the world of finance is coming to terms with the downturn of yet another mania, only marginally relevant to the thrust of this book, but presenting dynamics that are similar to those explored in section 2: the crypto-mania.[121] While the swings between periods of boom and bust may be an inevitable feature of economies with open and fully liberalized financial markets, the question that needs to be posed at the end of this chapter, and reprised in greater detail over the next two, concerns the role that regulation should and could take in mitigating the impact of crises, and perhaps preventing some of them.

History teaches us that between the enactment of New Deal legislations in the US in the early 1930s, and the initial liberalization of that regulatory infrastructure in the mid-1980s, a period of financial peace endured.[122] Coincidentally, financial stability ended with the regulatory changes that transformed financial markets, in the US and the UK initially, and then progressively at the global level.[123] After three decades of scandals and crises, a number of recurring patterns and common denominators can be recognized, and some were discussed in this chapter. One critical aspect of financial markets, identified recently by both policy-makers and academics, is the soaring level of private debt, which coincides with the huge expansion of some segments of debt capital markets.[124] In particular, the renaissance of the structured credit market since 2014 coincided with the rise of collateralized loan obligations (CLOs). CLOs came with the same promises of their predecessors, hiding in the process very similar structural flaws, and hard to quantify levels of leverage. At the same time, securitization also restarted as a vehicle to repackage

[121] See for instance Robert Reich, 'The Crypto Crash: all Ponzi schemes topple eventually', *The Guardian* (19 June 2022); Merryn Somerset Webb, 'Time to cut your stock market losses — or not?', *Financial Times* (17 June 2022); Siddarth Venkataramakrishnan and Robin Wigglesworth, 'Inside the cult of crypto', *Financial Times* (10 September 2021).

[122] See for instance, in support of this statement Joseph Stiglitz, *Freefall: America, Free Markets, and the Sinking of the World Economy*, Penguin, 2010, chapter 1; Arthur Wilmarth, *Taming the Megabanks*, Oxford University Press, 2020, chapter 2.

[123] These regulatory changes were detailed in Chapter 2.

[124] See IMF, 'Global Financial Stability Report 2019', chapter2; and Wilmarth, *Taming the Megabanks* (n122), chapter 12.

risky assets with opaque underlying credit ratings, such as loans originated through FinTech-based platforms (P2P).

The conceptualization of financial crises through different types of cycles proposed in this chapter reveals that debt capital markets have been invested by a new wave of innovation in the post-2008 years.[125] The hype behind new products and markets has come with a mania that has led to higher levels of private debt, unsustainable leverage, and risk-taking. While this is becoming apparent to most commentators, little has been done to mitigate the effects of the cycle that inevitably follow the upward swing. Along this line of thinking, concerns about post-crisis regulation were raised, among others, by Adair Turner and John Geanakoplos, and it is useful to signpost them here, as these regulatory concerns are reprised in the next two chapters.

In his book published in 2016, Turner questioned the state of the financial system after 2008, putting particular emphasis on the private debt creation effect that has continued unchallenged. Critically, policies directed at increasing the financial system's leverage are still informed by the belief that market discipline will suffice in mitigating risks and ensuring financial stability.[126] In an article published in 2014, Geanakoplos reiterated the damage caused by the swings of the leverage cycle on the real economy. He stressed the inadequate ex-post reactions of regulatory interventions that typically follow the crash, and the need to rely instead on more proactive forms of regulation aimed at mitigating the intensity of the cycle.[127] These regulatory and policy questions are reprised in greater detail in the next two chapters.

[125] Some of the new products and markets were detailed in the last chapter of this monograph. Their development was engineered during the post-2008 years, as memories of the GFC subsided, and some of them were at the very heart of the panic of 2020.

[126] Adair Turner, *Between Debt and the Devil*, Princeton University Press, 2016. A critique of market discipline is developed in the next chapter of this book.

[127] John Geanakoplos, 'Leverage, Default and Forgiveness: Lessons from American and European Crises' (2014) 39 Journal of Macroeconomics 320.

PART III

UNDERSTANDING HOW DEBT CAPITAL MARKETS ARE REGULATED

6
The regulatory framework of debt capital markets

1 Introduction

This chapter follows from the discussion conducted in Chapter 5 on the proneness of debt capital markets to lead to crises. That analysis developed a taxonomy of crises and led to some preliminary conclusions on the need for regulatory intervention in order to mitigate both the frequency and intensity of financial instability. Part III of this book engages with critical regulatory and policy questions that are conceptually linked with the conclusions reached at the end of Part II, and also with the framework (both historical and theoretical) developed in Part I.

This chapter provides an analytical discussion on the regulatory architecture that has permeated debt capital markets, with a specific focus on the period preceding the global financial crisis (GFC) of 2008.[1] The purpose of this analysis therefore is to draw a picture of how neoclassical economics (and neoliberal policy-making) influenced regulatory strategies, and how in turn regulatory tools reflected the application of the conceptual framework discussed in Chapter 3. The emphasis of this analysis is also on the effects of this regulatory design, which are reflected in the accounts provided in Chapters 4 and 5, respectively dealing with the development and innovation of debt products, and with how those innovated markets are causes of fragilities in the financial system. The key contention of this discussion is that the regulatory architecture developed between the 1980s and 2008 was instrumental to the growth of capital markets, and particularly its debt segments.

In particular, certain arear of debt capital markets remained only loosely and indirectly regulated, or to be more specific, they were regulated through market discipline mechanisms,[2] instead of being covered by more specifically tailored banking or capital markets rules. One prominent example of this approach is represented by the panoply of securitization-type transactions, which blossomed outside the perimeter of financial regulation and supervision. As will be explained later in this chapter, the standard disclosure rules applicable to bonds did not apply

[1] The discussion developed in Chapter 7 though shows that this focus is still very relevant, permeating post-2008 regulatory discourses.

[2] The concept of market discipline is expounded in section 2 of this chapter.

Debt Capital Markets. Vincenzo Bavoso, Oxford University Press. © Vincenzo Bavoso 2024.
DOI: 10.1093/oso/9780198893257.003.0006

in most securitizations, which would fall under exceptions of private placement or institutional investors.[3] Attendant areas of capital markets, such as repo transactions or derivatives, similarly remained regulated indirectly, through market discipline mechanisms. It is important to note here that both repo contracts and derivatives have been traditionally envisaged as areas of financial markets where counterparties are assumed capable of dealing with each other at arm's length, and rationally, by virtue of their access to disclosed information.

As will be illustrated in this chapter, disclosure has been the centrepiece of financial regulation since the New Deal legislation of the 1930s.[4] With the renewed emphasis on informational efficiency in the 1980s, disclosure became the main focus of regulatory efforts, perhaps to the detriment of other important strategies. Debt products for instance, from the simplest (plain vanilla) bonds to the most innovated securitized bonds, were the offspring of transactional innovation based on bundles of contractual relationships. It is interesting to note that despite the growth of debt finance, these contractual relationships remained only indirectly scrutinized, and were instead regulated through principles of market discipline and private ordering (see for instance the application of margin requirements in repo contracts).[5] With the benefit of hindsight, it is quite astonishing that this increasingly central area of capital markets did not receive more direct regulatory scrutiny, especially given its importance in the financial system as a whole. The post-2008 literature has reiterated the systemic dimension of integrated financial systems, where debt capital markets represent their critical fulcrum.[6] Thus, leaving fundamental problems of systemic risk and financial stability to be policed by principles of market discipline and private ordering seems today at odds with the priorities of financial regulation.

This chapter focuses on one main enquiry which is developed through a general discussion on market discipline, with three more specific analyses looking into applications of market discipline as regulatory tools: disclosure, private ordering, and credit rating agencies. Section 2 of this chapter focuses on the importance that market discipline acquired as an overarching regulatory principle in capital markets. In explaining the role of specific regulatory mechanisms (disclosure, private ordering, credit rating agencies) to advance the orthodoxy of market discipline, section 3 provides an illustration of the regulatory framework of capital markets, emphasizing a) the quasi-normative role that market actors have in it, and b) the overarching reliance on assumptions of efficient markets and rational market participants.

[3] Prospectus rules and relevant exceptions are analysed in Chapter 7.

[4] This was enshrined in the Securities Act 1933.

[5] Repo contracts were explained in the context of Chapter 4 (section 4.2).

[6] See for instance, Markus Brunnermeier, Andrew Crockett, Charles Goodhart, Avinash Persaud, and Hyun Song Shin, *The Fundamental Principles of Financial Regulation*, Geneva Reports on the World Economy 11, Centre for Economic Policy Research, 2009, chapters 2 and 3.

The more conceptual analysis conducted in this chapter is complemented by the normative study developed in Chapter 7, where attention is drawn to regulations dealing specifically with debt capital markets. In that context, a critical appraisal is done with respect to the edifice of post-2008 regulation and its impact, including current policy and regulatory exercises.

2 Regulating through market discipline

It is often observed that capital markets have developed along the lines of market-based finance, and in fact its segments and products (analysed in Chapter 4) represent the quintessential form of disintermediation from banks.[7] Intermediation here is to be understood as the process whereby borrowers access channels of funding by tapping the ultimate source, namely investors in capital markets, rather than the more traditional banking system.[8] It is also important to remember what was explained in Chapter 3 of this book, about the conceptual foundation upon which market-based channels of finance developed. The undisputed orthodoxy was (and to some extent still is) that regulation[9] could not improve overall economic welfare[10] and that the only exception to that would be the occurrence of a market failure, simply because the latter would be more costly than regulatory intervention.[11] This policy stance was consistent with the overall prioritization of efficiency goals, which is something that was also central to the analysis conducted in Chapter 3.[12]

The orthodoxy centred on efficiency resulted in a regulatory architecture devoid of strong regulatory oversight, where market forces and market participants were instead relied upon as a discipline mechanism, and importantly also as an efficiency engine, through their capacity (and freedom) to engineer new transactions and products.[13] This balance of forces reflects the process that from the 1980s until

[7] See on this Steven Schwarcz, 'Framing Address: A Framework for Analysing Financial Markets Transformation' (2013) 36 Seattle University Law Review 299, 303.

[8] This distinction points at the source of funding, whether this is banks or investors in capital markets. In both cases there are forms of intermediation, and in both scenarios banks are active in different ways, as providers of finance in the former scenario, as underwriters or brokers in the latter.

[9] Regulation to be intended here as rules that come from outside of the market, as a form of government intrusion, in other words.

[10] It will be remembered that this coincided under neoclassical economics with Pareto efficiency.

[11] On the broader regulatory debate, see Anthony Ogus, *Regulation: Legal Form and Economic Theory*, Hart Publishing, 2004, 4.

[12] As is detailed later in this chapter, prioritizing efficiency goals resulted in a specific regulatory focus on informational efficiency in particular. This was directed at ensuring the flow of information in capital markets, chiefly through disclosure mechanisms.

[13] This being at the very heart of that same efficiency rationale, because more financial products were thought to contribute to financial deepening and market completion, two concepts that are instrumental to achieving Pareto equilibrium. See Kenneth Arrow and Gerard Debreu, 'Existence of an Equilibrium for a Competitive Economy' (1954) 22(3) Econometrica 265.

the present day spurred financial innovation. What may appear as an unfettered innovation process found its legitimacy in the same conceptual foundations discussed earlier, namely the idea that a wider and more diversified range of financial products would complete markets. Deeper markets in turn would facilitate a more effective allocation of resources, and a more efficient diversification of risks.[14]

As was illustrated throughout Chapter 4, financial innovation was also the engine that allowed financial institutions to engage with extremely high levels of leverage (particularly before 2008) and increase in the process both their profits but critically also their risk-taking.[15] This trend too was widely accepted by mainstream academics and policy-makers, who maintained that high levels of leverage were a prerequisite for efficient financial markets. In line with the efficiency functions attributed to market participants, it was believed that leverage could positively impact on banks' allocative efficiency, because it would lower the cost of capital for the same banks.[16] Ideally, this would enable banks to extend more credit to the real economy, and at more favourable rates, ensuring in the process broader access to finance and economic development.[17] This line of thinking also suggested that regulating leverage would negatively impact on the capacity of financial institutions to extend credit, and it would also create regulatory costs on regulated financial institutions and competitive advantages for entities operating outside the same regulatory framework[18] (what in the post-2008 regulatory discussions is commonly referred to as the non-bank sector[19]).

It is important to stress that policies focused on efficiency underscored the regulatory agenda in the pre-2008 years, and to a great degree this direction does not seem to have changed after the global financial crisis (something that is appraised in Chapter 7). Instead, some of the regulatory measures introduced as reactions

[14] This ideology found a springboard in the neoliberal orthodoxy disseminated chiefly with the work of Milton Friedman, *Capitalism and Freedom*, University of Chicago Press, 1962, where the idea of free market was championed, and particularly the role of the market for regulatory purposes. This proposition in turn advanced the concept of rational utility-maximizers who would lead to a state of competitive equilibrium (optimal allocation of resources, or Pareto efficiency) in the context of efficient markets. Attaining this idealized state of competitive equilibrium represented another justification for preferring policies that facilitated the interaction between rational utility-maximizers and the market, with limited regulatory interference in the process.

[15] See John Kenneth Galbraith, *A Short History of Financial Euphoria*, Penguin, 1990, explaining at p 19: 'the world of finance hails the invention of the wheel over and over again, often in a slightly more unstable version ... most forms of financial innovation involve the creation of debt secured in greater or lesser adequacy by real assets'. The same type of debt creation was involved within the subsequent innovation which was centred on the use of leverage and the collateralization of assets.

[16] Banks in pre-crisis years expanded their balance sheets chiefly through debt rather than equity. See Harry De Angelo and René Stulz, 'Liquid Claim Production, Risk Management, and Bank Capital Structure: Why High Leverage is Optimal for Banks', Fisher College of Business, Working Paper 2013-03-08, October, 2014.

[17] ibid. It was contended that a wider extension of credit would ensure that the best projects would be adequately financed and this would of course contribute to economic growth.

[18] ibid.

[19] See on this Sirio Aramonte, Andreas Schrimpf, and Hyun Song Shin, 'Non-bank financial intermediaries and financial stability', BIS Working Paper No 972, October 2021.

to the 2008 crisis have been framed and critiqued precisely within that narrative, and have been deemed anti-efficient.[20] One of the consequences of the efficiency-centric approach is that leverage and other forms of risk-taking are assumed to be monitored by market participants. This idea was clearly reflected in regulatory approaches, most prominently under the third pillar of Basel II, where the supervision of the overall framework was to be left to market discipline.[21] Under Basel, market discipline consisted in the development of a set of disclosure recommendations, which, in line with the tenets of informational efficiency, were assumed to enable market participants to access and process information, and take informed actions.[22] Information gathered through this disclosure process was supposed to allow the necessary risk-assessment and risk-management procedures in relation to financial institutions' capital adequacy.[23] In essence, financial institutions were put in charge of policing each other and the overall market.

An important corollary of this regulatory strategy was the emphasis that was laid on banks' internal risk methodologies. These often highly complex quantitative formulae effectively empowered large financial institutions[24] to develop a high degree of discretion in assessing and applying capital requirements.[25] To further reiterate what was explained earlier, this design was seen as a cost-effective form of supervision, whereby market participants could police themselves. The underlying hypothesis was grounded on the same principles of informational efficiency explored earlier (and in Chapter 3), whereby depositors and other bank creditors were assumed capable, and willing, to play a role in monitoring banks' risk-taking. In this context, market discipline would materialize in two main ways: either through investors who would react to excessive levels of risk-taking, by for instance withdrawing funds or demanding a higher return for their investment; or through wider market reactions that would signal excessive risk-taking, such as for instance

[20] A key example here has been the discussion around Basel III and some of its measures. It has been observed that the leverage ratio and the higher capital requirements may limit the ability of banks to extend credit, and this could in turn have consequences in terms of GDP decline. See Institute of International Finance, 'The Cumulative Impact on the Global Economy of Changes in the Financial Regulatory Framework', September 2011.

[21] It is to be noted that Basel III has not changed its approach under the third pillar. The third pillar was premised on the assumption that the timely disclosure of banks' regulatory capital and risk exposure would enable the market (as in other market participants) to take cautionary actions and thereby restrain the excessive risk-taking of a specific bank. See 'Basel II: The New Basel Capital Accord—Third Consultative Paper', April 2003, Part 4.

[22] For a critique of the disclosure paradigm as a regulatory mechanism, see Emilios Avgouleas, 'The Global Financial Crisis and the Disclosure Paradigm in European Financial Regulation: The Case for Reform' (2009) 4 European Company and Financial Law Review 440–475; and Martin Hellwig, 'Market Discipline, Information Processing and Corporate Governance', Max Planck Institute for Research on Collective Goods, No 2005/19, 2005.

[23] Basel Committee on Banking Supervision, 'Consultative Document—Pillar 3 (Market Discipline)—Supporting Document to the New Basel Capital Accord', Bank for International Settlements, January 2001, 5–6.

[24] Large financial institutions in particular were able to develop in-house their own mathematical models for the calculation of risk models.

[25] This point will be expounded in section 4.

changes in the value of a bank's liabilities.[26] As the events of 2008 demonstrated, this hypothesis proved to be flawed for multiple reasons, chiefly due to the inability of market participants to provide the assumed monitoring, and importantly because the excessive focus placed on individual financial institutions prevented a more proactive approach towards detecting systemic risk.[27]

Outside of the Basel framework, of which more will be said in the next chapter, market discipline materialized in the years before 2008 with an ever-increasing trust in supervisory processes. These stemmed from market mechanisms and governance arrangements that did not derive from direct state intervention or actions from competent regulatory agencies. The orthodoxy in regulatory discourses was that market forces were better at allocating resources through an assessment of the relevant risks and returns, and that the same forces could exercise discipline across financial institutions.[28] This narrative however, came from the outset with a number of caveats. In a 2001 speech at the Bank for International Settlements, Andrew Crockett (at that time head of the Financial Stability Board) noted that, in spite of the accepted narrative, there were shortcomings related to market discipline, particularly with respect to its suitability to deal with systemic risk and the way it evolves.[29] Crockett further pointed out that market discipline is naturally hindered by a number of shortcomings that are typically associated with market forces. These were linked with the difficulty to disclose full information under market mechanisms (something that is analysed in greater details in the next section of this chapter), and the related problematic assessment of the value of assets and their risk.[30] These limitations have been further worsened by the incentive structure that is in place in financial institutions, and that impedes the timely and accurate exercise of the above assessments.[31]

An important aspect of the market discipline orthodoxy is the bias it promoted towards debt finance and generally towards the increase of debt in the financial system. The rationale behind this policy stance has its roots in the savings and loans crisis in the US in the mid-1980s. The widespread perception at that time

[26] See David Min, 'Understanding the Failures of Market Discipline' (2015) 92 Washington University Law Review 1421.

[27] Saule Omarova, 'Wall Street as Community of Fate: Toward Financial Industry Self-Regulation' (2011) 159 University of Pennsylvania Law Review 441. Omarova argues that this approach put banks in a self-regulatory position, where banks were lacking the necessary 'community of fate'.

[28] See on this Andrew Crockett, 'Market Discipline and Financial Stability', BIS Speech, 23 May 2001, available at www.bis.org/speeches/sp010523.htm. Crockett warns that for it to be effective, market discipline rests upon various conditions, namely that market participants have sufficient information to reach informed judgements, that they have the ability to process information, that they have the right set of incentives, and that they have the mechanisms to exercise discipline.

[29] ibid.

[30] ibid. Crockett notes that as opposed to market mechanisms, supervisory authorities can be better placed in a number of situations, given that they have preferential access to information, face different incentive structure, and may also be better at dealing with risks that affect the system as a whole.

[31] See Emilios Avgouleas and Jay Cullen, 'Excessive Leverage and Bankers' Pay: Governance and Financial Stability Costs of a Symbiotic Relationships' (2015) 21(1) Columbia Journal of European Law.

was that the system designed to regulate and supervise banks was not sufficient to monitor and limit banks' risk-taking. It was believed instead that market discipline had a role to play in complementing the regulation and supervision of banks' risk exposures. More specifically, bondholders were seen as best placed to exert discipline on banks and generally on financial institutions.[32]

This aspect of the market discipline orthodoxy should help contextualizing the development of debt capital markets that was analysed from different angles in the previous chapters of this book. It is useful in this respect to link the present analysis with some specific developments in the securitization and repo markets. Before 2008, the regulation of these two segments of capital markets was at best indirect.[33] Their development was chiefly driven by contractual innovations, which went unfettered and were instead facilitated by a liberal legal approach towards financial innovation.[34] To put this in the wider context of the efficiency rationale that is being discussed here, securitization became instrumental in providing originators with a tool to optimize their balance sheet, and this was possible due to two commercial law features: the legal characterization of the transfer of receivables from originator to SPV as a true sale;[35] and the bankruptcy remoteness of the SPV from the originator, which prevents the substantive consolidation of originator's and SPV's estates in the event of the originator's insolvency.[36]

Similarly, the repo market flourished in the pre-2008 years chiefly due to the flexibility that was afforded to lenders (money market mutual funds), and the money-like claims that they have against their borrowers (banks).[37] This is because in a repo transaction, title to the underlying collateral passes to the lender (as if it were a sale rather than a secured financing), providing as a result much

[32] See on this Robert Avery, Terrence Belton, and Michael Goldberg, 'Market Discipline in Regulating Bank Risk: New Evidence from the Capital Markets' (1988) 20(4) Journal of Money, Credit and Banking.

[33] As an illustration, the first attempt to regulate repos came in 2015 at the EU level with the Securities Financing Transaction Regulation; in the context of securitization, this was partly regulated through capital requirements, but a more targeted regulatory effort only started around 2014, and flowing at the EU level into the STS Regulation (and into the STC Framework as part of the Basel III package), analysed in the next chapter.

[34] See Dan Awrey, 'Complexity, Innovation, and the Regulation of Modern Financial Markets' (2012) 2 Harvard Business Law Review 235, 258–262.

[35] There is a long-standing academic debate as to whether the transfer of receivables to the SPV should instead be configured as a secured financing, where the assets are pledged as security. This characterization of the transaction would of course be detrimental to the goal of securitization, which is to move assets off the originator's balance sheet. See Steven Schwarcz, Bruce Markell, and Lissa Lamkin Broome, *Securitisation, Structured Finance and Capital Markets*, LexisNexis, 2004, 37–43 and 69–70; Philip Wood, *Project Finance, Securitisations, Subordinated Debt*, Sweet & Maxwell, 2007, 112.

[36] Again, allowing upon insolvency the creditors of the originator to lodge claims on the assets held by the SPV would defy the purpose of securitization because it would drastically compromise the interests of SPV investors. Moreover, the likelihood of substantive consolidation would highly affect the rating of securitized bonds, thereby hindering investor appetite. See Schwarcz and others, *Securitisation* (n 35), 69–70; and Wood, *Project Finance* (n 35), 125.

[37] See Morgan Ricks, 'Regulating Money Creation after the Crisis' (2011) 1 Harvard Business Law Review 89; and Gary Gorton and Andrew Metrick, 'Regulating the Shadow Banking System' (2010) 41(2) Brookings Papers on Economic Activity 264.

security to lenders in the event of borrowers' default in the repurchase agreement, and also giving them freedom to reuse the same collateral in other transactions.[38] More significantly, in the US, where title to collateral does not pass from borrower to lender, transactional efficiency is still preserved due to the 'automatic stay' exception under US bankruptcy law.[39] While achieving efficiency for market participants, these contractual arrangements did not capture system-wide concerns, such as the increase in risk and debt-creation that they elicited.

While the space of this contextualization becomes clearer in the next section, particularly through the discussion on private ordering, it is important to stress that the merit and effectiveness of market discipline have been questioned even by its proponents. It is recognized in fact that the signalling functions attributed to market discipline, and particularly the general monitoring by market participants, are constrained by impediments, such as the pervasive incentives in the banking industry.[40] This line of critique insists on praising the potential of market discipline, and its capacity to reduce bank failures and systemic risks. However, it also recognizes that the intrinsic structural features of the financial system, together with some incomplete regulatory structures (analysed later in this chapter, and in their normative specificities in the next chapter), prevent market discipline from accomplishing its regulatory functions.[41]

To further elaborate on this analysis, this chapter delves in the next section into the contextual and specific critique of three central applications of market discipline in the area of debt capital markets. This is done by exploring the mechanics of 1) disclosure, 2) private ordering and 3) credit ratings. Chapter 7 completes this study by looking into specific regulations in areas of debt capital markets, thereby permitting an assessment of whether the combination of market discipline and regulatory intervention is suited to prevent crises in this area of financial markets.

[38] At the EU level this was regulated through the EU Financial Collateral Directive 2002/47/EC.

[39] In the US, an 'automatic stay' is imposed during bankruptcy proceedings on the assets of the defaulted party. This means that secured creditors have to wait for the commencement of the bankruptcy proceeding before being able to seize the relevant assets pledged as security. The 'automatic stay' however, does not apply in the context of repo transactions and derivatives, therefore allowing creditors to immediately use the collateral upon debtor's default in the repo contract. See Jay Cullen, 'The Repo Market: Collateral and Systemic Risk', in *Research Handbook on Shadow Banking*, edited by I Chiu and I MacNeil, Edward Elgar, 2017. Cullen explains that reforms in bankruptcy law led to an almost total exception related to all types of repo collateral in 2005.

[40] David Llewellyn, *Inside the 'Black Box' of Market Discipline*, Institute of Economic Affairs, 2005, 41–42.

[41] ibid, 42. Llewellyn argues that despite its potential, and its aim to prevent crises or minimize their costs, market discipline remains somewhat of a 'black box' because of the way in which its operational contours have remained undefined.

3 Market discipline through regulatory mechanisms

3.1 The role of disclosure

Disclosure has for a long time been a centrepiece in the architecture of financial regulation. In its contemporary form, it dates back to the New Deal legislation in the US in the 1930s, and particularly the Securities Act 1933, which set out the framework of the disclosure obligations for firms issuing securities to the market.[42] In the context of that regulatory exercise, disclosure was prioritized as the main tool to regulate issuing companies and their securities, ahead of other regulatory strategies, such as for instance more direct and substantive rules. This was the result of coordinated policy efforts in the aftermath of the 1929 Great Crash, at a time when the Roosevelt government engineered a paradigmatic shift in the governance of US financial markets. At the heart of that institutional and normative project there were academics such as James Landis[43] and Louis Brandeis[44] who strongly advocated the use of disclosure as the best way to control the behaviour of banks, and in particular the way in which they controlled money invested with them, but also more widely as the 'remedy for social and industrial diseases'.[45]

Beyond its historical roots in the US, disclosure has become widely employed in most advanced financial systems, for a variety of reasons. Its merits are typically associated with some of the efficiency axioms that have already been encountered in this book, and that can be summarized here under six headings: 1) the capacity of disclosure to disseminate information and enable market participants to make informed decision; 2) the better pricing of securities, and therefore the higher allocative efficiency, as a result of the wider availability of information; 3) the reduction of costs associated with acquiring information; 4) the promotion of fair, competitive and ethical markets, because disseminated information in principle nullifies the advantage of insiders; 5) the stability that disclosure brings to financial

[42] Pub. L. 73–22. This was followed by the Securities Exchange Act 1934 which, among other things, created the Securities and Exchange Commission.

[43] On the inputs of James Landis, see Justin O'Brien, *The Triumph, Tragedy and Lost Legacy of James M Landis*, Hart Publishing, 2014, particularly chapter 1, on Landis' contribution to shaping the underpinnings of the disclosure paradigm.

[44] See Louis Brandeis, *Other People's Money and how the Bankers Use it*, National Home Library Foundation, 1933, 60.

[45] ibid, 62–63. The complete sentence used by Brandeis was: 'Publicity is justly commended as a remedy for social and industrial diseases. Sunlight is said to be the best of disinfectants; electric light the most efficient policeman.' Years later, Roosevelt endorsed that view by stating that 'There is, however, an obligation upon us to insist that every issue of new securities to be sold in interstate commerce shall be accompanied by full publicity and information, and that no essentially important element attending the issue shall be concealed from the buying public.' See Troy Paredes, 'Speech by SEC Commissioner: Remarks before the Symposium on "The Past, Present, and Future of the SEC"', Securities and Exchange Commission, Pittsburgh 16 October 2009.

markets, due to the reduced market volatility (usually linked to limited information); 6) the pre-emption of frauds and abuses.[46]

Without going back to the analysis developed in Chapter 3, it is important to stress that the efficiency rationale associated with disclosure hinges specifically on a corollary of neoclassical economics, that is rational choice theory. Its central tenet is that human agents endeavour to maximize their economic utility from a set of defined preferences. To that end, they acquire an optimal amount of information in different ways, and on the basis of that information they will opt for a strategy that maximizes their expected utility.[47] Rational choice theory led eventually to the concept of homo economicus, an idealized economic actor assumed capable of assessing probability distributions in accordance with the level of knowledge acquired through information.[48]

Despite remaining the foundation of financial regulation, disclosure has attracted widespread criticism over the years, and particularly in the aftermath of the 2008 GFC. Crises in financial markets have been repeatedly associated with shortcomings in the various regulatory obligations based on disclosure,[49] and this has coincided with the period of financial transformation that was illustrated in Chapter 2, and specifically with the growth of debt capital markets. While the critique against disclosure as a regulatory technique has revolved around a number of specific themes, they can all be understood as a reflection of the changing nature of capital markets. For the purpose of this analysis, the critique against disclosure can be conceptualized under three streams, namely a) problems associated with the complexity of information, b) problems of information overload, c) problems of information processing.

The first stream is associated most prominently with the work of Steven Schwarcz, who started looking at complexity as an invalidating factor of disclosure in the aftermath of the Enron scandal.[50] He was perhaps the first to ask the very critical and fundamental question concerning the suitability of disclosure rules in the context of innovated debt transactions.[51] More specifically, Schwarcz questioned whether investors would still be capable of processing information and making

[46] For a full conceptualization of these merits, see Emilios Avgouleas, *The Mechanics and Regulation of Market Abuse, a Legal and Economic Analysis*, Oxford University Press, 2005, particularly chapter 2.3.

[47] In this sense, see Richard Posner, *Economic Analysis of Law*, Aspen Law and Business, 2003, chapters 1 and 2.

[48] This is explained by Emilios Avgouleas, 'What Future for Disclosure as a Regulatory Technique? Lessons from Behavioural Decision Theory and the Global Financial Crisis', in *The Future of Financial Regulation*, edited by Iain MacNeil and Justin O'Brien, Hart, 2010, chapter 12. Avgouleas also explains that this configuration of human behaviour was refined by game theorists in the 1940s and then embedded into neoclassical economics.

[49] Such as most prominently initial disclosure obligations through the prospectus, or continuing disclosure through transparency obligations.

[50] See Steven Schwarcz, 'Rethinking the Disclosure Paradigm in a World of Complexity' (2004) 1 University of Illinois Law Review.

[51] ibid, 4.

informed decisions in the arena of disintermediated products, such as securitized bonds issued by special purpose vehicles, or debt products layered with complex derivatives. In the specific context of Enron, Schwarcz argued, there was no dispute as to whether information concerning the various SPVs had been disclosed to investors. The problem was instead that information about the underlying transactions was so complex that investors (regardless of their sophistication) were unable to make informed decisions.[52] In other words, the effect of disclosure was nullified by complexity.

Schwarcz developed a similar line of critique after 2008 to explain the wider information failure that affected the structured credit market in the years prior to the crisis.[53] His analysis explaining the increase in complexity is compelling,[54] and so is the clarification of how complexity exacerbates information failures in financial markets.[55] What perhaps emerges less clearly from these studies is the effective impact of disclosure obligations on complex products. In the context of structured products, for instance, they very often fall under exceptions that allow, across most jurisdictions, these products to be issued in so-called private placements.[56] Similarly, before 2008 (and the introduction of clearing requirements afterwards), most derivatives were traded over-the-counter,[57] and therefore their complexity was not testing any particular standard of disclosure. If at all, these exceptions confirm the rationale that permeates capital markets regulation, and the overarching prioritization of speed and cost-effectiveness over greater marketability and liquidity.

The second line of critique against disclosure is also closely related to changes in capital markets over the past four decades and the attendant shifts in the quality and quantity of information that investors have to digest.[58] On the latter in particular, it is often noted that prospectus documents are several hundred pages long and include complex details in relation to the issuing entity and the product issued. Moreover, where securities are issued by an SPV, the information is further

[52] ibid, 5.

[53] See Steven Schwarcz, 'Regulating Complexity in Financial Markets' (2009) 87(2) Washington University Law Review.

[54] ibid, 213–214, where Schwarcz explains the incentives, both on the supply side and on the demand side, that propelled the industry towards ever more innovated and complex securities.

[55] ibid, 236.

[56] In the US this is known as Rule 144A and it represents an exception to the requirement under s 5 of the Securities Act 1933 for issuers to register securities with the Securities and Exchange Commission. At the EU level, similar mechanisms are in place, whereby no prospectus is required under the EU Regulation 2017/1129 (art 1), for securities issued, among others, to qualified investors or in private placements. See also in the UK, FCA PRR 1.2.

[57] See Lynn Stout, 'Regulate OTC Derivatives by Deregulating Them' (Fall 2009) Regulation 30–33.

[58] See on this claim Troy Paredes, 'Blinded by the Light: Information Overload and its Consequences for Securities Regulation' (2003) 81 Washington University Law Quarterly 417.

layered, embedding several degrees of complexity, due to underlying contractual structures.[59]

Finally, problems of information processing are more closely related to the capacity of investors to process and make decisions on the basis of the complex information they acquire. This line of critique is in plain contradiction to the assumption of efficient markets examined in Chapter 3, and also with the rational theory proposition presented earlier in this section. It has become incontrovertible though that both the complexity and the volume of disclosed information are found to increase the impact of cognitive bias on investor decision-making processes.[60] Different manifestations of cognitive bias have emerged from studies in behavioural decision theory, which postulate that human preferences are not constant, and choices can be manipulated through the framing of information. In other words, the evaluation of gains and losses under this proposition can be the result of changes in reference points for the decision-maker, which in turn will affect the capacity to make calculated (informed) decisions.[61]

Two related aspects of human decision-making are identified in behavioural science as factors that limit the effectiveness of disclosure: bounded rationality and herding.[62] The former refers to the limited capacity of individuals to process information because of their limited computational and mnemonic abilities. This can explain investors' flawed understanding of disclosed information, particularly as regards complex financial products.[63] Herding in financial markets is typically ascribed to peer pressure, as well as reputational and career motivations (such as most prominently compensation packages in financial institutions) which push decision-makers to ignore disclosed information, and rely instead on the safer (in the short-term) follow-the-herd strategy.[64]

What can probably be observed is that the role of disclosure, while remaining central within the overall functioning of financial markets, has become residual in the context of debt capital markets. This is all the more visible once the transactional and product evolutions, discussed in Chapter 4, are taken under consideration. Debt capital markets have evolved in a dramatic way, particularly if

[59] See Erik Gerding, 'Disclosure 2.0: Can Technology Solve Overload, Complexity, and Other Information Failure' (2016) 90 Tulane Law Review 1143, 1155–1156, noting the different level of information included for instance in shares, preference share, bonds and so on.

[60] See Avgouleas, 'What Future for Disclosure' (n 48).

[61] See Daniel Kahnemann and Amos Tversky, 'Prospect Theory: An Analysis of Decision under Risk' (1979) 47 Econometrica; Amos Tversky and Daniel Kahnemann, 'Rational Choice and the Framing of Decisions' (1986) 59 Journal of Business. All this means that individual choices can be manipulated by the way in which information is presented, and the framing is of course stronger with less sophisticated decision-makers.

[62] See Emilios Avgouleas, 'The Global Financial Crisis and the Disclosure Paradigm in European Financial Regulation: The Case for Reform' (2009) 6 European Company and Financial Law Review 440, 453.

[63] ibid. See also Steven Schwarcz, 'Disclosure's Failure in the Subprime Mortgage Crisis' (2008) Utah Law Review 1109.

[64] See Avgouleas, 'The Global Financial Crisis' (n 62), 453–454.

compared to equity capital markets, and the structure of disclosure regulation may well be out of synch with the challenges presented by innovated debt products. This is of course the reality of capital markets dominated by dynamics of private ordering, which are discussed in the next section.

3.2 The role of private ordering

The dynamics of product innovation examined in Chapter 4 of this book need to be understood as the result of a very specific process that relies on the input of market participants—indeed private ordering. This concept may be subject to slightly different understandings across areas of law, but generally speaking it is conceived as a form of delegation of certain areas of regulation from public authorities to private market actors.[65] It is also important to understand it as a form of legal decentralization, both in the sense of rule-making being shifted from the public to the private sphere, and also in terms of creating spaces for contractual forms and relationships arising out of private groups.[66]

The rationale for private ordering resides in some of the efficiency goals analysed in Chapter 3 of this book, and particularly in the opportunity to reduce costs associated with regulation.[67] In the specific area of business law, this cost-saving rationale acquires an even greater magnitude, because private market actors have traditionally been deemed capable of operating more efficiently (and effectively) than public authorities.[68]

Delving further into the context of finance law, the development of specific segments, such as the structured credit market or derivatives, was very much the result of the prioritization of the same efficiency rationale. In this context, efficiency was upheld through legislative processes and at common law.[69] Above everything else though, it was very much the case of practices coming from the industry and

[65] See Avery Katz, 'Taking Private Ordering Seriously' (1996) 144(5) University of Pennsylvania Law Review.

[66] ibid, 1745–1746. Katz points to a number of useful works in this area, among which Lisa Bernstein, 'Opting Out of the Legal System: Extralegal Contractual Relations in the Diamond Industry' (1992) 21 Journal of Legal Studies 115; Alan Schwartz and Robert Scott, 'The Political Economy of Private Legislation' (1995) 143 University of Pennsylvania Law Review 595.

[67] On the more general scope and aims of private ordering, see Clark Havinghurst, 'Foreword: The Place of Private Accrediting Among the Instruments of Government' (1994) 57 Law and Contemporary Problems 9–10.

[68] See Steven Schwarcz, 'Private Ordering' (2002) 97(1) Northwestern University Law Review 319, 322. Schwarcz explains that this is why in the sphere of business law this delegation has occurred with very limited procedural constraints. In the context of corporate law, the presumed efficiency of private ordering is recognized with the capacity of contractual rules to respond to market forces better than mandatory rules. See for a critique Michael Galanis, 'Vicious Spirals in Corporate Governance: Mandatory Rules for Systemic (Re)Balancing' (2011) 31(2) Oxford Journal of Legal Studies.

[69] On the efficiency of common law doctrines, see the explanation by Eric Posner, 'Law, Economics and Inefficient Norms' (1996) 144(5) University of Pennsylvania Law Review 1703.

market participants (banks, investment firms, lawyers) becoming crystallized into legislation or common law doctrine. Without too much repetition,[70] the development of securitization in the UK and in the US was the result of two legal constructions: true sale and bankruptcy remoteness.[71] These two legal characterizations epitomize the extent to which the efficiency rationale was endorsed at common law level. As an illustration, characterizing the transfer of assets from the originator to the SPV as a true sale provided efficiency to the originator's balance sheet;[72] similarly, recognizing the bankruptcy remoteness of the SPV from the originator had the effect of preventing the substantive consolidation of the two entities' estates, in the event of the originator's insolvency.[73]

As a consequence of this legal and regulatory approach, structured finance remained at best indirectly regulated before 2008, being outside the remit of more traditional statutory regulation.[74] At the same time, relevant contractual developments, which need to be understood as the effect of private ordering, went unfettered and were instead facilitated by a regulatory approach that remained geared towards economic efficiency rationales.[75]

The same rationale explains the trajectory of the securitization market, which grew to optimize the capital efficiency of originators' (chiefly banks) balance sheets. Attendant areas of capital markets developed in accordance with similar

[70] Similar discussions on securitization and the repo market have been conducted in greater details in Chapter 4 of this book, and earlier in this chapter as an illustration of market discipline.

[71] These were examined in Chapter 4.

[72] There is a long-standing academic debate as to whether the transfer of receivables to the SPV should instead be configured as secured financing, where the assets are pledged as security. This characterization of the transaction would of course be detrimental to the goal of securitization, which is to move assets off the originator's balance sheet. Risks of recharacterization are very rare in English courts, where the tendency is to uphold the contractual structure devised by the parties. See as an illustration *Mahonia Ltd v JP Morgan Chase Bank* [2004] EWHC 1938. The situation is somewhat different in the US, where this area of law is governed by Art 9 of the UCC, and courts have to assess whether a transfer of risks and receivables has actually occurred (the criteria for which were outlined in *Fox v Peck Iron and Metal Company Inc.*, 25 B.R. 674 (Bankr. S.D.Cal. 1982); *Matter of Bevil, Bresler & Shulman Asset Management Corporation*, 67 B.R. 557, 559 (D.N.J. 1986)). See also Steven Schwarcz, Bruce Markell, and Lissa Lamkin Broome, *Securitisation, Structured Finance and Capital Markets*, LexisNexis, 2004, 37–43 and 69–70; Philip Wood, *Project Finance, Securitisations, Subordinated Debt*, Sweet & Maxwell, 2007, 112.

[73] Allowing upon insolvency the creditors of the originator to lodge claims on the assets held by the SPV would defy the purpose of securitization because it would drastically compromise the interests of SPV investors. Moreover, the likelihood of substantive consolidation would highly affect the rating of securitized bonds, thereby hindering investor appetite. Substantive consolidation is not a risk in English law, given courts' undisputed reliance on the *Salomon* doctrine, which emerged in cases such as *Re Polly Peck International Plc* [1996] 1 BCLC 428. In the US, courts employ the doctrine of fraudulent transfer (*Sampsell v Imperial Paper & Color Corp.* 313 U.S. 215 (1941)) whereby they grant consolidation of two entities' assets as a remedy for a fraudulent transfer. The risk of this approach is mitigated by the inclusion of so-called separateness covenants. See Schwarcz and others, *Securitisation* (n 72), 69–70; Wood, *Project Finance* (n 72), 125; Kettering Kenneth, 'Securitization and its Discontents: The Dynamics of Financial Product Development' (2008) 29(4) Cardozo Law Review 1553.

[74] Posner, 'Law, Economics' (n 69), 1702, explaining, from a US standpoint, the typical features of statutory regulation and the interest groups that are taken under consideration in the process.

[75] See Dan Awrey, 'Complexity, Innovation, and the Regulation of Modern Financial Markets' (2012) 2 Harvard Business Law Review 235, 258.

legal and regulatory mechanisms, and notable examples can be made with respect to the repo market and derivatives. The former prospered before 2008 due to the flexibility afforded to lenders (money market mutual funds)[76] and the level of security that they received through the rehypothecation of collateral in the event of the borrower's default.[77] Derivatives represent an even greater manifestation of the application of private ordering, particularly once over-the-counter (OTC) trading became the established practice in the fifteen years prior to the global financial crisis. In essence, OTC derivatives are bilateral contracts and their liberalization in the early 2000s[78] was justified by the belief that contractual relationships established by market participants[79] would lead to efficient outcomes, both for the parties in the contract and the market as a whole.[80] In this context, the role of the International Swaps and Derivatives Association (ISDA), a trade organization representing the participants in the derivatives market since 1985,[81] were instrumental to the development and standardization of relevant legal documentation, and to address legal and operational issues in the market.[82] At the same time, the OTC market was heavily shaped by the role of influential market participants, namely the big dealer banks, who contributed to the standardization of attendant derivatives contracts and to spur liquidity in the market.[83]

Consistent with what has been said so far is the widely held belief that parties in financial contracts can fend for themselves through arm's-length contracting. This refers to the assumption that parties are able to protect their own interests by negotiating terms in good faith.[84] This orientation has been supported at common

[76] In the US for instance, where title to the collateral does not pass from borrower to lender, transactional efficiency is preserved due to the 'automatic stay' exception under US bankruptcy law. See Cullen, 'The Repo Market' (n 39).

[77] Gorton and Metrick, 'Regulating the Shadow Banking System' (n 37), 276–279. At the EU level this was regulated through the EU Financial Collateral Directive 2002/47/EC.

[78] Critically, the difference between hedging and speculative derivatives vanished gradually in pre-crisis years, giving way to the wider application of OTC deals. See Lynn Stout, 'Derivatives and the Legal Origins of the 2008 Credit Crisis' (2011) 1 Harvard Business Law Review 1.

[79] It will be remembered that the standard contractual form employed in derivatives contracts is the so-called ISDA Master Agreement, whereby ISDA is the prime example of a trade organization that reflects the interests and inputs of participants in the OTC market. See www.isda.org (last accessed on 22/04/2024).

[80] See for an explanation Lynn Stout, 'Why the Law Hates Speculators: Regulation and Private Ordering in the Market for OTC Derivatives' (1999) 48 Duke Law Journal 701.

[81] See www.isda.org/about-isda/ (last accessed on 22/04/2024).

[82] Before the inception of the ISDA master agreement for instance, individual contracts were negotiated and drafted ad hoc, on a transaction basis, which of course hindered the necessary level of standardization and market development. See Norman Feder, 'Deconstructing Over-the-Counter Derivatives' (2002) 677 Columbia Business Law Review 736.

[83] See ISDA, 'Concentration of OTC Derivatives Among Major Dealers', ISDA Research Note, Issue 4, 2010, available at www.isda.org (last accessed on 22/04/2024), where it is confirmed that, as of June 2010, the largest dealer banks (also referred to as the big 14) were counterparties to around 82% of total outstanding swap contracts.

[84] In this sense *Katz v Oak Industries Inc.*, 508 A.2d 873 (Del. Ch. 1986), where it was clearly stated that 'Modern contract law has generally recognized an implied covenant to the effect that each party to a contract will act with good faith towards the other with respect to the subject matter of the contract',

law level, both in the US and the UK,[85] and it has become an ideal doctrine to legitimize avoiding regulatory intrusion in matters that are seen as the prerogative of transaction counterparties. To contextualize this contention, it is important to remember what was said in Chapter 5 about product innovation and its dynamics, particularly with respect to the parties that drive this process. Large financial institutions stand behind the standardization of contractual terms, and while their conduct in the process of selling financial products to the public is tightly regulated,[86] the design of the contractual terms remains shaped by private ordering mechanisms, which remain beyond the scope of regulatory intervention.[87] In the context of debt capital markets though, this arrangement has led to widening the information gap between different participants in the market, especially under conditions of complexity.[88] Post-2008 litigation shows very clearly that investors in structured products were unable to monitor the level of risk-taking that they were embarking on. Assumptions of arm's-length contracting were crashing against the highly complex transactions and products, which caused information failures even among sophisticated investors.[89]

The failure of private ordering in this context is best captured by Galanis, who addressed it as a process of rent expropriation at the expense of parties with a contractual power disadvantage.[90] As in other areas of capital markets, regulatory mechanisms flowing from the orthodoxy of economic efficiency have proven ineffective. Moreover, such orthodoxy proposes, in the specific context of private ordering, the question as to which institution should be in charge of setting norms

and also that 'The rights and obligations of the various parties are or should be spelled out in that documentation'.

[85] A similar orientation in the UK emerges from cases such as *JP Morgan Chase Bank v Springwell Navigation Corp.* [2008] EWHC (Comm) 1186; *Titan Steel Wheels Ltd v Royal Bank of Scotland Plc* [2010] EWHC (Comm) 211.

[86] This is covered by a variety of conduct rules which in the UK are enshrined in the FCA COB Rules (see www.handbook.fca.org.uk/handbook/COBS/1/?view=chapter (last accessed on 22/04/2024)), which flow from the EU MiFID and MiFID II instruments, while in the US relevant provisions were introduced under the Dodd-Frank Act 2010, Title VII.

[87] One argument here is that the complexity of financial products innovated in the pre-crisis years defied the ability of regulators to understand their consequence, and similarly it led investors to misprice the value and risks of the new product. See on this Wallace Turbeville, 'Derivatives Innovation in the Era of Financial Deregulation', Demos Report, June 2013.

[88] An illustration is the interest rate swap mis-selling scandal that, both in the UK and in the US, highlighted the input of financial institutions in the design of financial products, and in crafting contractual terms that would insulate them from liabilities. See Vincenzo Bavoso, 'Financial Innovation, Derivatives and the UK and US Interest Rate Swap Scandals: Drawing New Boundaries for the Regulation of Financial Innovation' (2016) 7(2) Global Policy.

[89] See Vincenzo Bavoso, 'Filling the Accountability Gap in Structured Finance Transactions: The Case for a Broader Fiduciary Obligation' (2017) 23(2) Columbia Journal of European Law. Most prominently, the action brought by the SEC against Goldman Sachs in 2010 epitomized the layers of complexities and conflicts of interest emerging in the context of structured products, and the ensuing information gap between parties in those contracts.

[90] Galanis, 'Vicious Spirals' (n 68), 361–362. More specifically, albeit in the context of corporate law, Galanis debunks the idea of spontaneous order, upon which private ordering stands.

(and which is best placed to do so): the legislation through Parliament, courts, or the community of market participants.[91] While answering this is outside the scope of this present discussion, it is important to conclude this section by stressing two points. First, there is little theoretical reason to presume that norms flowing from private groups tend towards efficiency more than those coming from government institutions.[92] Second, efficiency claims have very seldom found any empirical validation, beyond the cost-saving argument.

This discussion moves now to another critical element of market discipline regulation, which is represented by the employment of private credit ratings in debt capital markets.

3.3 The role of credit rating agencies

The presence of credit rating agencies in debt capital markets was encountered in Chapter 4 in connection with the mechanics of bond issues. Over the last four decades the relentless growth of these segments of financial markets has revealed the centrality and importance of these ratings, and particularly the entities issuing them. It is no exaggeration to say that credit rating agencies (CRAs) have progressively become the arbiters of debt capital markets, given that issuers typically rely on two ratings for the credit assessment of their securities.[93]

In the context of this discussion, it is important to point more specifically at the regulatory framework within which CRAs operate and the rationale for their role in debt capital markets. It is well known that CRAs became a more prominent feature in capital markets in connection with the growth of bond markets—again, a phenomenon explored both in Chapter 2 in its historical dimension, and in Chapter 4 where the transactional structure of bonds was examined. The development of debt securities in the 1980s spurred the necessity for a new type of informational intermediation between issuers and investors in capital markets,[94] a type of intermediation that is traditionally associated with the role of banks in the context of the relationship with their customers.[95] The steep growth of debt capital markets in that period also triggered a fundamental change in the revenue structure of CRAs, which until then had relied on fees from investor subscriptions,

[91] Katz, 'Taking Private Ordering Seriously' (n 65), 1747–1748.

[92] Posner, 'Law, Economics' (n 69), 1724. Posner explains that both sets of norms suffer from similar qualitative failures. See also Galanis, 'Vicious Spirals' (n 68), 361–362.

[93] See Steven Schwarcz, 'Private ordering and Public Markets: The Rating Agency Paradox' (2022) 2002(1) University of Illinois Law Review 2.

[94] The added value of this intermediation is the information that CRAs produce, to the extent that it improves investors' ability to assess risks. See Richard Herring and Edward Kane, 'How to Reform the Credit-Rating Process to Support a Sustainable Revival of Private-Label Securitization' (2012) 2(1) Quarterly Journal of Finance 2.

[95] Christopher Bruner, 'States, Markets, and Gatekeepers: Public-Private Regulatory Regimes in an Era of Economic Globalization' (2008) 30(125) Michigan Journal of International Law 134.

to eventually move to an issuer-pay model, whereby CRAs would be paid fees by the same entities whose debt securities they were rating.[96] Most importantly, CRAs were, and remained, private corporations that were entrusted with the crucial assessment of issuers' creditworthiness, that is, the likelihood of their timely payment on the securities. And that is precisely the information that they intermediate to investors through the ratings they issue.[97]

The essence of that function is a gatekeeping one, which is common to other areas of capital markets, and in fact arose conceptually in the 1930s with other New Deal reforms in the US. These were particularly aimed at maintaining fair and orderly markets and protecting investors, by inter alia requiring issuers of securities to disclose all material information, so that investors could reach informed decisions.[98] Gatekeepers in that context were entrusted with the task of serving investors by verifying or assessing the disclosure that they were receiving from issuers.[99] In defining that function, the SEC put further emphasis on the independence of specific professionals as gatekeepers to the public securities markets.[100] Independence here needs to be understood as a guarantee that the gatekeeper's verification (in this case the credit rating) is the offspring of its reputational credibility, and that the professional would not risk its reputational capital to favour one client.[101]

This form of regulation through private market actors is particularly evident in the context of the credit rating industry. In the US in particular, CRAs were given regulatory powers as a result of being designated as NRSROs (nationally recognized statistical rating organizations) in 1975.[102] By virtue of that designation, CRAs could issue ratings that would satisfy the requirements of the SEC.[103] Similarly, at the international level, the Basel Committee in its second iteration

[96] Frank Partnoy, 'How and Why Credit Rating Agencies Are Not Like Other Gatekeepers', University of San Diego, School of Law, Legal Studies Research Paper Series, No 07-46, 2006.

[97] Steven Schwarcz, 'Private Ordering of Public Markets: The Rating Agency Paradox' (2002) 2002(1) University of Illinois Law Review 6, where Schwarcz explains that CRAs formulate their ratings based on the information they receive from issuers, and the reliability of their rating is effectively dependent on how reliable is the information they receive from issuers.

[98] Comissioner Isaac C Hunt, Jr, 'Speech by SEC Commissioner: Accountants as Gatekeepers—Adding Security and Value to the Financial Reporting System', US Securities & Exchange Commission, Arlington Virginia, 26 October 2001.

[99] See John Coffee, 'The Attorney as Gatekeeper: An Agenda for the SEC' (2003) 103 Columbia Law Review 1293, 1296. Coffee provides examples of different types of gatekeepers, among which, auditors, securities analysis, as well as rating agencies.

[100] See Revision of the Commission's Auditor Independence Requirements, Securities Act Release No 33-7870, 65 Fed. Reg. 43,148, 43,150 July 12, 2000.

[101] Coffee, 'The Attorney as Gatekeeper' (n 99), 1297. Of course, the string of events in the early 2000s, culminating with the so-called accounting scandals in North America and Europe, proved this assumption to be completely misplaced.

[102] See 'Statement of Lawrence J White for the Committee on Banking, Housing, and Urban Affairs', US Senate, 26 September 2007.

[103] Under Rule 3a-7 of the Investment Company Act 1940, 15 USC, S80a (2000), investment grade credit ratings have the effect of exempting certain financings from the registration requirements under the same act.

of the Accords entrenched the importance of external credit ratings by allowing banks to employ them in order to calibrate the riskiness of their assets and determine the relevant risk weight.[104] In essence, Basel II induced an excessive reliance on credit ratings, and critically, on the underlying quantitative risk models, developed internally by the big banks.[105] At the EU level, for a long time, before the GFC of 2008, the EU Commission maintained that no specific legislation was needed in the area of CRAs, and instead it expressed confidence that the pre-eminently self-regulatory structure of the rating industry (chiefly revolving around the IOSCO code of conduct) would be sufficient.[106]

In line with the other discussions developed earlier in this chapter, the regulatory framework of credit ratings was informed by an economic efficiency rationale, aimed chiefly at reducing the information asymmetry between issuers of debt securities and investors.[107] Schwarcz explains that the same rationale is at the heart of securities regulation more generally, with the difference (crucial in this context) that while the function of securities regulation is to correct market failures, CRAs are driven by profit-making opportunities.[108] This observation is important to understand the development of the rating business and some of the regulatory problems that emerged from it over the past twenty years. These materialized at the apex of the 2008 GFC with a wave of rating downgrades that revealed the inaccuracy of CRAs' ratings in the period leading up to the crisis, particularly as regards the ratings of securitized bonds.[109] Of course, this was only a rehearsal of very similar failures that had been observed a few years earlier, with the sudden downgrades of corporate bonds during the wave of North American accounting scandals (Enron, WorldCom, and Tyco, among others, and then Parmalat in Italy).[110]

For the purpose of this discussion, emphasis is laid on specific regulatory issues that relate to the structured finance market, and which became more urgent in the pre-2008 years. The next chapter examines some relevant post-crisis regulatory corrections, among which those related to the CRA industry. The first concern here relates to the conflicting position that CRAs have with the entities whose products they rate. As announced earlier, this is the effect of the evolution of the

[104] This is in the context of the capital adequacy framework. See Basel Committee on Banking Supervision 'A New Capital Adequacy Framework', BIS, June 1999, 5.

[105] See Douglas Arner, 'The Global Credit Crisis of 2008: Causes and Consequences' (2009) 43(1) The International Lawyer 132. It needs to be noted that there is an attempt to reduce this reliance under the post-2008 Basel III framework.

[106] See ESME's report to the European Commission, 'Role of Credit Rating Agencies', June 2008, 7.

[107] See Schwarcz, 'Private Ordering' (n 97), 10.

[108] ibid.

[109] Herring and Kane, 'How to Reform the Credit-Rating Process' (n 94), 14. The authors explain that in the context of CDO tranches, nearly 60% of triple-A tranches were downgraded by at least three notches.

[110] ibid. For a discussion, see also Vincenzo Bavoso, *Explaining Financial Scandals: Corporate Governance, Structured Finance and the Enlightened Sovereign Control Paradigm*, CSP, 2013, chapter 4.

CRAs' business model (issuer-pay), and also of the transactional innovations in the structured finance market.[111] Conflicts of interest have been exacerbated by the complexity of structured products, and the ensuing increased asymmetry of information they created, because in that context CRAs not only provided a rating, but also a consulting service (so-called confirmation). This is an ancillary service whereby, before rating the product, CRAs advise the issuer during the structuring of the transaction, and essentially confirm the likelihood of a specific rating.[112] This practice led to the problematic alignment of commercial interests between issuers and agencies, because the latter were keen to pocket fees from issuers and avoid losing clients to other agencies, while the issuers were 'shopping' for the best possible ratings. In the process, the gatekeeping function attributed to CRAs became highly compromised, as confirmed by post-2008 studies.[113]

The second relevant concern is related to the way in which CRAs formulate their ratings, which is the result of rating methodologies developed in-house by the agencies. The rating of complex debt products became of course a multifaceted assessment, because it entailed moving from gauging the creditworthiness of single-asset corporate bonds, to pools of (fairly) homogeneous assets in plain vanilla securitized bonds, to CDO tranches with heterogenous assets pooled together in accordance with correlation formulae. The complexity and the range of variables to be taken into account in each specific situation can vary enormously[114], and this question is still pressing at present with respect to the rating of CLOs, and the claim of over-collateralization attached to CLOs' senior tranches.[115]

While differences in the structure and profile of these products should warrant the employment of bespoke methodologies, this has typically not been the case. Instead, the dynamics of ratings has been characterized by an inverted process, whereby the structuring exercise on the part of issuers was chiefly informed by the prospect of receiving a certain rating.[116] This 'rating game' was driven precisely by the underlying methodologies, which enabled awarding a triple-A rating to

[111] It should be noted that structured finance issuers pay the bulk of the fee upfront with an annual surveillance fee, whereas more traditional corporate bonds would have two or three CRAs rating their debt and an annual fee would be paid to each of them. See ESME's report, 'Role of Credit Rating Agencies' (n 106).

[112] Frank Partnoy, 'How and Why Credit Rating Agencies Are Not Like Other Gatekeepers', University of San Diego, Legal Studies Research Paper Series, No 07-46, 2006, 71.

[113] See John Coffee, 'What Went Wrong? An Initial Enquiry into the Causes of the 2008 Financial Crisis' (2009) 9(1) Journal of Corporate Law Studies.

[114] See ESME's report, 'Role of Credit Rating Agencies' (n 106), 4–5. See also Regulation (EC) No 1060/2009 L302/5 (40).

[115] See Fitch Ratings Inc, 'The Rating Process', Special Report, December 2011,17. On questions raised on this, see Rod Dubitski, 'CLOs, Private Equity, Pensions and Systemic Risk' (Spring 2020) The Journal of Structured Finance; Frank Partnoy, 'The Looming Bank Collapse' (July/August, 2020) The Atlantic.

[116] Andrew Johnston, 'Corporate Governance is the Problem, not the Solution: A Critical Appraisal of the European Regulation on Credit Rating Agencies' (2011) 11(2) Journal of Corporate Law Studies 409.

tranches whose underlying assets were predominantly triple-B (or worse). As a result, the design of new products was driven by the underlying methodologies, and became a sort of mathematical game (given the complex quantitative models) that a handful of dominant issuers (large financial institutions) knew how to master.[117]

Beyond compromising the assessment of the underlying assets' creditworthiness (and pricing), these rating methodologies became in essence a form of rating arbitrage that allowed a section of market participants to gain unfair advantages over investors, keeping in the process regulators in the dark due to the opaqueness and arbitrariness of the underlying rating methodologies.[118] The outcome of this process (an overarching mispricing of credit) counters the efficiency claims that are traditionally associated with market discipline and disclosure mechanisms.

4 Conclusion

This chapter provided a foundational understanding of the regulatory infrastructure permeating debt capital markets. It hinges on mechanisms of market discipline, which are discussed in the first part of this chapter, and on a number of applications of market discipline that are explored in the second part. After the GFC of 2008 this rather malleable architecture was increasingly supplemented by more direct legislation and substantive rules. These are analysed critically in the next chapter, which focuses also on the policy direction in debt capital markets, particularly in light of policy exercises conducted over the past ten years.

As was unveiled in this chapter, the overarching assumption at the heart of market discipline relies on a sequence of actions by market participants (a typical example is banks' bondholders), who are entrusted with the monitoring of the market, and with taking actions on the basis of the information gathered in the process. These actions are in turn supposed to result in corrective steps, such as, more immediately, prices moving in line with the actions of market participants, and then also reformed behaviour on the part of the monitored banks' management.[119] It will also be remembered from the discussion conducted in Chapter 3 that this idealized sequence of market-based actions is consistent with assumptions of efficient markets that flow from neoclassical economics, and whose underpinnings were explored in Chapter 3. It could easily be inferred that market discipline is in fact a further deployment of those hypotheses, resulting in the specific area of capital markets in the use of a number of regulatory tools, such as disclosure, private ordering, private credit ratings.

[117] Partnoy, 'How and Why Credit Rating Agencies' (n 112), 80. Partnoy argued that because of this fundamental fallacy, CRAs became 'gate-openers', rather than gatekeepers.

[118] ibid, 75.

[119] This process is well synthesized by Llewellyn, *Inside the 'Black Box'* (n 40), 44.

In this chapter's critical overview it was clearly put forward that both market discipline and its applications suffer from a number of shortcomings, and as a result that idealized sequence of actions remains in most cases unrealized. It is well documented that managers in financial institutions are constrained in their monitoring role due to various factors, chiefly related to their incentive structure,[120] which often do not favour incurring monitoring costs. Similarly, the assumption of efficient pricing, related to the tenet of informational efficiency, has proven unreliable, which raises the issue that management may not change behaviour in the face of changes in prices.[121] These concerns are coupled with evidence of cognitive bias and herding behaviour affecting market participants, which means that management may not react to market signals (such as price changes), while they may well take short cuts and engage in short-term strategies. All this defies the idea of market discipline.

In the same vein, questions related to the nature of financial innovation, which were raised in Chapter 5, are explained in this chapter through the discussion on private ordering, which revealed the fallacy at its heart and the resulting rent extraction from parties with information advantages. What also became evident from the transactional analysis in Chapter 4 is that products innovated by virtue of market participants' wisdom have become a source of systemic concerns, something that parties alone are not capable of mitigating. The critique on the role of credit rating agencies also reveals deep-seated problems associated with the function of private corporations acting as arbiters of debt capital markets, because problems of conflicts of interest and rating methodologies have arisen repeatedly over the past twenty years.

In light of this emerging dissatisfaction with the mechanics of market discipline, the key appraisal that needs to be conducted in Chapter 7 is the degree to which substantive regulation supplements the mechanics of market discipline. Or whether, conversely, the body of regulation, and particularly the post-2008 architecture, is still hinging on the same assumptions underscoring market discipline and information efficiency.

[120] Supra Avgouleas and Cullen, 'Excessive Leverage' (n 31).
[121] Llewellyn, *Inside the 'Black Box'* (n 40), 44.

7
Critiquing regulation and policy-making in debt capital markets

1 Introduction

This chapter takes stock of the analysis conducted in Chapter 6, complementing it by examining the relevant pieces of regulation in the area of debt capital markets. A number of regulatory interventions characterized the post-2008 period, attempting to correct the failures that were identified as causes of the global financial crisis (GFC). It is important to remember that this took the shape of a global exercise, with the Dodd-Frank Act[1] in the US enacted in 2010, various EU regulations and directives, and most importantly, transnational efforts championed by the Basel III framework.

Critically, in the post-2008 years there has been a strong policy push, particularly since 2014, to further empower capital markets in those regions that are still dominated by bank-based financial systems. These initiatives culminated with the EU Capital Markets Union (CMU), a project engineered originally by the European Central Bank and the Bank of England (before Brexit, of course),[2] aimed at fully harmonizing and integrating European capital markets, and in the process rebalancing the over-reliance of continental European economies on bank-based sources of finance.[3] While in principle this project encompassed the whole of capital markets channels of intermediation, it became evident from the outset that it was primarily aimed at fostering EU-wide markets for securitization and bonds-type products.[4] These segments of capital markets featured prominently in the ensuing regulatory efforts, which are detailed later in this chapter.

In light of the discussions conducted earlier in this book, and of the proneness of debt capital markets to lead to instability and crises,[5] it is legitimate to question

[1] Dodd-Frank Wall Street Reform and Consumer Protection Act, Pub. L. 111–203.

[2] See Bank of England and European Central Bank, 'The Impaired EU Securitisation Market: Causes, Roadblocks, and How to Deal with Them', April, 2014; Bank of England and European Central Bank, 'The Case for a Better Functioning Securitisation Market in the European Union', Discussion Paper, May 2014.

[3] EU Commission Green Paper, 'Building a Capital Markets Union', Com(2015) 63 Final.

[4] See Daniela Gabor and Jakob Verstergaard, 'Capital Markets Union: The Systemic Issues Buried deep in the Market Infrastructure Plan' (April 2015) FEPS Policy Brief; Vincenzo Bavoso, 'Market-Based Finance, Debt and Systemic Risk: A Critique of the EU Capital Markets Union' (2018) Accounting, Economics and Law: A Convivium.

[5] This was explored in Chapter 5.

Debt Capital Markets. Vincenzo Bavoso, Oxford University Press.
DOI: 10.1093/oso/9780198893257.003.0007

the capacity of the current regulatory infrastructure to withstand episodes of financial instability. At the time of writing this book, fears of systemic shocks are rising once again due to a sequence of banking failures in the spring of 2023, particularly with the near collapse of Credit Suisse followed by its coerced merger with UBS.[6] The crises of these large banking conglomerates should not be a surprise, despite the huge regulatory efforts and the attendant measures intended to improve capital and liquidity of systemic banks and limit their leverage.[7] The progressive implementation of these requirements led to the improved health of systemic banks' balance sheet, which in turn brought widespread optimism in the post-2008 period about the state of financial markets. What was being downplayed though is the migration of risks from systemic banks to non-bank channels of intermediation, a phenomenon epitomized by the panic of 2020 involving new financial products (such as CLOs) intermediated by private equity funds instead of the usual banks.[8] Yet that panic did not come unforeseen, because only a year earlier the IMF had raised red flags on the fragility of the financial system, chiefly due to the level of private debt creation and outstanding debt exposures.[9]

With these concerns in mind, and in light of the current banking crises, it is useful to remember that contemporary financial markets are the offspring of a functional integration of banking and capital markets activities,[10] whereby systemic financial institutions play a central role in capital markets, directly or indirectly, thereby augmenting the interconnectedness between different segments of the financial system. As an illustration, this hidden interconnectedness was at the heart of the panic of 2020 where large banking institutions were found to be exposed to the downgrades and defaults in the CLO market, despite not being directly part of those transaction chains.[11] In essence, the financial system is as interconnected as it was before 2008, and with shocks coming from hidden corners of the financial system,[12] the risk of a systemic crisis cannot be seen as remote.

These recent events provide further impetus to the discussion conducted in this chapter, whose thrust is centred on the appraisal of both the regulatory infrastructure of debt capital markets, and the policy direction permeating recent trends. In particular, doubts on the merits of the EU CMU, and its focus on securitization and bonds, become more pressing in the context of the current instability, and of

[6] See Anita Hawser, 'How does UBS's takeover of Credit Suisse stack up financially?', *The Banker* (2 May 2023); Basel Committee on Banking Supervision, 'Report on the 2023 Banking Turmoil', BIS October 2023.

[7] These requirements are analysed later in this chapter in the context of Basel III.

[8] The mechanics of CLOs were explained in Chapter 4.

[9] IMF, 'Global Financial Stability Report', 2019, chapter 2; Adair Turner, *Between Debt and the Devil*, Princeton University Press, 2015.

[10] See Robert Hockett and Saule Omarova (2017) 102 'The Finance Franchise', Cornell Law Review.

[11] See Vincenzo Bavoso, 'Hail the New Private Debt Machine: Private Equity, Leveraged Loans, and Collateralised Loan Obligations' (2020) 14(3) Law and Financial Markets Review.

[12] See Brooke Masters, 'We haven't reduced financial risk, just transformed it', *Financial Times* (10 December 2022).

the wider warning signs in relation to excessive levels of private debt creation. The rest of this chapter starts with the analysis of key disclosure standards which are traditionally embedded in the prospectus and transparency regimes. Critically, this discussion ties in with the critique developed in Chapter 6 on the role of disclosure as a regulatory technique; it also offers a first window over the policy direction in this area of capital markets, where reforms to the EU prospectus regime have sought a more facilitative regulatory framework. This chapter moves on to discuss in section 3 relevant regulatory interventions in debt capital markets in the post-2008 period, chiefly in the areas of securitization, repurchase agreements, credit derivatives, and credit rating agencies. This analysis is complemented in section 4 by a discussion on product regulation.

A crucial regulatory assessment in this chapter revolves around the transnational role of the Basel III framework, engineered in the post-GFC period, and still to be fully implemented. Its impact on debt capital markets is analysed in section 5, by examining new capital, leverage, and liquidity requirements and their effect on the balance sheet of large financial institutions. Section 6 concludes this chapter by providing an initial assessment of these regulatory exercises in debt capital markets. A full discussion is reprised in Chapter 8.

2 Disclosure in practice: prospectus and transparency regimes

Without repeating the conceptual discussion conducted in Chapter on the use of disclosure in financial regulation, this section looks at the more specific regulatory and policy functions that disclosure performs in capital markets, through the prospectus and transparency regimes. The regulatory functions of disclosure have typically been associated with the informational efficiency of securities markets, and the optimization of resource allocation for the benefit of issuing firms. This in turn reduces costs for the same firms that access capital markets for capital raising purposes.[13] The effectiveness of this regulatory framework is traditionally associated with the capacity of a jurisdiction to foster deep capital markets, and more specifically with the development of market-based forms of capital raising, as opposed to bank-based ones. This dichotomy is particularly relevant in the context of EU policy-making, where efforts to harmonize and integrate EU-wide capital markets go back at least to the mid-1980s,[14] and have more recently gained momentum with the EU CMU.[15] As anticipated, disclosure regulation results in

[13] See Niamh Moloney, *EU Securities and Financial Markets Regulation*, Oxford University Press, 2014, 48–49. See also on the general attributes of disclosure regulation, Bernard Black, 'The Legal and Institutional Preconditions for Strong Securities Markets' (2001) 48 UCLA Law Review 781.

[14] See the Internal Market White Paper in 1985, 'Completing the Internal Market', COM (85) 310.

[15] See EU Commission Green Paper, 'Building a Capital Markets Union', Com (2015) 63 Final.

mandatory rules that require issuers of securities to make comprehensive initial disclosures and subsequently periodic disclosures linked to the occurrence of material events.[16]

The question of mandatory disclosure has been at the heart of regulatory and policy debates. Both in the US and Europe mandatory disclosure has been traditionally seen as instrumental to mitigating problems of information asymmetry (between issuers and investors) and related risks of frauds, and as an efficient pricing mechanism.[17] Questions have increasingly been raised as regards the effectiveness of mandatory disclosure to promote market efficiency, particularly given on the one hand the regulatory costs associated with disclosure, and on the other hand the findings of behavioural economics, which challenge the axiom that information is essential for informed decisions.[18] As was discussed in Chapter 3 of this book, broader questions of informational efficiency have similarly reassessed the extent to which the disclosure of information leads to pricing and allocative efficiency.[19]

Restating these policy questions is important because of the role that disclosure regulation plays towards the integration of capital markets, particularly in the EU context.[20] The harmonization of disclosure rules has long been regarded in this sense as a precondition for achieving some degree of market integration and the growth of cross-border activities.[21] In the EU context in particular, integration has been a policy priority, particularly as it encompassed the access to finance agenda, and the attendant aim to facilitate market-based financing for the SME sector.[22] Promoting this agenda has often come at the expense of a tighter implementation of disclosure rules, and in fact it has admittedly required some degree of calibration of the same rules and at times their deregulation.[23] This is important for the purpose of appraising, later in this chapter, the impact of disclosure in the specific area of debt capital markets and debt products. Before getting there, it is important

[16] These obligations are the essence of the prospectus and transparency regimes, of which more is said later in this section.

[17] See for a discussion Louise Gullifer and Jennifer Payne, *Corporate Finance Law*, Hart, 2020, chapter 11.

[18] This discussion was conducted in the context of Chapter 6 of this book. See also ibid, 546–548; Donald Langevoort, 'Taming the Animal Spirits of the Stock Markets: A Behavioural Approach to Securities Regulation' (2002) 97 North Western University Law Review 135; Emilios Avgouleas, 'The Global Financial Crisis and the Disclosure Paradigm in European Financial Regulation: The Case for Reform' (2009) 6(4) European Company and Financial Law Review.

[19] For a critique, see Lynn Stout, 'The Unimportance of Being Efficient: An Economic Analysis of Stock Market Pricing and Securities Regulation' (1988) 87 Michigan Law Review 613.

[20] See the discussion conducted in Moloney, *EU Securities* (n 13), 61; and also Eilis Ferran, *Building an EU Securities Market*, Cambridge University Press, 2004.

[21] See in this sense the efforts of the International Organization of Securities Commissions (IOSCO) with initiatives such as 'International Disclosure Principles for Cross-Border Offerings and Listings of Debt Securities by Foreign Issuers', 2007.

[22] See in this sense Moloney, *EU Securities* (n 13), 70; and also EU Commission Green Paper 'Building a Capital Markets Union', Com(2015) 63 Final.

[23] Moloney, *EU Securities* (n 13), 70 and 77.

to stress that disclosure rules have a specific perimeter of application, which is typically referred to as public market. This refers in other words to securities that are offered to the public, on a regulated market.[24]

By contrast, private markets refer to all those exceptions to the disclosure regime, some of which have already been encountered in Chapters 4 and 6. These are situations where the type of (qualified) investors involved in the issue warrant the exemption, the so-called private placements.[25] The same rationale explains the treatment of many bond issues and the general regulatory framework around wholesale debt markets. These tend to be dominated by sophisticated investors, who are not deemed to require information disclosed through the prospectus. At the same time, promoting the development of cross-border bond markets at the EU level required this type of regulatory calibration.[26] This policy question is elaborated further later in this section.

2.1 The main regulatory requirements

Following from the previous discussion, it is useful to point at the specific framework of disclosure rules in the context of debt markets. This is done by looking chiefly at EU and UK rules, with some reference to US law, bearing in mind though that the regulatory approach in this area of capital markets is characterized by a substantial degree of convergence, if at all because of the cross-border ambitions of most developed capital markets, as well as the efforts of transnational regulatory actors, such as IOSCO.[27] In this sense, the EU regulatory framework represents a pioneering experience in the way a single rulebook was adopted, and with the 'passport' system, whereby the authorization issued by an individual member state to a financial institution is valid for the provision of services or the performance of activities across the whole EU.[28]

[24] At the EU level in particular, the designation of regulated market indicates a trading venue that is consistent with the objectives of promoting market efficiency, integration, and investor protection. This language is embedded in the most recent regulatory instrument, the EU Prospectus Regulation, Regulation (EU) 2017/1129, particularly, Arts 3 and 4. Importantly, for the purpose of MiFID II classifications and the transparency obligations that apply to trading venues, these include regulated markets, multilateral trading facilities, and organized trading facilities. See Moloney, *EU Securities* (n 13), 469–472.

[25] The specific cases under the Regulation are detailed later in the chapter.

[26] For a discussion, see Gullifer and Payne, *Corporate Finance Law* (n 17), 670, observing in particular how a limited application of disclosure requirements in the context of bond issues is counterbalanced by the higher sophistication of bond investors, and also by contractual arrangements that are included in bonds' financial covenants. See also the discussion conducted in chapter 4 on the bond market.

[27] See n 21.

[28] This system is also known as the 'home member state' system, because authorization and supervision of the financial institution remain the responsibility of the home member state's national competent authority. For a full discussion, see Pierre Schammo, *EU Prospectus Law*, Cambridge University Press, 2011, part II; Eilis Ferran *Building an EU Securities Market*, Cambridge University Press, 2004, chapter 6.

At the EU level the EU Prospectus Regulation[29] replaced the Prospectus Directive 2003, and it was accompanied by delegated legislation.[30] The UK has retained this framework in the aftermath of Brexit.[31] In the US, the Securities Act 1933 provided a blueprint for the way in which offers of securities to the public should be governed, and the contents that a final prospectus should incorporate.[32]

Before analysing the technicalities of the different level of disclosure that the prospectus regime requires, and the attendant exceptions, it is useful to remember the type of information that issuers have to disclose in the prospectus. The overarching aim of the disclosure is to provide investors with the information that is necessary to reach an informed appraisal of: a) assets and liabilities, b) financial position, c) profits and losses, d) the prospects of the issuer and of any guarantor attached to the issue, e) the rights attached to the securities, f) the reasons for the issue.[33] While this set of information is clearly intended to equip investors in the context of bond issues (and even more so in the case of equity), the issuance of asset-backed securities requires a different type of disclosure, centred on the assets themselves, rather than the issuer. It will be remembered from the discussion in Chapter 4 that asset-backed securities are issued by SPVs (chiefly shell entities set up for the purpose of the structured finance transaction), and information about the issuer in such cases needs to be supplemented with details of the asset pool held by the SPV and the structure of the transaction.[34]

The prospectus comes of course in different forms, each reflecting a level of disclosure that is commensurate to the amount of information that is required in the context of the issue. This depends on the type of investors and on the securities that are issued. Generally speaking, the highest level of disclosure is achieved with the issue of shares, then debt securities issued to retail investors, and the least burdensome disclosure is in the context of debt securities issued to wholesale investors.[35]

[29] Regulation (EU) 2017/1129.

[30] Commission Delegated Regulation (EU) 2019/980.

[31] See European Union (Withdrawal) Act 2018. More specifically, see also Official Listing of Securities, Prospectus and Transparency (Amendment etc) (EU Exit) Regulation 2019. In the UK, prospectus rules are incorporated into the Prospectus Regulation Rules, which are part of the FCA Handbook. It is to be noted that the UK started a process of regulatory review, referred to as UK Edinburgh Reforms, and as part of this it seeks to redesign its financial services framework to reflect more competitiveness. As part of this process, the UK FCA has conducted a review of the prospectus regime, resulting in a draft proposal that was to be published for consultation in the first half of 2024.

[32] This was enshrined in s 10(a) of the Act. SEC rulemaking and later amendments supplement the US discipline, including Title 15 of the US Code S77j, on the information required in a prospectus, and also relevant sections of the Securities Exchange Act 1934 providing a route for remedial actions. For an overview of applicable US rules, see Philip Wood, *Regulation of International Finance*, Sweet and Maxwell, 2019, 550–556.

[33] See Prospectus Regulation, Art 6(1). The equivalent reference in the UK is in s 87A(2) Financial Services and Markets Act (FSMA) 2000.

[34] See PR Regulation Annexes C(2019) 2020 final, annex 19, ss 2 and 3.

[35] See Gullifer and Payne, *Corporate Finance Law* (n 17), 681, 682, where specific examples of this different regulatory calibration are provided, particularly in terms of information required in the context of share issues, and not required (or required in less extensive form) in the context of debt securities.

The level of disclosure that applies in each issue is typically dependent on choices made by the issuer, revolving around the type of securities to be offered, to whom they are offered, and critically whether they are issued on a regulated market.[36] As was explained in Chapter 4, issuers' rationale in debt capital markets diverges from that in equity markets, because in the latter, issuing companies seek to reach the widest possible range of investors, and adherence with disclosure obligations is essential to that end. Conversely, in debt capital markets, speed of transactions is often crucial, and issuers' priority is to place the securities with a group of qualified investors, thereby attracting less onerous and time-consuming disclosure obligations.[37] Critically, these choices trigger exemptions (or different regulatory calibrations) under the prospectus regime, which are discussed in the next section.

Importantly, disclosure obligations are also in place throughout the life of securities, after they are issued, under transparency requirements. These were initially introduced at the EU level (and then transposed into UK law) under the Transparency Directive in 2004,[38] whose function was to impose obligations upon the issuer to disclose information to the marketplace concerning the issuer itself. More recently, these periodic obligations have been supplemented with obligations that more specifically capture the necessity to maintain transparency in the markets where securities are traded, ensuring therefore the efficiency of secondary markets. This was done in 2014 with the adoption of MiFID II and MIFIR.[39]

With respect to debt securities, ongoing disclosure requirements play a more limited role, because of the very nature of the information to be disclosed, which concerns primarily shareholders and their corporate governance role. Such information is likely to be relevant anyway in case the same firm issues equity securities on a regulated market.[40] In the UK, the FCA Handbook includes Disclosure Guidance and Transparency Rules (referred to as DTR in the Handbook) that apply to debt securities admitted to trading on the main market or the Professional Securities Market (PSM).[41] These requirements entail annual financial reports and half-yearly reports for issuers whose debt securities are traded on the main market, unless the securities are issued only as wholesale securities.[42] These

[36] One critical question is whether debt securities are traded on a regulated market, or a segment of a regulated market specifically suited for qualified investors. At the EU level, these differences and calibrations are captured in Art 6 of the Prospectus Regulation.

[37] Often, these securities are issued on the Professional Securities Market as far as the UK is concerned.

[38] Directive 2004/109/EC. This has now been amended by Directive (EU) 2022/2464 which also incorporates disclosure of corporate sustainability reporting.

[39] Respectively, Directive 2014/65/EU; and Regulation 648/2012.

[40] See Gullifer and Payne, *Corporate Finance Law* (n 17), 690. A similar rationale applies as regards pre- and post-trade transparency requirements imposed by MiFID II and MiFIR. See Moloney, *EU Securities* (n 13), 503–505.

[41] This is by virtue of the UK Listing Rules, LR 17.3 as the requirement extends beyond the definition of regulated market.

[42] See DTR 4, and particularly 4.4.2 for the case of wholesale securities.

requirements are less onerous for issuers whose securities are listed only on the PSM.[43]

As anticipated earlier, post-trade transparency requirements have been extended to debt securities with the inception of MiFID II and MIFIR, which have essentially brought different trading venues under the same regulatory remit.[44] These trading venues, which include multilateral trading facilities (MTFs), the PSM in the UK, as well as organized trading facilities (OTFs), are under a duty to disclose to the public the price, volume, and time of transactions traded on that venue.[45]

2.2 Narrowing the perimeter of application: the exemptions

While in principle issuers of debt securities should have the interest to reach the widest possible range and volume of investors, the dynamics of bond markets are rather different. Eurobonds for instance (discussed in different contexts in Chapters 2 and 4) are in most cases not offered to the public but are instead more quickly and directly placed with a specific group of sophisticated investors. Wherever investors are classified as sophisticated (qualified), exceptions (or at least different calibrations) of disclosure requirements are triggered.

It is useful to examine the UK rulebook to understand the mechanics of these exceptions and when they are triggered.[46] Firstly, section 86 of FSMA stipulates that if the offer falls within the scope of Article 1(4) of the Prospectus Regulation, the obligation to publish a prospectus does not apply.[47] The list of cases where the obligation does not apply is exhaustive and it includes ten situations[48], but most critically, offers of securities addressed to: a) qualified investors only;[49] b) fewer than 150 persons other than qualified investors (sometimes referred to as private placements).[50] It needs to be stressed, though, that notwithstanding these situations, if

[43] See LR 17.3.4.

[44] See MIFIR Art 8.

[45] ibid, Art 10. Art 21 extends the same obligation upon investment firms. See n 40.

[46] While this analysis does not focus specifically on US law, it was noted earlier that disclosure rules and their exceptions operate in similar ways. As was mentioned earlier in n 32, under US securities law offers of securities to the public must be either in compliance with prospectus requirements, and thus be registered with the US Securities and Exchange Commission (SEC), or alternatively they can fall under exemptions laid down under the Securities Act 1933. Among these exemptions, it is worth noting the sale to qualified institutional buyers (Rule 144A), and offerings to accredited investors (Section 4(a)(2)) and Regulation D.

[47] Financial Services and Markets Act 2000, s 86(1)(aa). Art 1(4) of the Prospectus Regulation is transposed into section 1.2.3 of the Prospectus Regulation Rules sourcebook in the UK. Section 1.2.3 provides a list of offers of securities to the public where the obligation to publish a prospectus does not apply.

[48] See Prospectus Regulation Rules sourcebook, section 1.2.3 (Art 1(4) of the Prospectus Regulation).

[49] Qualified investors are defined in Art 2(e) of the Prospectus Regulation.

[50] See Prospectus Regulation Art1(4). Other relevant exceptions refer to the size of the offer and the denomination of the securities.

the securities are admitted to trading on a regulated market (such as for instance the Main Market in the UK) the Prospectus Regulation Rules will still apply, again with a number of exceptions.[51]

The question of the market where debt securities are traded is an important one, and in the previous section it was reminded that some post-2008 regulatory changes have expanded the scope and meaning of 'regulated markets', which in some instances include multilateral trading facilities and organized trading facilities. What needs to be stressed here is that even where debt securities are traded 'over-the-counter' (OTC, as is most typically the case), they may still be listed on a market.[52] The choice of the trading venue is the issuer's and it determines the level of regulation that is required.

In the UK there are two main options: the LSE's Main Market, which is the regulated market for debt securities, and the Professional Securities Market, which stands as an MTF. If debt securities are admitted to trading on the former, publishing a prospectus is required unless an exemption under Article 1(2) or 1(5) of the Prospectus Regulation is triggered, and they refer chiefly to: debt securities issued by collective investment undertakings other than closed-end type; debt securities issued by a range of public entities and bodies; debt securities guaranteed by a government or local authority[53]; debt securities issued in a continuous or repeated manner by a credit institution, subject to limits on the total aggregated consideration.[54] Where debt securities are admitted to trading on the PSM, the publication of a prospectus is not required, unless of course the securities are issued to the public on that trading venue. Trading on the PSM will anyway require listing particulars, which represent a less onerous form of disclosure.[55]

Finally, it is also possible for issuers to have debt securities not admitted to trading on any market, without an offer to the public, in which case neither a prospectus nor listing particulars are required.

2.3 The EU policy agenda and different types of prospectuses

The growth agenda at the EU level, together with the policy drive of the CMU, have led to a strong focus on the place of SMEs in capital markets and their capital raising opportunities. As a result, designing efficient access to finance for SMEs has progressively become a central strategy of EU policy-makers.[56] In light of this, the

[51] See FSMA s 85(2), and also the Prospectus Regulation Art 1(2)(3)(5), outlining the case of debt securities issued by states or public authorities, or debt securities issued by banks in a continuous or repeated manner.

[52] The reasons for listing are explored in Chapter 4, section 2.

[53] See Prospectus Regulation, Art 1(2); and the equivalent in the UK FSMA, s 85(2) and (6).

[54] See Prospectus Regulation, Art 1(5)(i); and the equivalent in the UK FSMA, s 86(4a).

[55] These are detailed in the UK LR 4.2 and 4.2.2.

[56] While this policy agenda has long been at the heart of the EU Commission's priorities (see for instance Commission, 'Risk Capital: A Key to Job Creation in the EU', Sec (1998) 552), post-2008 policy

Prospectus Regulation included specifically calibrated provisions for two types of prospectuses,[57] namely the simplified prospectus for secondary issues, and the EU growth prospectus.[58] Generally speaking, the policy objective of these provisions is to facilitate access to capital markets for SMEs by simplifying the regulatory process and reducing capital raising costs.[59]

The facilitative agenda here is apparent, particularly in the context of debt securities. The simplified prospectus is available for secondary issues, where the securities have been admitted to trading on a regulated market, or an SME growth market, for at least eighteen months prior to the issuance, and where the issued securities are fungible with existing securities.[60] It is also to be noted that issuers of debt securities can use the simplified prospectus for secondary issues even where the issued securities are not fungible with any pre-existing securities, as long as they have had equity securities admitted to trading on a regulated market, or an SME growth market, for the previous eighteen months.[61]

With respect to the EU growth prospectus, this is a simple and standardized document, designed to be easy to complete by the issuer and easily accessible to investors.[62] This format can be used by a range of entities that do not have securities admitted to trading on a regulated exchange[63], hence it fulfils the objective of attracting new entities (and particularly SMEs) to capital markets. Apart from SMEs, other entities permitted to adopt this format are those whose securities are admitted to trading on an SME growth market, provided their market capitalization does not exceed EUR 500 million.[64]

discourses have emphasized the importance of facilitating SMEs' access to capital markets. See for instance the 'Europe 2020' strategy or the already announced CMU, of which more will be discussed later in this chapter.

[57] Typically, the form of the prospectus can vary, depending on whether the issue is part of a programme, or a stand-alone issue. Plain vanilla issues tend to align with a programme, and in such cases Art 8 of the Prospectus Regulation provides for debt securities to be issued with a 'base prospectus', which does not require a summary. For stand-alone issues, all the necessary information has to be included either in a composite prospectus, or divided into registration document, securities note, and summary, as per Arts 6 and 10 of the Prospectus Regulation. Also to be noted, Art 7(1) specifies that a summary is not required for issues of wholesale debt securities.

[58] See Prospectus Regulation, Arts 6 and 7 for general provisions on the general contents of prospectus, and Arts 14 and 15 for the simplified and EU growth formats.

[59] See Philip Wood, *Regulation of International Finance*, Sweet and Maxwell, 2019, 535–536. See also, for a critical appraisal, Pierre Schammo, 'Capital Markets Union and Small and Medium-sized Enterprises (SMEs): a Preliminary Assessment', in *The New financial architecture in the Eurozone*, edited by Allen, Carletti, and Gray, FIC Press, 2015, 137–176.

[60] See Art 14 Prospectus Regulation.

[61] ibid.

[62] See Art 15 of the Prospectus Regulation and Annex 25 and 27 of the Regulation for the relevant registration document and securities not applying for the issue of non-equity securities.

[63] ibid, Art 15.

[64] ibid, Art 15(b).

In terms of different forms of prospectuses, it is also worth remembering that the issue of wholesale debt securities can also benefit from a calibrated regulatory approach given that a simpler format is available for issuers in such situations.[65]

More critical and contextual discussions on the scope of these regulatory adjustments are conducted in section 6 of this chapter and in the next chapter.

3 Post-2008 corrections and debt capital markets regulation

This section deals with the rather difficult task of analysing the regulatory reforms that impacted key segments of debt capital markets, and it addresses the legal and regulatory issues that were raised in Chapters 4, 5 and 6. The task is difficult precisely because of the sheer volume of regulation that characterized the post-2008 period, in what proved to be the most crucial areas in international capital markets, namely: securitization, the repo market, credit derivatives, credit rating agencies. This discussion is complemented by addressing the critical question of product regulation, in relation to debt products, in section 4, while the Basel III framework is analysed later in this chapter.

3.1 Regulating securitization post-2008

The regulation of securitization has been at the heart of efforts to reform financial markets and prevent the build-up of excessive levels of risk-taking that characterized the pre-2008 years. These efforts have fluctuated across two ostensibly diverging policy objectives. On the one hand there has been some agreement in recognizing excesses in financial innovation, and particularly the unfettered development of plain vanilla securitization into products such as CDOs and synthetic CDOs, as key causes of the GFC.[66] This diagnosis is also mirrored in the analysis conducted in Chapters 4 and 5 of this monograph, which explained the legal structure of these complex products, and how they contributed to opaque chains of financial intermediation, and to ever increasing levels of risk-taking and leverage in the financial system.[67]

[65] ibid, Art 8, and Annex 7 where more specific information on the configuration of wholesale prospectus is given.

[66] See Adair Turner, *The Turner Review—A Regulatory Response to the Global Banking Crisis*, FSA, 2009, chapter1; Financial Crisis Inquiry Commission, 'The Financial Crisis Inquiry Report', January 2011, part II. Specifically, part II dealt with shadow banking, securitization and derivatives, deregulation redux, and subprime lending.

[67] ibid.

On the other hand, post-2008 regulatory efforts in this area also stemmed from the belief that restarting the securitization market[68] would be essential to the health of the financial system as a whole. The rationale behind this agenda coincides with some of the efficiency orthodoxies that were examined in earlier parts of the book,[69] hinging on the assumption that capital markets are more effective than banks at intermediating and allocating resources and diversifying risks.[70] As was discussed in the previous section, further integrating EU capital markets was always seen as a way to ensure a more diversified financial system, relieving in the process an overburdened banking sector.[71] Initiatives to promote well-functioning capital markets around a safer and more transparent securitization market became thus a priority both at the EU level,[72] and globally.[73]

Where there has been clearer agreement is on the need to canvass a regulatory framework that would allow securitization to work in a more sustainable way, aligning the interest of investors with those of originators.[74] These aims became encompassed at the EU level in the Securitization Regulation,[75] and more specifically in the STS framework (simple, transparent and standardized). This was conceived by the EU Commission as the catalyst of capital markets integration, and as the label under which securitizations would be deemed less risky and therefore attract a more favourable prudential treatment. The current regulatory framework comprises three elements: a) post-2008 provisions that apply to all securitization transactions (namely provisions on due diligence, risk retention, and transparency);

[68] It will be recalled from the analysis conducted in Chapter 2 that in the years following the crisis of 2008, the securitization market remained moribund, particularly in continental Europe, where it always lagged behind the more active US and UK markets. This trend only started to change around 2014.

[69] Specifically dealt with in Chapter 3 and also in Chapter 6.

[70] For a critique of this policy design, see Vincenzo Bavoso, *Capital Markets, Debt Finance and the EU Capital Markets Union: A law and finance critique*, Centre for European Policy Studies, 2017.

[71] See for instance, on the urgency for this shift to occur, a recent call by the Association for Financial Markets in Europe (AFME) to further facilitate the use of securitization in the EU. See Laura Noonan, 'EU and UK need to overhaul securitisation rules, finance group urges', *Financial Times* (6 June 2023).

[72] At the EU level, a revamped securitization market became immediately the central piece of the CMU puzzle, with the enactment of the new Securitization Regulation 2017/2402, and within it the STS brand (standing for simple, transparent and standardized), discussed later in this section.

[73] At the global level the Bank for International Settlements issued a similar framework called STC (standing for simple, transparent and comparable) 'Basel III Document: Revisions to the Securitisation Framework', 2014 (revised in 2016).

[74] For a critique of this regulatory goals: Vincenzo Bavoso, 'Good Securitisation, Bad Securitisation and the Quest for Sustainable EU Capital Markets' (2015) 4 Butterworth Journal of International Banking and Financial Law 221; Vincenzo Bavoso, 'High Quality Securitisation and EU Capital Markets Union—Is it Possible?' (2016) Accounting, Economics and Law, a Convivium.

[75] Securitization Regulation EU 2017/2402, in force since January 2018, and applicable one year later. It is important to note that the Regulation was conceived before Brexit, and in fact it stemmed from concerted efforts between the Bank of England and the European Central Bank. It remains central to the policy objectives of both the City of London, and EU financial markets. However, while starting from a unified approach, the Regulation is already starting to diverge in some areas, particularly in the context of level 2 measures, such as regulatory and implementing technical standards (RTS and ITS). See for an overview Clifford Chance, 'The Future of the Securitisation Regulation in the EU and UK: Brexit and Beyond', in *Structured Debt in a New World*, March 2022, 5–11.

b) the STS framework, which applies to transactions that comply with the criteria therein; c) outside of the Securitization Regulation, amendments to the prudential treatment of financial institutions that comply with the STS framework.[76] In the US, a number of relevant provisions were introduced with the Dodd-Frank Act, and are signposted below.[77]

The due diligence requirement was introduced under Article 5 of the Securitization Regulation, and it is central to the idea of creating a securitization market where investors can access all relevant information and make informed decisions, minimizing as a result the reliance on external credit ratings.[78] Under this requirement, institutional investors have a duty to assess the risks of the underlying securitization exposures,[79] and the originator's compliance with the STS criteria (if applicable). Moreover, institutional investors have to also conduct detailed ex post monitoring of the securitization performance.[80]

The risk retention requirement[81] involves the originator (or alternatively the SPV or the sponsor) maintaining on an ongoing basis a material net economic interest in the securitization of no less than 5%. This is calculated at the origination and is determined by the notional value of off-balance sheet items, with a specific list of items that qualify for the retention of the economic interest.[82] It is important to note that this 'skin-in-the-game' requirement revolves around specific rules set out in the regulatory technical standards (RTS), which include, inter alia, risk retention via liquidity facility, risk retention through the vertical tranche of securitized assets, and also the risk retention in the event of multiple originators, which is the case of CLO structures, examined in Chapter 4.[83]

An important piece of this regulatory architecture is the transparency requirement[84], which places an obligation on originators, sponsors and SPVs to make information available to investors and competent authorities.[85] Compliance with this process is supervised by competent national authorities, and the information is published on securitization repositories,[86] even though at the time of writing it

[76] This is part of the Capital Requirement Regulation 2017/2401.

[77] In particular, ss 941–946.

[78] A similar provision was introduced in the US with the Dodd-Frank Act, under s 945, whereby the SEC was instructed to issue rules with regards to the registration statement that issuers have to file. In essence, issuers have to provide a review of the assets that back the securitization.

[79] This includes a range of credit standards, risk retention rules, transparency requirements, as well as the compliance with the STS criteria. See Art 5(3).

[80] Art 5(4).

[81] While this analysis focuses on the EU regulatory framework, this provision has a parallel in the US, with s 941 of the Dodd-Frank Act.

[82] Art 6(1), and (3).

[83] Clifford Chance 'The Future of the Securitisation Regulation' (n 75), 6.

[84] A similar provision exists in the US, under s 942 of the Dodd-Frank Act, whereby the SEC was instructed to adopt regulations requiring securitization issuers to disclose, for each tranche or class of security, information in relation to the underlying assets.

[85] Art 7(1). This includes information on the underlying exposures and documentation that is essential for the understanding of the transaction. The STS notification, if applicable, is also part of this transparency requirement (under Art 7(1d)).

[86] See Art 10.

has not yet been finalized what the information to be published should amount to.[87] Transparency requirements are designed to apply to both private and public securitization—the distinction reflects the one introduced in relation to the prospectus regime in the previous section. In this context, it has been argued that private securitizations should perhaps be exempted from these requirements, especially where risks are transferred to well specified parties.[88] The problem with these orientations is that they further increase risks of regulatory arbitrage, which cannot be underplayed in a regulatory context dominated by a market discipline orthodoxy.[89]

Among the provisions applying to all securitizations, it is important to highlight the ban on re-securitizations, which means that the underlying exposures should not include securitization positions.[90]

Moving on to the STS framework, this was conceived as a label that could differentiate structured products because of their simplicity and transparency, vis-à-vis more complex ones. The STS (and similarly the STC at the Basel level) should in principle enable better predictability of risks and performances for investors, thus aligning their interests with originators'. The simplicity criterion is outlined in Article 20 of the Regulation, and it focuses on the requirements related to the securitization's underlying exposures, ensuring their accessible assessment on the part of investors. This is achieved firstly by mandating the transfer of receivables from originator to SPV by way of true sale, not to be impeded by clawback provisions.[91] This criterion also includes, among others, requirements to ensure the homogeneity of the underlying exposures (in terms of asset type and payment stream, and also excluding any securitization positions),[92] their eligibility criteria and creditworthiness.[93]

Standardization is the second criterion treated in the Regulation, at Article 21, and it focuses on the already discussed risk-retention requirement,[94] and on the mitigation of interest rate and currency risks, specifying though that the underlying exposures should not include derivatives.[95] This criterion also deals with

[87] At the time of writing, no securitization repositories is yet registered with ESMA. See ESMA, EBA, and EIOPA, 'Joint Committee Report on the Implementation and Functioning of the Securitization Regulation (article 44)', Final Report 17 May 2021, 25.

[88] ibid, 28.

[89] More on this overarching critique is developed said later in this chapter.

[90] Securitization Regulation, Art 8(1). This is what in Chapter 4 was also referred to as 'securitization squared'. The prohibition is reiterated, in the context of the STS framework, at Art 20(9), where it is stated that for the purpose of the simplicity requirement, the underlying securitization exposures cannot contain any securitization positions.

[91] Art 20(1)(2).

[92] Art 20(8)(9).

[93] Art 20(7).

[94] Art 21(1).

[95] Art 21(2).

transactional standardization, setting out a number of requirements that the documentation should include.[96]

Transparency is dealt with at Article 22 of the Regulation and it is centred on requirements upon the originator and the sponsor to make available data on critical aspects of the securitization that should enable investors to correctly price it. Relevant data here include historical defaults and loss performance for exposures that are similar to those being securitized;[97] the verification (by an independent third party) of a sample of the underlying exposures;[98] a liability cash-flow model representing the contractual relationship between the exposures and the payment flows.[99]

Importantly, the STS framework is based on a notification system whereby originators and sponsors jointly notify ESMA where a transaction complies with the three criteria examined earlier.[100] ESMA would then publish the STS notification on its official website, with the originator and the sponsor informing the relevant competent authority (or authorities) of the notification.[101] While Article 29 designates competent national authorities[102] for the purpose of supervising compliance with the Regulation, Article 28 confers the more specific assessment of STS compliance to third party verifiers, who should in turn be authorized by competent authorities.

3.2 Regulating and deregulating synthetics

A much-awaited component of the post-2008 regulation of securitization was always going to be the treatment of synthetic transactions. This comes as a result of the widespread identification of synthetics as the most opaque segment of the securitization market, and also due to their capacity to elicit undue increases in risk-taking and leverage.[103] The draft proposal of the Securitization Regulation included a fairly clear ban on synthetics, because they would fall outside the true-sale character of the transfer between originator and SPV (under the then simplicity

[96] Such as early amortization provisions at Art 20(6); clarifications on the duties and responsibilities of servicers and trustees, at Art 20(7); and terms related to remedial actions related to the delinquency and default of debtors (Art 20(9)).

[97] Art 22(1).

[98] Art 22(2).

[99] Art 22(3).

[100] Art 27(1).

[101] Art 27(1).

[102] Whose powers are set out in Art 30. Member states are also responsible for setting out and enforcing administrative sanctions, as per Art 32.

[103] In this sense, see Turner, *The Turner Review* (n 66), chapter 1; Financial Crisis Inquiry Commission, 'The Financial Crisis Inquiry Report' (n 66), part II, which dealt with shadow banking, securitization and derivatives, deregulation redux, and subprime lending. See also Zoltan Pozsar, Tobias Adrian, Adam Ashcroft, and Hayley Boesky, 'Shadow Banking', Staff Report, Federal Reserve Bank of New York, no 458, 2010.

criterion). From the outset though, this approach appeared ambiguous, due to the Commission's openness to assess the possibility of introducing synthetics under the STS umbrella.[104] This ambivalence became manifested when a report released by the European Banking Authority drew a distinction between different types of synthetics, namely balance sheet synthetics and arbitrage synthetics.[105] Balance sheet synthetics are explained in the report as a form of credit risk management driven by originators, whereby they achieve capital relief.[106] Arbitrage synthetics instead create arbitrage opportunities for originators, due to the high spread they achieve from the underlying low quality assets, and the low spread they pay on the transaction structure.[107] Arbitrage synthetics are typically driven by investors' preferences.[108]

Following huge lobbying pressure from the banking industry,[109] the EU Parliament mandated the Commission to draft a legislative proposal aimed at extending the STS framework to synthetics, with the original ban only applying to arbitrage synthetics, whereas balance sheet synthetics are to be included in a specific framework.[110] The opportunity to develop such a framework came with the Capital Markets Recovery Package,[111] which included the required amendments to the Securitization Regulation and a framework for STS criteria to be applied to balance sheet synthetics. The rationale for this inclusion, it is worth reiterating, is the importance that these transactional structures have for banks, particularly in the way synthetics facilitate the origination of high-risk assets—the case of SME loans being particularly resonant.[112] Moreover, synthetics enable banks to manage more efficiently their credit risk and capital profiles, and also optimize transaction costs in situations where true sale securitizations may be less practical.[113] In its

[104] See for a discussion, Bavoso, 'High Quality Securitisation' (n 74).

[105] EBA, 'The EBA Report on Synthetic Securitisation', December 2015. See also EU Parliament Briefing, 'Synthetic Securitisation. A Closer Look', June 2016.

[106] In this case, the securitization provides the originator with a hedge against the default of the asset pool, whereby the hedge is performed through a CDS. See on this Orcun Kaya, 'Synthetic Securitisation: Making a Silent Comeback', Deutsche Bank, EU Monitor Global Financial Markets (21 February 2017), 2.

[107] ibid. In this case, the originator does not hold the underlying asset pool, but enters into a credit protection arrangement, via a CDS, related to the asset pool, for arbitrage purposes.

[108] ibid.

[109] See EU Commission Consultation Document, 'An EU Framework for Simple, Transparent and Standardised Securitisation', February 2015, 15.

[110] See Securitization Regulation, Art 45.

[111] This was adopted in February 2021 and the aim of this package is to facilitate the economic recovery from the pandemic through capital markets. With this aim in mind, a number of amendments were adopted, among which, the Prospectus Regulation and the Securitization Regulation. See Council of the EU Press release 15 February 2021, at www.consilium.europa.eu/en/press/press-releases/2021/02/15/capital-markets-recovery-package-council-adopts-first-set-of-measures-to-help-companies-access-funding/ (last accessed on 06/05/2024).

[112] EU Commission, 'An EU Framework' (n 109), 15.

[113] EBA, 'Report on STS Framework for Synthetic Securitisation under Article 45 of Regulation (EU) 2017/2402', EBA/OP/2020/07, 6 May 2020, 34.

2020 report, EBA also claimed that the performance of synthetics had presented very low loss rates across all asset classes.[114]

In many ways the framework for balance sheet synthetics replicates the STS label, having however to take into consideration some extra factors due to the specific features and risks that are typical of synthetics. In particular, as was also recognized in EBA's report, the transactional structure of synthetics is characterized by the presence of a credit default swap, and as explained in Chapter 4 of this book, this increases counterparty credit risk. Attendant features that are typical of synthetics include the definition of the credit events that impact on the risk transfer mechanism (again the credit default swap), and more generally the approach to distinguish in practice balance sheet synthetics from their arbitrage counterparts so that the STS framework only applies to the former.[115]

To address these issues, and adapt the STS framework to synthetics, the amendments have inserted a new section in the Regulation to deal with general requirements, and then more specifically with simplicity (Art 26b), standardization (Art 26c) and transparency (Art 26d) in the context of balance sheet synthetics. Amendments also include specific requirements on credit protection agreements and synthetic excess spread (Art 26e).[116] An important aspect of this regulatory framework is that its compliance is not treated in the same way as the traditional (true sale) STS, where the regulatory capital benefits are available to any holder of any position in the securitization. With the balance sheet STS instead, capital benefits are only available to originator, and for the most senior tranche in the structure.[117]

Finally, it is important to point out that a regulatory framework for synthetic STS was not developed under the Basel III standards, where the STC framework only covers true sale securitizations. The risk here is, as is the case with any regulatory framework offering lower capital requirements, that it may attract opportunistic behaviour on the part of banks, to pursue arbitrage strategies and economize on their capital. This, in turn, could lead to excessive leverage on banks' balance sheet, and to the same dynamics that lead to financial instability and crises, examined in Chapter 5.[118]

[114] ibid, 26.

[115] ibid, 34 and 39–40.

[116] See EBA, 'Guidelines on the STS criteria for on-balance-sheet securitisation', Consultation Paper, 21/04/2023, 7. It is worth noting that the determination of the synthetic excess spread was clarified by EBA in a draft RTS on 24 April 2023, with possible solutions towards the calculation of the level of capital that originators should hold against the exposures. See on this Clifford Chance, 'Synthetic Securitisation: Completing the EU Regulatory Puzzle', in *Securitisation Markets and Regulation: Choosing Different Paths?*, July 2023.

[117] See Clifford Chance, 'STS for Synthetics: A Long Journey Finally Nearing Completion', in *Structured Debt in a New World*, March 2022.

[118] EBA, Report on STS Framework (n 113), 39. The argument here is that this framework could represent for banks a substitution of regulatory capital, through the use of risk mitigation strategies.

3.3 Regulating the repo market

While technically repurchase agreements are not debt products for the purpose of this treatise, their synergy with securitization chains requires some degree of analysis here. In the decades preceding the GFC of 2008, the repo market had become the channel of intermediation that magnified the interconnectedness between large financial institutions and wholesale (unregulated) sources of funding. Banks were able to borrow large volumes of short-term money from money market mutual funds (MMF), by pledging debt securities they had on their books.[119] The symbiosis between securitization and repos was highlighted in Chapter 2 of this book, where it was shown how these two segments of capital markets followed very similar boom-and-bust cycles before and after 2008. It is also important to remember that the repo market, notwithstanding its increasing centrality in capital markets, operated historically on the basis of market discipline mechanisms, and outside the umbrella of regulatory standards.[120]

It was only in 2015 that this regulatory vacuum was partly filled with the enactment at the EU level of the Securities Financing Transaction Regulation,[121] and at the same time with the Financial Stability Board's (FSB) regulatory framework for haircuts on non-centrally cleared SFTs.[122] Briefly, these two initiatives did tackle some of the problems that had emerged in the repo market in the previous decades. The EU instrument sought to address problems of transparency in the repo market, particularly with respect to the reuse (also known as rehypothecation) of the underlying collateral (the debt securities) as collateral in other transactions.[123] Long chains of rehypothecation became associated with huge increases in the level of leverage in a market that was virtually outside the scope of regulatory scrutiny.[124]

The other signposted regulatory initiative by the FSB sought to mitigate another severe problem that emerged from the repo market, namely the extreme spirals in the value of repo haircuts.[125] The FSB framework sought to limit the

[119] Pozsar and others, 'Shadow Banking' (n 103), 7–11.

[120] For a critique of the legal and regulatory preconditions of the repo market, see Vincenzo Bavoso, 'Basel III and the Regulation of Market-Based Finance: The Tentative Reform' (2021) 18(1) NYU Journal of Law & Business 107; to fully understand the shadow banking character of the repo market, and the money claims within it, see Morgan Ricks, 'Regulating Money Creation after the Crisis' (2011) 1 Harvard Business Law Review 103–104.

[121] EU Regulation 2015/2365. Securities financing transaction being the way in which repurchase agreements are referred to in Europe.

[122] FSB, 'Transforming Shadow Banking into Resilient Market-Based Finance: Regulatory Framework for Haircuts on Non-Centrally Cleared Securities Financing Transactions', November, 2015.

[123] Regulation 2015/2365 (n 121), Art 15. This needs to be understood in conjunction with Arts 4 and 13, which set out reporting requirements for counterparties in repo contracts.

[124] For a more detailed analysis of these provisions, see Bavoso, 'Market-Based Finance' (n 4), s 5.2.

[125] In a repurchase agreement, the haircut is the difference (typically expressed as a percentage) between the market value of the asset pledged as collateral (debt securities), and the purchase price paid for that asset in the repo contract. This difference can be understood as the representation of the credit quality of the underlying collateral, but also the price volatility and the overall market liquidity for those securities used as collateral. In the pre-2008 years it was possible for banks to borrow 100% of the value of the securities they were pledging as collateral (CDO tranches), whereas once the crisis hit, it was

procyclicality of haircut fluctuations in two ways, first, by improving the quantitative methodologies employed by repo counterparties to calculate haircuts, and second, by applying de minimis through-the-cycle haircut floors.[126] Another element of the FSB framework is conceived to limit the amount that non-bank entities can borrow against different types of securities in repo transactions. This is a provision designed to constrain the amount of leverage outside of the regulated banking sector, and at the same time reduce the pro-cyclicality of leverage.[127] It is worth noting that the FSB's recommendations on minimum haircuts rely on market participants establishing internal processes and procedures in accordance with the framework, while the monitoring of margin requirements is to be coordinated by relevant regulators together with the Basel Committee and IOSCO.[128]

When discussing the regulation of repurchase agreements, it needs to be remembered that they exist in the more common bilateral legal from, discussed thus far, but also as tri-party transactions, where an agent bank is interposed between the two repo counterparties. In the latter scheme, collateral cannot be rehypothecated outside of the tri-party venue, a feature that facilitates regulators' access to information, and the overall stability of repos.[129] The stability of tri-party repos contributed to inform, both in the EU and in the US, the choice of managing repo transactions through central clearing counterparties (CCP). These have the essential function of mitigating counterparty credit risk by guaranteeing the performance of the underlying obligations in the event of counterparties' default.[130]

no longer possible to use the same securities in the repo market. This hugely exacerbated funding and liquidity problems for individual banks, and eventually for the financial system as a whole. Moreover, pro-cyclical fluctuations in haircuts contribute to financial instability, and worsen the impact of leverage cycles (examined in Chapter 5). See Ana Fostel and John Geanakoplos, 'Reviewing the Leverage Cycle', Cowles Foundation for Research in Economics, Discussion Paper no 1918, 2013.

[126] FSB, 'Transforming Shadow Banking' (n 122), 5. The latter only applies to non-centrally cleared repos.

[127] ibid, 7. The haircut floors within this provision vary according to the category of the security pledged, its market risk and historical performance.

[128] FSB, 'Transforming Shadow Banking' (n 122). The FSB has been coordinating monitoring exercises on the implementation of these measures, and on the financial stability risks posed by repo-type transactions, particularly in the non-banking sector. See FSB, 'Implementation of G20 Non-Bank Financial Intermediation Reforms', Progress Report, 18 January 2023.

[129] See Adam Copeland, Antoine Martin, and Michael Walker, 'Repo Runs: Evidence from the Tri-Party Repo Market', Federal Reserve Bank of New York, Staff Reports 506, July 2011. The authors of this paper provided evidence suggesting that tri-party repos are more stable than bilateral ones and in fact performed better during the global financial crisis.

[130] This regulatory mechanism is explored in more details in the next section on the regulation of credit derivatives.

3.4 Regulating credit derivatives through clearing (and margin) requirements

As was explained in Chapter 4, two main legal and regulatory problems emerged from the liberalized derivatives market in the pre-2008 years, namely, the opaqueness of the OTC market, where it had become virtually impossible to access information as regards counterparties in derivatives contracts (for both regulators and other market participants); and the related question of counterparty credit risk (that is the risk of default of a counterparty in a derivative contract, and the knock-on effects that the default would have on other market participants). The regulatory response to these problems was centred on the interposition of central clearing counterparties (CCP, already encountered in the previous section) and trade repositories in the structure of bilateral OTC transactions.

The clearing obligation was introduced in the EU with EMIR[131] and in a very similar fashion in the US with the Dodd-Frank Act,[132] and in both regimes there are a number of exemptions to the clearing requirement.[133] EMIR defined clearing as the process of establishing positions (including the calculation of net obligations) and ensuring that financial instruments are available to backstop the exposures that arise from the derivatives positions. The effect of the clearing mechanism is the shift in the bilateral contractual character of derivatives, due to the role of CCPs which act as a counterparty of last resort in the contract. In other words, CCPs stand between the two counterparties and guarantee the performance of the two respective obligations, a function that was conceived to mitigate counterparty credit risk and the occurrence of systemic shocks.[134] Post-2008 reforms also sought to address the problem of opaqueness, and this was done by introducing trade repositories (TR) which are designed to serve as central data collectors and maintain records on derivatives positions.[135]

The clearing obligation is engineered with an attendant requirement whereby counterparties have to post initial and subsequent collateral—what is referred to as margin, mentioned also in the previous section.[136] The function of margin requirements is to absorb potential future losses, and mitigate the knock-on effects

[131] European Market Infrastructure Regulation, Regulation (EU) No 648/2012.

[132] Dodd-Frank Wall Street Reform and Consumer Protection Act, s 723, which delegated the Commodities Futures Trading Commission to issue rules establishing clearing requirements for certain categories of credit default swaps and interest rate swaps to be cleared by derivatives clearing organizations (DCOs) registered with the Commission.

[133] See ESMA, 'The Clearing Obligation under EMIR', Discussion Paper 12 July 2013, 2013/925; see also Dodd Frank Act, s 723. The definition of which types of swaps and which counterparties should be exempted from clearing requirements has been made by the SEC and the Commodity Futures Trading Commission.

[134] EMIR (n 131), Art 4. As in the US, under EMIR CCPs are authorized by the relevant regulator: ESMA in the EU and now the FCA in the UK.

[135] EMIR (n 131), Art 2.

[136] EMIR (n 131), Art 41.

of counterparties' defaults on their respective obligations. In essence, CCPs collateralize their exposure to clearing members, with margin requirements reflecting the riskiness of each derivative position.[137]

Notwithstanding the compelling rationale, the mechanics of margin requirements have been exposed as sources of instability. In the context of the recent collapse of US hedge fund Archegos for instance, the use of collateral and margin calls proved to be the cause of liquidity spirals. This is because margin requirements are designed to factor in changes in the price of the underlying assets; this in turn can trigger higher initial or subsequent margin requirements, due to the increased volatility in the asset market, which can result in larger than expected margin calls.[138] Similar dynamics were at the heart of the recent LDI (liability-driven investment) crisis in the UK pension system,[139] where margin calls (caused by sharp increases in interest rates, and the subsequent collapse in the value of gilts) forced counterparties in swap contracts to access credit facilities in order to meet calls for collateral. With counterparties unable to cover these margin calls, two prospects typically emerge, both disastrous: either defaulting, or resorting to asset sales. The latter option of course further depresses the underlying asset market.[140]

Dynamics of liquidity spirals are among the sources of systemic instability, because margin calls, by causing either defaults among counterparties or fire-sales, have the effect of perpetuating the collapse in the underlying asset market. These shocks do not remain isolated, but instead reveal the many layers of interconnectedness among market participants. While both *Archegos* and the LDI crisis are recent illustrations of this instability, problems associated with the pro-cyclicality of margin calls have been recognized in the past as central components of leverage cycles.[141]

Inevitably, the system of regulation centred on clearing and margin requirements has attracted criticism,[142] which to some extent is validated by the episodes

[137] EMIR (n 131). Margins are based on the calculation of the risk characteristics of the products cleared.

[138] In the *Archegos* case, for instance, the decline in the value of the stock that Archegos was exposed to via total return swaps triggered the request of huge variation margins by Archegos' counterparties. See ESMA, 'Leverage and Derivatives—The Case of Archegos', May 2022, 8. See also Satyajit Das, 'The risks from derivatives have morphed', *Financial Times* (7 October 2022).

[139] For a detailed analysis of the LDI crisis and the role of derivatives in it, see Vincenzo Bavoso, 'The LDI (Liability-Driven Investment) Debacle, Derivatives and Systemic Risk: There You Go Again!', forthcoming, European Business Organization Law Review, September 2023.

[140] Which was precisely what happened at the height of the LDI crisis in the UK. See Das, 'The risks from derivatives' (n 138); and ESMA, 'The Clearing Obligation' (n 133), 8.

[141] John Geanakoplos for instance observed that pro-cyclicality is the key element of these rapid swings and associated calls for cash, which initially affect the most leveraged counterparties, but eventually affect a wider spectrum of market participants with prices spiralling down, and reinforcing a dynamic that leads to a crisis situation. See John Geanakoplos, 'Solving the present crisis and managing the leverage cycle' (2010) Economic Policy Review, Federal Reserve Bank of New York, 104.

[142] In this vein, Steven Schwarcz, 'Post-Crisis Derivatives Regulation: What Went Right (and What Went Wrong)' (January 2023) Science Po Law Review (Biennial issue on Financial Regulation after the 2008 Crisis); speech by Sarah Breeden, 'Risks from leverage: How did a small corner of the pension industry threaten financial stability?', Bank of England, 7 November 2022.

illustrated earlier. Moreover, it is also true that CCPs have become concentrations of mutualized risks, which unavoidably contribute to moral hazard.[143] Notwithstanding this criticism, while they remain an important part of the framework designed to mitigate systemic risks, clearing requirements have not addressed two fundamental questions related to derivatives, namely: a) the excessive levels of leverage elicited by derivatives, and b) their role as mechanisms of risk transmission in the financial system. The second problem has become particularly sensitive because, as reflected in the two cited episodes, leveraged positions and attendant risks emanated from the non-banking sector[144] (hedge funds and pension funds in the above examples), which does not fall under the relevant leverage and liquidity provisions developed by Basel III (examined later in this chapter).

The problem with the use and function of derivatives in capital markets is that, while they are traditionally understood as instruments of risk mitigation and risk management, over recent decades they have clearly morphed into speculative tools. Beyond eliciting market participants' speculative bets, derivatives have also become channels for the transmission of systemic vulnerabilities, due to the way in which they expose banks to highly leveraged counterparties in the non-banking sector.[145] Later analyses in this chapter, on product intervention and the Basel III framework, clarify the extent to which these problems are addressed.

3.5 The new discipline on credit rating agencies

The role and function of credit rating agencies in capital markets was explored in Chapter 6 of this book, where emphasis was laid on two overarching problems: a) the shifts in the business model of CRAs, and their resulting inability to attend their gatekeeping functions; and b) the question related to the methodologies they employed to rate complex structured products. As has been the case in other areas of debt capital markets, regulatory responses in the post-2008 period were prompt, and in this area the EU Commission enacted a specific regulation in 2009 (followed by a number of amendments),[146] while in the US the Dodd-Frank Act included specific provisions on the regulation of CRAs.[147]

[143] On the role of clearinghouses, see Yesha Yadav, 'The Problematic Case of Clearinghouses in Complex Markets' (2013) 101 Georgetown Law Journal 387.

[144] See Sirio Aramonte, Andreas Schrimpf, and Hyun Song Shin, 'Non-bank financial intermediaries and financial stability', BIS Working Paper no 972, October 2021. See also Bank for International Settlements, 'Newsletter on bank exposures to non-bank financial intermediaries', 24 November 2022, where it is specifically observed that systemic vulnerabilities arise due to banks' exposures to channels of non-bank intermediation, and particularly to highly leveraged counterparties due to derivatives and securities financing (repo facilities).

[145] See Financial Stability Board, 'Implementation and Effects of the G20 Financial Regulatory Reforms', 5th Annual Report, 2019, 22–26.

[146] Regulation 1060/2009, followed by amendments with Regulation 513/2011 to incorporate the supervisory role of ESMA; Regulation 462/2013 and Directive 2013/14/EU.

[147] Dodd-Frank Act 2010, ss 931–939.

In the aftermath of the 2008 GFC some commentators called for radical reforms of the rating industry, going as far as advocating the establishment of a public rating agency.[148] The gist of these proposals was essentially aimed at breaking down the regulatory paradox of private entities acting as arbiters of debt capital markets. While regulatory reforms did not go that far, some of the problems experienced in the pre-2008 years have been addressed by regulators. With respect to the EU, the initial strategy was to bring all CRAs operating in the EU under a registration system, and then eventually, with the establishment of ESMA in 2011, under its direct supervision.[149] The Regulation specified though, that despite ESMA's powers with regards to the registration process, neither ESMA nor any public agency has powers to interfere with the content of credit ratings or the underlying methodologies.[150]

The arbitrariness of CRAs with respect to rating methodologies was however mitigated through a duty to disclose to the public methodologies, mathematical models, and assumptions employed, and these have to be reviewed at least on an annual basis.[151] In the context of this duty, CRAs have to ensure that their ratings are based on thorough analysis and reliable sources, and they also have to state (as is done elsewhere too in the Regulation) that ratings are mere opinions and should only be relied upon to a limited degree.[152]

The question of CRAs' conflicts of interest with the firms they rate was dealt with through various provisions. First, the Regulation states that CRAs must take all necessary steps to ensure that any rating is not affected by existing or potential conflicts of interest, which include business relationships involving a range of persons, among which are shareholders, managers, as well as employees.[153] A second provision is represented by the mandated rotation of a CRA after it rates a re-securitization. In other words, the CRA should not issue a credit rating on a new re-securitization with the underlying assets from the same originator, for a period of four years.[154]

The specific context of structured finance is also addressed by the Regulation, which prescribes a regime of extra disclosure. It mandates for the originator and the sponsor to jointly publish information on the credit quality and performance of the underlying assets, and also on the structure of the transaction, the cash flow, and the collateral support. In other words, this set of information is designed to

[148] See Elizabeth Warren, 'Unsafe at Any Rate' (Summer 2007) 5 Democracy; see also Vincenzo Bavoso, *Explaining Financial Scandals: Corporate Governance, Structured Finance and the Enlightened Sovereign Control Paradigm*, CSP, 2013, chapter 7.

[149] Regulation 1060/2009, Art 10. Before being able to operate in the EU, a CRA has to apply for registration (Art 2).

[150] ibid, Art 23.

[151] ibid, Art 8.

[152] ibid.

[153] ibid, Art 6. Detailed requirements on conflicts of interest are set out in Annex I, sections A and B of the Regulation.

[154] ibid, Art 6b.

provide the necessary elements to conduct a stress test on the creditworthiness of the underlying exposures.[155]

From a broader regulatory standpoint, the post-2008 years have seen a concerted effort to curb the reliance that financial institutions have traditionally placed on credit ratings,[156] whereby they are now specifically required to make their own credit risk assessments without solely relying on CRAs. This is an interesting development, because in a sense it reinforces large financial institutions' role in developing their own risk models, which was one of the regulatory problems within the Basel framework, leading to arbitrary risk assessments, and overall to a micro-prudential approach to risk regulation.[157] The second dimension of this strategy seeks to reduce the reliance on credit ratings also on the part of regulators, and it is specifically stated that the EU supervisory agencies[158] must not refer to credit ratings in their guidelines and technical standards, where such reference could lead to a mechanistic reliance.[159]

A final point to be made with respect to the new EU discipline is the attempt to create some degree of accountability in the event that CRAs commit infringements intentionally or with gross negligence.[160] Accountability should in principle flow from the facilitated configuration of civil liability, whereby both investors and issuers can claim damages under this provision. The latter have to establish that with respect to financial instruments they issued, which are rated by a CRA, the infringement was not caused by misleading or inaccurate information provided by the issuer to the CRA. Investors will have to establish that they have relied, with due care, on a credit rating for a decision to invest in (or divest from) a financial product. While the configuration of these liability routes is facilitated under the Regulation, actions will have to be brought in accordance with national laws, where the relevant legal system inevitably provides for very specific burdens of proof to establish reliance. Under English law for instance, as was briefly explained in Chapter 4, the claimant has to prove proximity to establish whether a duty of care arises for the CRA. This test is informed by the precedent set in *Caparo v Dickman*, where the House of Lords, upholding the Court of Appeal's test of proximity, denied that a relationship of proximity would be substantiated between auditors on the one hand and existing shareholders and/or future investors on the other.[161] This test, and the same outcome, was employed in later cases.[162]

155 ibid, Art 8b.

156 ibid, Art 5a.

157 For a critique, Bavoso, 'High Quality Securitisation' (n 74), 21–23.

158 The three EU supervisory agencies are the European Securities and Markets Authority (ESMA), the European Banking Authority (EBA), and the European Insurance and Occupational Pensions Authority (EIOPA). The scope of this specific provision is extended to the European Systemic Risk Board.

159 Regulation 1060/2009, Art 5b.

160 ibid, Art 35a, where the specific infringements are listed in Annex III.

161 *Caparo Industries Plc v Dickman* [1990] UKHL 2.

162 Most prominently in *Her Majesty's Commissioner of Customs and Excise v Barclays Bank Plc* [2006] UKHL 28. It could be argued that the criteria employed in the *Caparo* test highlight the idea

To briefly sketch the US reforms in this area, a number of provisions in the Dodd-Frank Act moved away from the pre-crisis configuration of NRSRO (nationally recognized statistical rating organizations), which were admittedly lightly regulated, and recognized instead the systemic importance of credit ratings and the crucial gatekeeping function of CRAs.[163] As its counterpart at the EU level, the new US regulation hinges on a registration requirement, whereby the SEC is attributed powers to suspend or revoke the registration of CRAs.[164] This is supplemented by rules aimed at minimizing the conflicts of interest between CRAs and their clients, where the regulation introduced clear distinctions between rating services and attendant sales and marketing ones.[165] Importantly, the regulation instructed the SEC to set up an Office of Credit Ratings[166] which would have a range of powers vis-à-vis CRAs, among which, to prescribe rules on rating methodologies.[167] Finally, the US framework also chose to reduce regulatory reliance on CRAs, particularly for government authorities, and as a result statutory references to credit ratings were removed.[168]

4 The conundrum of product regulation

The analyses conducted in Chapters 4 and 5 of this book highlighted the importance of financial innovation as a driver of growth in debt capital markets. Innovated financial products, from securitization to CLOs, have also been repeatedly identified as causes of financial instability, chiefly due to their opaqueness and capacity to increase leverage and foster interconnectedness between market participants operating in different segments of financial markets. Moreover, beyond the efficiency justification (their alleged capacity to improve risk-management and capital allocation), they were employed by large financial institutions for regulatory arbitrage purposes, as means to optimize, or completely bypass, regulatory costs.[169]

of limiting the range of circumstances in which a liability for careless acts can arise. It should be noted though that in later cases the proposition that there is a *Caparo* test that applies to all cases of negligence has been questioned. In particular, in *Robinson v Chief Constable of West Yorkshire* [2018] UKSC 4 it was affirmed, albeit in a very different factual context, that 'the concepts of proximity and fairness . . . are not susceptible of any such precise definition as would be necessary to give them utility as practical tests'.

163 See on this, s 931 Dodd-Frank Act 2010 which lays out the rationales for regulating CRAs.
164 ibid, s 932(2).
165 ibid, s 932(3).
166 ibid, s 932.
167 ibid.
168 ibid, s 939.
169 See the discussion conducted in Chapter 5, section 3.

As was clearly explained in both Chapters 2 and 4, after remaining dormant in the immediate aftermath of 2008, the ferment of financial innovation restarted with vigour after 2014. This may have been partly the result of the overall policy direction, particularly at the EU level, where the prioritization is to facilitate the growth of capital markets, which transpired from the earlier analysis of the prospectus regime and the EU CMU. It is equally important though in the context of this chapter to assess the safeguards that are currently in place to prevent the system from generating the same level of risk-taking and opaqueness that existed in the pre-2008 years. One such assessment was already conducted earlier in this chapter, with the discussion on the STS framework for securitization. The remainder of this section looks beyond that, at the rationale for regulating (or rather not regulating) financial innovation.

The EU regulatory framework presents some interesting provisions, in principle, because the Market in Financial Instrument Regulation[170] empowered ESMA[171] to restrict or prohibit a range of practices: a) the sale and distribution of certain financial instruments; b) a type of financial activity or practice.[172] It is crucial though to understand the scope and the context of application of these powers, which are delineated in the Regulation through three conditions that have to be satisfied for ESMA to act. First, ESMA's action should address a significant investor protection concern, or more generally, a threat to the integrity and stability of financial markets (or a specific commodity market). Second, other applicable regulatory requirements under EU law should not address the specific threat. Third, the relevant national competent authority has not taken action (or an adequate action) to address the threat.[173] Linked to the last point, ESMA's action prevails over a previous one issued by a national authority, however, ESMA needs to renew its action after three months, whereas prohibitions or restrictions issued by a national authority do not expire after three months.[174] Beyond ESMA and national authorities, the same powers are extended under MiFIR to the EBA (European Banking Authority[175]) and other competent authorities,[176] under the same conditions listed earlier.

To understand the scope of these intervention powers, it is useful to look again at the thrust of MiFIR's Article 40, which crucially states that the action should not have detrimental effects on market efficiency, and in weighing up the opportunity to exercise this power, ESMA should prioritize issues of market efficiency and investor protection.[177] The stance in this statutory provision reflects the efficiency

[170] MiFIR, Regulation (EU) No 648/2012, Art 40.

[171] ESMA's powers flow from Regulation (EU) No 1095/2010, Art 9(5).

[172] Regulation (EU) No 648/2012, Art 40(1)(a) and (b).

[173] ibid, Art 40(2).

[174] ibid, Art 40(6,7).

[175] ibid, Art 41.

[176] ibid, Art 42.

[177] ibid, Art 40(3)(a) and (b). Subsection (a) mentions market efficiency and also investor interest, while subsection (b) also mentions risks of regulatory arbitrage that the action may create.

rationale that was explored throughout Chapter 3 of this monograph, as well as the conceptual foundations of capital markets regulation analysed in Chapter 6. The question that needs to be asked then is whether product regulation can represent an effective regulatory strategy while it remains constrained by the logics of market efficiency. This question becomes particularly pressing in the context of debt capital markets, which are chiefly characterized by wholesale products, and as a result investor protection concerns are hardly triggered.

Following from the previous question, it is equally important to assess the range of debt products that fall within the scope of the above intervention powers, given the already stated focus of this provision on investor protection and retail markets. A clarification in this sense came from ESMA in 2019—bearing in mind that ESMA's intervention powers became effective in January 2018. It was then stated that products defined under MiFID as shares, bonds, derivatives, or funds (such as UCITS or alternative investment funds), are all subject to this provision. It was added that a prohibition or restriction could extend to a type of financial activity or practice, and it can apply to any person marketing, distributing or selling financial instruments, including banks and investment firms.[178]

At the time of writing, ESMA only adopted product intervention measures on two occasions. This first one was a temporary prohibition on the marketing, distribution, or sale of binary options[179] to retail investors, which ran between July and August 2018. The second measure was a temporary restriction on the marking, distribution, or sale of contracts for difference (CfD)[180] to retail investors, from August 2018.[181] ESMA agreed to renew these product intervention measures for additional three-month periods, respectively in August 2018 and March 2019.[182] ESMA's chair at that time, Steven Maijoor, confirmed on the occasion the overarching emphasis of these measures on investor protection. He stated for instance that the restriction on the use of CfD was aimed at ensuring that 'investors cannot lose more money than they put it'; similarly, the prohibition related to binary

[178] ESMA Product Intervention, available at www.esma.europa.eu/policy-activities/mifid-ii-and-investor-protection/product-intervention (last accessed on 07/05/2024).

[179] Binary options are a type of derivatives that try to predict whether the value of a certain asset will be above or below a certain point after a fixed period of time. The period of time can be as short as 60 seconds, and what is also peculiar with this type of investment is that the prediction is either right or wrong, in which case the investor loses the entire amount invested.

[180] Contracts for difference, unlike other derivatives such as futures, for instance, are open-ended contracts with no fixed settlement date, and can be closed out by the holder on demand. Typically, they offer exposure to a wide range of financial assets, such as share indices, debt securities, commodities, and currencies. See Practical Law, 'Contract for Difference (CFD)', Thomson Reuters.

[181] ESMA Adopts Final Product Intervention Measures on CFDs and Binary Options, available at www.esma.europa.eu/press-news/esma-news/esma-adopts-final-product-intervention-measures-cfds-and-binary-options (last accessed on 07/05/2024).

[182] See ESMA, 'Product Intervention', at www.esma.europa.eu/investor-corner/product-intervent ion (last accessed on 07/05/2024).

options addressed 'investor protection concerns that are caused by the characteristics of these products'.[183]

It needs to be noted in this analysis that intervention powers are also configured under MiFIR Article 45, in the context of commodity derivatives markets. These powers are designed to mitigate excessive volatility in the underlying commodity price, and ESMA can, in principle, take action with respect to all derivatives positions.[184] Under this provision, ESMA has powers to request information on the size and exposure of a derivative position; to request a reduction in the size of the derivative position, or to eliminate it; to limit, as a last resort measure, the ability of a person to enter into a commodity derivative.[185] Given the lack of action taken under this measure, it is difficult to speculate on the effective role that this provision can play in the wider context of product regulation.

Questions on ESMA's powers are central to this discussion, and instrumental to assess the extent to which product intervention can effectively rein in excesses in debt capital markets. Some wider considerations on ESMA's powers in the context of EU capital markets are reprised later in this chapter, but to understand the limits of its product intervention powers it is useful to look at the criteria laid out in the 2017 Delegated Regulation.[186] This clarifies the conditions that need to be satisfied under MiFIR Article 40(2), and in particular whether questions of investor protection are triggered, the integrity of financial markets, or their stability as a whole. What is particularly interesting here is the first condition laid out in the Delegated Regulation, which focuses on the degree of complexity of the financial instrument or financial activity, and which ESMA has to evaluate in relation to the type of client involved.[187] More specifically, ESMA needs to consider the type of underlying assets and the degree of transparency associated with it, as well as the transparency of the costs flowing from the same asset, the complexity of the performance calculation, the nature and scale of risks, whether the instrument is bundled with other products or services, and the complexity of terms and conditions.[188]

The gist of these conditions seems to clearly point at a retail rationale informing ESMA's powers, with little or no emphasis placed on the exercise of these powers for the purpose of addressing financial stability concerns. This was confirmed by Niamh Moloney, who explained that ESMA's powers were tested during the mis-selling scandals that occurred in the UK and the EU between 2014 and 2017,

[183] ESMA Adopts Final Product Intervention Measures on CFDs and Binary Options, available at www.esma.europa.eu/press-news/esma-news/esma-adopts-final-product-intervention-measures-cfds-and-binary-options (last accessed on 07/05/2024).

[184] See Directive 2014/65 on Markets in Financial Instruments (MiFID II) [2014] OJ L173/349, Arts 57–58 and 69.

[185] Regulation (EU) No 648/2012, Art 45.

[186] Commission Delegated Regulation (EU) 2017/567 supplementing Regulation (EU) No 600/2014.

[187] ibid, Art19(2a).

[188] ibid.

in relation to complex interest rate swaps sold to retail investors.[189] Moreover, in a statement in 2017, ESMA clearly indicated that the purpose behind the exercise of these intervention powers was ultimately to mitigate risks arising from the mis-selling of complex products to retail clients.[190]

As a final reflection on this regulatory toolkit, it seems squarely directed at the retail market, and as an investor protection mechanism. Normative references to market efficiency and its preservation seem to suggest that configuring the exercise of these powers in the context of wholesale debt products is currently unlikely (albeit not impossible under the normative framework). With a relative resurgence of the structured credit market, and red flags being raised by global policy-makers on the increasing level of private debt,[191] the limited extent of these powers seems to be at odds with the traditional objectives of financial regulation, which hinge on financial stability as well.

The picture emerging from the US regulatory landscape is not substantially different. In fact, powers aimed at regulating financial products essentially overlap with the panoply of disclosure-based measures explored in the previous sections, bearing in mind that with institutional investors and hedge funds representing the backbone of the investor population, most transactions fall under the private placement exemption.[192] In the specific context of structured finance, the Dodd-Frank Act has expanded the authority of the SEC with regard to asset-backed securities. In essence, this has resulted in more disclosure-based rules, such as the rule requiring issuers to review the underlying securities and disclose the nature of the review.[193] This is coupled with the rules adopted by the SEC on the use of representations and warranties that are designed to provide assurance that the disclosure of the underlying assets is accurate.[194]

A more direct measure, which mirrors the already analysed EU provision, is the so-called skin-in-the-game rule which requires securitizers or originators of asset-backed securities to retain at least 5% of the credit risk (that has to remain unhedged) of the asset portfolio.[195] In a similar vein, and in light of some of the lessons learned from the pre-2008 wave of financial innovation, the Dodd-Frank Act also attempted to reduce conflicts of interest arising from the vast web of relationships in structured transactions. Section 621 introduced a prohibition for a broad range of parties associated with the issue of asset-backed securities (such as

[189] Niamh Moloney, *The Age of ESMA—Governing EU Financial Markets*, Hart, 2018, 292.

[190] ibid. See also ESMA, 'Product Intervention', General Statement, 30 June 2017. This was later confirmed in an opinion issued by ESMA on 7 June 2021 in relation to product intervention measures by the Dutch Authority for Financial Markets.

[191] See IMF, *Global Financial Stability Report*, 2019, chapter 2; IMF, *Global Financial Stability Report*, 2024, chapter 2.

[192] See Regulation D, Rule 506, which was promulgated on the basis of s 4(a)(2) of the Securities Act 1933.

[193] Dodd-Frank Act 2010, s 945.

[194] ibid, s 943. The SEC has adopted Rule 193 to implement this requirement.

[195] ibid, s 941(b), adding s 15G of the Securities Exchange Act 1934.

underwriters, sponsors, placement agents, purchasers, or other parties affiliated to them) from engaging in any transaction for one year after the closing of the sale of the asset-backed security.[196]

It has been observed, particularly by US commentators, that the direction of financial innovation over the past forty years has created financial products that, despite being recognized as securities, are far more complex than those securities (shares and bonds) that were at the heart of historical, disclosure-based techniques.[197] This comment reflects the analysis conducted in Chapter 6, which explained how debt capital markets are permeated by a market discipline, disclosure-based regulatory approach, and this has not changed much since 2008. The next section on the Basel III framework will complete this assessment.

5 The new Basel framework

The launch of the Basel III framework[198] (still partly under implementation, and partly already superseded by what is called Basel 3.5[199] and Basel III Endgame[200]) was a vital part of the post-2008 regulatory infrastructure. While not specifically aimed at debt capital markets, its emphasis on large banks means that relevant areas of debt capital markets are captured by specific Basel III provisions, whereas the main shortcoming of the new framework is that it does not apply to non-bank entities, where a large chunk of private debt creation has migrated in the post-2008 period.[201] Full coverage of the Basel framework is beyond the scope of this chapter, and this section instead focuses on a critical appraisal of Basel III, pointing at its useful contribution towards the stability of the financial system, as well as its shortcomings.

[196] ibid, s 621, adding s 27B of the Securities Act 1933.

[197] For some useful discussions, see: Henry Hu, 'Too Complex to Depict? Innovation, "Pure Information", and the SEC Disclosure Paradigm' (2011) 90 Texas Law Review 1601; Dan Awrey, 'Complexity, Innovation and the Regulation of Modern Financial Markets' (2012) 2 Harvard Business Law Review; Saule Omarova, 'Licence to Deal: Mandatory Approval of Complex Financial Products' (2012) 90 Washington University Law Review 63.

[198] Bank for International Settlements, 'Basel III: International Regulatory Framework for Banks', at www.bis.org/bcbs/basel3.htm (last accessed on 07/05/2024).

[199] See for instance Deloitte, 'Basel III to 'Basel IV': What changed?', available at www2.deloitte.com/mm/en/pages/risk/articles/basel-iii-to-basel-iv.html (last accessed on 07/05/2024).

[200] A very current development in the Basel III implementation is the so-called Basel III 'Endgame', which has been hailed as the most ambitious reform package in banking history. This additional Basel package will significantly increase the capital requirements that banks have to keep on their books, and it will also substantially reduce the variability of risk-weighted assets through their further standardization. See for an overview Guowei Zhang and Peter Ryan, 'How the Basel III "Endgame" Reforms Will Transform US Capital Requirements', *SIFMA* (27 February 2023); Alexandra Scaggs, 'Basel III: Endgame', *Financial Times* (31 July 2023).

[201] See Antonio Garcia Pascual, Fabio Natalucci, and Thomas Piontek, 'Nonbank Financial Sector Vulnerabilities Surface as Financial Conditions Tighten', IMF Blog, 4 April 2023.

First, it needs to be noted that notwithstanding the addition of new provisions and the strengthening of existing ones, Basel III is a development of the earlier iteration (Basel II), rather than a restructuring of the previous architecture. This is so because of the policy-making at the Bank for International Settlement (BIS) which remained fixed in the belief that a regulatory framework built around risk models was still valid, despite the failures associated with it after the 2008 crisis. This stance was based on the distinction between the method employed for the risk analysis on the one hand, which was considered correct, and the statistical risk modelling on the other hand, which was deemed flawed. The regulatory failures of 2008 were attributed by BIS to the latter specifically.[202] As a result, Basel III builds on its predecessor. It is grounded on three pillars for the regulation of capital: Pillar 1, centred on different capital ratios, including countercyclical buffers and capital conservation buffers, risk coverage, and the leverage ratio; Pillar 2 focused on risk management and supervision; and Pillar 3 dealing with market discipline.[203] The three pillars are supplemented with a new set of liquidity standards.[204]

Overall, the revamped capital requirements reflect a substantially higher level (and better quality) of capital that banks have to maintain,[205] and include measures specifically designed to tackle pro-cyclical trends.[206] Moreover, global systemically important banks (G-SIB) are under further loss absorbency requirements aimed at strengthening their capital, and which are designed to reduce their probability of failure as well as the impact of their failure.[207]

The critical aspect of the Basel framework is the way in which capital is calculated. The capital ratio is calculated by dividing the bank's tier-1 and tier-2 capital by the bank's risk-based assets.[208] It follows that the determination of a bank's risk-weight assets (RWA) is instrumental to calculate how much capital a bank has to post. Traditionally, under Basel, risk-weighting has been problematic, first because

[202] See Simon Gleeson, *Gleeson on the International Regulation of Banking*, Oxford University Press, 2018, 27–33.

[203] Bank for International Settlements, 'Basel III: High-Level Summary of Basel III Reforms', 2017.

[204] An essential map of the new Basel framework is provided in Bank for International Settlements, 'Basel III Summary Table', available at www.bis.org/bcbs/basel3/b3_bank_sup_reforms.pdf (last accessed on 07/05/2024).

[205] Bank for International Settlements, 'Basel III: A Global Regulatory Framework for More Resilient Banks and Banking System', June 2011, para 69. This involves greater focus on common equity as tier-1 risk-weighted assets, which must be at least 4.5% (6% since 2019). The total of tier-1 and tier-2 capital must be not less than 8%.

[206] See Bank for International Settlements, 'Basel III: A Global Regulatory Framework for More Resilient Banks and Banking System', June 2011, paras 128, 129–132, and 137–139. This is particularly the result of the new capital conservation buffer (2.5% of tier-1 risk-weighted assets); and the countercyclical buffer (extra buffer of 2.5% of tier-1 risk-weighted assets).

[207] These involve additional tier-1 risk-weighted assets ranging between 1% and 2.5%. See Bank for International Settlements, 'Global Systemically Important Banks: Updated Assessment Methodology and the Higher Loss Absorbency Requirement', 2013, para 46.

[208] See on this. Adrian Blundell-Wignall and others, 'Assessing the Finalised Basel III Banking Regulation Regime', in *Globalisation and Finance at the Crossroads*, edited by Blundell-Wignall and others, Palgrave Macmillan, 2018, chapter 8.

of the weakness of the data employed, and secondly because of the freedom that banks have enjoyed in determining risk weights. The regulatory mechanism that elicited this practice is the use of the internal risk-based approach (IRB),[209] which effectively allowed sophisticated financial institutions to develop in-house internal models for regulatory capital charges.[210] This self-referential model emerged in the aftermath of the 2008 global crisis as unreliable, due to the excessive variability of RWAs calculated by banks.[211]

Basel III was developed with the awareness that internal models had caused the uneven application of capital weights among similar banks, resulting therefore in problems of regulatory arbitrage. The Basel Committee however, did not prohibit internal models, but instead opted to restrict their use.[212] Effectively, banks are still able to use the advanced IRB approach in cases where robust estimates are considered more likely. In such cases though, a more conservative output is ensured through the application of input floors,[213] which means that banks resorting to internal models are anyway subject to an alternative minimum capital requirement.[214] Undoubtedly, this represents a limit to banks' opportunities to achieve regulatory arbitrage through the use of internal models.[215] From a different angle, it has been observed that sophisticated banks are still likely to be able to benefit from the use of internal models, because they can estimate the probability of default, which remains a key variable, even in the foundation IRB approach.[216] In this sense, Blundell-Wignall argued that some of the problems commonly associated with internal models may well remain, and banks' resilience may depend on other regulatory tools, such as the leverage ratio.[217]

[209] The alternative of the IRB being the standardized approach (SA). Under the SA, banks employ a prescribed risk weight for the calculation of the RWA. See Bank for International Settlements, Basel Committee on Banking Supervision, 'Overview of the revised credit risk framework – Executive Summary', 28 February 2018.

[210] See on this Blundell-Wignall and others, 'Assessing the Finalised Basel III Banking Regulation Regime' (n 208), chapter 8.

[211] Bank for International Settlements, Basel Committee on Banking Supervision, 'Basel III: Finalising Post-Crisis Reforms', December 2017, 1.

[212] See Blundell-Wignall and others, 'Assessing the Finalised Basel III Banking Regulation Regime' (n 208), 208–209. Under Basel III the advanced IRB approach won't be available for banks' exposures to other banks and financial institutions, on the ground that exposures to these entities are too difficult for banks to model. Banks will be allowed to employ a foundation IRB approach for these exposures, under which they can still estimate the probability of default, while other risk-weights will be calculated according to parameters determined by the Committee.

[213] Blundell-Wignall and others, 'Assessing the Finalised Basel III Banking Regulation Regime' (n 208), 209.

[214] Essentially where banks use internal models, they are subject to an alternative minimum capital requirement—the so-called Basel III output floor. This is calculated using the standardized approach, in a way that minimizes the regulatory benefits that banks using internal models would gain, compared to those using the standardized approach. See on this Bozena Gulija, 'Basel III Finalisation: Completing the Jigsaw', *International Financial Law Review* (8 August 2019).

[215] *Gleeson on the International Regulation of Banking* (n 202), 49.

[216] Blundell-Wignall and others, 'Assessing the Finalised Basel III Banking Regulation Regime' (n 208), 209.

[217] Ibid.

While the regulation of securitization was discussed earlier in this chapter, it is useful to note here that Basel III introduced a new securitization framework to strengthen capital standards for securitization exposures.[218] These are risk-weighted under a specific regime that includes exposures from interest rates and currency derivatives, and credit protection to an SPV. The effect of this is that once a securitization exposure arises through an off-balance sheet SPV, that exposure is converted into an on-balance sheet one.[219]

As stated earlier, the leverage ratio was introduced to complement the capital requirements and it represents a limit to the total amount of leverage that banks can operate with. It requires banks with a high share of high-risk weighted assets to have additional loss-absorbing capacity, including both on-balance and off-balance sheet exposures.[220] In practical terms, non-GSIB entities have to maintain a leverage ratio under 3%, while for GSIB there is a buffer at 50% of their risk-weighted higher loss-absorbing requirement.[221]

Upon its inception, a number of criticisms were made as regards the leverage ratio. Its main limitation though manifested itself over the past few years, with repeated shocks in the financial system that initiated in the non-bank sector only to spread to banks, given the exposures that banks still have to the non-bank sector.[222] One more specific critique of the leverage ratio is its configuration as a non-risk-based capital measure. This risk insensitivity means that assets with the same nominal value, but different riskiness, are treated equally and attract the same capital charge. In turn, this may lead some banks with low risk-weighted assets to increase their risk-taking beyond a desirable level, offsetting in the process the benefit of the leverage ratio.[223] Perhaps, more substantially, it has been argued that the leverage ratio should have been designed as the main regulatory tool to mitigate risk-taking in the banking business, instead of being the backstop of capital.[224]

Finally, the Basel III framework was equipped with new liquidity measures designed to mitigate banks' over-reliance on, and exposure to wholesale sources of funding. These were aimed at limiting the interconnectedness between regulated banks and other channels of financial intermediation that do not fall under the

[218] See Basel Committee on Banking Supervision 'Basel III Document: Revision to the Securitisation Framework', Bank for International Settlements, 11 December 2014 (revised July 2016), p.2.

[219] This is done through a credit conversion factor of 100%. See *Gleeson on the International Regulation of Banking* (n 202), 350.

[220] Bank for International Settlements, Basel Committee on Banking Supervision 'Basel III Leverage Ratio Framework and Disclosure Requirements', January 2014.

[221] Blundell-Wignall and others, 'Assessing the Finalised Basel III Banking Regulation Regime' (n 208), 212.

[222] Two relevant examples in this sense are the panic of 2020, which involved stress and increasing defaults in the CLO market, and more recently, in the UK, the LDI crisis which initiated in the pension system.

[223] See in this sense Michael Grill, Jan Lang, and Jonathan Acosta Smith, 'The Leverage Ratio, Risk-Taking and Bank Stability' (2015) Special Feature EBA Staff Financial Stability Review 5–6.

[224] See Adrian Blundell-Wignall and Paul Atkinson, 'Thinking Beyond Basel III: Necessary Solutions for Capital and Liquidity' (2010) 1 OECD Journal: Financial Market Trends 14–15.

same regulation (such as the repo market). This regulatory approach was conceived to prevent the occurrence of liquidity crises such as those that hit many financial institutions in the run-up to the GFC of 2008.[225] The liquidity framework consists of two measures: the liquidity coverage ratio (LCR) and the net stable funding ratio (NSFR), which should improve the ability of banks to absorb shocks arising from financial stress, and reduce the possibilities of spill-overs.[226]

The LCR requires banks to maintain a minimum amount of high-quality liquid assets for the purpose of withstanding a thirty-day stress scenario, during which time the amount of high-quality liquid assets must remain at least 100% of the bank's total net cash outflows.[227] The key aspect of this ratio is that it tries to regulate short-term liquidity, by favouring specific assets that qualify as high-quality and liquid, such as government bonds, and disfavouring at the same time market-based assets such as asset-backed securities.[228] Similarly, the cash outflow is calculated by applying a presumed outflow percentage to the specific type of exposure, so-called run-off rates.[229] This essentially makes it more expensive for banks to hold liabilities other than deposits.

The NSFR supplements the LCR as a measure against extended liquidity shortages. Here banks are required to maintain a percentage of available stable funding, to match the amount of required stable funding.[230] The purpose of this ratio is to limit the way in which banks can finance long-term assets with short-term liabilities, limiting in the process the exposures that banks can have on their liabilities side (as they did in the pre-2008 period) to short-term funding from the shadow banking system.

While the new liquidity measures contributed to the safety of banks in the post-2008 period,[231] and to their reduced exposure to wholesale sources of funding,[232]

[225] See on this Gary Gorton and Andrew Metrick, 'Securitized Banking and the Run on the Repo' (2012) 104 Journal of Financial Economics.

[226] Bank for International Settlements, Basel Committee on Banking Supervision, 'Basel III: A global regulatory framework for more resilient banks and banking systems', June 2011.

[227] Bank for International Settlements, Basel Committee on Banking Supervision, 'Basel III: The Liquidity Coverage Ratio and Liquidity Risk Monitoring Tools', January 2013, para 17.

[228] ibid, para 24.

[229] ibid, paras 69–72. Stable retail deposits require 5% in the liquidity pool; less stable deposits require 10%; unsecured wholesale funding through operational relationship require 25%; unsecured wholesale funding from non-financial corporates require 75%; unsecured wholesale funding from all other customers require 100%.

[230] Bank for International Settlements, Basel Committee on Banking Supervision, 'Basel III: The Net Stable Funding Ratio', October 2014, paras 4, 9, and 17.

[231] During which time there was anyway a reduced volume of repo transactions. See www.federalreserve.gov/econresdata/notes/fedsnotes/2014/repurchase-agreements-in-the-financial-accounts-of-the-united-states-20140630.html (last accessed on 07/05/2024).

[232] Dealer Elizabeth Holmquist and Josh Gallin, 'Repurchase Agreements in the Financial Accounts of the United States', FEDS Notes, 30 June 2014, available at www.federalreserve.gov/econresdata/notes/fedsnotes/2014/repurchase-agreements-in-the-financial-accounts-of-the-united-states-20140630.html (last accessed on 07/05/2024). Banks have reduced their balance-sheet exposures to market-making, which some have argued may have detrimental effects on market liquidity. Tobias Adrian, John Kiff, and Hyun Song Shin, 'Liquidity, Leverage, and Regulation 10 Years After the Global Financial Crisis' (2018) 10(1–24) Annual Review of Financial Economics 9.

events such as the panic of 2020 and the LDI crisis show that banks are still fragile due to persisting, in some cases 'hidden', exposures to channels of intermediation that are not covered by banking regulation. In other words, with areas of financial intermediation having migrated towards non-bank entities (and with banks remaining interconnected with them, both on their liabilities side, but also on their assets side), the focus of Basel III, particularly as regards leverage and liquidity, may be insufficiently holistic.[233]

6 Conclusion

This chapter completes the discussion started in Chapter 6 on the regulation of debt capital markets. It analysed the relevant regulatory architecture, starting with disclosure requirements, and then moving on to examine more detailed provisions in the areas of bonds, securitization, repos, CRAs, credit derivatives, with an overview of the Basel III framework. Given the sheer size of post-crisis regulatory exercises, this can by no means be a comprehensive coverage. There is little reference here for instance to the regulation of covered bonds (a market analysed in Chapter 4), which was recently dealt with by an EU directive,[234] whereas emphasis was laid on more critical and problematic areas of debt capital markets.

Notwithstanding the post-2008 regulatory developments analysed in this chapter, the level of private debt creation, and attendant risk-taking in the financial system, has reached new heights, particularly through a revived shadow banking sector (now often called non-bank intermediation). Building on the analysis conducted in this chapter, a few points here can draw some conclusions as to why new regulatory exercises have not been successful in mitigating risks and instabilities arising from debt capital markets.

First, the architecture of global financial regulation has not sufficiently moved away from the pre-2008 orthodoxies. Unlike what had happened in the aftermath of the great crash of 1929, post-2008 policies have sought to fix the broken pre-crisis system, by adding new layers of regulation to the old regulatory infrastructure. The earlier discussion on Basel III is a perfect illustration of this trend. As a result, the system remains trapped in myopic assumptions that are proving, time and again, to be detached from the realities of financial markets. Second, and following from the previous point, regulation over-relies on assumptions of efficient markets and rational market participants. The issue is, even if they were rational, market participants would still act in their best interest, not in the interest of the

[233] See in this sense Yalman Onaran and Lauren Leatherby, 'Can We Survive the Next Financial Crisis?', Bloomberg, 10 September 2018.

[234] Directive (EU) 2019/2162. This attempted to harmonize the parameters of covered bonds across the EU.

system as a whole, which means that the assumed correcting power of the market remains at best an aspiration.[235] Reliance on market participants though, means that there is an insufficient focus on system-wide, macro-prudential priorities, despite a shift in macro-prudential policies having been on the radar of the main regulators globally.[236]

Third, many areas of debt capital markets remain regulated 'indirectly', via market discipline mechanisms that, again, rely chiefly on the wisdom of market participants. This point builds on the critique developed in Chapter 6, and on the analysis conducted in this chapter on segments such as the repo market and credit derivatives. Fourth, the financial system is still lacking the necessary institutional structure of supervision. This gap became more evident with the EU policy design to further implement the CMU. Many commentators expected this project to be accompanied by a strengthened EU-wide supervisory structure, either via a fully empowered ESMA, or through the creation of a new institutional body, akin to the SEC in the US. The fact that neither has been done (or initiated for that matter) may represent a problem in the context of debt capital markets. Segments such as securitization are by nature transnational, while the new Securitization Regulation, discussed in this chapter, relies chiefly on national competent authorities and market participants for the supervision and enforcement of its provisions. To even the most optimistic observer, this supervisory structure cannot appear adequately equipped to face the challenges and risks that emerge in debt capital markets.

Taking stock of these conclusions, the next chapter, which serves as the book's ending, draws a trajectory of debt capital markets at the time of writing, pointing to current developments and possible risks.

[235] This fallacy is often referred to as a tragedy-of-commons situation.

[236] See as an illustration FSB, '2023 Bank Failures: Preliminary lessons learnt for resolution', 10 October 2023; Bank of England, 'Financial Stability in Focus: The FPC's approach to assessing risks in market-based finance', 10 October 2023.

8

Muddling through crises: Ways forward in debt capital markets

1 Where are we now in debt capital markets?

The global financial crisis of 2008 was followed by substantial efforts to bring stability into the financial system. Initiatives took the shape of regulatory reforms, some of which were closely analysed in the previous chapter; some regulatory corrections, such as the upgrade of Basel III capital rules (called 'Endgame'), are still in the pipeline.[1] The purpose of this discussion is to assess the extent to which the post-2008 regulatory architecture is suited to meet the challenges posed by ever growing debt capital markets. Before delving into this assessment, it is important to understand the nature of the problem. After all, regulatory corrections have already been tested repeatedly after 2008, and particularly in recent years, with the panic of 2020 and the banking crises of 2023.

The 2020 episode is crucial to understand current dynamics in capital markets, because it shows where risk-taking and leverage have been shifted. Despite banks being better capitalized than they were in the pre-2008 years,[2] the panic of 2020, and the current prolonged instability, show that some of their root causes were never dealt with. The level of private debt creation, hailed by commentators such as Adair Turner as one of the main causes of financial instability,[3] did not subside

[1] Sonali Basak, 'New Capital Rules Bring Marvel-Like Drama to Banking', Bloomberg, 28 July 2023; Huw Jones, 'Bank of England delays final Basel bank capital rules to July 2025', Reuters, 27 September 2023.

[2] This was of course the effect of banks' progressive compliance with the Basel III standards as regards capital, liquidity and leverage. Yalman Onaran and Lauren Leatherby, 'Can We Survive the Next Financial Crisis?', Bloomberg, 10 September 2018, where it is noted that, in the US, the average level of capital of top banks was 2.5% in 2007, against 6.6% in 2018; similarly, in 2007 the same banks were over-reliant on short-term repos for funding, which represented 44% of their liabilities, whereas exposures to the repo market went down to 24% by 2018.

[3] See Adair Turner, *Between Debt and the Devil*, Princeton University Press, 2016, chapters 3 and 4. Turner notes that private sector debt in the UK increased from 50% of GDP in 1964, to 180% of GDP in 2007. Moreover, the majority of this debt was channelled towards the purchase of already existing assets, chiefly real estate, contributing therefore to asset bubbles instead of funding the real economy. See also Arthur Wilmarth, 'The Pandemic Crisis Shows that the World Remains Trapped in a "Global Doom Loop" of Financial Instability, Rising Debt Levels, and Escalating Bailouts' (2021) 40(8) Banking & Financial Services Policy Report, where Wilmarth notes that private debt increased in the US, as a percentage of GDP, from 169% in 1991, to 212% in 1999, to 288% in 2007.

Debt Capital Markets. Vincenzo Bavoso, Oxford University Press. © Vincenzo Bavoso 2024.
DOI: 10.1093/oso/9780198893257.003.0008

after 2008. Instead, it kept rising, chiefly through the non-bank financial system (ie, shadow banking). This is indeed puzzling and requires some further explaining.

While between 2007 and 2014 the level of private debt kept increasing, the fragility in the financial system was clearly moving away from banks, which were looking stronger and stable.[4] Red flags were, however, raised by the IMF in 2019 in their Global Financial Stability Report. It was stressed that post-crisis facilitative financial conditions were eliciting risk-taking beyond a desirable level, and more specifically the IMF highlighted alarming levels of speculative debt in the corporate system, debt originated chiefly through highly leveraged loans issued by non-bank intermediaries.[5] The IMF stressed that this level of indebtedness was leading to vulnerabilities because the rising debt burden was accompanied by a general weakening of debt servicing capacity (noting that this was before the pandemic).[6] Finally, the IMF also emphasized the systemic nature of these risks, given the exposures of financial institutions to high-leveraged loans.[7]

The question then is: how would these credit risks affect banks, given that they were not exposed on paper to these highly leveraged loans? An answer to this came from the FSB that clarified how excessive risk-taking in 'remote' corners of capital markets, and specifically, increasing defaults in high-leveraged loans (and related CLO market), would have spill-over effects across the financial system.[8] The FSB detailed the different layers of interconnectedness that can exist between banks and non-bank channels of intermediation,[9] and it stressed that while the implementation of the Basel III standards improved the capacity of banks to withstand shocks, exposures to certain markets may be difficult to model and monitor for banks, given the opacity of products (such as CLOs, analysed in Chapter 4), and the uncharted interconnectedness between banks and non-bank intermediation.[10]

What this means is that the shadow banking sector (ie non-bank intermediation) has kept growing in the post-2008 years. As an indication of that growth, assets held globally by money market mutual funds (MMF) have gone from $5.3 trillion in 2008, to $8.8 trillion in 2020, and over the same period the repo market expanded from $6 trillion to $11 trillion.[11] Moreover, after 2010, and more drastically

[4] ibid.

[5] IMF, *Global Financial Stability Report*, 2019, 27–28.

[6] ibid, 31. Effectively, the IMF represented the equivalent of a Minsky moment (briefly explained in Chapter 5 of this book), particularly in the way it stated that in the event of an economic slowdown (which eventually did happen, due to the pandemic) the level of corporate debt-at-risk (which refers to debt owed by firms that cannot cover their interest expenses with their earnings) could rise to nearly 40% of total corporate debt in major economies.

[7] ibid, 33. Similar concerns were raised by the IMF also in its 2022 and 2024 Reports.

[8] FSB, 'Vulnerabilities associated with leveraged loans and collateralized loan obligations', 19 December 2019, 1–2.

[9] ibid, 18–19. In particular, the FSB recognized a) direct exposures to leveraged loans and other credit facilities; b) exposures arising in the process of arranging the syndication of leveraged loans; c) direct exposures to third parties CLOs; and d) exposures through more indirect functions, such as sponsoring or warehousing facilities.

[10] ibid, 22.

[11] Wilmarth, 'The Pandemic Crisis' (n 3), 7.

since 2015, the shadow banking system has overtaken the banking system in size.[12] To be clear, this is very relevant to the context of debt capital markets, because the main component of the shadow banking sector is the bond market itself (in its wider meaning), with the volume of bonds having multiplied nearly five times between 1998 and 2022, and with banks having progressively retreated from this channel of intermediation, in favour of asset managers and private equity firms.[13]

To add to this problematic picture, the links between banks and non-banks have often turned into synergies, because banks have started sponsoring MMFs, in the process bypassing capital, leverage, and liquidity regulation while still earning fees, thereby capturing regulatory arbitrage opportunities.[14] A similar argument can be made with respect to banking-type intermediation conducted through FinTech services,[15] which has had the effect of creating a plethora of deposit-like money claims in the shadow banking sector.[16]

One of the consequences of the crisis of 2008, which reverberated in the 2020 panic, is the policy of bailing out failed, or about-to-fail, financial institutions. If in 2008 this happened in a more obvious fashion (particularly given the disastrous decision of letting Lehman Brothers go down), bailouts have taken a more subtle shape in recent years. This is primarily due to the policies enacted by central banks and governments (primarily the UK, US, and EU) in connection with the pandemic. Central banks started operating as market-makers of last resort[17] by buying distressed assets from a variety of financial institutions, such as broker-dealers, repo counterparties, MMFs, with the result of bailing out the financial system as a whole.[18] As was observed by Arthur Wilmarth, this general infusion of liquidity allowed large banks to escape bailouts, simply because their counterparties, both in the banking system and in the shadow banking system, were bailed out.[19] Effectively, these policies have entrenched the position of entities in the shadow banking system, given that in conditions of stress government safety nets have expanded beyond the boundaries of banks.[20]

[12] Robin Wigglesworth, 'How Bonds Ate the Entire Financial System', *Financial Times* (3 August 2023).

[13] ibid.

[14] Wilmarth, 'The Pandemic Crisis' (n 3), 7.

[15] The synergy between banks and FinTech firms, or FinTech channels of intermediation, is explored in Vincenzo Bavoso, 'The promise and perils of alternative market-based finance: the case of P2P lending in the UK' (November 2019) Journal of Banking Regulation.

[16] See also on the concept of money claims in the shadow banking system Morgan Ricks 'Regulating Money Creation after the Crisis' (2011) 1 Harvard Business Law Review.

[17] On this expanded policy framework of central banks, see Willem Buiter, Stephen Cecchetti, Kathryn Dominguez, and Antonio Sanchez Serrano, 'Stabilising financial markets: Lending and market making as a last resort', *Vox/CEPR* (6 February 2023).

[18] Wilmarth, 'The Pandemic Crisis' (n 3), 11–12.

[19] ibid, 12.

[20] ibid, 9.

The fragility of this system became even more evident during the banking crises in the spring of 2023, with failures of mid-size US banks, and more critically with the near-collapse of Swiss giant Credit Suisse.

2 Identifying shortcomings in the regulatory architecture

It is hard to reconcile the period of prolonged financial instability unleashed during the panic of 2020, and then the banking crises in 2023, with the gargantuan regulatory efforts of the post-2008 years. The reality is that the financial system has remained fragile and over-reliant on forms of public backstop that guarantee its functioning. One explanation for this is that, echoing what Adair Turner stated in 2011,[21] post-2008 reforms have not been radical enough, and more specifically they have not rethought the regulatory architecture that led to the crisis of 2008. This contention is further developed in the remaining of this section, which builds on the analysis conducted in Chapter 7.

Starting with Basel III, this added important layers of regulation (chiefly in terms of higher capital buffers, the leverage ratio, and the liquidity framework) which had some tangible effects on the business model of large banks. As was stressed in the previous section, after 2008 banks partly moved away from the pre-crisis securitized banking model, because both securitization and repo exposures became costly on banks' balance sheets.[22] Moreover, there are signs of a further strengthening of the Basel framework, with the inception of the so-called Basel 'Endgame'.[23] This should further limit regulatory arbitrage opportunities for banks, chiefly due to three prospective provisions, namely: a) the standardization of operational risk-weight assets, which is designed to hinder the use of internal models for the calculation of operational risk; b) the inclusion of cross-jurisdictional derivatives claims for the calculation of global systemically important banks' (GSIBs') capital requirements[24]; c) a significant increase of capital requirements for GSIBs.[25]

The clear drawback of the Basel approach is its focus on large banks,[26] which risks further shifting areas of financial intermediation away from banks, towards

[21] See Adair Turner, 'Lord Turner's Lecture – Reforming Finance: Are We Being Radical Enough?', Clare Distinguished Lecture in Economics, Cambridge, 18 February 2011.

[22] For a discussion, see Vincenzo Bavoso, 'Basel III and the Regulation of Market-Based Finance: The Tentative Reform' (2021) 18(1) NYU Journal of Law and Business, part IV.

[23] Alexandra Scaggs, 'Basel III: Endgame', *Financial Times* (31 July 2023).

[24] One criticism of the Basel III reform was that large banks would still be able to reduce their capital exposure to a certain debt by using derivatives (CDSs in particular) to reduce the risk weight of a specific asset. See Adrian Blundell-Wignall and Paul Atkinson, 'Thinking Beyond Basel III: Necessary Solutions for Capital and Liquidity' (2010) OECD Journal of Financial Markets Trends 12. Admittedly, the implementation of these provisions would limit these arbitrage opportunities.

[25] Scaggs, 'Basel III: Endgame' (n 23).

[26] This became evident in the US with the collapse of mid-size banks in the spring of 2023, such as Silicon Valley Bank. It needs to be borne in mind though that a number of initiatives to bring other

segments of financial markets that are not covered by banking regulation—the shadow banking system. This has already been happening, and there are signs that non-bank intermediation has been growing, while remaining highly interconnected with the banking system. This trend can lead to major stress, and as tested during the banking crises in March 2023, banks proved fragile to shocks coming from the non-bank sector. In other words, this is a structural issue that neither Basel III, nor any other post-crisis regulation, has addressed.

A more specific critique of the Basel framework revolves around its reliance on market discipline, and attendant regulatory techniques. Without rehearsing the critique put forward in Chapter 6 (on disclosure and generally the expected rational behaviour of market participants), it is worth contextualizing the risks of that approach. Market discipline is precisely what allows banks to resort to internal models, and particularly to a regime centred on risk regulation, which has proven incomplete. Similarly, the reliance on market discipline has pre-empted—historically, but particularly after 2008—mitigating risks in the financial system through more diversified strategies, such as for instance structural reforms concerning banks, or more robust supervisory structures. If one lesson can be drawn from the panic of 2020 and the banking crises of 2023, it is that market discipline has not curbed the excesses flowing from market participants' tendencies, whether that be excessive leverage or liquidity mismatches.

Moving on to the regulatory and policy package brought by the EU CMU, the most critical elements to be evaluated for the purpose of this analysis are: a) the bond market, b) the regulation of securitization; and c) the overall supervisory structure of debt capital markets. Starting with the bond market, Chapter 7 identified two main themes that characterize the regulatory trend in this area. First, there is a clear policy priority to expand the opportunities for access to finance through capital markets vis-à-vis banks, and this applies primarily to SMEs. As a result, much of the regulatory efforts in this area have sought to lower the regulatory barriers that SMEs face in accessing the bond market. It is worth reiterating that this policy is informed by the same efficiency rationale that was examined earlier in this book (in Chapters 3 and 6).[27] Second, the ensuing regulatory calibration is reflected in the already examined EU growth prospectus, which is designed to reduce regulatory costs for issuing firms, and attract new entities to capital markets.

financial institutions, such as hedge funds, under the same level of scrutiny are being contemplated. Brooke Masters, 'US regulators impose tougher disclosure rules on private funds', *Financial Times* (23 August 2023); Costas Mourselas and Will Louch, 'EU tightens rules on leverage for private credit funds', *Financial Times* (21 July 2023).

[27] For a critical discussion on the overall policy thrust of the EU CMU, see Vincenzo Bavoso, 'Market-Based Finance, Debt and Systemic Risk: A Critique of the EU Capital Markets Union' (2018) Accounting, Economics and Law: A Convivium.

This regulatory and policy strategy can be critiqued on two grounds. First, at a higher policy level, there is no conclusive evidence that capital markets represent a more efficient system of access to finance. There is instead literature indicating that SMEs, which admittedly are the backbone of economic activities across the EU (and beyond), prosper in financial ecosystems characterized by small local banks.[28] Moreover, the presumed efficiency of capital markets is impaired by the huge information costs that are typically associated with SMEs.[29] This entails that assessing their credit risk and translating that into information for investors in capital markets remains difficult, and investors would likely have to take high risks to fund SME projects. Second, and flowing from the first point, a facilitated access to the bond market would inevitably lead to increasing levels of private debt. Incidentally, risks related to the tightening of the credit cycle were recently identified by the IMF, which pointed at the contraction of profit margins particularly for smaller firms. For this segment of the economy, higher borrowing costs are already causing increasing levels of insolvencies.[30] The scenario portrayed by the IMF is one where the increase in the amount of debt that is at risk can cause system-wide losses for both bank and non-bank entities, resulting in financial instability.[31]

With respect to securitization, similar observations on its capacity to lead to problematic levels of debt and leverage in the financial system need to be made. The assessment of the new regulatory framework (the STS (Simple, Transparent, Standardized) at the EU level and the STC (Simple, Transparent, Comparable) as part of Basel III) hinges precisely on its capacity to elicit the growth of securitization, while fostering at the same time a market that does not lead to the same risks that characterized the pre-2008 period. This is admittedly a balancing act, because the industry has kept pushing for less stringent regulation,[32] whereas commentators and policy-makers have raised concerns on some of the criteria within the STS framework.[33] Chief among them was the reintroduction of synthetics, which were initially to remain outside the framework (as discussed in Chapter 7).

[28] See in this sense Iftekhar Hasan, Krzysztof Jackovicz, Oskar Kowalewski, and Lukasz Kozlowski, 'Bank Ownership Structure, SME Lending and Local Credit Markets', Bank of Finland, Research Paper 22, 2014; Deutsche Bundesbank Eurosystem, Time series database BBK01.PQ1601: Lending to domestic enterprises and self-employed persons/Total/Credit cooperatives, at www.bundesbank.de/dynamic/action/en/statistics/time-series-databases/time-series-databases/745582/745582?tsId=BBK01.PQ1601&listId=www_+s104_vjkre_15&dateSelect=2023 (last accessed on 19/05/2024).

[29] See Pierre Schammo, 'Market Building and the Capital Markets Union: Addressing Information Barriers in the SME Funding Market' (2017) 14(2) European Company and Financial Law Review.

[30] IMF, 'Global Financial Stability Report', October 2022, 26.

[31] ibid. As stated previously in this chapter, this outlook is consistent with the cycle of instability proposed by Minsky, analysed in Chapter 5 of this book.

[32] See Laura Noonan, 'EU and UK need to overhaul securitisation rules, finance group urges', *Financial Times* (6 June 2023). Some of the advocated changes would involve lower compliance costs, and would probably allow CLOs to be included among the transactions that comply with the STS criteria.

[33] See Vincenzo Bavoso, 'High Quality Securitisation and EU Capital Markets Union—Is it Possible?' (2016) Accounting, Economics and Law: A Convivium; Finance Watch, 'A Missed Opportunity to Revive Boring Finance', December 2014.

A similar concern can be raised with respect to tranching, particularly due to the transactional complexity that this practice elicits. Moreover, Chapter 4 explained the rationale behind this earlier innovation, that of stimulating the origination and repackaging of poor-quality assets, which end up receiving triple-A credit ratings due to complex underlying correlation formulas.[34] Tranching, in other words, is a transactional device that has the potential to augment interconnectedness in the financial system, and homogeneity between banks' balance sheets. All this is redolent of pre-2008 risk-taking,[35] and it is surprising that no regulatory framework has addressed these concerns.

Overall, and this point is expanded upon in the following section, the regulation of securitization is over-reliant on the role of market participants to monitor and supervise the new regulatory framework, with only marginal powers attributed to national and supranational authorities. Most prominently, this is evident with respect to verification of compliance with the STS criteria, which hinges on a private notification process handled by originators/sponsors,[36] while investors are left with a duty to exercise due diligence before they invest in securitized products. As is discussed later in this section, this design is not supplemented by a harmonized supervisory framework, because the relevant EU supervisor (the European Securities and Markets Authority—ESMA[37]) is only attributed a coordination role, while national regulators are competent for sanctioning breaches of the STS regulation.[38]

To conclude, while the STS framework has been widely employed across the EU, the overall securitization market in Europe has not seen the substantial broadening that was hoped for.[39] This may partly be due to Brexit, which has created a further fragmentation in European capital markets,[40] but also to the limited employment

[34] See for a critique Finance Watch, 'A Missed Opportunity' (n 33), 35; and Bavoso, 'High Quality Securitisation' (n 33), 16–17.

[35] See for instance the critique put forward by Joshua Coval, Jakub Jurek, and Erik Stafford, 'The Economics of Structured Finance' (2009) 23(1) Journal of Economic Perspectives, where they observe that risks related to senior tranches in the past were highly underrated, because the exposure of underlying assets to market or systematic risks could not be eliminated through diversification. In a similar fashion, Adair Turner argued that the process of 'slicing and dicing' led investors to believe that safe investment products could be created from risky underlying assets. See FSA, 'The Turner Review', March 2009.

[36] EU Regulation 2017/2402, Art 14. This essentially empowers originators and/or sponsors to notify national competent authorities whether the transaction complies with the STS label. Another example can be drawn from the due diligence requirement under Art 5 of the Regulation, which rests solely on market discipline mechanisms.

[37] ESMA was created with Regulation (EU) 1095/2010, as a supervisory authority for financial markets.

[38] EU Regulation 2017/2402, Art 29.

[39] ESMA, EBA, EIOPA, 'Joint Committee Report on the Implementation and Functioning of the Securitisation Regulation (article 44)', Final Report 17 May 2021, 42.

[40] It is trite to state that without a system of equivalence in place with major jurisdictions, STS securitizations may eventually stagnate, because from the buy side investors would not be able to receive the preferential prudential treatment associated with the STS brand; from the sell side, issuers would also be limited to a smaller investor base.

of securitization to advance economic goals, such as the already discussed securitization of SME loans.

Finally, with respect to the overall supervisory structure of debt capital markets, concerns need to be raised with respect to their institutional structure, particularly in light of the efforts at the EU level to fully implement EU-wide capital markets. Incidentally, the CMU project was not accompanied by the creation of an EU supervisory agency, and neither was ESMA fully empowered to act as such.[41] It must be remembered that after the crisis of 2008, policy efforts at the EU level were directed at bridging the gap between rule-making and supervision,[42] resulting in the establishment of the three ESAs in 2011, among which was ESMA, and the setting up of the European Systemic Risk Board.[43] Despite further commitments to strengthen these supervisory agencies and harmonize supervisory strategies,[44] the analysis conducted in Chapter 7 shows that in the context of debt capital markets, regulatory and supervisory mechanisms rely chiefly on the wisdom, and input, of market participants, through market discipline.

Similar concerns were voiced already in the post-2008 years. Emilios Avgouleas framed his critique of the GFC through the lack of an adequate governance and institutional framework in global finance,[45] expressing in the process doubts in a regulatory architecture informed by principles of efficient markets.[46] It is therefore compelling to question the main features of the regulatory framework of debt capital markets, given that they remain strongly reliant on the same principles (efficient markets) and mechanisms (market discipline).

The lack of a fully empowered supervisory authority in the more specific context of debt capital markets is particularly problematic, due to their inherently wholesale and transnational character. In this landscape, relying on the wisdom of market participants can easily lead to a lack of sufficient macroprudential focus[47], which was exactly one of the main problems experienced in the pre-2008 period.[48] This concern emerges through the analysis of different areas of regulation explored

[41] Bavoso, 'High Quality Securitisation' (n 33), 23–24.

[42] See the discussion conducted by Eilis Ferran, 'Understanding the New Institutional Architecture of EU Financial Markets Supervision', University of Cambridge, Legal Studies Research Paper, 29/2011.

[43] See Regulation (EU) No 1092/2010 establishing the ESRB; Regulation (EU) No 1095/2010 establishing ESMA; Regulation (EU) No 1093/2010 establishing the EBA (European Banking Authority); Regulation (EU) No 1094/2010 establishing the EIOPA (European Insurance and Occupational Pensions Authority).

[44] For instance the European Parliament and the Council signed Regulation (EU) 2019/2175, which reviews the powers, governance and funding of the ESAs.

[45] See Emilios Avgouleas, *Governance of Global Financial Markets—The Law, the Economics, the Politics*, Cambridge University Press, 2012, chapter 5, where emphasis is laid on the role of transnational regulatory actors (such as the Basel Committee, the IMF, or the Financial Stability Board), and the shortcomings associated with a system of soft law organizations.

[46] ibid, chapter 2.

[47] Despite the inclusion in the Securitization Regulation of Art 31 dealing with macroprudential oversight in the securitization market, and the role of the European Systemic Risk Board.

[48] John Armour, Dan Awrey, Paul Davies, Luca Enriques, Jeffrey Gordon, Colin Mayer, and Jennifer Payne, *Principles of Financial Regulation*, Oxford University Press, 66.

in Chapters 6 and 7, whereby a consistent pattern is the quasi-supervisory role attributed to market mechanisms and market participants (exemplified by the trust in third party verifiers, used by originators to provide opinions of adherence to the STS criteria, in the context of the securitization framework).[49]

Similarly, in the context of the repo market the same mechanisms emerge, with the insistence on a system of information disclosure among transaction counterparties that relies again on the assumption that the same parties act rationally on the back of that information. This is the mechanism that informs the regulation of collateral reuse (rehypothecation), which is the main engine of leverage and a critical contributor to systemic instability. Arguably, an important policy priority, such as financial stability, could have featured more clearly in this regulation, ahead of market efficiency.[50]

A last assessment here needs to look at the overarching rationale permeating financial regulation, particularly at the EU level, that emerged from the analysis of product regulation conducted in Chapter 7. The relevant EU legislation[51] clearly set out the scope for ESMA's intervention, stating that it should not be detrimental to market efficiency. This, in other words, is seen by the EU policy-maker as the utmost policy priority. While in the same statute this priority is accompanied by investor protection[52] (it will be recalled that under neoclassical economics market efficiency is considered tantamount to investor welfare), there is no indication of financial stability as a policy priority.

3 Policy trends in debt capital markets

Writing in the aftermath of the first noticeable financial shock in contemporary history (that is, after 1929), the 'Black Monday' of 1987, John Kenneth Galbraith focused his critique on the capacity of finance to disguise through financial innovation the accumulation of more risk-taking and leverage.[53] At that time, it was the growing employment of credit derivatives that came to the fore as the key innovation. Namely, the deployment of contractual instruments conceived as risk-management techniques. Credit derivatives developed eventually as a key

[49] See the analysis conducted in Chapter 7, section 3.1.

[50] In this sense, see Victor Constancio, 'Challenges for the European Banking Industry', Lecture at the conference on European Banking Industry: What's Next?, University of Navarra, Madrid, July 2016; Morgan Ricks *The Money Problem: Rethinking Financial Regulation*, University of Chicago Press, 2016.

[51] The Market in Financial Instruments Regulation (MiFIR), Regulation (EU) No 648/2012, Art 40(1)(a) and (b).

[52] ibid, art 40(3)(a) and (b). Subsection (a) mentions market efficiency and also investor interest, while subsection (b) also mentions risks of regulatory arbitrage that the action may create.

[53] In his own words, 'Only in the financial world is there such an efficient design for concealing what, with the passage of time, will be revealed as self- and general delusion'. John Kenneth Galbraith, *A Short History of Financial Euphoria*, Penguin, 1990, 19–20.

component of complete financial markets, capable in the process of multiplying both gains and losses, and creating layers of synthetic leverage.[54] Galbraith proved to be a visionary of what was to come in the following decade, with more drastic innovations unleashed by the panoply of securitization-type products. These too came with the promise of more efficient risk management and risk diversification, only to reveal a dark side represented by massive increases in private debt creation, and the systemic transmission of leverage through the shadow banking system.[55]

It is crucial to stress that the same priorities hinging on efficiency rationales are currently underscoring policy-making efforts at the transnational level. This is particularly evident with respect to the various attempts to shape narratives around shadow banking, whose growth was widely identified as the main source of financial instability and the direct cause of the GFC of 2008. Post-2008 regulation has engaged with the difficult task of bringing shadow banking into the realm of resilient market-based finance.[56] This has resulted in a rebranding exercise, which is particularly visible in the context of the EU CMU.[57] Here the rebranding was represented initially by the inclusion of SMEs among the main beneficiaries of the project, with new (market-based) channels of capital raising providing SMEs with much needed sources of finance, alternative to bank lending.[58] Four years later, with the CMU project struggling to take off, a prominent EU think-tank engaged with a task force aimed at rebranding the CMU, and making it more palatable for member states to conduct relevant reforms.[59] Key components of this task force were identified, again, with funding sources for SMEs (including start-ups, and high-growth companies); the creation of a euro area safe asset (in the shape of short-term treasury bills) to enhance private sector risk-sharing; supporting investment fund markets as vehicles that can channel retail investments into capital markets.[60]

[54] See Vincenzo Bavoso, 'The LDI (Liability-driven Investment) Debacle, Derivatives and Systemic Risk: There You Go Again!', forthcoming, European Business Organization Law Review, October 2023.

[55] Bengt Holmstrom, 'Understanding the Role of Debt in the Financial System', BIS Working Paper no 479, January 2015, 20.

[56] As an illustration, G30, 'Shadow Banking and Capital Markets: Risks and Opportunities', Washington, November 2016; FCA, 'Market-Based Finance: Its Contribution and Emerging Issues', May 2016.

[57] Notably, the CMU hinged on the same assumptions of efficient markets, which were clearly laid out in the relevant policy documents, such as: EU Commission, 'Building a Capital Markets Union—Accompanying the Green Paper', COM 2015/63; Niki Anderson, Martin Brooke, Michael Hume, and Miriam Kürtösiová, 'A European Capital Markets Union: implications for growth and stability', Bank Of England Financial Stability Paper No 33, 2015.

[58] EU Commission, 'Building a Capital Markets Union' (n 57), 9, where it is stressed that capital markets represent the ideal platform for the quickest development of business ides and entrepreneurial risk-taking activities.

[59] The difficulties encountered with the implementation of the CMU include the deep integration that is entailed, and which requires political willingness among member states. This should translate into reforms in areas such as tax law, company law, insolvency law, and a greater harmonization of supervision, which is still lacking as was observed earlier in this chapter. See CEPS-ECMI, 'Rebranding Capital Markets Union: A Market Finance Action Plan', Brussels, June 2019, iv, v.

[60] ibid.

While the success of the EU CMU is still at best marginal,[61] what is interesting for the purpose of this discussion is the overarching aim to facilitate the (re-)expansion of channels of financial intermediation that have been identified as sources of instability—channels that by design contribute to private debt creation, leverage, and risk-taking. This confirms the sovereignty of market orthodoxies at the heart of policy-making, at the EU level, as well as globally. To be clear, these policies flow from the set of neoclassical assumptions discussed in Chapter 3 of this book.

The repeated occurrence of periods of instability and crises in the years after 2008 shows two things: 1) the current regulatory infrastructure, built on the same foundations that were in place before 2008, is falling short in preserving the stability of the financial system; 2) the underlying policy direction is somewhat misguided, because it remains informed by a set of assumptions that do not reflect the mechanics of debt capital markets.

With soaring levels of private debt at the global level,[62] and with expanding shadow banking markets,[63] another global financial crisis cannot be ruled out. This would likely be of greater magnitude than the previous one, and the reasonable fear is that this level of systemic dislocation would lead to a complete and disordered fragmentation of the financial system.[64]

4 Future directions in debt capital markets

The arguments laid out in the previous sections draw a picture of a regulatory framework that is not suited to govern debt capital markets. Chapter 6 of this book explored the fundamental principles that underpin that framework, namely the use of market discipline, and the attendant deployment of regulatory techniques such as disclosure and private ordering. All this is supplemented by an institutional infrastructure that has not adjusted to the growth of debt capital markets over the past decades. This lacuna was highlighted earlier in this chapter, as well as in Chapter 7, where the absence of a supranational authority was noted—a deficiency particularly macroscopic in the EU, given the ambition to further integrate capital markets under the aegis of the CMU.

Concerns expressed in this book, on the structure of financial regulation, and specifically on the balance of powers between regulators and market participants, are not new. More radical and pre-emptive regulatory interventions have been

[61] See EU Commission, 'Monitoring Progress Towards a Capital Markets Union: A Toolkit of Indicators', SWD(2021)544 final/2, 2021.

[62] Vitor Gaspar, Paulo Medas, and Roberto Perrelli, 'Global Debt Reaches a Record $226 Trillion', IMF Blog, 15 December 2021.

[63] Wilmarth, 'The Pandemic Crisis' (n 3), 1.

[64] Iris Chiu, 'Prospects for International Financial Deglobalisation and its Potential Impact on International Financial Regulation' (2022) 16 Law and Financial Markets Review.

advocated by John Geanakoplos in the context of the leverage cycle. He highlighted the shortcomings of ex-post regulatory reactions, and made the case for measures that can curb cycles, preventing the economic and social dislocations that follow different phases of the cycle.[65] In the same vein, in his 2016 book Adair Turner targeted the unchallenged increases in private debt and leverage. Much of his criticism focused on the use of market discipline and the belief that it could result in an effective system of risk governance.[66] While these remarks are consistent with the thrust of this book's analysis, they remain largely frustrated in current regulatory discourses. Some of the reasons for this were explored in chapter five of this book and are worth reprising here.

The discussion in Chapter 5, on the proneness of debt capital markets to lead to instability and crises, unveiled the critical role of financial innovation in spurring cycles of instability. Financial innovation, in its modern dynamics, found legitimization in the orthodoxy of private ordering, whereby it was assumed that market participants' inputs would lead to an optimal allocation of resources (Pareto optimality). As a result, regulatory interference into the innovation process remained undesirable, because inconsistent with efficiency goals.[67] Unfettered financial innovation in the last four decades (detailed in Chapter 4) resulted however in the crafting of financial techniques that proved to be aimed at regulatory arbitrage goals: these were achieved either by maximizing profits via recharacterization of underlying risks, or by moving risks to less regulated areas of the financial system.[68] Moreover, new financial products were designed inhouse by large financial institutions, only to reflect their strategic priorities in terms of regulatory arbitrage and profit maximization.[69] It was hardly the case of innovation geared towards wider economic or welfare goals, unlike what neoclassical economics predicated.

Framing this analysis of financial innovation through the criteria elaborated in chapter five, and particularly the last criterion, finality, helps identifying the character of the innovation process, and its impact on the financial system. In essence, finality can contribute to designing a risk-benefit test for the specific financial innovation process, and designate its capacity to realize welfare goals, or conversely achieve arbitrage gains and lead to instability. What also follows from the analyses

[65] John Geanakoplos, 'Leverage, Default and Forgiveness: Lessons from American and European Crises' (2014) 39 Journal of Macroeconomics 320.

[66] Adair Turner, *Between Debt and the Devil*, Princeton University Press, 2016.

[67] The difficulty in regulating financial innovation is best captured by Cristie Ford, who observes that regulation that facilitates private sector innovation is often seen as 'better regulation', whereas this equation leaves out of the policy spectrum important aspects of accountability, transparency, and social welfare. Cristie Ford, 'Innovation-Framing Regulation' (2013) 649(1) The Annals of the American Academy of Political and Social Science.

[68] These were typically achieved either through collateralization techniques employing special purpose vehicles, or credit derivatives.

[69] As an illustration of this process, see Vincenzo Bavoso, 'Financial Innovation, Derivatives and the UK and US Interest Rate Swap Scandals: Drawing New Boundaries for the Regulation of Financial Innovation' (2016) 7(2) Global Policy.

conducted in this book is that two specific elements of the financial innovation dynamic need to be singled out. The first one is the liturgy and agenda that accompanies the innovation process, with the various efficiency-related promises finding their roots in the well-known neoclassical assumptions. The second one is the role of private ordering which is central (because of the same assumptions and promises) in shaping the innovation process and crafting the resulting products. Both of these elements should be revisited in current regulatory discussions.

A regulatory approach to financial innovation in line with that emerging from Chapter 5 is not likely to be implemented under the current conceptual foundations underpinning capital markets. The crux of the matter is that the growth of debt capital markets revolves around contractual developments, the evolution of which is part of the innovation process. How differently should these dynamics be regulated to prevent the cycles of instability discussed thus far? One problem clearly emerging from the analysis in Chapter 7 is that the challenges posed by transactions and products in debt capital markets are not captured by the principles of financial regulation and attendant techniques (such as disclosure). Therefore, if any meaningful shift is to happen in the way debt capital markets operate, and create instability, such shift should entail a paradigmatic departure from: a) the conceptual foundation upon which debt capital markets rest, and b) the ensuing way to understand financial innovation, and the powers of market participants within it.

While the aim of this book is to unveil the lingering fragilities in debt capital markets and the inadequate regulatory architecture engineered after 2008, it is useful to point at future directions of research in this area, and possible avenues for reform. Law and regulation have a fundamental role to play in effecting the necessary changes—should there ever be political consensus to that end. Three directions of reform are singled out here.

First, in line with the analysis conducted in Chapter 5, one possible regulatory adjustment could be the establishment of a product approval agency, which is consistent with a proposal by Saule Omarova.[70] This would have to operate globally, as a result of a multi-lateral treaty, something that sounds revolutionary under current regulatory and institutional models in financial markets. However, the prescriptive function that this agency would exert on market participants (such as banning transactions and products) would need to be complemented by substantial regulatory powers. This would clearly be a challenge at present.

Second, along the same trajectory of reform, debt products could be wholly reconfigured by redeploying legal doctrines in contract and property law. This draws on some of the discussions conducted in Chapters 2 and 4, on the evolution of derivatives more specifically. Many transactional forms whose employment is today

[70] See Saule Omarova, 'From Reaction to Prevention: Product Approval as a Model of Derivatives Regulation' (2013) 3 Harvard Business Law Review Online.

given for granted by both regulators and market participants (ie, contracts for difference) were in fact ostracized by established legal principles that configured wagers and speculation as illegal practices.[71] Reintroducing these legal doctrines today would have the effect of constraining private ordering, and limiting risk-taking by restricting the scope for speculation and leverage.[72]

Finally, structural reforms have clearly been the missing ingredient among the post-2008 regulatory interventions.[73] The analysis conducted in Chapter 2 revealed how regulatory changes in the late 1990s elicited the emergence of large (too-big-to-fail) financial institutions. These were built on the funding base of large commercial banks, and importantly on the regulatory backstops that they benefit from, adding to that business model the much riskier (and profitable) investment one.[74] In essence, large megabanks became the centre of the innovation process and engines of risk propagation, a process that has continued post-2008, as explained earlier in this chapter. It will also be remembered that commercial and investment banks used to operate as separate businesses, and the latter were organized as partnerships. Surely, that structural arrangement represented an ideal constraint to the capacity of those entities to generate excessive levels of risks, leverage and financial instability.[75]

Sceptics of such drastic shifts would certainly invoke the chilling effect that they would have on capital markets and financial innovation. And they are right. However, the choice today is between the power of inaction on the one hand, namely pursuing the same old policy agenda, muddling through and watching the huge debt bubble grow. With the understanding though that the next crisis will likely be of much greater magnitude than any previous one, and lead to a chaotic fragmentation of the financial (and economic, and most likely social) system. Alternatively, on the other hand, more drastic policies would lead to an ordered shrinking of debt capital markets, reduced in their capacity to generate risk-taking, leverage and instability. After all, this is the cure that can be extrapolated from the reading of Minsky's instability hypothesis,[76] which seems to inform today important policy exercises such as the cited IMF Global Financial Stability Reports.[77]

[71] It will be remembered from the discussions in Chapters 2 and 4, that contracts for difference were seen as wagers by both UK and US courts, given that parties in these contracts were not interested in the delivery of the underlying goods, and would settle the transaction by paying the difference between the strike price and the market price.

[72] A similar approach is put forward in Bavoso, 'The LDI Debacle' (n 54).

[73] With the timid exception of ring-fencing in the UK, initially advocated under the Vickers Report. See 'The Independent Commission on Banking: The Vickers Report', House of Commons Library, December 2013. This eventually flowed into the Financial Services (Banking Reform) Act 2013, *c* 33 Part 1.

[74] See on this Arthur Wilmarth, *Taming the Megabanks*, Oxford University Press, 2020, particularly chapters 7, 8, 9.

[75] This type of structural reform would go even further that the proposal put forward by Morgan Ricks in *The Money Problem*, University of Chicago Press, 2016, which advocated the prohibition of non-banks issuing deposit substitutes.

[76] This was examined in Chapter 5.

[77] Particularly in 2019, 2022, and 2024.

Bibliography

Acharya, Viral, Philipp Schnabl, and Gustavo Suarez 'Securitization without Risk Transfer' (2013) 107(3) Journal of Financial Economics 515–536

Adrian, Tobias, John Kiff, and Hyun Song Shin 'Liquidity, Leverage, and Regulation 10 Years After the Global Financial Crisis' (2018) 10 Annual Review of Financial Economics 1–24

Aldasoro, Inaki, Wenqian Huang, and Esti Kemp, 'Cross-border links between banks and non-bank financial institutions' (2020) BIS Quarterly Review 1–14

Anderson, Niki, Martin Brooke, Michael Hume, and Miriam Kürtösiová, 'A European Capital Markets Union: implications for growth and stability', Bank of England Financial Stability Paper No. 33, 2015

Anderson, Richard and Charles Gascon 'The Commercial Paper Market, the Fed, and the 2007-2009 Financial Crisis' (November/December 2009) Federal Reserve Bank of St. Louis Review 589–612

Aramonte, Sirio, Andreas Schrimpf, and Hyun Song Shin, 'Non-bank financial intermediaries and financial stability', BIS Working Paper no 972, October 2021

Armour, John, Dan Awrey, Paul Davies, Luca Enriques, Jeffrey Gordon, Colin Mayer, and Jennifer Payne, *Principles of Financial Regulation*, Oxford University Press, 2016

Arner, Douglas 'The Global Credit Crisis of 2008: Causes and Consequences' (2009) 43(1) The International Lawyer 91–136

Arner, Douglas, Janos Barberis, and Ross Buckley, 'The Evolution of FinTech: A New Post-Crisis Paradigm?', University of New South Wales Law Research Series, no 62, 2016

Arrow, Kenneth and Gerard Debreu, 'Existence of an Equilibrium for a Competitive Economy' (1954) 22 Econometrica 3

Association for Financial Markets in Europe, 'Securitisation Data Report', Q1:2018

Avery, Robert, Terrence Belton, and Michael Goldberg, 'Market Discipline in Regulating Bank Risk: New Evidence from the Capital Markets' (1988) 20(4) Journal of Money, Credit and Banking 597–610

Avesani, Renzo, Antonio Garcia Pascual, and Elina Ribakova, 'The Use of Mortgage Covered Bonds', IMF Working Paper Series, January 2007

Avgouleas, Emilios, *The Mechanics and Regulation of Market Abuse, a Legal and Economic Analysis*, Oxford University Press, 2005

Avgouleas, Emilios, 'The Global Financial Crisis, Behavioural Finance and Financial Regulation: In Search of a New Orthodoxy' (2009) 9/1 Journal of Corporate Law Studies 23–59

Avgouleas, Emilios, 'The Global Financial Crisis and the Disclosure Paradigm in European Financial Regulation: The Case for Reform' (2009) 4 European Company and Financial Law Review

Avgouleas, Emilios, 'What Future for Disclosure as a Regulatory Technique? Lessons from Behavioural Decision Theory and the Global Financial Crisis', in *The Future of Financial Regulation*, edited by Iain MacNeil and Justin O'Brien, Hart, 2010

Avgouleas, Emilios, 'The Reform of "Too-Big-To-Fail" Bank: A New Regulatory Model for the Institutional Separation of "Casino" from "Utility" Banking', February 2010, available at SSRN https://papers.ssrn.com/sol3/papers.cfm?abstract_id=1552970

Avgouleas, Emilios, *Governance of Global Financial Markets – The Law, the Economics, the Politics*, Cambridge University Press, 2012

Avgouleas, Emilios and Jay Cullen, 'Market Discipline and EU Corporate Governance Reforms in the Banking Sector: Merits, Fallacies and Cognitive Boundaries' (2014) 41 Journal of Law and Society 28

Avgouleas, Emilios, 'Regulating Financial Innovation', in *The Oxford Handbook of Financial Regulation*, edited by Moloney, Ferran, Payne, Oxford University Press, 2015

Avgouleas, Emilios, 'Bank Leverage Ratios and Financial Stability: A Micro- and Macroprudential Perspective', Levy Economics Institute Working Paper no 849, October 2015

Avgouleas, Emilios and Jay Cullen, 'Excessive Leverage and Bankers' Pay: Governance and Financial Stability Costs of a Symbiotic Relationship' (2015) 21(1) Columbia Journal of European Law 2–44

Avgouleas, Emilios and Charles Goodhart, 'Critical Reflections on Bank Bail-ins' (2015) 1(1) Journal of Financial Regulation 3–29

Awrey, Dan, 'Complexity, Innovation, and the Regulation of Modern Financial Markets' (2012) 2 Harvard Business Law Review 236–293

Bamford, Alice and Donald MacKenzie, 'Counterperformativity' (Sept/Oct 2018) New Left Review 113

Bamford, Colin, *Principles of International Financial Law*, Oxford University Press, 2011

Bank for International Settlements, 'History of the Basel Committee', at www.bis.org/bcbs/history.htm

Bank for International Settlements, 'Basel III: International Regulatory Framework for Banks', at www.bis.org/bcbs/basel3.htm

Bank for International Settlements, 'Basel III Summary Table', available at www.bis.org/bcbs/basel3/b3_bank_sup_reforms.pdf

Bank for International Settlement, 'Basel III: A Global Regulatory Framework for More Resilient Banks and Banking System', June 2011

Bank for International Settlements, 'Global Systemically Important Banks: Updated Assessment Methodology and the Higher Loss Absorbency Requirement', 2013

Bank for International Settlements, 'Basel III Document: Revisions to the Securitisation Framework', 2014 (revised in 2016)

Bank for International Settlements, 'Basel III: High-Level Summary of Basel III Reforms', 2017

Bank for International Settlements, 'Newsletter on bank exposures to non-bank financial intermediaries', 24 November 2022

Bank of England, 'What are Cryptoasset (cryptocurrencies)?', 19 May 2020

Bank of England, 'Financial Stability in Focus: The FPC's approach to assessing risks in market-based finance', 10 October 2023

Bank of England and European Central Bank, 'The Impaired EU Securitisation Market: Causes, Roadblocks, and How to Deal with Them', April 2014

Bank of England and European Central Bank, 'The Case for a Better Functioning Securitisation Market in the EU', Discussion Paper, May 2014

Baron, Neil, 'The Role of Rating Agencies in the Securitization Process', in *A Primer on Securitization*, edited by Kendall and Fishman, MIT Press, 2000

Basak, Sonali, 'New Capital Rules Bring Marvel-Like Drama to Banking', Bloomberg, 28 July 2023

Bank for International Settlements, Basel Committee on Banking Supervision, 'A New Capital Adequacy Framework', June 1999

Bank for International Settlements, Basel Committee on Banking Supervision, 'Consultative Document – Pillar 3 (Market Discipline) – Supporting Document to the New Basel Capital Accord', January 2001

Bank for International Settlements, Basel Committee on Banking Supervision, 'Basel III: The Liquidity Coverage Ratio and Liquidity Risk Monitoring Tools', January 2013

Bank for International Settlements, Basel Committee on Banking Supervision, 'Basel III: The Net Stable Funding Ratio', October 2014

Bank for International Settlements, Basel Committee on Banking Supervision, 'Basel III Leverage Ratio Framework and Disclosure Requirements', January 2014

Bank for International Settlements, Basel Committee on Banking Supervision 'Basel III: Finalising Post-Crisis Reforms', December 2017

Bank for International Settlements, Basel Committee on Banking Supervision 'Implications of fintech developments for banks and bank supervisors', February 2018

Bank for International Settlements, Basel Committee on Banking Supervision 'Overview of the revised credit risk framework - Executive Summary', 28 February 2018

Bank for International Settlements, Basel Committee on Banking Supervision 'Report on the 2023 Banking Turmoil', October 2023

Basel Committee on Banking Supervision, 'Core Principles for Effective Banking Supervision', September 1997

Basel Committee on Banking Supervision, 'Basel II: The New Basel Capital Accord - Third Consultative Paper', April 2003

Basel Committee on Banking Supervision, 'Basel III: A Global Regulatory Framework for More Resilient Banks and Banking Systems', 2011

Bavoso, Vincenzo, 'Financial Innovation and Structured Finance: The Case of Securitisation' (2013) 34(1) The Company Lawyer 3–12

Bavoso, Vincenzo, 'HSH v. UBS – Lessons from New York' (2013) 28(6) Journal of International Banking and Financial Law 377–379

Bavoso, Vincenzo, *Explaining Financial Scandals: Corporate Governance, Structured Finance and the Enlightened Sovereign Control Paradigm*, Cambridge Scholars Publishing, 2013

Bavoso, Vincenzo, 'Good Securitisation, Bad Securitisation and the Quest for Sustainable EU Capital Markets' (2015) 4 Butterworth Journal of International Banking and Financial Law 221

Bavoso, Vincenzo, 'High Quality Securitisation and EU Capital Markets Union – Is it Possible?' (July 2016) Accounting Economics and Law: A Convivium

Bavoso, Vincenzo, 'Financial Innovation, Derivatives and the UK and US Interest Rate Swap Scandals: Drawing New Boundaries for the Regulation of Financial Innovation' (2016) 7(2) Global Policy 227–236

Bavoso, Vincenzo, 'Filling the Accountability Gap in Structured Finance Transactions: The Case for a Broader Fiduciary Obligation' (2017) 23(2) Columbia Journal of European Law 369–400

Bavoso, Vincenzo, 'Capital Markets, Debt Finance and the EU Capital Markets Union: A law and finance critique', Centre for European Policy Studies, 2 October 2017

Bavoso, Vincenzo, 'Market-Based Finance, Debt and Systemic Risk: A Critique of the EU Capital Markets Union' (October 2018) Accounting Economics and Law: A Convivium 1–26

Bavoso, Vincenzo, 'The Promise and Perils of Alternative Market-Based Finance: The Case of P2P Lending in the UK' (2019) 21 Journal of Banking Regulation 395–409

Bavoso, Vincenzo, 'Hail the New Private Debt Machine: Private Equity, Leveraged Loans and Collateralised Debt Obligations' (2020) 14(3) Law and Financial Markets Review 141–150

Bavoso, Vincenzo, 'Regulating Complex Financial Products Post-Crisis: Between the STS Regulation and ESMA Product Intervention Powers', in *Regulation and the Global Financial Crisis*, edited by Daniel Cash and Robert Goddard, Routledge, 2021

Bavoso, Vincenzo, 'Financial Intermediation in the Age of Fintech: P2P Lending and the Reinvention of Banking' (2021) 2(1) Oxford Journal of Legal Studies 48–75

Bavoso, Vincenzo, 'Basel III and the Regulation of Market-Based Finance: The Tentative Reform' (2021) 18(1) NYU Journal of Law & Business n.2 241–278

Bavoso, Vincenzo, 'The LDI (Liability-Driven Investment) Debacle, Derivatives and Systemic Risk: There You Go Again!', European Business Organization Law Review, 2023 (forthcoming), available at https://papers.ssrn.com/sol3/papers.cfm?abstract_id=4372485

Berg, Alan, 'Recharacterisation after Enron' (May 2003) Journal of Business Law 205

Bernstein, Lisa, 'Opting Out of the Legal System: Extralegal Contractual Relations in the Diamond Industry' (1992) 21 Journal of Legal Studies 115–157

Bhattacharya, Sudipto, Charles Goodhart, Dimitrios Tsomocos, and Alexandros Vardoulakis, 'Minsky's Financial Instability Hypothesis and the Leverage Cycle', London School of Economics FMG Special Paper, September 2011

Biais, Bruno, Florian Heider, and Marie Hoerova, 'Risk-sharing or Risk-taking? Financial Innovation, Margin Requirements and Incentives', ECB working paper, 2010

Biondi, Yuri, 'Empowering Market-Based Finance: A Note on Bank Bailouts in the Aftermath of the North Atlantic Financial Crisis of 2007' (February 2016) Accounting, Economics and Law: A Convivium

Black, Bernard, 'The Legal and Institutional Preconditions for Strong Securities Markets' (2001) 48 UCLA Law Review 781–856

Black, Fisher and Myron Scholes, 'The Valuation of Option Contracts and a Test of Market Efficiency' (1972) 27 Journal of Finance 399–417

Black, Fisher and Myron Scholes, 'The Pricing of Options and Corporate Liabilities' (1973) 81(3) Journal of Political Economy 637–654

Blair, Margaret, 'Financial Innovation, Leverage, Bubbles and the Distribution of Income' (2010–2011) 30 Review of Banking and Financial Law 225–311

Blair, Margaret, 'Making Money: Leverage and Private Sector Money Creation' (2013) 36 Seattle University Law Review 417–454

Blundell-Wignall, Adrian and Paul Atkinson, 'Thinking Beyond Basel III: Necessary Solutions for Capital and Liquidity' (2010) 1 OECD Journal: Financial Market Trends 9–34

Blundell-Wignall, Adrian, Paul Atkinson, and Caroline Roulet, 'Assessing the Finalised Basel III Banking Regulation Regime', in *Globalisation and Finance at the Crossroads*, edited by Blundell-Wignall et al, Springer/Palgrave Macmillan, 2018

Bohmann, Marc, David Michayluk, and Vinay Patel, 'Price Discovery in Commodity Derivatives: Speculation or Hedging?' (2019) 39(9) The Journal of Futures Markets 1107–1121

Bolton, Patrick, Wei Jiang, and Anastasia Kartasheva, 'The Credit Suisse CoCo wipeout: Facts, misperceptions, and lessons for financial regulation' (2023) 35(2) Journal of Applied Corporate Finance 66–74

Bord, Vitaly and Joao Santos, 'The Rise of the Originate-to-Distribute Model and the Role of Banks in Financial Intermediation' (July 2012) Federal Reserve Bank of New York, Economic Policy Review 21–34

Bouchaud, Jean-Philippe, 'Economics Needs a Scientific Revolution' (October 2008) 455 Nature 1181

Boyer, Robert, 'The Global Financial Crisis in Historical Perspective: An Economic Analysis Combining Minsky, Hayek, Fisher, Keynes and the Regulation Approach' (May 2013) Accounting, Economics and Law: A Convivium

Brandeis, Louis, *Other People's Money and how the Bankers Use it*, National Home Library Foundation, 1933

Bratton, William and Adam Levitin, 'A Transactional Genealogy of Scandal: From Michael Milken to Enron to Goldman Sachs' (2013) 86 Southern California Law Review 783

Braun, Benjamin and Daniela Gabor, 'Central Banking, Shadow Banking and Infrastructural Power', in *International Handbook of Financialisation*, edited by Philip Made and others, Routledge, 2020

Brealey, Richard, Stewart Myers, and Franklin Allen, *Corporate Finance*, McGraw-Hill, 2006

Breeden, Sarah, Speech: 'Risks from Leverage: How did a small corner of the pension industry threaten financial stability?', Bank of England, 7 November 2022

Breuer, Peter, 'Measuring Off-Balance-Sheet Leverage', International Monetary Fund, Working Paper no 00/202, 2000

Brummer, Chris, *Soft Law and the Global Financial System*, Cambridge University Press, 2012

Bruner, Christopher, 'States, Markets, and Gatekeepers: Public-Private Regulatory Regimes in an Era of Economic Globalization' (2008) 30(125) Michigan Journal of International Law 125–176

Brunetti, Anna, 'Funding Circle's SME securitisation wins higher ratings', *Peer2Peer Finance News* (16 March 2017), at www.p2pfinancenews.co.uk/2017/03/16/funding-circles-sme-securitisation-wins-higher-ratings/

Brunnermaier, Markus, 'Deciphering the Liquidity and Credit Crunch 2007-2008' (2009) 23 Journal of Economic Perspectives 77–100

Brunnermeier Markus, Andrew Crockett, Charles Goodhart, Avinash Persaud, and Hyun Song Shin, 'The Fundamental Principles of Financial Regulation' (2009) Geneva Reports on the World Economy 11, Centre for Economic Policy Research 1–98

Buchanan, Bonnie, *Securitization and the Global Economy – History and Prospects for the Future*, Palgrave Macmillan, 2017

Buckley, Ross, 'The Changing Nature of Banking and Why it Matters', in *Rethinking Global Finance and its Regulation*, edited by Buckley, Avgouleas, and Arner, Cambridge University Press, 2015

Buckley, Ross, Douglas Arner, Dirk Zetzsche, *FinTech: Finance, Technology and Regulation*, Cambridge University Press, 2023

Buiter. Willem, Stephen Cecchetti, Kathryn Dominguez. and Antonio Sanchez Serrano. 'Stabilising financial markets: Lending and market making as a last resort', *Vox/CEPR* (6 February 2023)

Burrell, Maddie, Mikhail Kleptsov, Adam Craig, Jonathan Lewis, and Julia Tsybina, 'ESG Securitisation: Weathering the Storm' (June 2023) Clifford Chance, Securitisation Markets and Regulation: Choosing Different Paths? 1–80

Calomiris, Charles, 'Financial Innovation, Regulation and Reform' (2009) 29 Cato Journal 65

Carney, Mark, Speech: 'The Promise of FinTech – Something New under the Sun', 25 January 2017

Casey, Jean-Pierre and Karel Lannoo, *Europe's Hidden Capital Markets: Evolution, Architecture and Regulation of the European Bond Market*, Centre for European Policy Studies, 2005

Centeno, Miguel Angel, 'The New Leviathan: The Dynamics and Limits of Technocracy' (1993) 22(3) Theory and Society 307–335

CEPS-ECMI, *Rebranding Capital Markets Union: A Market Finance Action Plan*, Brussels, 2019

Chance, Don, 'A Brief History of Derivatives', in *Essays in Derivatives*, edited by Don Chance, Frank Fabozzi Associates, 2008

Chancellor, Edward, *The Price of Time: The Real Story of Interest*, Penguin, 2023

Chimianti, Maria Teresa, Urszula Kochanska, and Andrea Pinna, 'Understanding the Crypto-asset Phenomenon, its Risks and Measurement Issues' (2019) 5 European Central Bank Economic Bulletin 1–149

Chiu, Iris, 'Prospects for International Financial Deglobalisation and its Potential Impact on International Financial Regulation' (2022) 16 Law and Financial Markets Review 1–19

City AM, 'London fintech star Monzo is fending off one takeover offer each month' *City AM* (10 October 2017)

Claessens, Stijn, Ashoka Mody, and Shahin Vallee, 'Paths to Eurobonds', Bruegel Working Paper 2012/10, July 2012

Clausen, Nis Jul and Karsten Engsig Soerensen, 'Reforming the Regulation of Trading Venues in the EU under the Proposed MiFID II – Levelling the Playing Field and Overcoming Market Fragmentation?' (2012) 9(3) European Company and Financial Law Review 275–306

Clifford Chance, 'The Future of the Securitisation Regulation in the EU and UK: Brexit and Beyond', in *Structured Debt in a New World*, Clifford Chance, 2022

Clifford Chance, 'STS for Synthetics: A Long Journey Finally Nearing Completion', in *Structured Debt in a New World*, Clifford Chance, 2022

Clifford Chance, 'Synthetic Securitisation: Completing the EU Regulatory Puzzle', in *Securitisation Markets and Regulation: Choosing Different Paths?*, Clifford Chance, 2023

Coffee, John, 'The Attorney as Gatekeeper: An Agenda for the SEC' (2003) 103 Columbia Law Review 1293

Coffee, John, 'What Went Wrong? An Initial Enquiry into the Causes of the 2008 Financial Crisis' (2009) 9(1) Journal of Corporate Law Studies 1–22

Comotto, Richard, 'Haircuts and Initial Margins in the Repo Market', ICMA European Repo Council, 8 February 2012

Constancio, Victor, 'Challenges for the European Banking Industry', Lecture at the conference on European Banking Industry: What's Next?, University of Navarra, Madrid, July 2016

Cootner, Paul, *The Random Character of Stock Market Prices*, MIT Press, 1964

Copeland, Adam, Antoine Martin, and Michael Walker, 'Repo Runs: Evidence from the Tri-Party Repo Market', Federal Reserve Bank of New York, Staff Reports 506, July 2011

Corporate Finance Institute, 'What is a Total Return Swap (TRS)?', available at https://corporatefinanceinstitute.com/resources/knowledge/finance/total-return-swap-trs/

Council of the EU, Press release 15 February 2021, at www.consilium.europa.eu/en/press/press-releases/2021/02/15/capital-markets-recovery-package-council-adopts-first-set-of-measures-to-help-companies-access-funding/

Coval, Joshua, Jakub Jurek, and Erik Stafford, 'The Economics of Structured Finance' (2009) 23(1) Journal of Economic Perspectives 3–25

Craughan, Julian, David Palmer, and Emily Reid, 'Online lending platforms and securitisation: Bringing the wholesale market to the Individual' (2015) 6 Journal of International Banking and Financial Law 1–6

Criado, Sarai and Adrian Van Rixtel, 'Structured Finance and the Financial Turmoil of 2007-2008: An Introductory Overview', Banco de España Occasional Paper No 0808, 2008

Crockett, Andrew, Speech: 'Market Discipline and Financial Stability', BIS, 23 May 2001, available at www.bis.org/speeches/sp010523.htm

Cullen, Jay, 'The Repo Market, Collateral and Systemic Risk: In Search of a Regulatory Coherence', in *Research Handbook on Shadow Banking*, edited by Iris Chiu and Iain MacNeil, Edward Elgar, 2018

Cummans, Jared, 'A Brief History of Bond Investing', 1 October 2014, at http://bondfunds.com/education/a-brief-history-of-bond-investing/

Darrat, Alif, 'Are Financial Deepening and Economic Growth Causally Related? Another Look at the Evidence' (1999) 13(3) International Economic Journal 19

Das, Satyajit, 'The risks from derivatives have morphed', *Financial Times* (7 October 2022)

Davies, Paul, Sarah Worthington, and Christopher Hare, *Gower: Principles of Modern Company Law*, Sweet & Maxwell, 2021

De Angelo, Harry and René Stulz, 'Liquid-Claim Production, Risk Management, and Bank Capital Structure: Why High Leverage is Optimal for Banks', Fisher College of Business Working Paper no 2013-03-08, 2014

De Haan, Jakub, Sander Oosterloo, and Dirk Schoenmaker, *Financial Markets and Institutions – A European Perspective*, Cambridge University Press, 2012

De Haan, Jakub, Dirk Schoenmaker, and Peter Wierts, *Financial Markets and Institutions*, Cambridge University Press, 2020

De Larosiere, Jacques, 'The High-Level Group on Financial Supervision in the EU', Brussels, 25 February 2009

Deloitte, 'Basel III to 'Basel IV': What changed?', available at www2.deloitte.com/mm/en/pages/risk/articles/basel-iii-to-basel-iv.html

Deutsche Bundesbank Eurosystem, Time series BBK01.PQ1601: Lending to domestic enterprises and self-employed persons/Total/Credit cooperatives, at www.bundesbank.de/dynamic/action/en/statistics/time-series-databases/time-series-databases/745582/745582?tsId=BBK01.PQ1601&listId=www_+s104_vjkre_15&dateSelect=2023

Devasabai, Kris, 'A Loan in the Dark', *Risk* (October 2014)

Diffie, Whitfield and Martin Hellman, 'New Directions in Cryptography' (1976) 22 IEEE Transactions on Information Theory 644

Dubitsky, Rod, 'CLOs, Private Equity, Pensions and Systemic Risk' (Spring 2020) 26(1) The Journal of Structured Finance 8–28

EBA, 'The EBA Report on Synthetic Securitisation', December 2015

EBA, 'Report on STS Framework for Synthetic Securitisation under Article 45 of Regulation (EU) 2017/2402', EBA/OP/2020/07, 6 May 2020

EBA, 'Guidelines on the STS criteria for on-balance-sheet securitisation', Consultation Paper, 21/04/2023

The Economist, 'Sachs and the Shitty' (29 April 2010)

The Economist Special Report: Financial Innovation 'The Ferment of Finance' (25 February 2012)

Eichengreen, Barry, *Globalizing Capital: A History of the International Monetary System*, Princeton University Press, 2008

Eisinger, Jesse and Jake Bernstein, 'The Magnetar Trade: How One Hedge Fund Helped Keep the Bubble Going', *ProPublica* (9 April 2010)

Engelen, Ewald, Ismail Ertürk, Julie Froud, Sukhdev Johal, Adam Leaver, Mick Moran, Adriana Nilsson, and Karel Williams, *After the Great Complacence*, Oxford University Press, 2011

Epstein, Gerard, *Financialization and the World Economy*, Edward Elgar, 2005

Erturk, Ismail, Julie Froud, Sukhdev Johal, Adam Leaver, and Karel Williams, 'The Democratization of Finance? Promises, Outcomes and Conditions' (2007) 14(4) Review of International Political Economy 553–575

ESMA, 'The Clearing Obligation under EMIR', Discussion Paper 12 July 2013, 2013/925

ESMA, 'Product Intervention', General Statement, 30 June 2017

ESMA, 'EU Securities Markets', ESMA Annual Statistical Report, 18 November 2020

ESMA, 'Leverage and Derivatives – The Case of Archegos', May 2022

ESMA, 'Product Intervention', available at www.esma.europa.eu/policy-activities/mifid-ii-and-investor-protection/product-intervention

ESMA, 'ESMA Adopts Final Product Intervention Measures on CFDs and Binary Options', available at www.esma.europa.eu/press-news/esma-news/esma-adopts-final-product-intervent ion-measures-cfds-and-binary-options

ESMA's report to the European Commission, 'Role of Credit Rating Agencies', June 2008

ESMA, EBA, and EIOPA, 'Joint Committee Report on the Implementation and Functioning of the Securitisation Regulation (article 44)', Final Report 17 May, 2021

EU Commission, Internal Market White Paper 'Completing the Internal Market', COM (85) 310, 1985

EU Commission, 'Risk Capital: A Key to Job Creation in the EU', Sec (1998) 552

EU Commission Green Paper, 'Building a Capital Markets Union', Com(2015) 63 Final

EU Commission, 'Building a Capital Markets Union – Accompanying the Green Paper', COM 2015/63

EU Commission Consultation Document 'An EU Framework for Simple, Transparent and Standardised Securitisation', February 2015

EU Commission, 'Monitoring Progress Towards a Capital Markets Union: A Toolkit of Indicators', SWD(2021)544 final/2, 2021

EU Parliament Briefing, 'Synthetic Securitisation. A Closer Look', June 2016

European Central Bank, 'Trading European Sovereign Bonds: The Microstructure of the MTS Trading Platform', ECB Working Paper Series no 432, 2005

European Central Bank, 'The Euro Bonds and Derivatives Markets', June 2007

European Environment Agency, 'Green Bonds', 28 April 2023

Fabbro, Daniel, 'The Australian Credit Default Market' (December 2011) Reserve Bank of Australia Bulletin 57–66

Fabozzi, Frank and Franco Modigliani, *Mortgage and Mortgage-Backed Securities Markets*, Harvard Business School Press, 1992

Fabozzi, Frank and Vinod Kothari, 'Securitization: The Tool for Financial Transformation', Yale ICF Working Paper no 07-07, 2007

Fabozzi, Frank, Henry Davis, and Moorad Choudhry, *Introduction to Structured Finance*, Wiley, 2006

Fama, Eugene, 'The Behaviour of Stock Market Prices' (1965) 38(1) The Journal of Business 34–105

Fama, Eugene, 'Random Walks in Stock Market Prices', in *Selected Papers of the Graduate School of Business*, University of Chicago, 1965

Fama, Eugene, 'Efficient Capital Markets: A Review of Theory and Empirical Work' (1970) 25(2) The Journal of Finance 383–417,

Featherstone, Kevin, 'The Greek Sovereign Debt Crisis and EMU: A Failing State in a Skewed Regime' (2011) 49(2) Journal of Common Market Studies 193–217

Feder, Norman, 'Deconstructing Over-the-Counter Derivatives' (2002) 3 Columbia Business Law Review 677–747

Federal Reserve Bank of San Francisco, 'What are the differences between debt and equity markets?', October 2005, available at www.frbsf.org/education/publications/doctor-econ/2005/october/debt-equity-market/

Federal Reserve Board, 'Remarks by Chairman Alan Greenspan, before the Futures Industry Association', Boca Raton Florida, 19 March 1999
Ferran, Eilis, *Building an EU Securities Market*, Cambridge University Press, 2004
Ferran, Eilis, 'Understanding the New Institutional Architecture of EU Financial Markets Supervision', University of Cambridge, Legal Studies Research Paper, 29/2011
Ferran, Eilis and Look Chan Ho, *Principles of Corporate Finance Law*, Oxford University Press, 2014
Ferrarini, Guido and Paolo Saguato, 'Reforming Securities and Derivatives Trading in the EU: From Emir to MiFIR' (2013) 13(2) Journal of Corporate Law Studies 319–359
Finance Watch, 'A Missed Opportunity to Revive Boring Finance', December 2014
Financial Conduct Authority, 'Market-Based Finance: Its Contribution and Emerging Issues', Occasional Paper 18, May 2016
Financial Conduct Authority, 'Innovate and Innovation Hub', 20/09/2018, available at www.fca.org.uk/firms/innovate-innovation-hub
Financial Crisis Inquiry Commission, 'Financial Crisis Inquiry Report', January 2011
Financial Stability Board, 'Transforming Shadow Banking into Resilient Market-Based Finance: Regulatory Framework for Haircuts on Non-Centrally Cleared Securities Financing Transactions', November, 2015
Financial Stability Board, 'Financial Stability Implications from FinTech – Supervisory and Regulatory Authorities Issues that Merit Authorities' Attention', 27 June 2017
Financial Stability Board, 'Vulnerabilities associated with leveraged loans and collateralised loan obligations', 19 December 2019
Financial Stability Board, 'Implementation and Effects of the G20 Financial Regulatory Reforms', 5th Annual Report, 2019
Financial Stability Board, 'Global Monitoring Report on Non-Bank Financial Intermediation', 20 December 2022
Financial Stability Board, 'Implementation of G20 Non-Bank Financial Intermediation Reforms', Progress Report, 18 January 2023
Financial Stability Board, '2023 Bank Failures: Preliminary lessons learnt for resolution', 10 October 2023
Financial Stability Board and the Committee on the Global Financial System (CGFS), 'FinTech Credit: Market Structure, Business Models and Financial Stability Implications', 22 May 2017
Fitch Ratings Inc, 'The Rating Process', Special Report, December 2011
Foley, Stephen and Henny Sender, 'Private equity firms fuel demand for CLOs', *Financial Times* (20 December 2012)
Fostel, Ana and John Geanakoplos, 'Reviewing the Leverage Cycle', Cowles Foundation for Research in Economics, Discussion Paper no 1918, 2013
Friedman, Milton, *Capitalism and Freedom*, The University of Chicago Press, 1962
Froud, Julie, Adriana Nilsson, Michael Moran, and Karel Williams, 'Stories and Interests in Finance: Agendas of Governance before and after the Financial Crisis' (2012) 25(1) Governance: An International Journal of Policy, Administration, and Institutions 35–59
G30, 'Shadow Banking and Capital Markets: Risks and Opportunities', Washington, 2016
Gabor, Daniela and Jakob Verstergaard, 'Capital Markets Union: The Systemic Issues Buried deep in the Market Infrastructure Plan', FEPS Policy Brief, April 2015
Gabriel, Douglas, 'The History of Italian Banking', American Almanac, 4 September 1995, at https://truthbitsblog.files.wordpress.com/2019/03/history-of-italian-banking.pdf
Galanis, Michael, 'Vicious Spirals in Corporate Governance: Mandatory Rules for Systemic (Re) Balancing' (2011) 31(2) Oxford Journal of Legal Studies 327–363
Galbraith, John Kenneth, *A Short History of Financial Euphoria*, Penguin, 1990
Gallagher, Paul, 'How Venice Rigged the First, and Worst, Global Financial Collapse', reprinted from Fidelio Magazine 1995, at https://archive.schillerinstitute.com/fid_91-96/954_Gallagher_Venice_rig.html
Gallino, Luciano, *Finanzcapitalismo*, Einaudi, 2011

Garcia, Pascual Antonio, Fabio Natalucci, and Thomas Piontek, 'Nonbank Financial Sector Vulnerabilities Surface as Financial Conditions Tighten', IMF Blog, 4 April 2023

Gaspar, Vitor, Paulo Medas, and Roberto Perrelli, 'Global Debt Reaches a Record $226 Trillion', IMF Blog, 15 December 2021

Geanakoplos, John, 'The Leverage Cycle', in *NBER Macroeconomics Annual 2009,* edited by D Acemoglu, K Rogoff, and M Woodford , Vol. 24, NBER, 2010

Geanakoplos, John, 'Solving the Present Crisis and Managing the Leverage Cycle' (August 2010) Federal Reserve Bank of New York, Economic Policy Review 101–131

Geanakoplos, John, 'Leverage, Default and Forgiveness: Lessons from American and European Crises' (2014) 39 Journal of Macroeconomics 313–333

Gerding, Erik, 'Disclosure 2.0: Can Technology Solve Overload, Complexity, and Other Information Failure' (2016) 90 Tulane Law Review 1143

Gilligan, George, 'Bad Behaviour in International Financial Markets: National and Multilateral Perspectives', in *Integrity Risk and Accountability in Capital Markets: Regulating Culture*, edited by J O'Brien and G Gilligan, Hart, 2013

Gilson, Ronald and Rainer Kraakman, 'The Mechanisms of Market Efficiency' (1984) 70(4) Virginia Law Review 549

Gilson, Ronald and Rainer Kraakman, 'Market Efficiency after the Financial Crisis: It's still a Matter of Information Costs' (2014) 100 Virginia Law Review 313

Giudici, Paolo, 'Fin-Tech: Research Challenges in Financial Supervision and Technological Compliance' (November 2018) Frontiers in Artificial Intelligence

Gleeson, Simon, *Gleeson on the International Regulation of Banking*, Oxford University Press, 2018

Gorton, Gary and Andrew Metrick, 'Regulating the Shadow Banking System' (2010) Brookings Papers on Economic Activity 1–52

Gorton, Gary and Andrew Metrick, 'Securitized Banking and the Run on the Repo' (2012) 104(3) Journal of Financial Economics 425–451

Gorton, Gary and Nicholas Souleles, 'Special Purpose Vehicles and Securitization', in *The Risks of Financial Institutions*, edited by Mark Carey and René Stulz, University of Chicago Press, 2007

Gower, Laurence, 'Big Bang and City Regulation' (1988) 51(1) The Modern Law Review 1–22

Graeber, David, *Debt: The First 5000 Years*, Melville House, 2011

Greenspan, Alan, 'Risk Transfer and Financial Stability: Remarks by Chairman Alan Greenspan to the Federal Reserve Bank of Chicago's Forty-first Annual Conference on Bank Structure', 5 May 2005, available at www.federalreserve.gov/Boarddocs/Speeches/2005/20050505/default.htm

Grill, Michael, Jan Lang, and Jonathan Acosta Smith, 'The Leverage Ratio, Risk-Taking and Bank Stability', Special Feature EBA Staff Financial Stability Review, 2015

Gulija, Bozena, 'Basel III Finalisation: Completing the Jigsaw' (August 2019) International Financial Law Review 8

Gullifer, Louise and Jennifer Payne, *Corporate Finance Law*, Hart, 2020

Guggenheim Investments, 'Understanding Collateralized Loan Obligations', May 2019

Hahn, Thomas, 'Commercial Paper', in *Instruments of the Money Market*, edited by Timothy Cook and Robert Laroche, Federal Reserve Bank of Richmond Special Report, 1998

Haldane, Andrew, Speech: 'Rethinking the Financial Network', 2009, at https://www.bankofengland.co.uk/speech/2009/rethinking-the-financial-network

Haldane, Andrew and Robert May, 'Systemic Risk in Banking Ecosystems' (January 2011) 469 Nature 351–355

Hale, Thomas, 'Debut securitisation for Zopa loans', *Financial Times* (26 September 2016)

Hasan, Iftekhar, Krzysztof Jackovicz, Oskar Kowalewski, and Lukasz Kozlowski, 'Bank Ownership Structure, SME Lending and Local Credit Markets', Bank of Finland, Research Paper 22, 2014

Havinghurst, Clark, 'Foreword: The Place of Private Accrediting Among the Instruments of Government' (1994) 57 Law and Contemporary Problems 1–14

Hawser, Anita, 'How does UBS's takeover of Credit Suisse stack up financially?', *The Banker*, 2 May 2023

Hellwig, Martin, 'Market Discipline, Information Processing and Corporate Governance', Max Planck Institute for Research on Collective Goods, No 2005/19, 2005

Herring, Richard and Edward Kane, 'How to Reform the Credit-Rating Process to Support a Sustainable Revival of Private-Label Securitization' (2012) 2(1) Quarterly Journal of Finance 1–25

Hockett, Robert and Saule Omarova, 'The Finance Franchise' (2017) 102 Cornell Law Review 1143

Holmquist, Elizabeth and Josh Gallin, 'Repurchase Agreements in the Financial Accounts of the United States', FEDS Notes, June 30 2014, available at www.federalreserve.gov/econresdata/notes/feds-notes/2014/repurchase-agreements-in-the-financial-accounts-of-the-united-states-20140630.html

Holmstrom, Bengt, 'Understanding the Role of Debt in the Financial System', BIS Working Paper no 479, January 2015

House of Commons, 'The Independent Commission on Banking: The Vickers Report', December 2013

House of Lords, Economic Affairs Committee, 'Quantitative easing: a dangerous addiction?', 16 July 2021

Hu, Henry, 'Too Complex to Depict? Innovation, 'Pure Information', and the SEC Disclosure Paradigm' (2011) 90 Texas Law Review 1601

Huang, Robin Hui, 'The Regulation of Shadow Banking in China: International and Comparative Perspectives' (2015) 30 Banking & Finance Law Review 481

Hudson, Alastair, *The Law of Finance*, Sweet & Maxwell, 2013

Hunt, Isaac C, Jr (Commissioner) 'Speech by SEC Commissioner: Accountants as Gatekeepers – Adding Security and Value to the Financial Reporting System', US Securities & Exchange Commission, Arlington Virginia, 26 October 2001

Jaffer, Sue, Nicholas Morris, and David Vines, 'Why Trustworthiness is Important', in *Capital Failure: Rebuilding Trust in Financial Services*, edited by N Morris and D Vines, Oxford University Press, 2014

Jaffer, Sue, Nicholas Morris, Edward Sawbridge, and David Vines, 'How Changes to the Financial Services Industry Eroded Trust', in *Capital Failure: Rebuilding Trust in Financial Services*, edited by N Morris and D Vines, Oxford University Press, 2014

Jobst, Andreas, 'Collateralised Loan Obligations (CLOs): A Primer', CFS Working Paper, No 2002/13, Goethe University, Center for Financial Studies (CFS), 2002

Johnson, Grahame and Eric Santor, 'Central Bank Liquidity Provision and Core Funding Markets', Reserve Bank of Australia, Conference 2013, available at www.rba.gov.au/publications/confs/2013/johnson-santor.html

Johnston, Andrew, 'Corporate Governance is the Problem, not the Solution: A Critical Appraisal of the European Regulation on Credit Rating Agencies' (2011) 11(2) Journal of Corporate Law Studies 395–441

Jones, Huw, 'Bank of England delays final Basel bank capital rules to July 2025', Reuters, 27 September 2023

Kaal, Wulf and Marco Dell'Erba, 'Initial Coin Offerings: Emerging Practices, Risk Factors, and Red Flags', in *Fintech Handbook*, edited by F Moeslein and S Omlor, Verlag C.H. Beck, 2008

Kahneman, Daniel, *Thinking Fast and Slow*, Penguin, 2012

Kahneman, Daniel and Amos Tversky, 'Prospect Theory: An Analysis of Decision under Risk' (1997) 47(2) Econometrica 263–292

Kara, Alper and Solomon Deku, 'Securitisation – the complex financial product that fuelled the financial crisis is making a comeback', The Conversation (14 September 2018), at https://theconversation.com/securitisation-the-complex-financial-product-that-fuelled-the-financial-crisis-is-making-a-comeback-93807

Kaserer, Christoph and Marc Rapp, 'Capital Markets and Economic Growth – Long-Term Trends and Policy Challenges', Research Report, March 2014, at www.europeanissuers.eu/_lib/newsflash/research_paper_-_release_version_-_march_2014.pdf

Katz, Avery, 'Taking Private Ordering Seriously' (1996) 144(5) University of Pennsylvania Law Review 1745–1763

Kaya, Orcun, 'Synthetic Securitisation Making a Silent Comeback' (February 2017) Deutsche Bank, EU Monitor Global Financial Markets

Kendall, Leon, 'Securitization: A New Era in American Finance', in *A Primer on Securitization*, edited by L Kendall and M Fishman, MIT Press, 2000

Kendall, Leon and Michael Fishman (eds), *A Primer on Securitization*, MIT Press, 2000

Kendall, Maurice, 'The Analysis of Economic Time Series, Part I, Prices' (1953) 116(1) Journal of the Royal Statistical Society 11–25

Kerr, Ian, *A History of the Eurobond Market: The First 21 Years*, Euromoney Publications, 1984

Kettering, Kenneth, 'Securitization and its Discontents: The Dynamics of Financial Product Development' (2008) 29(4) Cardozo Law Review 1553

Kindleberger, Charles, *Manias, Panics and Crashes*, Palgrave, 2011

Kodres, Laura, 'Shadow Banks: Out of the Eyes of Regulators', IMF, available at www.imf.org/en/Publications/fandd/issues/Series/Back-to-Basics/Shadow-Banks

Kothari, Vinod, *Securitization: The Financial Instrument of the Future*, Wiley Finance, 2006

Igan, Deniz and Thomas Lambert, 'Bank Lobbying: Regulatory Capture and Beyond', in *The Political Economy of Financial Regulation*, edited by E Avgouleas and D Donald, Cambridge University Press, 2018

Institute of International Finance, 'The Cumulative Impact on the Global Economy on Changes in the Financial Regulatory Framework', September 2011

International Capital Markets Association, 'History of the Eurobond market', available at www.icmagroup.org/About-ICMA/history/history-of-the-eurobond-market/

International Monetary Fund, *Global Financial Stability Report*, Washington, 2019

International Monetary Fund, *Global Financial Stability Report*, Washington, 2022

International Monetary Fund, *Global Financial Stability Report*, Washington, 2024

IOSCO, 'International Disclosure Principles for Cross-Border Offerings and Listings of Debt Securities by Foreign Issuers', 2007

ISDA, 'Concentration of OTC Derivatives Among Major Dealers', ISDA Research Note, Issue 4, 2010

Langevoort, Donald, 'Taming the Animal Spirits of the Stock Markets: A Behavioural Approach to Securities Regulation' (2002) 97 North Western University Law Review 135

Latham & Watkins, 'EU Risk Retention Rules and CLOs – the Journey's End?', *Commentary* (26 June 2014)

Latouche, Serge, *Farewell to Growth*, Polity Press, 2010

Levine, Ross, 'Financial Development and Economic Growth: Views and Agenda' (1997) 35(2) Journal of Economic Literature 688–726

Levitin, Adam, 'The Politics of Financial Regulation and the Regulation of Financial Politics: A Review Essay' (2014) 127 Harvard Law Review 1991

Lewis, Michael, *The Big Short*, Penguin, 2010

Llewellyn, David, *Inside the 'Black Box' of Market Discipline*, Institute of Economic Affairs, 2005

London Stock Exchange, 'Our History', available at www.londonstockexchange.com/products-and-services/ms/history/history.htm

Long, Douglas, 'Converging Developments in ABCP Conduits and SIV Markets' in *Asset Securitisation and Synthetic Structures: Innovations in the European Credit Markets*, edited by E Watson and J Carter, Euromoney, 2006

Low, Kelvin, 'Confronting Cryptomania: Can Equity Tame the Blockchain' (2020) 14 Journal of Equity 240,

Low, Kelvin and Elisa Mik, 'Pause the Blockchain Legal Revolution' (2020) 69(1) International & Comparative Law Quarterly 135

Lucas, Douglas, Laurie Goodman, and Frank Fabozzi, 'Collateralized Debt Obligations and Credit Risk Transfer', Yale IFC Working Paper no 07-06, 2006

MacKenzie, Donald, *An Engine, Not a Camera – How Financial Models Shape Markets*, MIT Press, 2008

MacKenzie, Donald, *Material Markets: How Economic Agents are Constructed*, Oxford University Press, 2009

MacKenzie, Donald and Yuval Millo, 'Constructing a Market, Performing Theory: The Historical Sociology of a Financial Derivatives Exchange' (July 2003) 109(1) American Journal of Sociology 107–145

Majone, Giandomenico, 'Europe's "Democratic Deficit": The Question of Standards' (1998) 4(1) 5–28 European Law Journal

Malkiel, Burton, *A Random Walk Down Wall Street*, WW Norton and Company, 1973

Markowitz, Harry, 'Portfolio Selection' (1952) 7(1) The Journal of Finance 77–91

Masters, Brooke, 'We haven't reduced financial risk, just transformed it', *Financial Times* (10 December 2022)

Masters, Brooke, 'US regulators impose tougher disclosure rules on private funds', *Financial Times* (23 August 2023)

Matlock, George, 'Reviving Securitisation in Europe for CMU', European Stability Mechanism, 15/07/2021

McCormack, Gerard, *Secured Credit under English and American Law*, Cambridge University Press, 2004

McDonough, Rob, 'Collateralised Loan Obligations', Global Financial Markets Institute, 9 April 2016, www.gfmi.com/articles/collateralized-loan-obligations/

McVea, Harry, 'Credit Rating Agencies, the Subprime Mortgage Debacle, and Global Governance: The EU Strikes Back' (2010) 59 International & Comparative Law Quarterly 701

Mehrling, Perry, Zoltan Pozsar, James Sweeney, and Daniel Neilson, 'Bagehot Was a Shadow Banker: Shadow Banking, Central Banking and the Future of Global Finance', 2013, available at SSRN http://papers.ssrn.com/sol3/papers.cfm?abstract_id=2232016

Merton, Robert, 'Theory of Rational Option Pricing' (1973) 4 Bell Journal of Economics and Management Science 141–183

Michie, Ranald, *The Global Securities Market – A History*, Oxford University Press, 2006

Michie, Ranald, 'Financial Capitalism', in *The Cambridge History of Capitalism*, Vol 2, edited by Larry Neal and Jeffrey G Williamson, Cambridge University Press, 2014

Milne, Alistair and Paul Parboteeah, 'The Business Models and Economics of Peer-to-Peer Lending', Research Report, European Credit Research Institute, No 17 May 2016

Min, David, 'Understanding the Failures of Market Discipline' (2015) 92 Washington University Law Review 1421

Minsky, Hyman, 'Financial Instability Revisited: The Economics of Disaster', Prepared for the Steering Committee for the Fundamental Reappraisal of the Discount Mechanism Appointed by the Board of Governors of the Federal Reserve System, January 1970

Minsky, Hyman, 'The Financial Instability Hypothesis: An Interpretation of Keynes and an Alternative to "Standard" Theory' (1977) 16(1) Nebraska Journal of Economics and Business 5–16

Minsky, Hyman, 'Capitalist Financial Processes and the Instability of Capitalism' (1980) 14(2) Journal of Economic Issues 505–523

Minsky, Hyman, 'The Financial Instability Hypothesis', Jerome Levy Economics Institute of Bard College, Working Paper no 74, May 1992

Mirowski, Philip, *More Heat Than Light: Economics as Social Physics, Physics as Nature's Economics*, Cambridge University Press, 1989

Mishkin, Frederic and Stanley Eakins, *Financial Markets and Institutions*, Addison Wesley, 2000

Mitchell, Lawrence, *The Speculation Economy – How Finance Triumphed over Industry*, Berrett-Koehler, 2007

Moloney, Niamh, *EU Securities and Financial Markets Regulation*, Oxford University Press, 2014

Moloney, Niamh, *The Age of ESMA – Governing EU Financial Markets*, Hart, 2018

Moloney, Niamh, *EU Securities and Financial Markets Regulation*, Oxford University Press, 2023
Moody's Investor Service, 'ABCP 2008 Year in Review and 2009 Outlook', Structured Finance: Special Report, February 2009
Moody's Investors Service, 'Structured finance in focus: a short guide to covered bonds', 1, 2 May 2010
Mourselas, Costas and Will Louch, 'EU tightens rules on leverage for private credit funds', *Financial Times* (21 July 2023)
Muth, John, 'Rational Expectations and the Theory of Price Movements' (July 1961) 29(3) Econometrica 315–335
NASDAQ, 'NASDAQ's Story', available at www.business.nasdaq.com/discover/nasdaq-story/index.html
Noonan, Laura, 'EU and UK need to overhaul securitisation rules, finance group urges', *Financial Times* (6 June 2023)
O'Brien, Justin, *The Triumph, Tragedy and Lost Legacy of James M Landis*, Hart Publishing, 2014
Ogus, Anthony, *Regulation: Legal Form and Economic Theory*, Hart Publishing, 2004
O'Malley, Chris, *Bonds without Borders*, Wiley, 2015
Omarova, Saule, 'Wall Street as Community of Fate: Toward Financial Industry Self-Regulation' (2011) 159 University of Pennsylvania Law Review 412–492
Omarova, Saule, 'Licence to Deal: Mandatory Approval of Complex Financial Products' (2012) 90(63) Washington University Law Review 64–140
Omarova, Saule, 'From Reaction to Prevention: Product Approval as a Model of Derivatives Regulation' (2013) 3 Harvard Business Law Review Online 1–14
Onaran, Yalman and Lauren Leatherby, 'Can We Survive the Next Financial Crisis?', Bloomberg, 10 September 2018
Pagano, Marco and Ernst-Ludwig Von Thadden, 'The European Bond Markets under EMU' (2004) 20(4) Oxford Review of Economic Policy 531–554
Paredes, Troy, 'Blinded by the Light: Information Overload and its Consequences for Securities Regulation' (2003) 81 Washington University Law Quarterly 417
Paredes, Troy, 'Speech by SEC Commissioner: Remarks before the Symposium on "The Past, Present, and Future of the SEC"', Securities and Exchange Commission, Pittsburgh, 16 October 2009
Park, Hyejin and Charles Kahn, 'Collateral, Rehypothecation, and Efficiency' (2019) 39 Journal of Financial Intermediation 34–46
Partnoy, Frank, 'How and Why Credit Rating Agencies Are Not Like Other Gatekeepers', University of San Diego Legal Studies Research Paper, no 07-46, 2006
Partnoy, Frank, 'Rethinking the Regulation of Credit Rating Agencies: An Institutional Investor Perspective', University of San Diego Legal Studies Research Paper, no 09-014, 2009
Partnoy, Frank, 'The Looming Bank Collapse' (July/August, 2020) The Atlantic
Partnoy, Frank and David Skeel, 'The Promise and Perils of Credit Derivatives' (2007) 75 University of Cincinnati Law Review 1020
Peer2Peer Finance News, 'UK P2P set for securitisation boom', 5 October 2016, available at www.p2pfinancenews.co.uk/2016/10/05/p2p-securitisation-moodys/
Petram, Ludewijk, *The World's First Stock Exchange*, Columbia University Press, 2014
Pistor, Katharina, 'On the Theoretical Foundations for Regulating Financial Market', Columbia Law School Public Law & Legal Theory Working Paper Group, 12-304, June 2012
Posner, Eric, 'Law, Economics and Inefficient Norms' (1996) 144(5) University of Pennsylvania Law Review 1697–1744
Posner, Richard, *Economic Analysis of Law*, Aspen Law and Business, 2003
Post, Mitchell, Michael Schoenbeck, and Joyce Payne, 'The Evolution of the U.S. Commercial Paper Market since 1980' (1992) 78 Federal Reserve Bulletin 879
Pozsar, Zoltan, 'Shadow Banking: The Money View', Office of Financial Research, Working Paper 14-04, July 2014
Pozsar, Zoltan and Manmohan Singh, 'The Nonbank-Bank Nexus and the Shadow Banking System', International Monetary Fund, Working Paper no 11/289, 2011

Pozsar, Zoltan, Tobias Adrian, Adam Ashcroft, and Hayley Boesky, 'Shadow Banking', Federal Reserve Bank of New York, Staff Report no 458, 2010
Practical Law, 'Contract for Difference (CFD)', Thomson Reuters
Ranieri, Lewis, 'The Origins of Securitization, Sources of its Growth, and its Future Potential', in *A Primer on Securitization*, edited by L Kendall and M Fishman, MIT Press, 2000
Rawlings, Philip, 'The Changing Role of the Trustee in International Bond Issues' (2007) 43 Journal of Business Law 43–66
Reich, Robert, 'The Crypto Crash: all Ponzi schemes topple eventually', *The Guardian* (19 June 2022)
Rennison, Joe and Robert Smith, 'CLOs: ground zero for the next stage of the financial crisis?', *Financial Times* (13 May 2020)
Rennison, Joe, Eric Platt, Colby Smith, and Philip Stafford, 'US put off derivatives rules for a decade before Archegos blew up', *Financial Times* (12 April 2021)
Revision of the Commission's Auditor Independence Requirements, Securities Act Release No 33-7870, 65 Fed. Reg. 43,148, 43,150 July 12, 2000
Ricks, Morgan, 'Regulating Money Creation after the Crisis' (2011) 1 Harvard Business Law Review 76–140
Ricks, Morgan, *The Money Problem: Rethinking Financial Regulation*, University of Chicago Press, 2016
Roche, Cullen, 'The rise of the Bond Market and its Impact on Portfolio Allocations', Pragmatic Capitalism, 25/02/2015, available at www.pragcap.com/the-rise-of-the-bond-market-its-impact-on-portfolio-allocation/
Rousseau, Peter and Paul Wachtel, 'What is Happening to the Impact of Financial Deepening on Economic Growth?' (2011) 49(1) Economic Enquiry 276
Salmon, Felix, 'A Formula for Disaster' (March 2009) Wired
Samuelson, Paul, 'Rational Theory of Warrant Pricing' (1965) 6(2) Industrial Management Review 13–39
Sapir, Andre, Nicolas Veron, and Guntram Wolff, 'Making a reality of Europe's Capital Markets Union', Bruegel Policy Contribution no 2018/07
Sargent, Patrick, 'Bankruptcy Remote Finance Subsidiary: The Substantive Consolidation Issue' (1989) 44 Business Lawyer 1223
Scaggs, Alexandra, 'Basel III: Endgame', *Financial Times* (31 July 2023)
Schammo, Pierre, *EU Prospectus Law*, Cambridge University Press, 2011
Schammo, Pierre, 'Capital Markets Union and Small and Medium-sized Enterprises (SMEs): a Preliminary Assessment', in *The New Financial Architecture in the Eurozone*, edited by Allen, Carletti, and Gray, FIC Press, 2015
Schammo, Pierre, 'Market Building and the Capital Markets Union: Addressing Information Barriers in the SME Funding Market' (2017) 14(2) European Company and Financial Law Review 271–313
Schillig, Michael, '"Lex Cryptographi(c)a", "Cloud Crypto Land" or What? – Blockchain Technology on the Legal Hype Cycle' (June 2022) Modern Law Review 31–66
Schuster, Edmund, 'Cloud Crypto Land' (December 2020) Modern Law Review 974–1004
Schwarcz, Steven, 'Structured Finance: The New Way to Securitize Assets' (1990) 11 Cardozo Law Review 607
Schwarcz, Steven, 'The Alchemy of Asset Securitization' (1994) 1 Stanford Journal of Law, Business and Finance 133–154
Schwarcz, Steven, 'Private Ordering' (2002) 97(1) Northwestern University Law Review 319–350
Schwarcz, Steven, 'Private Ordering of Public Markets: The Rating Agency Paradox' (2002) University of Illinois Law Review 1–28
Schwarcz, Steven, 'Enron and the Use and Abuse of Special Purpose Entities in Corporate Structures' (2002) 70 University of Cincinnati Law Review 1309–1318
Schwarcz, Steven, 'Commercial Trusts as Business Organizations: Unravelling the Mystery' (2003) 58 Business Lawyer 559–586

Schwarcz, Steven, 'Rethinking the Disclosure Paradigm in a World of Complexity' (2004) 1 University of Illinois Law Review 1–38
Schwarcz, Steven, 'Systemic Risk' (2008) 97(1) Georgetown Law Journal 193–249
Schwarcz, Steven, 'Disclosure's Failure in the Subprime Mortgage Crisis' (2008) Utah Law Review 1109–1122
Schwarcz, Steven, 'Regulating Complexity in Financial Markets' (2009) 87(2) Washington University Law Review 211–268
Schwarcz, Steven, 'Fiduciaries with Conflicting Obligations' (2010) 94Minnesota Law Review 1867–1913
Schwarcz, Steven, 'The Conundrum of Covered Bonds' (2011) 66 The Business Lawyer 561–586
Schwarcz, Steven, 'Structuring Responsibility in Securitization Transactions' (2012) 40 Capital University Law Review 803–819
Schwarcz, Steven, 'Controlling Financial Chaos: The Power and Limits of Law' (2012) Wisconsin Law Review 815–840
Schwarcz, Steven, 'Framing Address: A Framework for Analyzing Financial Markets Transformation' (2013) 36 Seattle University Law Review 299
Schwarcz, Steven, 'Securitization, Structured Finance, and Covered Bonds' (2014) 39 Journal of Corporation Law 130–154
Schwarcz, Steven, 'Post-Crisis Derivatives Regulation: What Went Right (and What Went Wrong)' (January 2023) Science Po Law Review (Biennial issue on Financial Regulation after the 2008 Crisis) 44–51
Schwarcz, Steven, Bruce Markell, and Lissa Lamkin Broome, *Securitisation, Structured Finance and Capital Markets*, LexisNexis, 2004
Schwartz, Alan and Robert Scott, 'The Political Economy of Private Legislation' (1995) 143 University of Pennsylvania Law Review 595
Sharpe, William, 'Capital Asset Prices: A theory of market equilibrium under conditions of risk' (1964) 19(3) The Journal of Finance 425–442
Sharpe, William, *Portfolio Theory and Capital Markets*, McGraw-Hill, 1970
Shenker, Joseph and Anthony Colletta, 'Asset Securitization: Evolution, Current Issues and New Frontiers' (1990–1991) 69 Texas Law Review 1369
Shiller, Robert, *Irrational Exuberance*, Princeton University Press, 2005
Shin, Hyun Song, 'Reflections on Northern Rock: The Bank Run that Heralded the Global Financial Crisis' (2009) 23(1) Journal of Economic Perspectives 101–119
Shoffman, Marc, 'P2P securitisation boom still on the cards', *Peer2Peer Finance News* (27 March 2018), available at www.p2pfinancenews.co.uk/2018/03/27/p2p-securitisation/
Shrout, Kurt, 'The U.S. Bond Market May Be Much Different Than You Think It Is', 30 May 2013, available at https://learnbonds.com/93027/how-big-is-the-bond-market/
Sissoko, Carolyn, 'The Collateral Supply Effect on Central Bank Policy', August 2020, available on SSRN https://ssrn.com/abstract=3545546
Slaughter and May, 'Model Guide to Securitisation Techniques', February 2010
Somerset, Webb Merryn, 'Time to cut your stock market losses — or not?', *Financial Times* (17 June 2022)
Standard & Poor's Global Market Intelligence, 'Leveraged Loan Primer', at www.spglobal.com/marketintelligence/en/pages/toc-primer/lcd-primer#sec1
'Statement of Lawrence J. White for the Committee on Banking, Housing, and Urban Affairs', US Senate, 26 September 2007
Stigler, George, 'The Theory of Economic Regulation' (1971) 2(1) The Bell Journal of Economics and Management Science 3–21
Stigler, George, *Memoirs of an Unregulated Economist*, Basic Books, 1988
Stiglitz, Joseph, 'Credit Markets and the Control of Capital' (1985) 17(2) Journal of Money, Credit and Banking 133–152
Stiglitz, Joseph, 'The Cases and Consequences of the Dependence of Quality on Price' (1987) 25(1) Journal of Economic Literature 1–48

Stiglitz, Joseph, *Freefall: America, Free Markets, and the Sinking of the World Economy*, Penguin, 2010

Stigum, Marcia, *The Money Market*, Dow Jones-Irwin, 1983

Stout, Lynn, 'The Unimportance of Being Efficient: An Economic Analysis of Stock Market Pricing and Securities Regulation' (1988) 87 Michigan Law Review 613–709

Stout, Lynn, 'Why the Law Hates Speculators: Regulation and Private Ordering in the Market for OTC Derivatives' (1999) 48 Duke Law Journal 701–786

Stout, Lynn, 'The Mechanisms of Market Inefficiency: An Introduction to the New Finance' (Summer 2003) The Journal of Corporation Law 635 636–666

Stout, Lynn, 'Regulate OTC Derivatives by Deregulating Them' (Fall 2009) Regulation 29–41

Stout, Lynn, 'Derivatives and the Legal Origin of the 2008 Credit Crisis' (2011) 1 Harvard Business Law Review 1–38

Stuart, Rebecca, 'Why did Credit Suisse fail and what does it mean for banking regulation?', *Economics Observatory* (13 April 2023)

Taggart Jr, Robert, 'The Growth of the "Junk" Bond Market and Its Role in Financing Takeovers', in *Mergers and Acquisitions*, edited by Alan J Auerbach, University of Chicago Press, 1988

Tayler, Graham, 'UK Building Society Demutualisation Motives' (2003) 12(4) Business Ethics: A European Review 394–402

Thomas, Geraint and Alastair Hudson, *The Law of Trusts*, Oxford University Press, 2010

Turbeville, Wallace, 'Derivatives Innovation in the Era of Financial Deregulation', Demos Report, June 2013

Turner, Adair, *The Turner Review – A Regulatory Response to the Global Banking Crisis*, FSA, 2009

Turner, Adair, 'Lord Turner's Lecture - Reforming Finance: Are We Being Radical Enough', Clare Distinguished Lecture in Economics, Cambridge, 18 February 2011

Turner, Adair, *Between Debt and the Devil*, Princeton University Press, 2016

Turner, John, 'Why did Silicon Valley Bank fail?', *Economics Observatory* (17 March 2023)

Tversky, Amos and Daniel Kahneman, 'Rational Choice and the Framing of Decisions' (1986) 59 Journal of Business 251–278

UK Finance, 'SME finance in the UK: past, present and future', December 2018, at www.ukfinance.org.uk/system/files/UK-Finance-SME-Finance-in-UK-AW-web.pdf

Uwaifo, Elisabeth, 'Key Issues in Structuring a Synthetic Securitisation Transaction – A European Perspective' (2001) 16(4) Journal of International Banking Law 98–104

Van Horn, Rob and Philip Mirowski, 'The Rise of the Chicago School of Economics and the Birth of Neoliberalism', in *The Road from Mont Pelerin The Making of the Neoliberal Thought Collective*, edited by Philip Mirowski and Dieter Plehwe, Harvard University Press, 2009

Venkataramakrishnan, Siddarth and Robin Wigglesworth, 'Inside the cult of crypto', *Financial Times* (10 September 2021)

Von Hayek, Friedrich, *The Road to Serfdom*, Routledge, 1944

Warren, Elizabeth, 'Unsafe at Any Rate' (Summer 2007) 5 Democracy

Weber, Ernst Juerg, 'A Short History of Derivative Security Markets', University of Western Australia, Discussion Paper 8/10, 2008

Wigglesworth, Robin, 'How Bonds Ate the Entire Financial System', *Financial Times* (3 August 2023)

Wigglesworth, Robin and Joe Rennison, 'Bond trading: Technology Finally Disrupt a $50tn Market', *Financial Times* (9 May 2018)

Wilmarth, Arthur, 'The Dark Side of Universal Banking: Financial Conglomerates and the Origins of the Subprime Financial Crisis' (2009) 41(4) Connecticut Law Review 963

Wilmarth, Arthur, *Taming the Megabanks*, Oxford University Press, 2020

Wilmarth, Arthur, 'The Pandemic Crisis Shows that the World Remains Trapped in a "Global Doom Loop" of Financial Instability, Rising Debt Levels, and Escalating Bailouts' (2021) 40(8) Banking & Financial Services Policy Report 1–28

Wood, Philip, *Project Finance, Securitisation, Subordinated Debt*, Sweet & Maxwell, 2007

Wood, Philip, *International Loans, Bonds, Guarantees, Legal Opinions*, Sweet & Maxwell, 2019

Wood, Philip, *Regulation of International Finance*, Sweet & Maxwell, 2019

World Economic Forum, 'The Complex Regulatory Landscape for FinTech: An Uncertain Future for Small and Medium-Sized Enterprises Lending', White Paper, August, 2016

Wright, Aaron and Primavera De Filippi, 'Decentralized Blockchain Technology and the Rise of Lex Cryptographia', March 10 2015, available at SSRN https://papers.ssrn.com/sol3/papers.cfm?abstract_id=2580664

Yadav, Yesha, 'How Algorithmic Trading Undermines Efficiency in Capital Markets' (2015) 68 Vanderbilt Law Review 1608–1670

Yadav, Yesha, 'The Problematic Case of Clearinghouses in Complex Markets' (2013) 101 Georgetown Law Journal 388–444

Zhang, Guowei and Peter Ryan, 'How the Basel III "Endgame" Reforms Will Transform US Capital Requirements', *SIFMA* (27 February 2023)

Zheng, Zibin, Shaoan Xie, Hongning Dai, Xiangping Chen, and Huaimin Wang, 'An Overview of Blockchain Technology: Architecture, Consensus, and Future Trends', 2017 IEEE 6th International Congress on Big Data 557–564

Index

For the benefit of digital users, indexed terms that span two pages (e.g., 52–53) may, on occasion, appear on only one of those pages.